CONSUMER GUIDE®

1990 CARS

P9-CRJ-796

Contents

Introduction

Each profile in *1990 Cars* lists the major changes for 1990 and a summary of available body styles, engines, and other key features. We have combined similar models produced by the same manufacturer, such as the Buick Electra and Oldsmobile Ninety-Eight, into one report. By combining similar cars into one report we can cover more vehicles in the same amount of space. Electra and Ninety-Eight are built from the same design, use the same engine and transmission, and have similar styling. The main differences between them are in interior trim, optional equipment, and prices, so we've provided separate price lists for each brand. We have not combined all similar vehicles, but in our reports we mention which other models are built from the same design. This should help you make a shopping list of cars that fit your needs and meet your budget.

Information in the specifications charts is provided by the manufacturers, except for the fuel economy estimates, which are furnished by the federal Environmental Protection Agency.

How Cars Are Rated

The Ratings Chart at the end of this book includes numerical ratings in 16 categories for each car line. In cases

---

KEY TO SPECIFICATIONS

Notchback = coupe or sedan with a separate trunk. **Hatchback** = coupe or sedan with a rear liftgate. **Wheelbase** = distance between the front and rear wheels. **Curb weight** = weight of base models, not including optional equipment. **Engines: ohv** = overhead valve; **ohc** = overhead cam; **dohc** = double overhead cam; **I** = inline cylinders; **V** = cylinders in V configuration; **flat** = horizontally opposed cylinders; **bbl.** = barrel (carburetor); **TBI** = throttle-body (single-point) fuel injection; **PFI** = port (multi-point) fuel injection; **rpm** = revolutions per minute; **S** = standard; **O** = optional; **OD** = overdrive transmission; **NA** = not available.

---

where a certain model, body style, engine, or other feature affected the ratings, that is noted in the chart. The ratings apply only to the specific model that was tested by the editors. For example, the ratings for the Acura Integra apply only to the GS 3-door hatchback, which has anti-lock brakes (ABS) standard. An Integra without ABS may not score as highly in braking.

The total points awarded to each model or car line is an important indicator of a vehicle's overall capabilities, but the editors encourage readers to examine the ratings in individual categories. Large cars tend to earn more points because they have spacious interiors, roomy trunks, and wide doorways that allow easy entry/exit. That gives them a built-in advantage over small cars in the rating scale. However, small cars typically earn higher marks for fuel economy, while sporty cars score well in steering/handling. The individual reader should determine which categories are the most important in making a buying decision.

Price Information

The latest available prices have been provided for all models and optional equipment offered by the manufacturers. In most cases, the editors were able to provide dealer invoice prices and our estimated low prices. In some cases, only suggested retail prices were available; with some models that hadn't yet gone on sale, no prices were available. In all cases, the prices are subject to change by the manufacturers. If the prices in this book don't match what you find in a dealer's showroom, or if a salesman claims our prices are incorrect, please contact us and we'll do what we can to help you out (the address is listed below). We have nothing to gain by giving you wrong information; a car salesman has much to gain by claiming our prices are incorrect.

Car dealers are under no legal obligation to sell a car at or below "manufacturer's suggested retail price." Dealers are free to sell their merchandise at whatever price people are willing to pay. The dealer invoice prices are what the dealer pays the manufacturer for the car and factory- or port-installed options. The dealer's costs of preparing a car for delivery to the consumer are included in the invoice price of all domestic cars. On some imported vehicles, this cost may not be included in the dealer invoice. The destination charge is not included in either the suggested retail or dealer invoice prices, so it must be added to the total cost of the vehicle.

The low prices listed in this book are estimates based on national market conditions for particular models. Cars that are in high demand and short supply will likely sell at or near suggested retail price. Cars in low demand and high supply will be sold at much larger discounts, or closer to dealer invoice. For example, the Mazda Miata is in such high demand that the low price is suggested retail, while a Mazda RX-7 can be purchased for well below retail.

Certain cars are in much higher demand in certain areas. For example, a 4-wheel-drive car will be in great demand in New England and the Rocky Mountain states, while there will be little interest in this 4WD model in the Sun Belt. You should expect to pay more in the areas where demand is high for a particular model. On the other hand, winter is a good time to buy a convertible in the midwest or New England, when there's little demand.

To determine local market conditions for the vehicles you're interested in, we encourage you to shop for the same car at three or more dealers. If all the dealers have only one or two models in stock and show little willingness to discount their prices, you're shopping in a seller's market, so you should expect to pay close to suggested retail. On the other hand, if all the dealers have lots of cars in stock and seem eager to bargain, then you should be able to get a big discount. With most cars these days, it is a buyer's market. Take advantage of this by letting the dealers know that you've been shopping elsewhere and that price will be an important factor in your decision.

Before you buy any car, test drive it. Don't choose your next car on our recommendations alone. Buy the car that feels right for you when you're behind the wheel. Since you're going to be the one who has to live with this vehicle, make sure that it fits your needs. We strongly suggest you test drive the same vehicle you're planning to buy. You may spot something you don't like about it before it's too late.

The editors invite your questions and comments. Address them to:

Consumer Guide
7373 N. Cicero Ave.
Lincolnwood, IL 60646

Acura Integra

Acura Integra LS

The 1990 Integra is built from a new design that is larger than the 1986-89 original and shares none of its major components. Model choices comprise a returning hatchback coupe and a new notchback 4-door instead of a 5-door hatchback. The Integra coupe has grown 3.9 inches in wheelbase and 4.2 inches longer overall. As before, 4-wheel disc brakes are standard; the brakes are larger than before and a Honda-designed anti-lock brake system (ABS) is available only on top-line GS models (as standard). Motorized front shoulder belts are standard on all Integras. A dual-cam 4-cylinder engine still drives the front wheels, but displacement grows from 1.6 to 1.8 liters and horsepower increases from 118 to 130. A 5-speed manual transmission remains standard; the optional 4-speed overdrive automatic now features a Sport mode with higher shift points. The new engine provides brisk pickup, at least with manual shift. We timed a 5-speed GS coupe at 9.0 seconds 0-60 mph. Informal clockings show the automatic sedan at 11.5 seconds—hardly great for a car with sporting intentions, but adequate. The new Integra feels more substantial than the old and suffers less road noise. Improved suspension damping makes for a smoother, more supple ride than on earlier Integras, while the new model has minimal body roll and impressive grip in turns. The GS's standard ABS has exceptional stopping ability; other models also have commendable braking. Inside, the new Integras offer about two inches more leg room and an inch more head room, but there's less rear shoulder room than before and the coupe loses some rear leg room. The sedan seats four adults without cramping, while the coupe is more of a 2 + 2, its back seat being best left to kids and cargo. The new Integras are refined, competent, well-made compacts that should be reliable and have good resale value.

Specifications

	3-door hatchback	4-door notchback
Wheelbase, in.	100.4	102.4
Overall length, in.	172.9	176.5
Overall width, in.	67.4	67.4
Overall height, in.	52.2	52.8
Turn diameter, ft.	33.1	33.7
Curb weight, lbs.	2544	2579
Cargo vol., cu. ft.	16.2	11.2
Fuel capacity, gals.	13.2	13.2
Seating capacity	5	5
Front headroom, in.	38.5	38.7
Front shoulder room, in.	52.7	52.5
Front legroom, max., in.	43.6	43.5
Rear headroom, in.	34.7	36.8
Rear shoulder room, in.	52.0	52.4
Rear legroom, min., in.	28.6	31.7

Powertrain layout: transverse front engine/front-wheel drive.

Engines

	dohc I-4
Size, liters/cu. in.	1.8/112
Fuel delivery	PFI
Horsepower @ rpm	130 @ 6000
Torque (lbs./ft.) @ rpm	121 @ 5000
Availability	S

EPA city/highway mpg

5-speed OD manual	24/28
4-speed OD automatic	23/27

Prices

Acura Integra

	Retail Price	Dealer Invoice	Low Price
RS 3-door hatchback, 5-speed	$11950	$10038	$10967
RS 3-door hatchback, automatic	12675	10647	11632
LS 3-door hatchback, 5-speed	13725	11529	12596
LS 3-door hatchback, automatic	14450	12138	13261
GS 3-door hatchback, 5-speed	15825	13293	14523
GS 3-door hatchback, automatic	16550	13902	15188
RS 4-door notchback, 5-speed	12850	10794	11793
RS 4-door notchback, automatic	13575	11403	12458
LS 4-door notchback, 5-speed	14545	12217	13348
LS 4-door notchback, automatic	15270	12826	14013
GS 4-door notchback, 5-speed	15950	13398	14637
GS 4-door notchback, automatic	16675	14007	15303
Destination charge	295	295	295

Standard equipment:

RS: 1.8-liter DOHC 16-valve PFI 4-cylinder engine, 5- speed manual or 4-speed automatic transmission, power steering, 4-wheel disc brakes, reclining front bucket seats, split folding rear seat, rear shoulder belts, tinted glass, remote fuel door and hatch releases, dual manual mirrors, fog lights, rear defogger, rear wiper/washer (hatchback), tachometer, coolant temperature gauge, tilt steering column, intermittent wipers, door pockets, cargo cover (hatchback), 195/60R14 tires. **LS** adds: power mirrors, power locks (4-door), power sunroof (hatchback), AM/FM cassette with power antenna, driver's seat lumbar support adjustment, cruise control, map lights (hatchback). **GS** adds: anti-lock braking system, power windows, map lights, adjustable side bolsters on driver's seat, alloy wheels.

OPTIONS are available as dealer-installed accessories.

Acura Legend

The Legend Coupe and Sedan are carried over with minor changes for what probably will be their final season in this form. The Sedan was introduced for 1986 when American Honda launched its Acura division and the Coupe arrived about a year later. New versions of both are expected for 1991. Changes for 1990 include a restyled grille for Coupes and a rear spoiler for the LS Coupe; burled-walnut center console trim for the flagship LS Sedan and Coupe; and new

Prices are accurate at time of printing; subject to manufacturer's change.

Acura Legend Coupe LS

Specifications

	2-door notchback	4-door notchback
Wheelbase, in.	106.5	108.7
Overall length, in.	188.0	190.6
Overall width, in.	68.7	68.9
Overall height, in.	53.9	54.7
Turn diameter, ft.	36.4	37.1
Curb weight, lbs.	3139	3170
Cargo vol., cu. ft.	14.7	16.6
Fuel capacity, gals.	18.0	18.0
Seating capacity	5	5
Front headroom, in.	37.2	38.4
Front shoulder room, in.	55.4	55.7
Front legroom, max., in.	42.9	43.4
Rear headroom, in.	36.3	36.5
Rear shoulder room, in.	54.3	55.4
Rear legroom, min., in.	30.3	34.5

Powertrain layout: transverse front engine/front-wheel drive.

Engines

	ohc V-6
Size, liters/cu. in.	2.7/163
Fuel delivery	PFI
Horsepower @ rpm	160 @ 5900
Torque (lbs./ft.) @ rpm	162 @ 4500
Availability	S

EPA city/highway mpg	
5-speed OD manual	19/24
4-speed OD automatic	18/22

front seats for all models. All Legends have front-wheel drive and a 160-horsepower 2.7-liter V-6 engine. A driver's-side airbag is standard on all models and anti-lock brakes are standard on L and LS models. Legend has reigned for four years as the most expensive, most prestigious Japanese car sold in the U.S., but for 1990 it has been surpassed in price, performance, and panache by two newcomers: Infiniti Q45 and Lexus LS 400. Legend still impresses us as an excellent all-around car, whether you want two doors or four. Acceleration is brisk from the smooth, eager V-6 engine; the ride is comfortable and the handling is competent; the anti-lock brakes on the L and LS provide short, safe stops; there's ample room inside for four adults; and assembly quality is top-notch. In addition, Acura has consistently scored at the top of customer-satisfaction surveys, Legend commands high resale value, and service and maintenance costs are low. All that makes Legend hard to beat.

Prices

Acura Legend	Retail Price	Dealer Invoice	Low Price
Sedan			
4-door notchback, 5-speed	$22600	$18532	$19532
4-door notchback, automatic	23400	19188	20188
4-door notchback w/sunroof, 5-speed . . .	23485	19257	20257
4-door notchback w/sunroof, automatic . .	24285	19913	20913
L 4-door notchback, 5-speed	25900	21238	22238
L 4-door notchback, automatic	26700	21894	22894
L w/leather trim, 5-speed	26850	22017	23017
L w/leather trim, automatic	27650	22673	23673
LS 4-door notchback, 5-speed	29610	24280	25280
LS 4-door notchback, automatic	30410	24935	25935
Coupe			
2-door notchback, 5-speed	24760	20303	22532
2-door notchback, automatic	25560	20959	23260
L 2-door notchback, 5-speed	27325	22406	24866
L 2-door notchback, automatic	28125	23062	25594
L w/leather trim, 5-speed	28275	23185	25730
L w/leather trim, automatic	29075	23841	26458
LS 2-door notchback, 5-speed	30690	25195	27943
LS 2-door notchback, automatic	31490	25821	28656
Destination charge	295	295	295

Prices are accurate at time of printing; subject to manufacturer's change.

Standard equipment:

Sedan: 2.7-liter SOHC 24-valve PFI V-6, 5-speed manual or 4-speed automatic transmission, power steering, 4-wheel disc brakes, driver's-side airbag, air conditioning, cruise control, power windows and locks, tilt steering column, remote fuel door and trunk releases, door pockets, lighted visor mirrors, rear defogger, map lights, illuminated entry system, reclining front bucket seats, moquette upholstery, driver's seat lumbar and thigh support adjustments, rear armrest, AM/FM ST ET cassette with EQ and power diversity antenna, maintenance interval reminder, tachometer, coolant temperature gauge, trip odometer, intermittent wipers, 205/60HR15 tires on alloy wheels; coupe has power sunroof, V-rated tires. **L sedan** has: anti-lock braking system, memory power driver's seat, security system; coupe adds power driver's seat, heated mirrors, driver's seatbelt presenter, driver's information center. **LS** has: automatic climate control, power passenger seat, Bose sound system, driver's information center.

OPTIONS are available as dealer-installed accessories.

Audi V8 Quattro

Audi V8 Quattro

The $47,450 V8 Quattro is Audi's new high-performance luxury sedan, powered by a 240-horsepower 3.6-liter aluminum engine with dual overhead cams. Power is routed through a 4-speed overdrive automatic transmission to a permanently engaged all-wheel-drive system. This is the first Audi Quattro with an automatic transmission; it has three shift modes: E for higher fuel economy; S for sportier performance; and M for manual. A standard automatic shift lock requires that the brake pedal be applied to shift into a drive gear. Anti-lock brakes, a driver's-side airbag, 2-sided galvanized steel body panels, leather upholstery, cellular telephone, and a Bose sound system are among the standard features. The V8 Quattro has some impressive qualities: Outstanding traction from its sophisticated all-wheel drive system; amazing stability at high speeds; precise, responsive steering; and strong brakes with anti-lock control. Too bad the V8 Quattro also has such a

Specifications

	4-door notchback
Wheelbase, in.	106.4
Overall length, in.	191.9
Overall width, in.	71.4
Overall height, in.	55.9
Turn diameter, ft.	34.4
Curb weight, lbs.	3946
Cargo vol., cu. ft.	17.0
Fuel capacity, gals.	21.1
Seating capacity	5
Front headroom, in.	37.8
Front shoulder room, in.	56.8
Front legroom, max., in.	41.7
Rear headroom, in.	37.5
Rear shoulder room, in.	55.3
Rear legroom, min., in.	35.0

Powertrain layout: longitudinal front engine/permanent 4WD.

Engines

	dohc V-8
Size, liters/cu. in.	3.6/217
Fuel delivery	PFI
Horsepower @ rpm	240 @ 5800
Torque (lbs./ft.) @ rpm	245 @ 4000
Availability	S

EPA city/highway mpg

4-speed OD automatic	14/18

Prices are accurate at time of printing; subject to manufacturer's change.

stiff ride, the product of a firm suspension and wide Z-rated tires (designed for speeds over 149 mph). While this combination provides reassuring stability at ultra high speeds, it is too harsh on bumpy roads taken at legal speeds. Highway fuel economy is disappointing; we didn't even reach 22 mpg. The well-designed interior offers plenty of room and comes with nearly every convenience feature standard equipment (a compact disc player is the main omission). On top of that, Audi's warranties cover scheduled maintenance for the first three years/50,000 miles. Despite all that, the new Lexus LS 400 and Infiniti Q45 are more tuned to American driving tastes, and are better values for the money.

Prices

Audi V8 Quattro	Retail Price	Dealer Invoice	Low Price
4-door notchback	$47450	$39424	—
Gas Guzzler Tax	1050	1050	1050
Destination charge	335	335	335

Low price not available at time of publication.

Standard equipment:

3.6-liter DOHC 32-valve PFI V-8, 4-speed automatic transmission, permanent 4-wheel drive, anti-lock 4-wheel disc brakes, power steering, driver's-side airbag, Kodiak leather power front sport seats (comfort seats are available at no charge), heatable front seats, automatic climate control, cruise control, power windows and locks, heated power mirrors, power sunroof, Audi-Bose AM/FM cassette with diversity antenna, tachometer, gauges (coolant temperature, oil pressure and temperature), trip odometer, 6-function trip computer, 10-function Auto Check System, cellular phone, headlamp washers, rear shoulder belts, seatback pockets, leather-wrapped steering wheel and shift knob, reading lamps, lighted visor mirrors, ski sack, anti-theft alarm, tinted glass, rear defogger, heated windshield washer nozzles and door locks, intermittent wipers, 215/60ZR15 tires on alloy wheels.

Optional equipment:

Connolly leather comfort seats	250	200	—
Pearlescent metallic paint	450	360	—
California compliance equipment	150	150	150

Audi 80/90 and Coupe Quattro

Audi Coupe Quattro

The all-wheel-drive Coupe Quattro is built on the same platform as the 80/90 sedans, but introduces a new dual-cam, 20-valve version of Audi's 2.3-liter 5-cylinder engine. The 2-door Coupe's engine makes 164 horsepower, 34 more than the single-cam version used in the 80 Quattro and the front-drive 90. For 1990, the 20-valve engine also becomes standard on the 90 Quattro. The front-drive 80 has a 108-horsepower 2.0-liter 4-cylinder. The Coupe uses the same permanently engaged AWD system as the 80/90 Quattros. As with the 80 and 90 Quattros, a 5-speed manual is the only transmission offered on the Coupe. Anti-lock brakes are standard on the Coupe and 90, and optional on the 80. All models now have a driver's-side airbag standard. Even with the standard airbag and other new features, Audi has cut prices on the 80/90 models because of sagging sales. Despite the price cut, these cars are hardly cheap. The base front-drive 80 starts at $19,000 and the Coupe Quattro is nearly $30,000. The 80/90 sedans and the new Coupe suffer from the same problem: not enough engine to justify their high prices. We clocked a front-drive 90 with the 130-horsepower engine and automatic transmission at 10.4 seconds (slower than a Hyundai Sonata V-6) and a

Coupe Quattro at 9.3 seconds (slower than a Mitsubishi Eclipse). We don't base all our conclusions on 0-60 times, but at these prices we expect to blow the doors off Hyundais and Mitsubishis. On the plus side, all models are well equipped, and we've also been impressed by the assembly quality and paint finishes on the cars we've tested recently, which shows that Audi is trying hard to win back buyers after surviving the sudden-acceleration issue. However, we aren't confident that the resale value of Audis will ever recover.

Specifications

	2-door notchback	4-door notchback
Wheelbase, in.	100.4	100.4
Overall length, in.	176.0	176.3
Overall width, in.	67.6	66.7
Overall height, in.	54.3	55.0
Turn diameter, ft.	33.8	33.8
Curb weight, lbs.	3171	2612[1]
Cargo vol., cu. ft.	24.0	10.2
Fuel capacity, gals.	18.5	15.9
Seating capacity	5	5
Front headroom, in.	35.1	35.1
Front shoulder room, in.	51.7	51.7
Front legroom, max., in.	42.2	42.2
Rear headroom, in.	35.4	35.4
Rear shoulder room, in.	50.6	51.7
Rear legroom, min., in.	32.6	32.6

1. 2954 lbs., Quattro.

Powertrain layout: longitudinal front engine/front-wheel drive or permanent 4WD (Quattro).

Engines	ohc I-4	ohc I-5	dohc I-5
Size, liters/cu. in.	2.0/121	2.3/141	2.3/141
Fuel delivery	PFI	PFI	PFI
Horsepower @ rpm	108 @ 5300	130 @ 5700	164 @ 6000
Torque (lbs./ft.) @ rpm	121 @ 3200	140 @ 4500	157 @ 4500
Availability	S[1]	S[2]	S[3]

EPA city/highway mpg			
5-speed OD manual	22/30	20/26	18/24
3-speed automatic	23/27	19/22	

1. 80.   2. 80 Quattro, 90.   3. Coupe, 90 Quattro.

Prices

Audi 80/90	Retail Price	Dealer Invoice	Low Price
80 4-door notchback, 5-speed	$18900	$16394	$16894
80 4-door notchback, automatic	19485	16929	17249
80 Quattro 4-door notchback, 5-speed . . .	22800	19539	20039
90 4-door notchback, 5-speed	23990	20197	20697
90 4-door notchback, automatic	24575	20732	21232
90 Quattro 4-door notchback	27500	23145	23645
Destination charge	335	335	335

Standard equipment:

80: 2.0-liter PFI 4-cylinder engine, 5-speed manual transmission, power steering, 4-wheel disc brakes, driver's-side airbag, air conditioning, tinted glass, rear defogger, cruise control, power windows and locks, AM/FM cassette with diversity antenna, power mirrors, velour reclining front bucket seats with height adjusters, rear head restraints, rear shoulder belts, tachometer, coolant temperature gauge, trip odometer, digital clock, intermittent wipers, lighted right visor mirror, 175/70SR14 SBR tires. **80 Quattro** adds: 2.3-liter PFI 5-cylinder engine, close-ratio 5-speed, permanent 4-wheel drive, rear spoiler, 195/60VR14 tires on alloy wheels. **90** has: 2.3-liter 5-cylinder engine with 5-speed or 2.0-liter 4-cylinder with 3-speed automatic, anti-lock braking system, fog lights, clearcoat metallic paint, wood dashboard trim, power sunroof, individual passenger reading lamps, Auto Check System, 195/60VR14 tires (H-rated on 4-cylinder). **90 Quattro** adds: DOHC 20-valve engine.

Optional equipment:

Anti-lock brakes, 80	1100	990	1020
Sport Pkg., 80 Quattro	760	608	667
Front sport seats, trip computer, auto check system, gauges.			
Anti-theft alarm, 80	265	212	233
Manual sunroof, 80	550	462	494
Ski sack, Quattros	130	104	114
All Weather Pkg.	415	332	364
Headlamp washers, heatable front seats, heated windshield washer nozzles and front door locks.			
175/70R14 all-weather tires, Quattros . . .	NC	NC	NC
Clearcoat paint, 80	395	316	347
Pearlescent metallic paint, 90	395	316	347
Leather upholstery, 90	1000	800	878
Electronics Pkg., 90	525	420	461
Trip computer, anti-theft alarm.			
Power seats w/driver's side memory, 90 .	825	660	724
California compliance equipment	125	125	125

Prices are accurate at time of printing; subject to manufacturer's change.

Audi Coupe Quattro

	Retail Price	Dealer Invoice	Low Price
3-door hatchback	$29750	$25030	—
Destination charge	335	335	335

Low price not available at time of publication.

Standard equipment:

2.3-liter DOHC 20-valve PFI 5-cylinder engine, 5-speed manual transmission, permanent 4-wheel drive, power steering, anti-lock 4-wheel disc brakes, driver's-side airbag (late availability), leather reclining front bucket seats with lumbar support and height adjustments, split folding rear seat with armrest, automatic climate control, power windows and locks, cruise control, heated power mirrors, power sunroof, AM/FM cassette, tachometer, coolant temperature and oil pressure gauges, voltmeter, trip odometer, 6-function trip computer, 10-function Auto Check System, rear shoulder belts and head restraints, Zebrano wood inlays, leather-wrapped steering wheel and shift knob, lighted visor mirrors, anti-theft alarm system, tinted glass, rear defogger, intermittent wipers, ski sack, 205/60VR15 tires on alloy wheels.

Optional equipment:

Cold Weather Pkg.	350	280	—
Heatable front seats, headlight washers, heated windshield washer nozzles and door locks.			
Power front seats w/driver's-side memory .	825	660	—
Pearlescent metallic paint	395	316	—
California compliance equipment	125	125	125

Audi 100/200

Audi 200 Quattro

The 100 and 200 lines have been streamlined, all remaining models have a driver's-side airbag as standard equipment, and prices have been cut across the board. Last year, the airbag was standard on 200 models and optional on 100 models. Last year's lowest-priced model, the 100E sedan, has been dropped. The 100 wagon also is gone. The 100 series now consists of a front-drive sedan with a 130-horsepower 2.3-liter 5-cylinder engine and 3-speed automatic transmission, and an all-wheel drive 100 Quattro sedan with the same engine and a 5-speed manual transmission. The 200 models are a front-drive sedan with a 162-horse-

---

Specifications

	4-door notchback	5-door wagon
Wheelbase, in.	105.6	105.6
Overall length, in.	192.7	192.7
Overall width, in.	71.4	71.4
Overall height, in.	55.9	55.9
Turn diameter, ft.	34.2	34.2
Curb weight, lbs.	2932[1]	3042[2]
Cargo vol., cu. ft.	16.7	75.4
Fuel capacity, gals.	21.1	21.1
Seating capacity	5	5
Front headroom, in.	37.5	36.5
Front shoulder room, in.	NA	NA
Front legroom, max., in.	NA	NA
Rear headroom, in.	36.5	36.5
Rear shoulder room, in.	NA	NA
Rear legroom, min., in.	NA	NA

1. 3306 lbs., Quattro.   2. 3439 lbs., Quattro.

Powertrain layout: longitudinal front engine/front-wheel drive or permanent 4WD (Quattro).

Engines

	ohc l-5	Turbo ohc l-5
Size, liters/cu. in.	2.3/141	2.2/136
Fuel delivery	PFI	PFI
Horsepower @ rpm	130 @ 5600	162 @ 5500
Torque (lbs./ft.) @ rpm	140 @ 4000	177 @ 3000
Availability	S	S
EPA city/highway mpg		
5-speed OD manual	18/24	17/25
3-speed automatic	18/22	18/22

Prices are accurate at time of printing; subject to manufacturer's change.

Audi 100 Quattro

power 2.2-liter turbocharged 5-cylinder engine and 3-speed automatic transmission, and AWD Quattro sedan and wagon models, both with the turbo engine and 5-speed manual transmission. The front-drive 200 sedan now has leather upholstery standard, while the 200 Quattros gain heated front and rear seats and heated front door locks as standard. Audi won a major victory in 1989 when the federal government ruled that unintended acceleration in the Audi 5000 (now called 100 and 200) was caused by drivers stepping on the wrong pedal, not by mechanical or electronic flaws in the cars. Now, Audi has an even greater obstacle to overcome: How to restore consumer confidence and regain sales momentum. That won't be easy. Other European luxury-car makers have been scrambling to maintain their sales and two Japanese newcomers, Lexus and Infiniti, have made the competition more cutthroat. European-style luxury reigned during the Eighties, but Japanese-style luxury may rule the Nineties. Try an Audi 100 or 200, and then drive the Lexus and Infiniti sedans to see which suits you best.

Prices

Audi 100/200	Retail Price	Dealer Invoice	Low Price
100 4-door notchback	$26900	$22372	$22872
100 Quattro 4-door notchback	29470	24505	25005

	Retail Price	Dealer Invoice	Low Price
200 4-door notchback	33405	27771	28271
200 Quattro 4-door notchback	35805	29763	30263
200 Quattro 5-door wagon	36930	30697	31197
Destination charge	335	335	335

Standard equipment:

100: 2.3-liter PFI 5-cylinder engine, 3-speed automatic transmission, power steering, anti-lock 4-wheel disc brakes, driver's-side airbag, automatic climate control, power windows and locks, heated power mirrors, velour reclining bucket seats with driver's-side height adjustment, folding rear armrest, rear shoulder belts, reading lamps, lighted visor mirrors, anti-theft alarm, ski/storage sack, tinted glass, rear defogger, cruise control, intermittent wipers, AM/FM cassette with diversity antenna, Zebrano wood inlays, rear head restraints, front seatback pockets, leather-wrapped steering wheel, power sunroof, 205/60VR15 SBR tires on alloy wheels. **100 Quattro** has 5-speed manual transmission, permanent 4-wheel drive. **200** adds to 100: 2.2-liter turbocharged PFI 5-cylinder engine, trip computer, leather upholstery, Audi/Bose music system.

Optional equipment:

Leather upholstery, 100	1250	1000	1098
Power seats w/driver's-side memory, 100 .	825	660	724
Front sport seats, 200 Quattro	365	292	320
Cold Weather Pkg.	350	280	307
Headlamp washers, heatable front and rear seats, heated windshield washer nozzles and front door locks.			
Trip computer, 100	260	208	228
Audi/Bose music system, 100	600	480	527
Pearlescent metallic paint, 100	900	720	790
200	450	360	395
California compliance equipment	150	150	150

BMW 3-Series

All 3-Series models gain a driver's-side airbag as standard equipment this year to satisfy the federal requirement for passive restraints. Come spring, BMW tries to recapture the spirit of former models such as the 2002 with a new entry-level model, the 318is, a 2-door with a 1.8-liter 4-cylinder engine. The 318is engine has dual overhead cams,

Prices are accurate at time of printing; subject to manufacturer's change.

BMW 325i

16 valves, and 134 horsepower, and is teamed only with a 5-speed manual transmission. The 318is' price was not available. The only other 4-cylinder model in recent years has been the high-performance, limited-production M3, which continues for 1990. Other changes for the 3-Series this year are that all models are prewired for a trunk-mounted compact-disc changer and a remote-control central locking system is a new option. The remote control system also arms a theft-deterrent system as it locks the doors. New options for the 325i and the all-wheel-drive 325iX models are leather upholstery and an electric sunroof (a manual sunroof is standard); an 8-speaker premium sound system is a new option for the 325is and 325iX. Both the 325i and the 325iX are available in 2- and 4-door styling; all other 3-Series models are 2-doors only. The 3-Series models haven't been selling well lately, mainly because they have small, rather Spartan interiors, but big price tags. Most 3-Series models are in the $25,000-$30,000 range, the same as the Acura Legend, which offers similar features in a roomier package. As Legend's sales have steadily increased, 3-Series sales have steadily dropped, perhaps an indication of a shift in American driving tastes. Aside from the cramped quarters, there's much to like about the 3-Series cars. BMW dealers should be more willing to discount prices these days.

CONSUMER GUIDE®

Specifications

	2-door notchback	4-door notchback	2-door conv.
Wheelbase, in.	101.2	101.2	101.2
Overall length, in.	170.2	170.2	175.2
Overall width, in.	64.8	64.8	64.8
Overall height, in.	54.3	54.3	53.9
Turn diameter, ft.	34.4	34.4	34.4
Curb weight, lbs.	2811[1]	2855[2]	2990
Cargo vol., cu. ft.	14.3	14.3	11.0
Fuel capacity, gals.	16.4	16.4	16.4
Seating capacity	5	5	4
Front headroom, in.	37.7	37.7	NA
Front shoulder room, in.	52.0	52.0	NA
Front legroom, max., in.	NA	NA	NA
Rear headroom, in.	36.4	36.4	NA
Rear shoulder room, in.	52.4	52.4	NA
Rear legroom, min., in.	NA	NA	NA

1. 3000 lbs., 325iX. 2. 3044 lbs., 325iX.

Powertrain layout: longitudinal front engine/rear-wheel drive or permanent 4WD (325iX).

Engines

	ohc I-6	dohc I-4
Size, liters/cu. in.	2.5/152	2.3/140
Fuel delivery	PFI	PFI
Horsepower @ rpm	168 @ 5800	192 @ 6750
Torque (lbs./ft.) @ rpm	164 @ 4300	170 @ 4750
Availability	S	S[1]

EPA city/highway mpg

5-speed OD manual	18/23	17/29
4-speed OD automatic	18/22	

1. M3.

Prices

BMW 3-Series	Retail Price	Dealer Invoice	Low Price
325i 2-door notchback	$24650	$20215	$22433
325i 4-door notchback	25450	20870	23160
325is 2-door notchback	28950	23740	26345
325i 2-door convertible	33850	27755	30803
325iX 2-door notchback	29950	24560	27255
325iX 4-door notchback	30750	25215	27983
M3 2-door notchback	34950	28660	31805

Prices are accurate at time of printing; subject to manufacturer's change.

	Retail Price	Dealer Invoice	Low Price
Destination charge	345	345	345

Standard equipment:

325i: 2.5-liter PFI 6-cylinder engine, 5-speed manual transmission, power steering, anti-lock 4-wheel disc brakes, driver's-side airbag, air conditioning, cloth or leatherette reclining bucket seats with height/tilt adjustments, outboard rear lap/shoulder belts, power windows and locks, cruise control, power mirrors, AM/FM cassette, power antenna, tinted glass, Service Interval Indicator, Active Check Control, manual sunroof, toolkit, 195/65VR14 tires on alloy wheels. **Convertible** adds: leather upholstery, map lights, trip computer, premium sound system, cross-spoke alloy wheels. **325is** adds: limited-slip differential, front and rear spoilers, power sunroof. **325iX** has: permanent 4-wheel drive, sill extensions, leatherette upholstery, manual sunroof, folding rear armrest with ski sack, 205/55VR15 tires. **M3** has 325is equipment plus 2.3-liter DOHC PFI 4-cylinder engine, sport suspension, 205/55VR15 tires.

Optional equipment:

4-speed automatic transmission (NA M3) .	700	590	645
Metallic paint	375	305	340
Leather upholstery, 325i exc. conv., iX . .	895	NA	NA
Power sunroof, 325i, 325iX	225	185	205
Glass sunroof, 325is	495	395	445
Limited-slip differential, 325i	400	345	373
Cross-spoke alloy wheels, conv.	500	415	458
Heated front seats	250	205	228
Not available on 325i hardtops.			
Premium sound system, 325is & iX	250	205	228
CD changer	780	545	663
Remote alarm system	515	300	408

BMW 5-Series

A driver's-side airbag is standard on the 525i this year as the major change for the 5-Series sedans, which were redesigned for 1989. Only the higher-priced 535i came with an airbag last year. The high-performance M5, derived from the 5-Series sedan and already on sale in Europe, comes to the U.S. next spring. The M5 uses a 311-horsepower,

BMW 535i

dual-cam 3.6-liter 6-cylinder engine and comes only with a 5-speed manual transmission and seats for four. The 525i and 535i have seats for five and are available with either a 5-speed manual or 4-speed automatic. A 168-horsepower 2.5-liter 6-cylinder powers the 525i and a 208-horsepower 3.4-liter 6-cylinder powers the 535i. Both models are now prewired for a cellular telephone and a trunk-mounted compact-disc changer. Newly optional is a remote-control feature for the central locking system that also activates a burglar alarm when it locks the doors. The 535i's interior gains more leather this year, plus new wood trim. BMW had announced plans to phase in a traction-control system as an option for the 535i, but that has been delayed until the 1991 model year. While we like the 535i a lot, we also like the Infiniti Q45 and Lexus LS 400, new Japanese luxury sedans that are invading BMW's domain. We like the 525i less because its 2.5-liter engine doesn't have the gusto you expect in this price range. By comparison, the Q45 and LS 400 cost about the same, but come with potent V-8 engines. Because of the new Japanese competitors, BMW has cut the 535i's base price by $2100 this year and the 525i's base price by $3800. Dealers might be willing to cut prices further.

Prices are accurate at time of printing; subject to manufacturer's change.

Specifications

	4-door notchback
Wheelbase, in.	108.7
Overall length, in.	185.8
Overall width, in.	68.9
Overall height, in.	55.6
Turn diameter, ft.	36.1
Curb weight, lbs.	3395[1]
Cargo vol., cu. ft.	16.2
Fuel capacity, gals.	21.1
Seating capacity	5
Front headroom, in.	38.5
Front shoulder room, in.	NA
Front legroom, max., in.	42.0
Rear headroom, in.	37.4
Rear shoulder room, in.	NA
Rear legroom, min., in.	25.5

1. 3530 lbs., 535i.

Powertrain layout: longitudinal front engine/rear-wheel drive.

Engines

	ohc I-6	ohc I-6
Size, liters/cu. in.	2.5/152	3.4/209
Fuel delivery	PFI	PFI
Horsepower @ rpm	168 @ 5800	208 @ 5700
Torque (lbs./ft.) @ rpm	164 @ 4300	225 @ 4000
Availability	S	S
EPA city/highway mpg		
5-speed OD manual	18/25	15/23
4-speed OD automatic	18/23	15/21

Prices

BMW 5-Series	Retail Price	Dealer Invoice	Low Price
525i 4-door notchback	$33200	$27225	$30213
535i 4-door notchback	41500	34030	37765
Destination charge	345	345	345
Gas Guzzler Tax, 535i 5-speed	650	650	650

Standard equipment:

525i: 2.5-liter PFI 6-cylinder engine, 5-speed manual transmission, power steering, anti-lock 4-wheel disc brakes, driver's-side airbag, air conditioning with individual temperature controls, leather power front bucket seats, folding center armrests, rear armrest with storage, rear shoulder belts, power windows and locks, heated power mirrors, fog lights, adjustable steering wheel, tinted glass, tachometer and coolant temperature gauge, rear defogger, seatback pockets, front and rear reading lights, dual LCD trip odometers, Service Interval Indicator, fuel economy indicator, trip computer, power sunroof, toolkit, 205/65VR15 tires on alloy wheels. **535i** adds: 3.4-liter engine, 5-speed manual or 4-speed automatic transmission, leather-wrapped steering wheel, automatic climate control, 225/60VR15 tires.

Optional equipment:	Retail Price	Dealer Invoice	Low Price
4-speed automatic transmission, 525i . . .	700	590	645
Leather upholstery, 525i	1100	915	1008
Limited-slip differential	400	350	375
Heated front seats	250	205	228
CD changer	780	545	663
Ski sack	160	135	148
Remote alarm system	515	300	408
Glass sunroof	810	645	728

BMW 7-Series

BMW 735i

Traction control is standard on the 750iL as the major change for 1990. BMW calls its traction-control system ASC, for automatic stability control. The system uses the anti-lock brake sensors at the rear wheels to detect wheel slip. If either rear wheel slips during acceleration, ASC limits the amount of power to that wheel (or both) until it regains traction. ASC was supposed to be offered as an option on the 735i and 735iL this year, but that has been postponed until 1991. The 735i and 735iL use a 208-horse-power 3.4-liter 6-cylinder engine; the 750iL has a 296-horse-power V-12. The "L" in the model names denotes a longer wheelbase, 116 inches instead of 111.5 on the 735i. No new 7-Series models are coming to the U.S. this year, but next June a new luxury coupe, the 850i, arrives to replace the 6-Series 2-door, which has ceased production. The 4-seat 850i will use the 750iL's V-12 engine, teamed with either a 4-speed automatic or new 6-speed manual transmission.

Specifications

	735i 4-door notchback	735iL/750iL 4-door notchback
Wheelbase, in.	111.5	116.0
Overall length, in.	193.3	197.8
Overall width, in.	72.6	72.6
Overall height, in.	55.6	55.1
Turn diameter, ft.	38.1	39.4
Curb weight, lbs.	3835	4015[1]
Cargo vol., cu. ft.	17.6	17.6
Fuel capacity, gals.	21.5	24.0
Seating capacity	5	5
Front headroom, in.	38.3	38.3
Front shoulder room, in.	NA	NA
Front legroom, max., in.	44.3	44.3
Rear headroom, in.	37.2	37.2
Rear shoulder room, in.	NA	NA
Rear legroom, min., in.	NA	32.8

1. 4235 lbs., 750iL.

Powertrain layout: longitudinal front engine/rear-wheel drive.

Engines	ohc I-6	ohc V-12
Size, liters/cu. in.	3.4/209	5.0/304
Fuel delivery	PFI	PFI
Horsepower @ rpm	208 @ 5700	296 @ 5200
Torque (lbs./ft.) @ rpm	225 @ 4000	332 @ 4100
Availability	S	S

EPA city/highway mpg

5-speed OD manual	15/23	
4-speed OD automatic	15/21	12/18

The $70,000 750iL effortlessly devours long stretches of highway while isolating its occupants from outside disturbances. Its only real competitor is the similarly priced, V-8-powered Mercedes 560SEL. It more than matches the 560SEL for acceleration, room, quietness, and snob appeal, plus, it's a newer design with a more sporting feel. The 735i is $21,000 cheaper than the 750iL but basically the same car except for some sacrifices in acceleration, features, and back-seat space. You don't have to spend this much to get a good luxury sedan. An Acura Legend costs less than half the price of a 750iL. Or, there are the new Lexus LS 400 and Infiniti Q45, which start out in the $35,000 to $38,000 range.

Prices

BMW 7-Series	Retail Price	Dealer Invoice	Low Price
735i 4-door notchback	$49000	$40180	$44590
735iL 4-door notchback	53000	43460	48230
750iL 4-door notchback	70000	56000	63000
Destination charge	345	345	345
Gas Guzzler Tax, 735i, 735iL	650	650	650
750iL	1500	1500	1500

Standard equipment:

3.4-liter PFI 6-cylinder engine, 4-speed automatic transmission, power steering, anti-lock 4-wheel disc brakes, driver's side airbag, automatic climate control system with separate left and right controls, power front bucket seats with 3-position driver's-side memory (including outside mirrors), leather upholstery, rear shoulder belts, cruise control, fog lamps, speed-sensitive intermittent wipers, heated wiper parking area, heated windshield washer jets, heated power mirrors, heated driver's door lock, power windows and locks, leather-wrapped steering wheel, rear head restraints, front center armrests, rear armrest with storage compartment, Bubinga wood trim, time-delay courtesy light, map lights, rear reading lights, tinted glass, tachometer and coolant temperature gauge, LCD main and trip odometers, Service Interval Indicator, fuel economy indicator, Active Check Control, trip computer, rear defogger, power sunroof, AM/FM cassette, power antenna, tool-kit, 225/60VR15 tires on cast alloy wheels. **735iL** adds: power rear seat, self-leveling rear suspension, remote alarm system. **750iL** adds: 5.0-liter PFI V-12, additional leather trim, Elmwood trim, cellular telephone, forged alloy wheels.

Prices are accurate at time of printing; subject to manufacturer's change.

Optional equipment:

	Retail Price	Dealer Invoice	Low Price
Limited-slip differential	400	350	375
Heated front seats, 735i, 735iL	250	205	228
Heated rear seats, 750iL	250	205	228
CD changer, 735i, 735iL	780	545	663
Ski sack	160	135	148
Roll-up rear sunshade, 735iL	140	115	128
Cellular telephone, 735i, 735iL	1205	1000	1103
Remote alarm system, 735i	515	300	408

Buick Electra/
Oldsmobile Ninety-Eight

Buick Electra T Type

Several minor changes are made to these full-size, front-drive luxury twins. The Electra line is topped by the Park Avenue Ultra, which was introduced in January 1989. Ultra's standard equipment includes a leather interior, 20-way power adjustments for the driver and front passenger seats, 2-tone paint, and 15-inch aluminum wheels. The other Electras continue as the Limited, the Park Avenue, and the sporty T Type. They share their 4-door sedan platforms and mechanical components with the Olds Ninety-Eight and its sporty variant, the Touring Sedan. For '90, all get body reinforcements intended to improve rough-road solidity and a revised power-steering valve designed to enhance road feel. A compact disc player is a new option. Anti-lock brakes are standard on the Buick Ultra and T Type and on the Olds Touring Sedan; they remain optional on the other Electras and Ninety-Eights. A driver's-side airbag is optional on all Ninety-Eights except the Touring Sedan. A 165-horsepower 3.8-liter V-6 and a 4-speed overdrive automatic is the only available powertrain. The basic design and powertrain of the Electra and Ninety-Eight also are used for the Buick LeSabre, Olds Eighty Eight, and Pontiac Bonneville. These cars are among General Motors' best, combining 6-passenger room and luxurious comfort with credible front-drive road manners and ample V-6 power. Unless you're enamored of the Ninety-Eight or Electra badges, however, we strongly recommend you consider the LeSabre, Eighty Eight, or Bonneville. They have all the dynamic virtues of the Electra and Ninety-Eight, but with fewer luxury amenities, they're priced lower.

Specifications

	4-door notchback
Wheelbase, in.	110.8
Overall length, in.	196.9
Overall width, in.	72.4
Overall height, in.	54.3
Turn diameter, ft.	39.4
Curb weight, lbs.	3288
Cargo vol., cu. ft.	16.4
Fuel capacity, gals.	18.0
Seating capacity	6
Front headroom, in.	39.3
Front shoulder room, in.	58.9
Front legroom, max., in.	42.4
Rear headroom, in.	38.1
Rear shoulder room, in.	58.8
Rear legroom, min., in.	41.5

Powertrain layout: transverse front engine/front-wheel drive.

Engines

	ohv V-6
Size, liters/cu. in.	3.8/231
Fuel delivery	PFI
Horsepower @ rpm	165 @ 4800
Torque (lbs./ft.) @ rpm	210 @ 2000
Availability	S

EPA city/highway mpg

4-speed OD automatic	18/27

Prices are accurate at time of printing; subject to manufacturer's change.

Prices

Buick Electra

	Retail Price	Dealer Invoice	Low Price
Limited 4-door notchback	$20225	$17454	$17704
T Type 4-door notchback	23025	19871	20121
Park Avenue 4-door notchback	21750	18770	19020
Park Avenue Ultra 4-door notchback	27825	23735	23985
Destination charge	550	550	550

Standard equipment:

Limited: 3.8-liter PFI V-6 engine, 4-speed automatic transmission, power steering, air conditioning, 55/45 cloth front seat with storage armrest, power driver's seat, tilt steering column, power windows, intermittent wipers, cruise control, AM/FM cassette, rear defogger, left remote and right manual mirrors, trip odometer, remote fuel door release, tinted glass, front reading and courtesy lights, rear shoulder belts, automatic level control, wire wheel covers, 205/75R14 all-season SBR tires. **T Type** adds: anti- lock braking system, Gran Touring suspension, sport steering wheel, floormats, overhead console, quartz analog gauge cluster (includes tachometer, voltmeter, coolant temperature and oil pressure gauges, low-fuel warning), rear headrests, lighted visor mirrors, power mirrors, 45/45 front seat with console and armrest, leather-wrapped steering wheel, power antenna, remote decklid release, 215/65R15 Goodyear Eagle GT+4 tires on alloy wheels. **Park Avenue** adds to base: cruise control, power locks, power mirrors, coach lamps, rear reading and courtesy lights, lighted right visor mirror, added sound insulation, floormats, upgraded carpet, WSW tires. **Ultra** adds: anti-lock braking system, 55/45 leather front seat with 20-way power adjustments, two-tone paint, rear armrest, 205/70R15 tires on alloy wheels.

Optional equipment:

Anti-lock brakes	925	786	833
Premium Pkg. SB, Limited	398	338	358

Power antenna, floormats, door edge guards, lighted right visor mirror, power right seatback recliner, remote decklid release.

Luxury Pkg. SC, Limited	1009	858	908

Pkg. SB plus automatic climate control, door courtesy/warning lights, power mirrors, power passenger seat.

Prestige Pkg. SD, Limited	2199	1869	1979

Pkg. SC plus cornering lights, automatic power locks, Twilight Sentinel, remote keyless entry, illuminated entry, light monitors, automatic day/night mirror, lighted left visor mirror, driver's seatback recliner, self-sealing tires, upgraded radio (includes AM stereo, EQ and tape search/repeat).

	Retail Price	Dealer Invoice	Low Price
Premium Pkg. SB, T Type	690	587	621

Automatic climate control, door edge guards, power passenger seat with power recliner, Concert Sound speakers.

Luxury Pkg. SC, T Type	1178	1001	1060

Pkg. SB plus cornering lights, Twilight Sentinel, illuminated entry, lamp monitors, door courtesy/warning lights, rear reading lights, low washer fluid indicator, power decklid pulldown.

Prestige Pkg. SD, T Type	2099	1784	1889

Pkg. SC plus automatic power locks, remote keyless entry, automatic day/night mirror, heated left mirror, power driver's seatback recliner, two-position driver's seat memory, deluxe trunk trim, upgraded radio (includes AM stereo, EQ and tape search/repeat).

Premium Pkg. SB, Park Ave	825	701	743
Ultra	410	349	369

Automatic climate control, door edge guards, Twilight Sentinel, Concert Sound speakers, power antenna, power passenger seat with power recliner.

Luxury Pkg. SC, Park Ave	1500	1275	1350
Ultra	1085	922	977

Pkg. SB plus cornering lights, automatic power locks, four-note horn, illuminated entry, remote keyless entry, light monitors, low fuel and washer fluid indicators, lighted left visor mirror, power decklid pulldown.

Prestige Pkg. SD, Park Ave	2306	1960	2075
Ultra	1596	1357	1436

Pkg. SC plus automatic day/night mirror, heated left mirror, two-position driver's seat memory, driver's seatback recliner, deluxe trunk trim, self-sealing tires, upgraded radio (includes AM stereo, EQ and tape search/repeat).

Gran Touring Pkg., Ltd & Park Ave	272	231	245
Ltd & Park Ave w/SD	122	104	110

Gran Touring suspension, HD cooling, 2.97 axle ratio, leather-wrapped steering wheel, 215/65R15 Eagle GT tires on alloy wheels.

2.97 axle ratio	NC	NC	NC
HD cooling (std. T Type)	40	34	36
Quartz analog gauge cluster (std. T Type) .	126	107	113
Park Ave & Ultra w/SC/SD	110	94	99
Electronic instruments, Park Ave & Ultra .	299	254	269
Park Ave & Ultra w/SC/SD	283	241	255
Decklid luggage rack	115	98	104
Firemist paint, exc. T Type	210	179	189
UX1 radio			
T Type, Park Ave & Ultra w/SB/SC	150	128	135

Includes AM stereo, EQ, tape search/repeat and Concert Sound speakers.

Bose music system (NA Ltd)	773	657	696
w/SB/SC	703	598	633
w/SD	553	470	498

Prices are accurate at time of printing; subject to manufacturer's change.

	Retail Price	Dealer Invoice	Low Price
CD player	454	386	409
T Type, Park Ave & Ultra w/SB/SC	384	326	346
w/SD	234	199	211
Includes AM stereo, EQ and Concert Sound speakers.			
Astroroof	1230	1046	1107
Theft deterrent system	159	135	143
Vinyl top, LTD & Park Ave	260	221	234
Ultra	895	761	806
Leather/vinyl 55/45 seat, Park Ave	450	383	405
T Type	395	336	356
Alloy wheels, Ltd & Park Ave	55	47	50
California emissions pkg.	100	85	90
Bodyside stripes, Ltd & T Type	45	38	41

Oldsmobile Ninety-Eight

	Retail Price	Dealer Invoice	Low Price
Regency 4-door notchback	$19995	$17256	$17456
Brougham 4-door notchback	21595	23124	23324
Touring Sedan 4-door notchback	26795	23124	23324
Destination charge	550	550	550

Standard equipment:

3.8-liter PFI V-6, 4-speed automatic transmission, power steering, air conditioning, tinted glass, power windows and locks, 55/45 seat with power driver's side and storage armrest, rear shoulder belts, remote mirrors, opera lamps, front and rear armrests, right visor mirrors, trip odometer, reading lamp, AM/FM cassette, automatic load leveling, 205/75R14 all-season SBR tires, wire wheel covers. **Brougham** adds: automatic climate control, cruise control, tilt steering column, cornering lamps, sail panel reading lamps, intermittent wipers, opera lamps, alloy wheels. **Touring Sedan** adds: anti-lock braking system, FE3 suspension, 215/65R15 Goodyear Eagle GT+4 tires on alloy wheels, front console with storage, Driver Information System (trip computer, service reminder), gauge cluster including tachometer, fog lamps, illumination package, power mirrors with heated left, AM/FM cassette w/EQ, Twilight Sentinel, steering wheel touch controls, remote decklid and fuel door releases.

Optional equipment:

Anti-lock brakes, base & Brougham	925	786	833
Inflatable Restraint System, base & Brougham	850	723	765
Option Pkg. 1SB, base	949	807	854
Intermittent wipers, cruise control, rear defogger, tilt steering column, power antenna, lighted visor mirrors, Remote Lock Control Pkg., floormats.			

	Retail Price	Dealer Invoice	Low Price
Option Pkg. 1SC, base	2068	1758	1861

Pkg. 1SC plus manual driver's seatback recliner, automatic climate control, power passenger seat, cornering lamps, steering wheel touch controls.

	Retail Price	Dealer Invoice	Low Price
Value Option Pkg., base & Brougham . . .	801	681	721

Convenience Value Group, custom leather trim, AM/FM cassette w/EQ.

	Retail Price	Dealer Invoice	Low Price
Padded vinyl roof, base & Brougham . . .	260	221	234
Power glass sunroof	1230	1046	1107
Rear defogger, base & Brougham	160	136	144
Accent stripe, base	45	38	41
FE3 suspension pkg., base	339	288	305
Brougham	246	209	221
Alloy wheels, base	103	88	93
Wire wheel covers, Brougham	NC	NC	NC
Convenience Value Group, base & Brougham	376	320	338
AM/FM cassette w/EQ, base & Brougham .	235	200	212
AM/FM radio w/CD player, base & Brougham	359	305	323
Touring Sedan	124	105	112
Delco/Bose music system, Touring Sedan .	523	445	471
Instrument panel cluster, base & Brougham .	66	56	59
Driver Information System, base & Brougham .	150	128	135
High-capacity cooling, base & Brougham .	66	56	59
Glamour metallic paint, base & Brougham .	210	179	189
Luggage rack, base & Brougham	115	98	104
Custom leather trim, base & Brougham . .	490	417	441
Engine block heater	18	15	16
California emissions pkg.	100	85	90

Buick LeSabre/ Oldsmobile Eighty Eight/ Pontiac Bonneville

These popular General Motors full-size, front-drive cars receive some exterior alterations and under-the-skin modifications. LeSabre and Eighty Eight get a restyled grille, headlamps, taillamps, and front and rear fascias. At Pontiac, Bonneville SE and LE versions get a new grille and taillamps similar to the top-of-the-line SSE's, while the SE also gets a rear spoiler in place of its previous rear-deck luggage rack. Buick's sporty T Type option packages have been discontinued, but most of the T Type equipment is

Buick Le Sabre

Specifications

	2-door notchback	4-door notchback
Wheelbase, in.	110.8	110.8
Overall length, in.	196.5	196.5
Overall width, in.	72.4	72.4
Overall height, in.	54.2	54.9
Turn diameter, ft.	39.4	39.4
Curb weight, lbs.	3242	3269
Cargo vol., cu. ft.	15.7	16.4
Fuel capacity, gals.	18.0	18.0
Seating capacity	6	6
Front headroom, in.	38.1	38.9
Front shoulder room, in.	59.0	59.5
Front legroom, max., in.	42.4	42.4
Rear headroom, in.	37.6	38.3
Rear shoulder room, in.	57.8	59.5
Rear legroom, min., in.	37.4	38.7

Powertrain layout: transverse front engine/front-wheel drive.

Engines

	ohv V-6
Size, liters/cu. in.	3.8/231
Fuel delivery	PFI
Horsepower @ rpm	165 @ 4800
Torque (lbs./ft.) @ rpm	210 @ 2000
Availability	S

EPA city/highway mpg

4-speed OD automatic	18/27

available in the Gran Touring package, which for '90 includes added automatic level control. Bonneville's front-seat lap belts are now mounted to the seats rather than to the inside of the roof pillar. All three cars have a stiffer front substructure for better over-the-road behavior and noise isolation. No changes have been made to their powertrain, which remains a 165-horsepower 3.8-liter V-6 coupled to a 4-speed automatic transmission. All three cars are available as 4-door notchback sedans, plus the LeSabre and Eighty Eight also have 2-door models, and all are available with optional anti-lock brakes (they're standard on the Bonneville SSE). The Pontiac is marketed as the sportiest of the bunch, while the Eighty Eight is the only one available with an optional driver's-side airbag. The 1989 LeSabre, meanwhile, was the top domestic model and ranked No. 2 among 154 domestic and imported cars in J.D. Power and Associates' initial quality survey. All three cars are stellar family automobiles, with front-wheel drive, a responsive engine, standard air conditioning, optional anti-lock brakes, and a big-car ride and feel. They're built from the same design as the more expensive Oldsmobile Ninety-Eight and Buick Electra, but we favor the Bonneville/LeSabre/Eighty Eight because there are no substantive differences on their plusher brethren.

Prices

Buick LeSabre	Retail Price	Dealer Invoice	Low Price
2-door notchback	$16145	$13933	$14133
Custom 4-door notchback	16050	13851	14051
Limited 4-door notchback	17400	15016	15216
Limited 2-door notchback	17300	14930	15130
Destination charge	505	505	505

Standard equipment:

Base and Custom: 3.8-liter PFI V-6, 4-speed automatic transmission, power steering, air conditioning, tilt steering column, cloth split bench seat with armrest, trip odometer, tinted glass, AM/FM radio, automatic front seatbelts, rear shoulder belts, 205/75R14 all-season SBR tires. **Limited** adds: 55/45 front seat with storage armrest, reclining seatbacks, wide lower bodyside moldings.

Prices are accurate at time of printing; subject to manufacturer's change.

Optional equipment:	Retail Price	Dealer Invoice	Low Price
Anti-lock brakes	925	786	833
Popular Pkg. SB, base & Custom	714	607	643
Floormats, cruise control, rear defogger, 55/45 seat with storage armrest, intermittent wipers, white-stripe tires.			
Premium Pkg. SC, base	1254	1066	1129
Custom	1294	1100	1165
Pkg. SB plus power locks, AM/FM cassette, wire wheel covers.			
Luxury Pkg. SD, base	1859	1580	1673
Custom	1974	1678	1777
Pkg. SC plus power driver's seat, power windows, door edge guards, manual seatback recliners.			
Prestige Pkg. SE, base	2218	1885	1996
Custom	2333	1983	2100
Pkg. SD plus lighted right visor mirror, power mirrors, power antenna, remote decklid release, Concert Sound speakers.			
Popular Pkg. SB, Ltd 2-door	1356	1153	1220
Ltd 4-door	1461	1242	1315
Floormats, cruise control, rear defogger, power windows and locks, power driver's seat, AM/FM cassette, intermittent wipers, white-stripe tires.			
Premium Pkg. SC, Ltd 2-door	1769	1504	1592
Ltd 4-door	1884	1601	1696
Pkg. SB plus door edge guards, lighted right visor mirror, power antenna, remote decklid release, wire wheel covers.			
Luxury Pkg. SD, Ltd 2-door	2261	1922	2035
Ltd 4-door	2376	2020	2138
Pkg. SC plus automatic climate control, door courtesy light and reflector, front and rear reading lights, power mirrors, power passenger seatback recliner, deluxe trunk trim.			
Prestige Pkg. SE, Ltd 2-door	2766	2351	2489
Ltd 4-door	2881	2449	2593
Pkg. SD plus power passenger seat, upgraded radio (includes AM stereo, EQ, tape search/repeat).			
Gran Touring Pkg.	738	627	664
w/SB	662	563	596
w/SC/SD/SE	447	380	402
Gran Touring suspension, 2.97 axle ratio, HD cooling, leather-wrapped steering wheel, automatic level control, 215/65R15 tires on alloy wheels.			
2.97 axle ratio	NC	NC	NC
Requires HD cooling.			
HD cooling	40	34	36
Power locks, base	175	149	158
Custom	215	183	194
Gauge pkg.	110	94	99
Tachometer, coolant temperature and oil pressure gauges, voltmeter.			
Decklid luggage rack	115	98	104
AM/FM cassette, Custom w/SA/SB	150	128	135

	Retail Price	Dealer Invoice	Low Price
AM/FM cassette w/EQ & AM ST	385	327	347
Custom w/SC/SD, Ltd w/SB/SC/SD . . .	235	200	212
Custom w/SE	150	128	135
Power antenna	75	64	68
Automatic level control	175	149	158
Vinyl top, 4-doors	200	170	180
55/45 seat w/storage armrest, base & Custom	183	156	165
Leather/vinyl 55/45 seat, Ltd	450	383	405
Alloy wheels, w/SA/SB	270	230	243
w/SC/SD/SE	55	47	50
Wire wheel covers, w/SA/SB	215	183	194
Power windows, 2-doors	230	196	207
4-doors	295	251	266
California emissions pkg.	100	85	90

Oldsmobile Eighty Eight

	Retail Price	Dealer Invoice	Low Price
Royale 2-door notchback	$15895	$13717	$13917
Royale 4-door notchback	15995	13804	14004
Brougham 2-door notchback	17295	14926	15126
Brougham 4-door notchback	17395	15012	15212
Destination charge	505	505	505

Standard equipment:

Royale: 3.8-liter PFI V-6, 4-speed automatic transmission, power steering, air conditioning, tinted glass, left remote mirror, AM/FM radio, bench seat with center armrests, rear shoulder belts, 205/75R14 tires. **Brougham** adds: Convenience Group (lamps, right visor mirror, chime tones), 55/45 front seat with storage armrest, remote decklid release.

Optional equipment:

	Retail Price	Dealer Invoice	Low Price
Anti-lock brakes	925	786	833
Inflatable Restraint System, 4-doors	850	723	765
Option Pkg. 1SB, Royale	839	713	755

Divided bench seat with dual controls, intermittent wipers, cruise control, tilt steering column, Convenience Group, rear defogger, floormats.

Option Pkg. 1SC, Royale 2-door	1389	1181	1250
Royale 4-door	1504	1278	1354

Pkg. 1SB plus power windows and locks, door edge guards, power antenna, driver's seatback recliner.

Option Pkg. 1SD, Royale 2-door . . .-. . . .	1905	1619	1715
Royale 4-door	2020	1717	1818

Pkg. 1SC plus Remote Control Lock Pkg., power driver's seat, Reminder Pkg.

Prices are accurate at time of printing; subject to manufacturer's change.

	Retail Price	Dealer Invoice	Low Price
Value Option Pkg., Royale	349	297	314

Alloy wheels, instrument panel cluster, decklid luggage rack.

	Retail Price	Dealer Invoice	Low Price
Option Pkg. 1SB, Brougham 2-door	1290	1097	1161
Brougham 4-door	1405	1194	1265

Intermittent wipers, cruise control, tilt steering column, power windows and locks, floormats, door edge guards, power driver's seat, rear defogger.

	Retail Price	Dealer Invoice	Low Price
Option Pkg. 1SC, Brougham 2-door	1661	1412	1495
Brougham 4-door	1776	1510	1598

Pkg. 1SB plus power antenna, Reminder Pkg., driver's seatback recliner, electronic air conditioning.

	Retail Price	Dealer Invoice	Low Price
Option Pkg. 1SD, Brougham 2-door	1936	1646	1742
Brougham 4-door	2051	1743	1846

Pkg. 1SC plus Driver Information System, Remote Control Lock Pkg.

	Retail Price	Dealer Invoice	Low Price
Value Option Pkg., Brougham	712	605	641

Convenience Value Group, AM/FM cassette with EQ, custom leather trim.

	Retail Price	Dealer Invoice	Low Price
Power passenger seat, Brougham	270	230	243
Power locks, Royale 2-door	175	149	158
Royale 4-door	215	183	194
Power windows, Royale 2-door	240	204	216
Royale 4-door	305	259	275
Rear defogger	160	136	144
FE3 Touring Car Ride & Handling Pkg.	779	662	701
Wire wheel covers, Royale	291	247	262
Brougham	215	183	194
Alloy wheels, Regency	368	313	331
Brougham	302	257	272
205/75R14 WSW tires, Royale	76	65	68
Convenience Value Group, Royale	317	269	285
Brougham	287	244	258
AM/FM cassette, Royale	140	119	126
w/EQ, Brougham	235	200	212
AM/FM radio w/CD player, Brougham	359	305	323
Instrument panel cluster	66	56	59
Driver Information System, Brougham	150	128	135
High-capacity cooling equipment	66	56	59
Decklid luggage rack	115	98	104
Towing Pkg.	271	230	244
Custom leather trim	490	417	441

Pontiac Bonneville

	Retail Price	Dealer Invoice	Low Price
LE 4-door notchback	$15774	$13613	$13813
SE 4-door notchback	19144	16521	16721
SSE 4-door notchback	23994	20707	20907
Destination charge	505	505	505

Standard equipment:

LE: 3.8-liter PFI V-6, 4-speed automatic transmission, power steering, air conditioning, tinted glass, cloth 45/55 seat with recliners, rear shoulder belts, left remote and right manual mirrors, wide bodyside moldings, AM/FM radio, coolant temperature gauge, 205/75R14 tires. **SE** adds: 2.97 axle ratio, storage armrest, cargo security net, intermittent wipers, cruise control, tilt steering column, tachometer and trip odometer, power windows, AM/FM cassette with EQ, Rally Tuned Suspension, 215/60R16 Eagle GT + 4 tires on alloy wheels. **SSE** adds: 3.33 axle ratio, anti-lock braking system, Electronic Ride Control, automatic air conditioning with steering wheel controls, electronic compass, Driver Information System, heated power mirrors, headlamp sentinel, headlamp washers, power seat adjustments (including lumbar support, recliners and head restraints), fog lamps, aero bodyside extensions, eight-speaker audio system with Touch Control, power antenna, rear storage armrest, rear defogger, lighted visor mirrors, leather-wrapped steering wheel, illuminated entry, remote decklid release, power locks, first aid and accessory kits, uprated suspension, 215/60R16 Eagle GT + 4 tires.

Optional equipment:	Retail Price	Dealer Invoice	Low Price
Anti-lock brakes, LE & SE	925	786	833
LE requires Pkg. 1SD or 1SE.			
Option Pkg. 1SB, LE	269	229	242
Tilt steering column, intermittent wipers, Lamp Group.			
Option Pkg. 1SC, LE	464	394	418
Pkg. 1SB plus cruise control.			
Option Pkg. 1SD, LE	1716	1459	1544
Pkg. 1SC plus power windows and locks, power driver's seat, remote decklid release, lighted visor mirrors, rally gauges with tachometer, AM/FM cassette.			
Option Pkg. 1SE, LE	2414	2052	2173
Pkg. 1SD plus illuminated entry, power mirrors, leather-wrapped steering wheel, power antenna, remote fuel door release, remote keyless entry, power passenger seat.			
Value Option Pkg. R6A, LE	940	799	846
w/Pkg. 1SD or 1SE	465	395	419
Custom interior trim, 215/65R15 tires on alloy wheels.			
Option Pkg. 1SB, SE	330	281	297
Lighted visor mirrors, illuminated entry, power mirrors, power antenna.			
Option Pkg. 1SC, SE	810	689	729
Pkg. 1SB plus remote fuel door release, remote keyless entry, power passenger seat, Twilight Sentinel.			
Value Option Pkg. R6A, LE	610	519	549
SE w/Pkg. 1SB or 1SC	535	455	482
Custom two-tone paint, AM/FM cassette with EQ.			
Value Option Pkg. R6A, SSE	1080	918	972
Power glass sunroof, theft deterrent system.			

Prices are accurate at time of printing; subject to manufacturer's change.

	Retail Price	Dealer Invoice	Low Price
Rear defogger, LE	160	136	144
Custom two-tone paint, LE & SE	105	89	95
Power locks, LE	215	183	194
Power windows, LE	375	319	338
Power antenna, LE	75	64	68
AM/FM cassette, LE	140	119	126
AM/FM cassette w/EQ, SE	655	557	590
SE w/Pkg. 1SB or 1SC	580	493	522
Includes electronic air conditioning, power antenna, anti-theft feature, Touch Control.			
AM/FM radio w/CD player & EQ, LE	1031	876	928
LE w/custom interior trim	931	791	838
LE w/Pkg. 1SD	891	757	802
LE w/Pkg. 1SD & custom interior trim .	791	672	712
LE w/Pkg. 1SE	766	651	689
LE w/Pkg. 1SE & custom interior trim .	666	566	599
SE	841	715	757
SE w/Pkg. 1SB or 1SC	766	651	689
SSE	186	158	167
Includes electronic air conditioning, leather-wrapped steering wheel, anti-theft feature, power antenna, Touch Control.			
Metrix 45/45 seat w/console, SE	235	200	212
Ventura leather trim, SSE	779	662	701
Custom interior trim, LE	705	599	635
LE w/Pkg. 1SD or 1SE	230	196	207
Metrix 45/45 seat, six-speaker performance sound system, gauges, power windows, trunk security net; requires Pkg. 1SC, 1SD or 1SE.			
Power driver's seat, LE	270	230	243
Power glass sunroof, SE & SSE	1230	1046	1107
WSW tires, LE	76	65	68
215/65R15 tires, LE	114	97	103
215/65R15 WSW tires, LE	184	156	166
LE w/Pkg. R6A	70	60	63
Diamond-spoke alloy wheels, LE	296	252	266
Requires 215/65R15 tires.			
Theft deterrent system, SSE	150	128	135

Buick Riviera and Reatta

A convertible joins the Reatta lineup in spring 1990 and both Reatta and Riviera get a new dashboard that eliminates the controversial video-screen control center. Reatta is a 2-seat coupe introduced in January 1988. It's built on

Buick Riviera

a shortened version of the 5-passenger Riviera's front-drive platform and shares most of Riviera's mechanical and comfort features. Both cars get a driver's-side airbag as standard for '90, but anti-lock brakes, standard on the Reatta, remain a Riviera option. A 3.8-liter V-6 engine and 4-speed overdrive automatic transmission comprise the only available powertrain. The Reatta ragtop is the first Buick convertible since the 1982-85 Riviera. Its soft top must be raised and lowered by hand from outside the car. A power pulldown snugs it against the hard rear tonneau cover, which is hinged and eliminates the need for a snap-on boot. The top is available in five colors and has a glass back window with an electric defogger. The convertible's price hadn't been announced. The video Electronic Control Center was introduced on the '86 Riviera and carried over to the Reatta. A small, touch-sensitive screen in the center of the dashboard replaced traditional gauges and switches for the climate system, stereo, and other functions. Critics said it was distracting, not helpful, for the driver. The new dashboard uses conventional buttons and slide levers. In addition, the previous digital speedometer, tachometer, and other gauges have been replaced by vacuum-fluorescent readouts made to look like analog instruments; a switch lets the driver choose a speedometer that's analog, digital, or both. A new center console and revised door panels complete the cabin's cosmetic make over. While the Reatta and the Riviera are competent on the road, both emphasize style and luxury over driving excitement.

Specifications

	Riviera 2-door notchback	Reatta 2-door notchback	Reatta 2-door conv.
Wheelbase, in.	108.0	98.5	98.5
Overall length, in.	193.3	183.7	183.7
Overall width, in.	71.7	73.0	73.0
Overall height, in.	53.6	51.2	51.2
Turn diameter, ft.	37.5	38.0	38.0
Curb weight, lbs.	3464	3379	3562
Cargo vol., cu. ft.	14.4	10.5	10.5
Fuel capacity, gals.	18.2	18.2	18.2
Seating capacity	5	2	2
Front headroom, in.	37.8	36.9	36.9
Front shoulder room, in.	57.9	57.0	57.0
Front legroom, max., in.	42.7	43.1	43.1
Rear headroom, in.	37.8	—	—
Rear shoulder room, in.	57.4	—	—
Rear legroom, min., in.	35.6	—	—

Powertrain layout: transverse front engine/front-wheel drive.

Engines

	ohv V-6
Size, liters/cu. in.	3.8/231
Fuel delivery	PFI
Horsepower @ rpm	165 @ 4800
Torque (lbs./ft.) @ rpm	210 @ 2000
Availability	S

EPA city/highway mpg

4-speed OD automatic	18/27

Prices

Buick Riviera

	Retail Price	Dealer Invoice	Low Price
2-door notchback	$23040	$19653	$19853
Destination charge	550	550	550

Standard equipment:

3.8-liter PFI V-6, 4-speed automatic transmission, power steering, 4-wheel disc brakes, driver's side airbag, power windows and locks, automatic level control, cloth reclining bucket seats, power driver's seat, AM/FM cassette, power antenna, rear shoulder belts, floormats, full-length console, cruise control, rear defogger, intermittent wipers, Pass Key theft deterrent system, door edge guards, electronic instrumentation (tachometer, coolant temperature and oil pressure gauges, voltmeter, trip odometer), remote fuel door and decklid releases, tinted glass, tilt steering column, leather-wrapped steering wheel, illuminated driver's door lock and interior light control, cornering lamps, coach lamps, door courtesy and warning lights, power mirrors, lighted visor mirrors, 205/70R15 all-season SBR tires, locking wire wheel covers.

Optional equipment:

	Retail Price	Dealer Invoice	Low Price
Anti-lock brakes	925	786	833
Prestige Pkg. SE	865	735	779

Twilight Sentinel, remote keyless entry, automatic power locks, heated left mirror, power decklid pulldown, power passenger seat with power recliner, automatic day/night mirror.

Gran Touring Pkg.	104	88	94

Gran Touring suspension, 2.97 axle ratio, leather-wrapped steering wheel and shift handle, fast-ratio power steering, 215/65R15 Goodyear Eagle GT + 4 tires on alloy wheels.

Riviera Appearance Pkg.	205	174	185

Firemist lower accent paint, bodyside stripe, painted alloy wheels.

Firemist or pearlescent paint	210	179	189
Lower accent paint	190	162	171
Delco/Bose Gold music system w/CD player .	1399	1189	1259
CD player w/EQ	516	439	464
Astroroof	1230	1046	1107

Buick Reatta

	Retail Price	Dealer Invoice	Low Price
2-door notchback	$23335	$24170	$25612
2-door convertible	NA	NA	NA
Destination charge	550	550	550

Standard equipment:

3.8-liter PFI V-6 engine, 4-speed automatic transmission, power steering, 4-wheel disc brakes, anti-lock braking system, driver's side airbag, automatic climate control, power windows and locks, power front bucket seats with recliners, leather upholstery, remote keyless entry, electronic instruments (tachometer, coolant temperature and oil pressure gauges, voltmeter, trip odometer), tinted glass, intermittent wipers, AM/FM cassette with EQ and power antenna, full-length console, lighted visor mirrors, intermittent wipers, tilt steering column, leather-wrapped steering wheel, rear defogger, digital clock, cruise control, remote fuel door and trunk releases, cornering lamps, fog lamps, Pass Key theft deterrent system, map lights, illuminated driver's door lock and interior light control, 215/65R15 Goodyear Eagle GT + 4 tires on alloy wheels.

Prices are accurate at time of printing; subject to manufacturer's change.

Optional equipment:	Retail Price	Dealer Invoice	Low Price
CD player	396	337	356
Sliding sunroof	895	761	806
16-way driver's seat	680	578	612
California emissions pkg.	100	85	90

Buick Skylark/
Oldsmobile Cutlass Calais

Buick Skylark

Oldsmobile revives the revered 442 name for 1990, while a new Luxury Edition sedan tops a revamped Skylark range. The Skylark and Cutlass Calais are front-drive compacts available as 2-door coupes or 4-door sedans. They share their design with the Pontiac Grand Am. Engine choices are a 2.5-liter 4-cylinder, a 3.3-liter V-6, and the Quad 4. The Quad 4 is a 2.3-liter, 16-valve 4-cylinder that makes 160 horsepower with automatic transmission and 180 with manual. The latter version is the HO (high-output) Quad 4; it's offered only on the Calais and only with manual transmission. The original 442 was a mid-1960s rear-drive, mid-size V-8 muscle car. It drew its name from its 4-barrel carburetor, 4-speed manual transmission, and dual exhausts. Today's 442 is an option package on the front-drive, compact Calais S 2-door coupe. Its name denotes the HO Quad 4, 4-valves per cylinder, and dual cam-

Specifications

	2-door notchback	4-door notchback
Wheelbase, in.	103.4	103.4
Overall length, in.	178.8	178.8
Overall width, in.	66.6	66.6
Overall height, in.	52.4	52.4
Turn diameter, ft.	35.4	35.4
Curb weight, lbs.	2518	2585
Cargo vol., cu. ft.	13.2	13.2
Fuel capacity, gals.	13.6	13.6
Seating capacity	5	5
Front headroom, in.	37.8	37.8
Front shoulder room, in.	53.9	53.9
Front legroom, max., in.	42.9	42.9
Rear headroom, in.	37.1	37.1
Rear shoulder room, in.	55.1	53.5
Rear legroom, min., in.	34.3	34.3

Powertrain layout: transverse front engine/front-wheel drive.

Engines	ohv I-4	dohc I-4	dohc I-4	ohv V-6
Size, liters/cu. in.	2.5/151	2.3/138	2.3/138	3.3/204
Fuel delivery	TBI	PFI	PFI	PFI
Horsepower @ rpm	110 @ 5200	160 @ 6200	180 @ 6200	160 @ 5200
Torque (lbs./ft.) @ rpm	135 @ 3200	155 @ 5200	150 @ 5200	185 @ 2000
Availability	S	O	S[1]	O

EPA city/highway mpg

5-speed OD manual	22/33		22/31	
3-speed automatic	23/31	23/31		20/27

1. Calais International Series and Quad 442.

shafts. The HO Quad 4 also is standard on the Calais International Series. Elsewhere in the Calais lineup, the S model gets a new instrument cluster and a remote keyless entry system is a new option on all models. The new Skylark Limited Edition has a full vinyl top, wire wheel covers, 2-tone paint, and bright exterior trim. Inside are a reclining cloth split front bench and split, folding rear seat. It shares with the rest of the Skylarks a new instrument panel that replaces digital readouts with analog gauges. Gone from the Skylark line are the Limited 4-door sedan and 2-door coupe. The 2- and 4-door Custom models return, one step up from the new base coupe and sedan. A

Prices are accurate at time of printing; subject to manufacturer's change.

Gran Sport Coupe rounds out the new Skylark models. Japanese rivals generally feel more refined and are more efficiently packaged than Calais and Skylark. With the V-6, they're potent entry-level models into the Olds and Buick lines. The Quad 4 offers lots of power, but no Calais or Skylark has road manners that do full justice to the engine's performance potential.

Prices

Buick Skylark	Retail Price	Dealer Invoice	Low Price
4-door notchback	$10465	$9659	$9859
2-door notchback	10565	9752	9952
Custom 4-door notchback	11460	10234	10434
Custom 2-door notchback	11460	10234	10434
Luxury Edition (LE) 4-door notchback*	13145	11738	11938
Gran Sport (GS) 2-door notchback	12935	11551	11751
Destination charge	425	425	425

Standard equipment:

2.5-liter TBI 4-cylinder engine, 3-speed automatic transmission, power steering, cloth split bench seat, tinted glass, trip odometer, AM/FM radio, 185/80R13 tires. **Custom** adds: front and rear center armrests, remote fuel door release, split folding rear seat, upgraded trunk trim. **Luxury Edition** adds: vinyl top, two-tone paint, wire wheel covers, reclining split bench seat, wide bodyside moldings, left remote and right manual mirrors. **Gran Sport** adds to Custom: Gran Touring suspension, AM/FM cassette, left remote and right manual mirrors, leather-wrapped steering wheel, wide black bodyside moldings, 215/60R14 Goodyear Eagle GT + 4 tires on alloy wheels.

Optional equipment:

2.3-liter Quad 4 engine	660	561	594
3.3-liter V-6	710	604	639
Air conditioning	720	612	648
Popular Pkg. SB, base 2-door	831	706	748
Base 4-door	921	783	829
Air conditioning, front center armrest, right visor mirror, upgraded trunk trim, remote fuel door release, seatback recliners (4-door).			
Premium Pkg. SC, base	856	728	770
Air conditioning, bodyside moldings, wheel opening and rocker panel moldings.			
Luxury Pkg. SD, base 2-door	967	822	870
Base 4-door	1057	898	951
Pkgs. SB and SC.			

	Retail Price	Dealer Invoice	Low Price
Prestige Pkg. SE, base 2-door	1155	982	1040
Base 4-door	1245	1058	1121

Pkg. SD plus tilt steering column, left remote and right manual mirrors.

	Retail Price	Dealer Invoice	Low Price
Elite Pkg. SF, base 2-door	1534	1304	1381
Base 4-door	1599	1359	1439

Air conditioning, power windows, cruise control, intermittent wipers, tilt steering column, left remote and right manual mirrors, bodyside moldings, wheel opening and rocker panel moldings.

	Retail Price	Dealer Invoice	Low Price
Popular Pkg. SB, Custom	1178	1001	1060

Air conditioning, rear defogger, tilt steering column, left remote and right manual mirrors, bodyside moldings, wheel opening moldings.

	Retail Price	Dealer Invoice	Low Price
Premium Pkg. SC, Custom	1473	1252	1326

Pkg. SB plus cruise control, intermittent wipers, floormats.

	Retail Price	Dealer Invoice	Low Price
Luxury Pkg. SD, Custom	1825	1551	1643

Pkg. SC plus AM/FM cassette, wire wheel covers, white-stripe tires, 4-way seat adjuster.

	Retail Price	Dealer Invoice	Low Price
Prestige Pkg. SE, Custom 2-door	2240	1904	2016
Custom 4-door	2345	1993	2111

Pkg. SD plus power windows and locks.

	Retail Price	Dealer Invoice	Low Price
Elite Pkg. SF, Custom 2-door	2718	2310	2446
Custom 4-door	2823	2400	2541

Pkg. SE plus power driver's seat, power antenna, lighted right visor mirror, remote decklid release, front reading lamps, wide rocker panel moldings.

	Retail Price	Dealer Invoice	Low Price
Popular Pkg. SB, LE	1015	863	914

Air conditioning, rear defogger, tilt steering column.

	Retail Price	Dealer Invoice	Low Price
Premium Pkg. SC, LE	1485	1262	1337

Pkg. SB plus cruise control, intermittent wipers, AM/FM cassette, 4-way seat adjuster, floormats.

	Retail Price	Dealer Invoice	Low Price
Luxury Pkg. SD, LE	2005	1704	1805

Pkg. SC plus power windows and locks.

	Retail Price	Dealer Invoice	Low Price
Prestige Pkg. SE, LE	2433	2068	2190

Pkg. SD plus power driver's seat, power antenna, lighted visor mirror, remote decklid release, front reading lamps.

	Retail Price	Dealer Invoice	Low Price
Premium Pkg. SB, GS	1015	863	914

Air conditioning, tilt steering column, rear defogger.

	Retail Price	Dealer Invoice	Low Price
Luxury Pkg. SC, GS	1345	1143	1211

Pkg. SB plus intermittent wipers, cruise control, 4-way seat adjuster, floormats.

	Retail Price	Dealer Invoice	Low Price
Prestige Pkg. SD, GS	1835	1560	1652

Pkg. SC plus power windows and locks, power antenna.

	Retail Price	Dealer Invoice	Low Price
Gran Touring Pkg., Custom w/SA/SB/SC .	565	480	509
Custom w/SD/SE/SF	320	272	288

Gran Touring suspension, leather-wrapped steering wheel, 215/60R14 tires on alloy wheels.

	Retail Price	Dealer Invoice	Low Price
WSW tires, base	68	58	61

Prices are accurate at time of printing; subject to manufacturer's change.

	Retail Price	Dealer Invoice	Low Price
185/75R14 WSW tires, Custom w/SA/SB/SC	68	58	61
Bucket seats & floorshift, base & LE	210	179	189
Wire wheel covers, Custom w/SA/SB/SC	177	150	159
Alloy wheels, Custom w/SA/SB/SC	346	294	311
Custom w/SD/SE/SF	169	144	152
Rear defogger	160	136	144
AM/FM cassette	140	119	126
Engine block heater	18	15	16
Decklid luggage rack	115	98	104
Lower accent paint	195	166	176

Oldsmobile Cutlass Calais

	Retail Price	Dealer Invoice	Low Price
2-door notchback	$9995	$9225	$9425
4-door notchback	9995	9225	9425
S 2-door notchback	10895	9729	9929
S 4-door notchback	10995	9819	10019
SL 2-door notchback	13195	11783	11983
LS 4-door notchback	13295	11872	12072
I Series 2-door notchback	14895	13301	13501
I Series 4-door notchback	14995	13391	13591
Destination charge	425	425	425

Standard equipment:

2.5-liter TBI 4-cylinder engine, 5-speed manual transmission, power steering, cloth front bucket seats (reclining on 2-door), AM/FM radio, trip odometer, dual outside mirrors, tinted glass, rear shoulder belts, 185/80R13 all-season SBR tires. **S** adds: full-length console with armrest and storage bin, left remote mirror, reclining front seatbacks. **SL** adds: 3-speed automatic transmission, Convenience Group (reading lights, lighted right visor mirror, misc. lights), 4-way driver's seat, split folding rear seat, upgraded steering wheel, two-tone paint, alloy wheels. **International Series** adds: 2.3-liter DOHC PFI HO Quad 4 engine, FE3 suspension, air conditioning, door pockets, floormats, fog lamps, rocker panel extensions and wheel flares, Driver Information System (trip computer, service reminder), rallye instruments (tachometer, coolant temperature, oil pressure, voltmeter), AM/FM cassette, tilt steering column, leather-wrapped steering wheel and shift handle, power decklid release, intermittent wipers, 205/55R16 tires on alloy wheels.

Optional equipment:

	Retail Price	Dealer Invoice	Low Price
3.3-liter V-6, SL	50	43	45
2.3-liter Quad 4, S	660	561	594
I Series	400	340	360
I Series includes 3-speed automatic transmission.			
3-speed automatic transmission, base & S	540	459	486

	Retail Price	Dealer Invoice	Low Price
Column shift, base (credit)	(110)	(94)	(94)
Air conditioning, base, S & SL	720	612	648
Quad 442 Sport Performance Pkg., S 2-door	1667	1417	1500

HO Quad 4 engine, 5-speed manual transmission, FE3 suspension, rallye instruments, rear spoiler, leather-wrapped steering wheel, 215/60R14 Goodyear Eagle GT tires on alloy wheels.

Value Option Pkg. I, S	166	141	149

Rallye instruments, decklid luggage rack.

Value Option Pkg. II, S	391	332	352

Pkg. I plus rallye instruments.

Value Option Pkg., SL	315	268	284

Removable glass sunroof, decklid luggage rack.

Option Pkg. 1SB, base	460	391	414

Tilt steering column, bodyside moldings, 4-way manual driver's seat, cruise control, floormats.

Option Pkg. 1SC, base 2-door	1410	1199	1269
Base 4-door	1450	1233	1305

Pkg. 1SB plus air conditioning, power locks, intermittent wipers.

Option Pkg. 1SB, S	965	820	869

Tilt steering column, air conditioning, remote mirrors, 4-way manual driver's seat, floormats.

Option Pkg. 1SC, S	1402	1192	1262

Pkg. 1SB plus intermittent wipers, visor mirrors, underhood lamp, cruise control, rear defogger.

Option Pkg. 1SD, S 2-door	2067	1757	1860
S 4-door	2172	1846	1955

Pkg. 1SC plus power windows, power antenna, remote lock control pkg.

Option Pkg. 1SB, SL 2-door	1590	1352	1431
SL 4-door	1630	1386	1467

Air conditioning, power locks, tilt steering column, intermittent wipers, cruise control, power antenna, rear defogger, remote mirrors, floormats.

Option Pkg. 1SC, SL 2-door	2460	2091	2214
SL 4-door	2565	2180	2309

Pkg. 1SB plus power windows, power driver's seat, Driver Information System, lighted visor mirrors, remote lock control pkg.

Option Pkg. 1SB, I Series 2-door	1235	1050	1112
I Series 4-door	1340	1139	1206

Power driver's seat, power windows, remote mirrors, cruise control, power antenna, rear defogger, remote lock control pkg.

Removable glass sunroof (NA base)	350	298	315
Power locks, base & S 2-doors	175	149	158
Base & S 4-doors	215	183	194
Rear defogger	160	136	144
FE3 suspension pkg., S	526	447	473
SL	182	155	164
Alloy wheels, S	354	301	319

Prices are accurate at time of printing; subject to manufacturer's change.

	Retail Price	Dealer Invoice	Low Price
185/75R14 WSW tires, base & S	68	58	61
Rallye instruments, S	126	107	113
AM/FM cassette, base, S & SL	165	140	149
AM/FM radio w/CD player, S & SL	421	358	379
I Series	274	233	247
AM/FM cassette w/EQ, I Series	150	128	135
Decklid luggage carrier, S & SL	115	98	104
Custom leather trim, I Series	400	340	360
Engine block heater	18	15	16
California emissions pkg.	100	85	90

Cadillac Allante

Cadillac Allante

Allante becomes the first front-drive car with traction control, a new standard feature for 1990. The traction-control system uses the sensors for the anti-lock brakes to detect wheel slip during acceleration or steady cruising. When one of the front wheels starts to slip, the system applies the brakes to that wheel to optimize traction. If the traction-control system is engaged for more than three seconds, the engine computer cuts fuel delivery to one of the cylinders. If traction control remains engaged, the computer cuts fuel to as many as four cylinders to minimize stress on the brakes, engine, and transmission. Cadillac has

Specifications

	2-door conv.
Wheelbase, in.	99.4
Overall length, in.	178.7
Overall width, in.	73.5
Overall height, in.	52.2
Turn diameter, ft.	40.2
Curb weight, lbs.	3466
Cargo vol., cu. ft.	16.2
Fuel capacity, gals.	22.0
Seating capacity	2
Front headroom, in.	37.2
Front shoulder room, in.	57.7
Front legroom, max., in.	43.2
Rear headroom, in.	—
Rear shoulder room, in.	—
Rear legroom, min., in.	—

Powertrain layout: transverse front engine/front-wheel drive.

Engines

	ohv V-8
Size, liters/cu. in.	4.5/273
Fuel delivery	PFI
Horsepower @ rpm	200 @ 4400
Torque (lbs./ft.) @ rpm	270 @ 3200
Availability	S

EPA city/highway mpg

4-speed OD automatic	15/22

added a lower-priced Allante model that comes only with a folding convertible top; the higher-priced version comes with the convertible top and a removable aluminum hardtop. Other changes for Allante are that a driver's-side airbag is now standard and the electronically controlled shock absorbers have been revised to improve ride quality. With an airbag now standard, Allante's steering column loses its telescoping feature, but retains a tilt feature. A compact disc player has been added to the standard sound system. Despite a slew of major changes to Allante last year, including a larger, more powerful engine, 1989 sales were stagnant. This year, Allante has a new problem to face: the new Mercedes-Benz SL, which offers more horsepower and greater prestige. Allante's main advantage over

Prices are accurate at time of printing; subject to manufacturer's change.

the Mercedes SL remains its lower price, but that hasn't helped before, so it probably won't now. The 1990 Allante is a much better car than the original version that debuted for 1987, but we're not convinced it's good enough to justify spending so much money.

Prices

Cadillac Allante	Retail Price	Dealer Invoice	Low Price
2-door convertible	$51500	$44068	$45068
2-door convertible w/hardtop	57813	48873	49873

Price includes $650 Gas Guzzler Tax and $550 destination charge.

Standard equipment:

4.5-liter PFI V-8 engine, 4-speed automatic transmission, power steering, anti-lock 4-wheel disc brakes, traction control system, driver's-side airbag, removable hardtop, folding convertible top, ten-way power Recaro seats with leather upholstery and driver's-side position memory, Delco-GM/Bose Symphony music system with cassette and CD player, tilt steering column, power mirrors, intermittent wipers, automatic day/night mirror, power decklid pulldown, theft deterrent system, 225/55VR16 Goodyear Eagle VL tires on alloy wheels.

OPTIONS prices not available at time of publication.

Cadillac Brougham

Anti-lock brakes are a new standard feature and a 5.7-liter V-8 engine is a new option for Brougham, Cadillac's rear-drive luxury sedan. The Brougham also wears revised exterior styling, though the changes aren't nearly as dramatic as on the arch rival Lincoln Town Car. At 221 inches overall, the 4-door Brougham edges the redesigned Town Car by less than in inch to remain the longest production car built in the U.S. Appearance changes include composite front headlamps, new bumper covers and rub strips, and a padded vinyl roof. The optional 175-horsepower 5.7-liter V-8 has single-point fuel injection and is available only with the Coachbuilder or Trailer Towing packages. The 5.7 V-8 carries an $850 gas-guzzler tax. A 140-horsepower 5.0-liter

Cadillac Brougham

Specifications

	4-door notchback
Wheelbase, in.	121.5
Overall length, in.	221.0
Overall width, in.	76.5
Overall height, in.	56.7
Turn diameter, ft.	40.5
Curb weight, lbs.	4283
Cargo vol., cu. ft.	19.5
Fuel capacity, gals.	25.0
Seating capacity	6
Front headroom, in.	39.0
Front shoulder room, in.	59.4
Front legroom, max., in.	42.0
Rear headroom, in.	38.1
Rear shoulder room, in.	59.4
Rear legroom, min., in.	41.2

Powertrain layout: longitudinal front engine/rear-wheel drive.

Engines

	ohv V-8	ohv V-8
Size, liters/cu. in.	5.0/307	5.7/350
Fuel delivery	4 bbl.	TBI
Horsepower @ rpm	140 @ 3200	175 @ 4200
Torque (lbs./ft.) @ rpm	255 @ 2000	295 @ 2000
Availability	S	O

EPA city/highway mpg

4-speed OD automatic	17/24	14/21

Prices are accurate at time of printing; subject to manufacturer's change.

V-8 with a 4-barrel carburetor and no guzzler tax remains standard. Other new standard features include front shoulder belts that can be left buckled for automatic deployment, an electronic instrument cluster, rear-window defogger, a cassette player and graphic equalizer, and black walnut burl trim for the interior. A revamped climate-control system now has three automatic settings and two manual settings. Prodded by the arrival of a redesigned Town Car, Cadillac has made some overdue changes on the Brougham, whose design dates to the 1977 model year. The standard anti-lock brakes fill a big void in the safety department, while the optional 5.7-liter V-8 gives Brougham the power it has desperately needed. Cadillac estimates Brougham does 0-60 mph in 10.5 seconds with the 5.7, versus 14.3 seconds with the standard 5.0 engine. Even so, we're not recommending you buy a Brougham because of this year's new brakes and larger engine, or a Town Car either. Both these cars are still overweight, clumsy, and inefficient.

Prices

Cadillac Brougham	Retail Price	Dealer Invoice	Low Price
4-door notchback	$27400	$23372	$24767
Destination charge	550	550	550
Gas Guzzler Tax, w/Trailer Towing or Coachbuilder Pkg.	850	850	850

Standard equipment:

5.0-liter 4bbl. V-8, 4-speed automatic transmission, power steering, anti-lock braking system, 55/45 cloth front seat with power driver's side (including recliner), storage armrest, seatback pockets, automatic climate control, power windows and locks, cruise control, automatic level control, AM/FM cassette with EQ and power antenna, rear defogger, power mirrors, illuminated entry, digital instruments, trip odometer, automatic parking brake release, tilt/telescopic steering column, remote decklid release, tinted glass, door edge guards, floormats, front and rear lamp monitors, cornering lights, right visor mirror, Uniroyal Royal Seal 225/75R15 tires.

Optional equipment:

Trailer Towing Pkg.	549	461	387

5.7-liter TBI V-8, 3.08 axle ratio, HD suspension, oil cooler, HD transmission and driveshaft, trailer wiring harness.

	Retail Price	Dealer Invoice	Low Price
Coachbuilder Pkg.	(139)	(117)	(117)

Same content as Trailer Towing Pkg. less trailer wiring harness.

	Retail Price	Dealer Invoice	Low Price
d'Elegance Pkg. w/cloth	2171	1824	1532
w/leather	2731	2294	1927

50/50 front seat, power passenger seat, lighted visor mirrors, illuminated entry, rear reading lamps.

	Retail Price	Dealer Invoice	Low Price
Option Pkg. B	768	645	542

Lighted visor mirrors, rear reading lamps, power passenger seatback recliner, power passenger seat, power decklid pulldown, Twilight Sentinel.

	Retail Price	Dealer Invoice	Low Price
Option Pkg. C	1243	1044	877

Pkg. B plus automatic power locks, remote fuel door release, theft deterrent system.

	Retail Price	Dealer Invoice	Low Price
d'Elegance Pkg. C	475	399	335

Automatic power locks, remote fuel door release, theft deterrent system.

	Retail Price	Dealer Invoice	Low Price
Astroroof	1355	1138	956
Gold Ornamentation Pkg.	395	332	279
Livery Pkg.	299	251	211
Leather seating area	560	470	395
Automatic day/night mirror	80	67	56
Firemist paint	240	202	169
CD player	296	249	209
Leather-wrapped steering wheel	115	97	81
Wire wheel covers	445	374	314
Wire wheels	1000	840	706
California emissions pkg.	100	84	71

Cadillac De Ville/Fleetwood

The front-drive De Ville and Fleetwood have 25 more horsepower this year, thanks to multi-point fuel injection and other changes to their 4.5-liter V-8 engine. A driver's-side airbag and GM's Pass Key theft-deterrent system are new standard features. Last year's 5-model lineup returns: base Sedan de Ville and Coupe de Ville, plusher Fleetwood sedan and coupe, and top-shelf Fleetwood Sixty Special, available only as a 4-door. All now have 180 horsepower and one fuel injector for each cylinder; last year's 155-horsepower V-8 had two injectors mounted atop the engine. With an airbag now standard across the board, all models lose the telescoping feature for the steering column, but a standard tilt feature returns. Anti-lock brakes remain standard on the Fleetwoods, optional on the De Villes. We were impressed

Prices are accurate at time of printing; subject to manufacturer's change.

Cadillac Sedan de Ville

Specifications

	2-door notchback	4-door notchback
Wheelbase, in.	110.8	113.8
Overall length, in.	202.7	205.6
Overall width, in.	71.7	71.7
Overall height, in.	54.9	55.2
Turn diameter, ft.	39.8	41.0
Curb weight, lbs.	3466	3546
Cargo vol., cu. ft.	18.1	18.4
Fuel capacity, gals.	18.0	18.0
Seating capacity	6	6
Front headroom, in.	39.3	39.3
Front shoulder room, in.	59.0	59.0
Front legroom, max., in.	42.4	42.4
Rear headroom, in.	38.0	38.1
Rear shoulder room, in.	57.6	59.3
Rear legroom, min., in.	40.3	43.6

Powertrain layout: transverse front engine/front-wheel drive.

Engines

	ohv V-8
Size, liters/cu. in.	4.5/273
Fuel delivery	PFI
Horsepower @ rpm	180 @ 4300
Torque (lbs./ft.) @ rpm	240 @ 2600
Availability	S

EPA city/highway mpg

4-speed OD automatic	16/25

with the acceleration from last year's 4.5-liter V-8, and we're more impressed with the 1990 version, which moves these luxury cars with even more authority. There's ample power for brisk takeoffs from stoplights and for quick, safe highway passing. Fuel economy was disappointing last year (we averaged just 15.7 mpg from a mix of city and highway driving), and we don't expect any improvement this year, plus you now have to buy more expensive premium gas. However, there are other reasons why we like the De Ville and Fleetwood. The wheelbase on the sedans was stretched three inches last year so even back-seat passengers can stretch out. The wide doors allow easy entry/exit and the trunk provides ample cargo capacity. Because of the strong, refined engine, abundant comfort and convenience features, and Cadillac's improved quality, we urge you to check out De Ville and Fleetwood before you buy a European or Japanese luxury car. You might be surprised.

Prices

Cadillac De Ville/Fleetwood	Retail Price	Dealer Invoice	Low Price
Coupe de Ville 2-door notchback	$26960	$22997	$23297
Sedan de Ville 4-door notchback	27540	23492	23792
Fleetwood 2-door notchback	32400	27637	27937
Fleetwood 4-door notchback	32980	28132	28432
Fleetwood Sixty Special 4-door notchback .	36980	31544	31844
Destination charge	550	550	550

Standard equipment:

De Ville: 4.5-liter PFI V-8, 4-speed automatic transmission, power steering, driver's-side airbag, 45/45 front seat, power driver's seat, storage armrest, seatback pockets, automatic climate control, power windows and locks, cruise control, power mirrors, intermittent wipers, automatic level control, Fuel Data Center (instantaneous and average fuel economy, distance to empty), automatic parking brake release, Pass Key theft deterrent system, AM/FM cassette with EQ and power antenna, tilt steering column, trip odometer, remote decklid release, tinted glass, door edge guards, retainer for garage door opener, visor mirrors, leather-wrapped steering wheel, 205/70R15 tires. **Fleetwood** adds: anti-lock brakes, power passenger seat, digital instruments, walnut appliques, fender skirts, remote fuel door release, power decklid pulldown, illuminated entry, rear overhead mirrors (4-door), opera lamps (2-door), formal cabriolet roof (2-door), padded vinyl roof (4-door), Twilight Sentinel, lace alloy wheels. **Sixty Special** adds: leather interior,

Prices are accurate at time of printing; subject to manufacturer's change.

heated front seats with power lumbar, thigh, and lateral supports, automatic day/night mirror, rear passenger foot rests, rear overhead console, vinyl top.

Optional equipment:

	Retail Price	Dealer Invoice	Low Price
Anti-lock brakes, De Ville	925	777	823
De Ville Option Pkg. B	356	299	317
Floormats, power passenger seat, trunk mat.			
De Ville Option Pkg. C	771	648	686
Pkg. B plus illuminated entry, lighted visor mirrors, power decklid pulldown, Twilight Sentinel.			
De Ville Option Pkg. D	961	807	855
Remote fuel door release, automatic day/night mirror, trumpet horn.			
De Ville Option Pkg. E	1146	963	1020
Pkg. D plus automatic power locks.			
Fleetwood/Sixty Special Option Pkg. B . . .	410	344	365
Automatic power locks, theft deterrent system.			
Astroroof (NA Sixty)	1355	1138	1206
Rear defogger	195	164	174
Gold Ornamentation Pkg.	395	332	352
Digital instruments, De Ville	250	210	223
Leather seating areas (std. Sixty)	560	470	498
Memory power driver's seat, Fleetwood & Sixty	235	197	209
Automatic day/night mirror, Fleetwood & Sixty	80	67	71
Firemist paint	240	202	214
Delco-Bose sound system	576	484	513
w/CD player	872	732	776
Power recliners (each), Fleetwood	95	80	85
Formal cabriolet roof, De Ville	825	693	734
Vinyl roof delete (credit), Fleetwood 4-door & Sixty	(374)	(314)	(314)
Theft deterrent system, De Ville	225	189	200
Wire wheel covers (credit), Fleetwood & Sixty	(115)	(97)	(97)
Lace alloy wheels, De Ville	480	403	427
ElectriClear windshield	250	210	223
Engine block heater	45	38	40

Cadillac Eldorado/Seville

More horsepower, a standard driver's-side airbag, and new exterior styling touches are the major changes for the Eldorado coupe and the Seville sedan, which are built on the same front-drive platform. Both use a 4.5-liter V-8 that

Cadillac Seville STS

gains multi-point fuel injection this year (one injector for each cylinder) instead of throttle-body injection (two injectors mounted on top of the engine). Horsepower grows from 155 to 180 and the compression ratio increases from 9.0:1 to 9.5:1, so the 4.5 now requires premium unleaded gas. The EPA city fuel-economy estimate has dropped one mpg to 16, while the highway estimate is unchanged at 25. To accommodate the standard airbag, the telescoping feature for the steering column has been dropped, but a tilt feature returns. Last year the Seville Touring Sedan (STS) was an option package; this year it's a regular model. Both Seville and Eldorado have new bumper moldings, taillamps, and other minor styling changes. A new feature for the optional automatic door locks is "central unlocking;" all doors are unlocked if the key is held in a turned position for 1.5 seconds in either front door. A rear window defogger, heated outside mirrors, and illuminated entry system are now standard on all models, while the standard climate-control system now has three automatic settings and two manual settings. Anti-lock brakes are standard on the STS, optional on the other models. We're enthused about this year's more powerful 4.5-liter V-8, based on our brief exposure to it at Cadillac's preview, though the 1990 models may be less economical than previous versions, which weren't economy champs. Eldorado and Seville now offer a dash of performance with their usual large helping of luxury features.

Prices are accurate at time of printing; subject to manufacturer's change.

Specifications

	Eldorado 2-door notchback	Seville 4-door notchback
Wheelbase, in.	108.0	108.0
Overall length, in.	191.4	190.8
Overall width, in.	72.4	72.0
Overall height, in.	53.7	53.7
Turn diameter, ft.	39.4	39.4
Curb weight, lbs.	3426	3480
Cargo vol., cu. ft.	14.0	14.0
Fuel capacity, gals.	18.8	18.8
Seating capacity	5	5
Front headroom, in.	37.8	37.8
Front shoulder room, in.	57.6	57.2
Front legroom, max., in.	42.4	42.5
Rear headroom, in.	37.8	37.9
Rear shoulder room, in.	57.5	57.2
Rear legroom, min., in.	36.1	36.1

Powertrain layout: transverse front engine/front-wheel drive.

Engines

	ohv V-8
Size, liters/cu. in.	4.5/273
Fuel delivery	PFI
Horsepower @ rpm	180 @ 4300
Torque (lbs./ft.) @ rpm	240 @ 2600
Availability	S

EPA city/highway mpg

4-speed OD automatic	16/25

Prices

Cadillac Eldorado/Seville	Retail Price	Dealer Invoice	Low Price
Eldorado 2-door notchback	$28885	$24613	$24913
Seville 4-door notchback	31830	27151	27451
Seville STS 4-door notchback	36320	30981	31281
Destination charge	550	550	550

Standard equipment:

Eldorado: 4.5-liter PFI V-8, 4-speed automatic transmission, power steering, 4-wheel disc brakes, driver's-side airbag, cloth and leather reclining front bucket seats, power front seats, automatic climate control, power windows and locks, cruise control, heated power mirrors, intermittent wipers, tilt steering column, rear defogger, Driver Information Center (outside temperature, engine data, instantanious and average fuel economy, distance to empty), oil life indicator, trip odometer, automatic level control, remote fuel door and decklid releases, power decklid pulldown, AM/FM cassette with EQ and power antenna, illuminated entry, automatic parking brake release, Pass Key theft deterrent system, lighted visor mirrors, front and rear reading lamps, floormats, cornering lights, front and rear lamp monitors, retainer for garage door opener, door edge guards, tinted glass, leather-wrapped steering wheel, Twilight Sentinel, 205/70R15 tires on alloy wheels. **Seville** adds: birdseye maple trim, two-tone paint. **Seville STS** adds: anti-lock brakes, 3.31 axle ratio, leather interior with elm burl accents, rear console, automatic power locks, theft deterrent system, 215/65R15 tires.

Optional equipment:

	Retail Price	Dealer Invoice	Low Price
Anti-lock brakes (std. STS)	925	777	823
Option Pkg. B, exc. STS	410	344	365
Automatic power locks, theft deterrent system.			
Biarritz Pkg., Eldo	3180	2671	2830
Leather upholstery, power front recliners and lumbar support adjusters, power passenger seat, seatback pockets, walnut on instrument panel, console and door panels, cabriolet roof with opera lamps, two-tone paint, closed-in backlight treatment, wire wheel discs, accent molding, reversible floormats.			
Birdseye maple appliques, Eldo	245	206	218
Astroroof	1355	1138	1206
Gold Ornamentation Pkg.	395	332	352
Leather seating area, Seville	450	378	401
Eldo	545	458	485
Eldo includes power passenger seatback recliner.			
Automatic day/night mirror	80	67	71
Firemist paint, Seville & STS	240	202	214
Firemist primary paint, Eldo & Seville			
w/2-tone	190	160	169
Secondary	50	42	45
White diamond paint, Eldo & Seville	240	202	214
Two-tone paint, STS	225	189	200
Delco-Bose sound system	576	484	513
w/CD player	872	732	776
Padded vinyl roof, Eldo	1095	920	975
Cabriolet roof, Seville	1095	920	975
Phaeton roof, STS	1195	1004	1064
215/65R15 WSW tires, Eldo & Seville . . .	76	64	68
Touring suspension, Eldo & Seville	155	130	138
Wire wheel covers, Eldo & Seville	235	197	209
Alloy wheels, Eldo	115	97	102
California emissions pkg.	100	84	89

Prices are accurate at time of printing; subject to manufacturer's change.

Chevrolet Astro/GMC Safari

Chevrolet Astro

General Motors' compact-van twins are scheduled to get a
4-wheel-drive option in January, followed in the spring of
1990 by an extended-length model and a more powerful
optional engine. This fall, a 4-wheel anti-lock feature is
added as standard equipment to the front disc/rear drum
brakes. Astro, sold by Chevrolet dealers, and Safari, sold
by GM dealers with GMC truck franchises, are identical
except for names, series designations, and slightly higher
base prices on Safari. The new permanently engaged 4WD
system will augment the standard rear-wheel drive and
will be available on both the standard- and extended-length
versions. The 4WD system normally sends 65 percent of
the power to the rear wheels and 35 percent to the front;
it automatically transfers more power to the axle with the
best grip when there's wheel slip. The extended model will
increase cargo capacity nearly 19 cubic feet by adding 10
inches behind the rear wheels. It rides the standard 110-
inch wheelbase. Standard on all Astros and Safaris is a
4.3-liter V-6 rated at 150 horsepower. In January, 2WD
models will be available with a 175-horsepower version of
that engine. The 5-speed manual transmission is no longer
available, so all Astros and Safaris have a 4-speed overdrive

automatic as standard. All models also get a restyled instrument panel with a larger glovebox. Astro/Safari is similar to the Ford Aerostar as a smaller interpretation of the traditional rear-drive van. That's in contrast to the new front-drive minivans marketed by Chevrolet, Pontiac, and Oldsmobile which, like the Dodge Caravan, Plymouth Voyager, and Mazda MPV, are lighter-duty vehicles designed to drive like cars. The extended-length body, available 4WD, and anti-lock brakes increase Astro/Safari's appeal. But these GM twins remain relatively truck-like, and thus better suited to heavy-duty work than as substitutes for the family station wagon.

Specifications

	5-door van	5-door van
Wheelbase, in.	110.0	110.0
Overall length, in.	177.0	187.0
Overall width, in.	77.0	77.0
Overall height, in.	74.1	74.1
Turn diameter, ft.	39.5	39.5
Curb weight, lbs.	3084	NA
Cargo vol., cu. ft.	151.8	170.4
Fuel capacity, gals.	27.0	27.0
Seating capacity	8	8
Front headroom, in.	39.2	39.2
Front shoulder room, in.	64.0	64.0
Front legroom, max., in.	41.6	41.6
Rear headroom, in.	37.9	37.9
Rear shoulder room, in.	67.8	67.8
Rear legroom, min., in.	36.5	36.5

Powertrain layout: Longitudinal front engine/rear-wheel drive or permanent 4WD.

Engines

	ohv V-6	ohv V-6
Size, liters/cu. in.	4.3/262	4.3/262
Fuel delivery	TBI	TBI
Horsepower @ rpm	150 @ 4000	175 @ 4600
Torque (lbs./ft.) @ rpm	230 @ 2400	230 @ 2800
Availability	S	O[1]

EPA city/highway mpg

4-speed OD automatic	17/22	16/20

1. 2WD models only.

Prices are accurate at time of printing; subject to manufacturer's change.

Prices

Chevrolet Astro/GMC Safari Passenger Van

	Retail Price	Dealer Invoice	Low Price
Astro CS	$13790	$12314	$12514
Astro CL	14830	13243	13443
Astro LT	16325	14088	14288
Safari SLX	14003	12505	12705
Safari SLE	15043	13433	13633
Safari SLT	16538	14768	14968
Astro CS AWD	15765	14078	14278
Astro CL AWD	16805	15007	15207
Astro LT AWD	18300	16342	16542
Safari SLX AWD	15827	14133	14333
Safari SLE AWD	16867	15062	15262
Safari SLT AWD	18362	16397	16597
Destination charge	500	500	500

Standard equipment:

CS/SLX: 4.3-liter TBI V-6 engine, 4-speed automatic transmission, 4-wheel anti-lock brakes, coolant temperature and oil pressure gauges, voltmeter, trip odometer, tinted glass, intermittent wipers, AM radio, highback bucket seats, 5-passenger seating, rubber floor covering, remote fuel door release, 205/75R15 tires. **CL/SLE** adds: air dam with fog lamps, floormats, visor mirror, custom steering wheel, auxiliary lighting, carpet, wide bodyside moldings, rally wheels. **LT/SLT** adds: velour seat and door panel trim, upgraded front bucket seats with recliners, integrated armrests and adjustable headrests, split-back center bench seat with integrated armrests, headrests, recliners and fold-down center console with convenience tray and cup pockets; right-hand seat folds forward for access to rear, deep-tinted glass. **AWD** models have permanent 4-wheel drive.

Optional equipment:

Air conditioning, front	820	697	738
Front & rear	1343	1142	1209
Optional axle ratio	38	32	34
Locking differential	252	214	227
Sport Pkg., CL/SLE	905	769	815
Others	1309	1113	1178
Sport suspension, sport steering wheel, color-keyed bumpers, wide bodyside molding.			
Convenience Group ZQ2	411	349	370
Power windows and locks.			
Convenience Group ZQ3	346	294	311
Cruise control and tilt steering column.			

	Retail Price	Dealer Invoice	Low Price
Power door locks	211	179	190
7-passenger seating, CS/SLX	1069	909	962
CL/SLE	981	834	883
LT/SLT	878	746	790
8-passenger seating, CS/SLX	344	292	310
CL/SLE	396	337	356
LT/SLT	878	746	790
Custom vinyl bucket seats, w/8-pass.	158	134	142
w/5-pass.	106	90	95
Custom cloth bucket seats, w/8-pass.	158	134	142
w/5-pass.	106	90	95
Deluxe bumpers, CS/SLX	128	109	115
Others	76	65	68
Cold Climate Pkg.	46	39	41
Engine block heater, antifreeze protection to −32 degrees F.			
Roof console	83	71	75
Includes dome and reading lights, two storage compartments.			
Engine oil cooler	135	115	122
HD radiator	56	48	50
HD radiator & trans oil cooler	118	100	106
w/F&R A/C	63	54	57
Complete body glass	157	133	141
Deep tinted glass, w/o body glass	161	137	145
w/body glass	290	247	261
Rear heater	267	227	240
Electronic instruments	88	75	79
Auxiliary lighting	129	110	116
Deluxe outside mirrors	52	44	47
Power mirrors	150	128	135
AM/FM radio	151	128	136
AM/FM cassette	273	232	246
AM/FM cassette w/EQ	423	360	381
AM radio delete (credit)	(95)	(81)	(81)
Seatback recliner & armrests	241	205	217
Power driver's seat	240	204	216
HD shock absorbers	40	34	36
Sport suspension, CS/SLX	509	433	458
Others	417	354	375
HD Trailering Special Equipment	564	479	508
w/F&R A/C	507	431	456
LD Trailering Special Equipment	109	93	98
Alloy wheels, CS/SLX	325	276	293
Others or w/sport suspension	233	198	210
Argent rally wheels, CS/SLX	92	78	83
Deluxe two-tone paint, CL/SLE	172	146	155
Others	334	284	301

Prices are accurate at time of printing; subject to manufacturer's change.

	Retail Price	Dealer Invoice	Low Price
Special two-tone paint	172	146	155
Custom two-tone paint, CS/SLE	187	159	168
Others	329	280	296
Luggage carrier	126	107	113
California emissions pkg.	100	85	90

Chevrolet Camaro/ Pontiac Firebird

Chevrolet Camaro IROC-Z

These rear-drive ponycars head into the ninth model year for this design with a larger standard engine for their base versions and a driver's-side airbag for all models. Besides appearance and brand loyalty, the only notable difference between Camaro and Firebird is that the Chevy is available in a convertible body style. Around January, both the Camaro and the Firebird will get a minor facelift comprised of a reshaped nose and a new tail. They'll be sold as '90½ models. For fall, the entry-level Firebird and Camaro coupe trade last year's 2.8-liter V-6 for a 3.1-liter V-6; horsepower increases by five and torque by 20 pounds/feet. Horsepower is up slightly on some versions of the 5.0- and 5.7-liter V-8 engines that power the other models. As before, the 5.7 is available with automatic transmission only; the other engines come standard with a 5-speed manual. The airbag is accompanied by slightly altered interior accommodations, including a standard tilt wheel for the Camaro and the elimination of the Firebird's optional steering-wheel stereo-system controls. Leather upholstery is a new Camaro option, while all Firebirds get the sport front seats from last year's Trans Am and those with power windows get door map pockets with integral cup holders. A theft-deterrent system that disables the starter unless the proper ignition key is used remains standard on both the Camaro and Firebird. The larger V-6 should give the base models

Specifications

	3-door hatchback	2-door conv.
Wheelbase, in.	101.1	101.1
Overall length, in.	192.0	192.0
Overall width, in.	72.8	72.8
Overall height, in.	50.0	50.3
Turn diameter, ft.	36.9	36.9
Curb weight, lbs.	3077	3263
Cargo vol., cu. ft.	31.0	5.2
Fuel capacity, gals.	15.5	15.5
Seating capacity	4	4
Front headroom, in.	37.0	37.1
Front shoulder room, in.	57.5	58.6
Front legroom, max., in.	43.0	42.9
Rear headroom, in.	35.6	36.1
Rear shoulder room, in.	56.3	48.1
Rear legroom, min., in.	29.8	28.3

Powertrain layout: longitudinal front engine/rear-wheel drive.

Engines

	ohv V-6	ohv V-8	ohv V-8	ohv V-8
Size, liters/cu. in.	3.1/191	5.0/305	5.0/305	5.7/350
Fuel delivery	PFI	TBI	PFI	PFI
Horsepower @ rpm	140 @ 4400	170 @ 4000	210 @ 4400	245 @ 4400
Torque (lbs./ft.) @ rpm	180 @ 3600	255 @ 2400	285 @ 3200	345 @ 3200
Availability	S[1]	S[2]	S[3]	O[4]

EPA city/highway mpg

5-speed OD manual	19/27	17/25	16/26	
4-speed OD automatic	18/27	17/26	17/24	16/24

1. Camaro RS coupe, base Firebird. 2. Camaro RS conv., Firebird Formula; optional, RS coupe. 3. Camaro IROC-Z, Firebird Trans Am; optional, Firebird Formula, GTA.
4. IROC-Z, Firebird Formula and Trans Am; std., GTA.

Prices are accurate at time of printing; subject to manufacturer's change.

more pep, but the true nature of these cars is realized with a V-8. Thus equipped, they promise classic American ponycar fun, but pay the price with a punishing ride, poor wet-weather traction, lousy fuel economy, and high insurance premiums.

Prices

Chevrolet Camaro	Retail Price	Dealer Invoice	Low Price
RS 3-door hatchback	$10995	$9819	$10019
RS 2-door convertible	16880	15074	15274
IROC-Z 3-door hatchback	14555	12998	13198
IROC-Z 2-door convertible	20195	18034	18234
Destination charge	439	439	439

Standard equipment:

RS: 3.1-liter PFI V-6 engine (hatchback; convertible has 5.0-liter TBI V-8), 5-speed manual transmission, power steering, driver's-side airbag, AM/FM radio, left remote and right manual mirrors, cloth reclining front bucket seats, folding rear seat, rear shoulder belts, tilt steering column, intermittent wipers, tinted glass, Pass Key theft deterrent system, power hatch pulldown, tachometer, coolant temperature and oil pressure gauges, voltmeter, 215/65R15 tires on alloy wheels. **IROC-Z** adds: 5.0-liter TPI V-8 engine, limited-slip differential, right visor mirror, fog lamps; convertible has 245/50ZR16 tires.

Optional equipment:

5.0-liter TBI V-8, RS hatchback	350	298	315
5.7-liter PFI (TPI) V-8, IROC	300	255	270
4-speed automatic transmission	515	438	464
Air conditioning	805	684	725
Performance axle ratio & dual exhaust	466	396	419
Preferred Group 1, RS hatchback	1410	1199	1269

Air conditioning, AM/FM cassette, power locks, cruise control, bodyside moldings, floormats.

Preferred Group 2, RS hatchback	1782	1515	1604

Group 1 plus power windows and locks, remote hatch release, cargo cover, reading lamps.

Preferred Group 1, IROC hatchback	865	735	779

Air conditioning, bodyside moldings.

Preferred Group 2, IROC hatchback	1759	1495	1583

Group 1 plus AM/FM cassette, power windows and locks, cruise control, remote hatch release, cargo cover, floormats.

	Retail Price	Dealer Invoice	Low Price
Preferred Group 3, IROC hatchback	2143	1822	1929
Group 2 plus power driver's seat, power mirrors, reading lamps.			
Preferred Group 1, RS convertible	1040	884	936
Air conditioning, AM/FM cassette, bodyside moldings, floormats.			
Preferred Group 2, RS convertible	1640	1394	1476
Group 1 plus power windows and locks, cruise control.			
Preferred Group 1, IROC convertible	865	735	779
Air conditioning, bodyside moldings.			
Preferred Group 2, IROC convertible	1640	1394	1476
Group 1 plus AM/FM cassette, power windows and locks, cruise control, floormats.			
Preferred Group 3, IROC convertible	2001	1701	1801
Group 2 plus power driver's seat and power mirrors.			
Custom cloth bucket seats	327	278	294
Leather bucket seats	800	680	720
Rear defogger	160	136	144
Power locks	175	149	158
Remote hatch release	50	43	45
Rear window louvers	210	179	189
Power mirrors	91	77	82
Removable glass roof panels	866	736	779
245/50ZR16 tires on alloy wheels	520	442	468
AM/FM cassette	140	119	126
Delco-Bose audio system	1015	863	914
Sound system prices are for base models; prices vary with option package content.			
Engine block heater	20	17	18
California emissions pkg.	100	85	90

Pontiac Firebird

3-door hatchback	$11320	$10109	$10309
Formula 3-door hatchback	14610	13047	13247
Trans Am 3-door hatchback	16510	14743	14943
GTA 3-door hatchback	23320	20825	21025
Destination charge	439	439	439

Standard equipment:

3.1-liter PFI V-6, 5-speed manual transmisson, power steering, driver's-side airbag, cloth reclining front bucket seats, rear shoulder belts, power hatch pulldown, AM/FM radio, gauge cluster including tachometer, Pass Key theft-deterrent system, left visor mirror, 215/65R15 tires on alloy wheels. **Trans Am** adds: 5.0-liter PFI V-8, F41 suspension. **Formula** adds: 5.0-liter TBI V-8, dual exhaust, air conditioning, WS6 performance suspension, 245/50ZR16 tires on alloy wheels. **GTA** adds: 5.7-liter PFI V-8, 4-speed automatic

Prices are accurate at time of printing; subject to manufacturer's change.

transmission, 4-wheel disc brakes, limited-slip differential, rear defogger, power windows and locks, tinted glass, cruise control, tilt steering column, articulated bucket seats with inflatable lumbar support and thigh bolsters, floormats, upgraded upholstery, cargo cover, AM/FM cassette with EQ and Touch Control.

Optional equipment:

	Retail Price	Dealer Invoice	Low Price
5.0-liter TBI V-8, base	350	298	315
Requires air conditioning.			
5.0-liter PFI V-8, Formula	745	633	671
GTA (credit)	(300)	(255)	(255)
5.7-liter PFI V-8, Formula	1045	888	941
T/A	300	255	270
Requires 4-speed automatic transmission, engine oil cooler, 4-wheel disc brakes, limited-slip axle and 245/50ZR16 tires.			
5-speed manual transmission, GTA w/5.0 (credit)	(515)	(438)	(438)
4-speed automatic transmission, exc. GTA .	515	438	464
Air conditioning, base	805	684	725
Limited-slip differential, base & Formula . .	100	85	90
4-wheel disc brakes, Formula & T/A	179	152	161
Option Pkg. 1SB, base w/V-6	865	735	779
Air conditioning, bodyside moldings.			
Option Pkg. 1SC, base w/V-6	1603	1363	1443
Pkg. 1SB plus power windows and locks, 4-way manual driver's seat, door pockets, cruise control, remote hatch release, reading lamps.			
Option Pkg. 1SB, base w/V-8, Formula & T/A	495	421	446
Bodyside moldings, power windows and locks, door pockets.			
Option Pkg. 1SC, base w/V-8, Formula . .	889	756	800
T/A	854	726	769
Pkg. 1SB plus 4-way manual driver's seat, cruise control, remote hatch release, power mirrors, reading lamps.			
Value Option Pkg. (VOP), base & Formula .	820	697	738
T-top roof, AM/FM cassette.			
Value Option Pkg., T/A	889	756	800
T-top roof, AM/FM cassette, cargo screen.			
Value Option Pkg., GTA	1020	867	918
T-top roof, leather interior.			
Rear defogger, exc. GTA	160	136	144
Dual converter exhaust	155	132	140
Engine oil cooler, Formula & T/A	110	94	99
Hatch roof (T-tops)	920	782	828
Two-tone paint, base	150	128	135
Delete lower accent paint, Formula (credit) .	(150)	(128)	(128)
Power locks, exc. GTA	175	149	158
Power windows, exc. GTA	260	221	234

	Retail Price	Dealer Invoice	Low Price
Power antenna, exc. GTA	75	64	68
AM/FM cassette, exc. GTA	150	128	135
AM/FM cassette w/EQ, exc. GTA	300	255	270
w/VOP	150	128	135
AM/FM radio w/CD player, exc. GTA	526	447	473
w/VOP	376	320	338
GTA	226	192	203
Cargo security screen, exc. GTA	69	59	62
Ventura leather trim, GTA	450	383	405
Sport Appearance Pkg., base	450	383	405
Trans Am fascias, fog lamps, sill moldings; available only with V-6.			
245/50ZR16 tires, T/A	385	327	347
Includes WS6 performance suspension.			
Warranty enhancements for New York . . .	65	55	59
California emissions pkg.	100	85	90

Chevrolet Caprice/
Buick Estate Wagon/
Oldsmobile Custom Cruiser

Chevrolet Caprice Classic Brougham

General Motors' sole remaining full-size rear-drive cars coast into 1990 with few changes in anticipation of a major restyling for 1991. All three are available as station wagons with a rear-facing third seat for 8-passenger capacity. The

Caprice is the only one also offered as a 4-door sedan. The wagons use a carbureted 307-cubic-inch V-8 rated at 140 horsepower; the Caprice sedan's fuel-injected 305-cubic-inch V-8 makes 170 horsepower. A 4-speed overdrive automatic is the only transmission. For '90, all three get door-mounted automatic front seatbelts. The Buick is now offered in a single, luxury model called the Estate Wagon. The less plush LeSabre Estate is discontinued, and "Electra" has been trimmed from the surviving model's name. The Olds Custom Cruiser gains an aluminum wheel option. The redesigned 1991 models are set for a spring 1990 debut. They'll retain the current cars' full-size, rear-drive underpinnings, but wear curvy new aerodynamic

Specifications

	4-door notchback	5-door wagon
Wheelbase, in.	116.0	116.0
Overall length, in.	212.2	215.7
Overall width, in.	75.4	79.3
Overall height, in.	56.4	58.2
Turn diameter, ft.	38.7	39.7
Curb weight, lbs.	3693	4192
Cargo vol., cu. ft.	20.9	87.9
Fuel capacity, gals.	24.5	22.0
Seating capacity	6	8
Front headroom, in.	39.5	36.9
Front shoulder room, in.	60.5	60.9
Front legroom, max., in.	42.2	42.2
Rear headroom, in.	38.2	39.3
Rear shoulder room, in.	60.5	60.9
Rear legroom, min., in.	39.1	37.2

Powertrain layout: longitudinal front engine/rear-wheel drive.

Engines	ohv V-8	ohv V-8
Size, liters/cu. in.	5.0/305	5.0/307
Fuel delivery	TBI	4 bbl.
Horsepower @ rpm	170 @ 4000	140 @ 3200
Torque (lbs./ft.) @ rpm	255 @ 2400	255 @ 2000
Availability	S[1]	S[2]

EPA city/highway mpg

4-speed OD automatic	16/25	17/24

1. Sedans.   2. Wagons.

bodies and have updated interiors. Unchanged will be the ability of these cars to transport families and their luggage, plus tow a trailer, all with traditional American big-car bearing. We're curious to see how GM might address their vices, which include ponderous handling, a floaty ride, and poor fuel economy. Today's only direct rivals are the Ford LTD Crown Victoria and Mercury Grand Marquis. Ford's wagons are marginally more pleasant to drive than the GM wagons, thanks to a fuel-injected V-8 with slightly more power and a little more refinement, but otherwise the choice is mostly one of brand loyalty.

Prices

Chevrolet Caprice	Retail Price	Dealer Invoice	Low Price
4-door notchback	$14525	$12535	$12735
Classic 4-door notchback	15125	13053	13253
Classic Brougham 4-door notchback	16325	14088	14288
Classic Brougham LS 4-door notchback	17525	15124	15324
Classic 5-door wagon	15725	13571	13771
Destination charge	505	505	505

Standard equipment:

5.0-liter (305-cid) TBI V-8 engine (4-doors; 307-cid 4bbl. on wagon), 4-speed automatic transmission, power steering, air conditioning, left remote and right manual mirrors, tinted glass, rear shoulder belts, AM/FM radio, knit cloth bench seat, 205/75R15 all-season SBR tires (4-doors; wagon has 225/75R15). **Classic** adds: wheel opening moldings, Quiet Sound Group, vinyl door pull straps, bright wide lower bodyside moldings, hood ornament, carpeted lower door panels. **Brougham** adds: upgraded carpet, front door courtesy lights, vinyl roof, 55/45 cloth front seat with center armrest. **LS** adds: Landau-style vinyl roof, sport mirrors, tinted glass.

Optional equipment:

Limited-slip differential	100	85	90
Performance axle ratio	21	18	19
Vinyl bench seat, base 4-door	28	24	25
Wagon (credit)	(172)	(146)	(146)
Vinyl 50/50 seat, base 4-door	305	259	275
Wagon	103	88	93
Cloth 50/50 seat	275	234	248
Leather 45/55 seat	550	468	495

Prices are accurate at time of printing; subject to manufacturer's change.

	Retail Price	Dealer Invoice	Low Price
Preferred Group 1, base 4-door	170	145	153

Bodyside moldings, floormats, extended-range speakers, wheel opening moldings.

Preferred Group 2, base	820	697	738

Group 1 plus power locks, cruise control, tilt steering column, intermittent wipers, auxiliary lighting.

Preferred Group 1, Classic 4-door	713	606	642

Cruise control, tilt steering column, 205/75R15 white-stripe tires, bodyside moldings, intermittent wipers, remote decklid release, auxiliary lighting, floormats, extended-range speakers, remote mirrors.

Preferred Group 2, Classic 4-door	2087	1774	1878

Group 1 plus AM/FM cassette with power antenna, power windows and locks, power front seats, deluxe luggage compartment trim, intermittent wipers, remote decklid release, lighted right visor mirror.

Preferred Group 1, wagon	211	179	190

Bodyside moldings, auxiliary lighting, load floor carpet, remote mirrors.

Preferred Group 2, wagon	1556	1323	1400

Group 1 plus AM/FM cassette with power antenna, power windows and locks, cruise control, tilt steering column, luggage rack, intermittent wipers, floormats.

Preferred Group 3, wagon	2475	2104	2228

Group 2 plus AM/FM cassette with EQ, power front seats, deluxe rear compartment decor, gauge package with trip odometer, Twilight Sentinel, cornering lamps, lighted right visor mirror.

Preferred Group 1, Brougham	470	400	423

205/75R15 white-stripe tires, gauge package with trip odometer, bodyside moldings, Twilight Sentinel, remote decklid release, lighted right visor mirror, floormats, extended-range speakers, remote mirrors.

Preferred Group 2, Brougham	2384	2026	2146

Group 1 plus AM/FM cassette with power antenna, power windows and locks, power front seats, cruise control, wire wheel covers, tilt steering column, deluxe luggage compartment trim, intermittent wipers, cornering lamps.

Preferred Group 1, LS	2270	1930	2043

AM/FM cassette with power antenna, power windows and locks, power front seats, cruise control, wire wheel covers, tilt steering column, 205/75R15 white-stripe tires, gauge package with trip odometer, bodyside moldings, Twilight Sentinel, intermittent wipers, remote decklid release, lighted right visor mirror, floormats, remote mirrors.

Preferred Group 2, LS	2494	2120	2245

Group 1 plus AM/FM cassette with EQ, deluxe luggage compartment trim, cornering lamps.

Rear window air deflector, wagon	65	55	59
Trunk cargo net	30	26	27
HD cooling	40	34	36
Rear defogger	160	136	144

	Retail Price	Dealer Invoice	Low Price
Power locks, 4-doors	215	183	194
Wagon	290	247	261
AM/FM cassette	175	149	158
AM/FM cassette w/EQ	285	242	257

Sound system prices are for base models; prices vary with option package content.

	Retail Price	Dealer Invoice	Low Price
Estate equipment, wagon	307	261	276
F40 HD suspension, 4-doors	26	22	23
F41 sport suspension	49	42	44
Inflatable rear shock absorbers	64	54	58
205/75R15 white-stripe tires, 4-doors	76	65	68
225/70R15 white-stripe tires, 4-doors	188	160	169
Wheel covers, base & Classic	65	55	59
Wire wheel covers, Brougham	150	128	135
Others	215	183	194
Custom 2-tone paint	141	120	127
Vinyl roof	200	170	180
California emissions pkg.	100	85	90
Engine block heater	20	17	18
Pinstriping	61	52	55

Buick Estate Wagon

	Retail Price	Dealer Invoice	Low Price
5-door wagon	$17940	$15482	$15682
Destination charge	505	505	505

Standard equipment:

5.0-liter 4bbl. V-8, 4-speed automatic transmission, power steering, air conditioning, 55/45 cloth front seat with manual passenger recliner, tinted glass, tilt steering column, trip odometer, intermittent wipers, front reading lamps, AM/FM radio, 2-way tailgate with power window, 225/75R15 WSW tires on alloy wheels.

Optional equipment:

	Retail	Dealer	Low
Popular Pkg. SB	1150	978	1035

Floormats, cruise control, rear defogger, power locks, remote tailgate lock release, roof rack, woodgrain vinyl applique, door edge guards.

Preimum Pkg. SC	1965	1670	1769

Pkg. SB plus air deflector, bodyside moldings, power driver's seat, power windows, AM/FM cassette.

Luxury Pkg. SD	2208	1877	1987

Pkg. SC plus lighted right visor mirror, Exterior Molding Pkg., power antenna.

Prices are accurate at time of printing; subject to manufacturer's change.

	Retail Price	Dealer Invoice	Low Price
Prestige Pkg. SE	2766	2351	2489

Pkg. SD plus automatic climate control, cornering lights, Twilight Sentinel, illuminated entry, power mirrors, front light monitors, power passenger seatback recliner.

	Retail Price	Dealer Invoice	Low Price
AM/FM cassette	150	128	135
AM/FM cassette w/AM ST & EQ, w/SA/SB .	300	255	270
w/SC/SD/SE	150	128	135
Power antenna	75	64	68
Power passenger seat	270	230	243
Delete third seat (credit)	(215)	(183)	(183)
Trailer Towing Pkg.	215	183	194
Leather/vinyl 55/45 seat	450	383	405
Limited-slip differential	100	85	90

Requires Trailer Towing Pkg.

	Retail Price	Dealer Invoice	Low Price
Wire wheel covers	215	183	194
Delete woodgrain, base & w/SB (credit) . .	(345)	(293)	(293)
w/SC/SD/SE	(320)	(272)	(272)
California emissions pkg.	100	85	90

Oldsmobile Custom Cruiser

5-door wagon	$17595	$15185	$15385
Destination charge	505	505	505

Standard equipment:

5.0-liter 4bbl. V-8, 4-speed automatic transmission, power steering, power tailgate window, air conditioning, tinted glass, left remote and right manual mirrors, trip odometer, AM/FM radio, right visor mirror, locking rear storage compartment, 55/45 bench seat, rear shoulder belts, rear-facing third seat, P225/75R15 tires.

Optional equipment:

Option Pkg. 1SB	1078	916	970

Driver Convenience Pkg., power mirrors, passenger seatback recliner, power antenna, Reminder Pkg., rear defogger, luggage rack, accent stripe, door edge guards, floormats.

Option Pkg. 1SC	2237	1901	2013

Pkg. 1SB plus power windows and locks, lower bodyside moldings, lighted visor mirrors, power driver's seat, AM/FM cassette.

Option Pkg. 1SD	3084	2621	2776

Pkg. 1SC plus automatic climate control, reading lamps, Illumination Pkg., cornering lamps, exterior lamp monitor, automatic day/night mirror, power passenger seat, wire wheel covers.

Bodyside & tailgate paneling	255	217	230

	Retail Price	Dealer Invoice	Low Price
Rear defogger	160	136	144
Automatic leveling system	175	149	158
Limited-slip differential	100	85	90
Alloy wheels	320	272	288
Instrument panel cluster	66	56	59
Trailering Pkg.	96	82	86
Engine block heater	18	15	16
California emissions pkg.	100	85	90

Chevrolet Cavalier/ Pontiac Sunbird

Chevrolet Cavalier

These are the surviving members of the J-car family of front-drive subcompacts, which once boasted a representative in each General Motors division. For '90, the Cavalier convertible is dropped, but the remaining models get larger engines. Sunbird, meanwhile, gets a slightly revised exterior. Both cars have 2-door coupe and 4-door sedan versions; Cavalier also is available as a 5-door wagon, while Sunbird continues to offer a convertible. The stripper Cavalier VL (Value Leader) model, offered previously only on the coupe, is now available on all body styles, as is the optional RS package. All except VL models get power steering and tinted glass as standard for '90, while all Cavaliers gain new seats. Sunbird SE and GT models get a new hood, front fenders, front fascia, and semi-hidden headlamps for '90; the GT also gets new rear-fender and side-rocker extensions. All '90 Cavaliers and Sunbirds get automatic front seat belts. With the Cavalier Z24 convertible replaced by the Beretta ragtop in the Chevy line for '90, the Sunbird LE becomes the sole J-car convertible. Pontiac had previously offered the Sunbird soft top in GT trim, but the con-

Specifications

	2-door notchback	4-door notchback	5-door wagon	2-door conv.
Wheelbase, in.	101.2	101.2	101.2	101.2
Overall length, in.	178.4	178.4	174.5	178.2
Overall width, in.	66.0	66.3	66.3	65.0
Overall height, in.	52.0	52.1	52.8	51.9
Turn diameter, ft.	34.7	34.7	34.7	34.7
Curb weight, lbs.	2436	2444	2529	2662
Cargo vol., cu. ft.	13.2	13.7	64.4	10.4
Fuel capacity, gals.	13.6	13.6	13.6	13.6
Seating capacity	5	5	5	4
Front headroom, in.	37.9	39.7	38.3	38.5
Front shoulder room, in.	53.7	53.7	53.7	53.7
Front legroom, max., in.	42.9	42.2	42.2	42.2
Rear headroom, in.	36.1	37.9	38.8	37.4
Rear shoulder room, in.	52.0	53.7	53.7	38.0
Rear legroom, min., in.	30.5	34.3	33.7	31.8

Powertrain layout: transverse front engine/front-wheel drive.

Engines

	ohv I-4	ohv V-6	ohc I-4	Turbo ohc I-4
Size, liters/cu. in.	2.2/133	3.1/191	2.0/121	2.0/121
Fuel delivery	TBI	PFI	TBI	PFI
Horsepower @ rpm	95 @ 5200	135 @ 4500	96 @ 4800	165 @ 5500
Torque (lbs./ft.) @ rpm	120 @ 3200	180 @ 3600	118 @ 3600	175 @ 4000
Availability	S[1]	S[2]	S[3]	S[4]

EPA city/highway mpg

5-speed OD manual	25/36	19/28	26/36	21/30
3-speed automatic	25/33	20/27	24/32	21/28

1. Cavalier.   2. Cavalier Z24; optional, wagon.   3. Sunbird.   4. Sunbird GT; optional conv.

vertible drops a notch to the LE level for 1990 in a price-reducing move. The convertible has a power top and for 1990 has a new snap-on boot to cover the lowered roof. A 2.2-liter 4-cylinder replaces a 2.0-liter four as Cavalier's standard engine. Optional on the Cavalier wagon and standard on the Z24 is a 3.1-liter V-6. It replaces a 2.8-liter V-6. Sunbird retains its choice of a naturally aspirated or turbocharged 2.0-liter four. Entering their ninth model year, the J-cars can't compete with newer Japanese rivals in refinement or cabin space. They are priced attractively, however, and a Z24 or a Sunbird GT makes an enjoyable baby muscle car. The Sunbird ragtop is one of the least-expensive 4-seat convertible cars.

Prices

Chevrolet Cavalier	Retail Price	Dealer Invoice	Low Price
VL 2-door notchback	$7577	$7145	$7345
VL 4-door notchback	7777	7334	7534
VL 5-door wagon	8165	7700	7900
2-door notchback	8620	7956	8156
4-door notchback	8820	8141	8341
5-door wagon	9195	8487	8687
Z24 2-door notchback	11505	10274	10474
Destination charge	425	425	425

Standard equipment:

VL: 2.2-liter TBI 4-cylinder engine, 5-speed manual transmission, cloth front bucket seats, rear shoulder belts, remote tailgate lock release (wagon), 185/80R13 tires on styled steel wheels. **Base** adds: power steering, tinted glass, easy-entry passenger seat (2-door), AM/FM radio, wheel trim rings. **Z24** adds: 3.1-liter PFI V-6, front sport seats, center console, FE3 sport suspension, 215/60R14 Goodyear Eagle GT + 4 tires on alloy wheels.

Optional equipment:

3.1-liter V-6	685	582	617
3-speed automatic transmission	465	395	419
Air conditioning	720	612	648
Preferred Group 1, VL	275	234	248
Power steering, bodyside moldings.			
Preferred Group 2, VL	443	377	399
Group 1 plus tinted glass, left remote and right manual mirrors, floormats.			

Prices are accurate at time of printing; subject to manufacturer's change.

	Retail Price	Dealer Invoice	Low Price
Preferred Group 1, base	318	270	286

Split folding rear seat, intermittent wipers, left remote and right manual mirrors, bodyside moldings, floormats.

| Preferred Group 2, base 2- & 4-door | 1368 | 1163 | 1231 |
| Base wagon | 1483 | 1261 | 1335 |

Group 1 plus air conditioning, cruise control, tilt steering column, roof rack (wagon).

Preferred Group 3, base 2-door	1913	1626	1722
Base 4-door	2018	1715	1816
Base wagon	2133	1813	1920

Group 2 plus AM/FM cassette, power windows and locks.

| Preferred Group 1, Z24 | 744 | 632 | 670 |

Air conditioning, dome reading lamp.

| Preferred Group 2, Z24 | 1302 | 1107 | 1172 |

Group 1 plus AM/FM cassette, cruise control, tilt steering column, intermittent wipers, floormats.

| Preferred Group 3, Z24 | 1907 | 1621 | 1716 |

Group 2 plus AM/FM cassette with EQ, power windows and locks, remote decklid release.

AM/FM radio, VL	332	282	299
AM/FM cassette, VL	472	401	425
Base & Z24	140	119	126
AM/FM cassette w/EQ, Z24	290	247	261

Sound system prices are for base models; prices vary with option package content.

Rear defogger	160	136	144
Power locks, 2-doors	175	149	158
4-doors & wagons	215	183	194
Tinted glass, VL	105	89	95
RS Pkg.	405	344	365

Black exterior accents, dual mirrors, FE2 sport suspension, tachometer and trip odometer, 195/70R14 tires on rally wheels.

Removable sunroof	350	298	315
185/80R13 white-stripe tires	68	58	61
195/70R14 tires	156	133	140
215/60R14 OWL tires, Z24	102	87	92
Alloy wheels	265	225	239

Pontiac Sunbird

LE 2-door notchback	$8799	$7858	$8058
LE 4-door notchback	8899	7947	8147
LE 2-door convertible	13934	12434	12634
SE 2-door notchback	9204	8219	8419
GT 2-door notchback	11724	10470	10670
Destination charge	425	425	425

Standard equipment:

LE: 2.0-liter TBI 4-cylinder engine, 5-speed manual transmission, power brakes, rear deflector (wagon), reclining front bucket seats, outboard rear lap/shoulder belts, AM/FM radio, 185/75R14 tires; convertible has power top, power windows and locks. **SE** adds: moldings, rally gauges with tachometer, 195/70R14 tires. **GT** adds: turbo engine, rally suspension, console, engine block heater, rally gauges with tachometer and trip odometer, tinted glass, AM/FM cassette, left remote and right manual mirrors, 215/60R14 Goodyear Eagle GT tires on alloy wheels.

Optional equipment:

	Retail Price	Dealer Invoice	Low Price
2.0-liter non-turbo engine, GT (credit) . . .	(768)	(653)	(653)
2.0-liter turbo engine pkg., LE conv.	1402	1192	1262
LE conv. w/VOP	1023	870	921
Includes rally gauge cluster, engine block heater, FE3 suspension, 215/60R14 tires on alloy wheels.			
3-speed automatic transmission	465	395	419
Air conditioning	720	612	648
Option Pkg. 1SB, LE	416	354	374
Tinted glass, power steering, left remote and right manual mirrors, floormats.			
Option Pkg. 1SC, LE 2-door	1462	1243	1316
LE 4-door	1468	1248	1321
Pkg. 1SB plus air conditioning, tilt steering column, intermittent wipers, lamp group, front seat armrest, rally gauges.			
Option Pkg. 1SD, LE 2-door	1857	1578	1671
LE 4-door	1863	1584	1677
Pkg. 1SC plus cruise control, remote decklid release, split folding rear seat.			
Option Pkg. 1SB, LE conv.	1046	889	941
Air conditioning, tilt steering column, intermittent wipers, lamp group, front seat armrest, rally gauges.			
Option Pkg. 1SC, LE conv.	1369	1164	1232
Pkg. 1SB plus cruise control, remote decklid release, tachometer.			
Option Pkg. 1SB, SE	416	354	374
Power steering, tinted glass, left remote and right manual mirrors, floormats.			
Option Pkg. 1SC, SE	1413	1201	1272
Pkg. 1SB plus air conditioning, tilt steering column, intermittent wipers, lamp group, front seat armrest.			
Option Pkg. 1SD, SE	1886	1603	1697
Pkg. 1SC plus cruise control, remote decklid release, rally gauges with tachometer, split folding rear seat.			
Option Pkg. 1SB, GT	1122	954	1010
Air conditioning, tilt steering column, floormats, lamp group, intermittent wipers, split folding rear seat.			
Option Pkg. 1SC, GT	1367	1162	1230
Pkg. 1SB plus cruise control and remote decklid release.			

Prices are accurate at time of printing; subject to manufacturer's change.

	Retail Price	Dealer Invoice	Low Price
Value Option Pkg. (VOP), LE	374	318	337
SE	469	399	422
AM/FM cassette, 195/70R14 tires on alloy wheels.			
Cruise control, LE	195	166	176
Rear defogger	160	136	144
Power locks, 2-door	175	149	158
4-door	215	183	194
Power windows, 2-door	230	196	207
4-door	295	251	266
AM/FM cassette, LE & SE	170	145	153
AM/FM radio w/CD player, SE & LE . . .	396	337	356
SE & LE w/VOP, GT	192	163	173
Decklid spoiler, LE conv.	70	60	63
Removable sunroof, SE & GT	350	298	315
195/70R14 tires, LE & SE	114	97	103
14" alloy wheels, LE	265	225	239
SE (includes rear spoiler)	335	285	302
Two-tone paint, LE	101	86	91

Chevrolet Celebrity/ Pontiac 6000

Chevrolet Celebrity

Chevy continues to pare the Celebrity line while Pontiac has surrendered the 6000's STE badge to the new Grand Prix. These front-drive intermediates are sister ships to the Buick Century and Oldsmobile Cutlass Ciera. At Chevy, however, Lumina is now the mid-size standard-bearer. That

CONSUMER GUIDE®

costs the Celebrity its 4-door sedan body style and leaves it with only a 5-door wagon in base and sporty Eurosport trim. Meanwhile, Pontiac still offers the 6000 as 4-door sedan or a 5-door wagon, but it has transferred the top-of-the-line STE label from the 6000 to the new Grand Prix sedan. The 6000 STE last year came standard with 4-wheel drive. All-wheel drive remains exclusive to the 6000, but now it's an option and is available only on the S/E sedan. The S/E retains most of the 6000 STE's standard equipment, while the 4WD hardware itself is unchanged, remaining a permanently engaged system that splits engine torque 60 percent front/40 percent rear. Standard 4-wheel

---

Specifications

	4-door notchback	5-door wagon
Wheelbase, in.	104.9	104.9
Overall length, in.	188.8	193.2
Overall width, in.	72.0	72.0
Overall height, in.	53.7	54.1
Turn diameter, ft.	37.0	37.0
Curb weight, lbs.	2843	3162
Cargo vol., cu. ft.	15.2	74.4
Fuel capacity, gals.	15.7	15.7
Seating capacity	6	8
Front headroom, in.	38.5	38.6
Front shoulder room, in.	56.3	56.2
Front legroom, max., in.	42.2	42.1
Rear headroom, in.	37.8	38.9
Rear shoulder room, in.	56.5	56.2
Rear legroom, min., in.	36.5	34.7

Powertrain layout: transverse front engine/front-wheel drive or permanent 4WD (6000 S/E sedan).

Engines

	ohv I-4	ohv V-6
Size, liters/cu. in.	2.5/151	3.1/191
Fuel delivery	TBI	PFI
Horsepower @ rpm	110 @ 5200	135 @ 4400
Torque (lbs./ft.) @ rpm	135 @ 3200	180 @ 3200
Availability	S	O

EPA city/highway mpg

3-speed automatic	23/31	20/27
4-speed OD automatic		19/30

Prices are accurate at time of printing; subject to manufacturer's change.

anti-lock disc brakes are an S/E AWD exclusive. For '90, a 3.1-liter V-6 replaces a 2.8-liter V-6 as the standard engine on all 6000 S/E models, as well as on the LE wagon and on the Celebrity Eurosport. The 3.1 is optional the base LE sedan and base Celebrity. Its 135 horsepower is 10 more than the 2.8 made. The 2.5-liter 4-cylinder in the LE and base Celebrity has 110 horsepower, up from last year's 98. Air conditioning is now standard on all 6000s except the LE sedan, and all Celebritys get heavy-duty suspension components, intermittent wipers, a split, folding second seat, and front-door map pockets. Though they were introduced for the '82 model year, 6000 and Celebrity remain decent value for the money. The wagons' appeal is enhanced by a rear-facing third seat (standard on 6000, optional on Celebrity) that gives them 8-passenger capacity.

Prices

Chevrolet Celebrity	Retail Price	Dealer Invoice	Low Price
5-door 2-seat wagon	$12395	$10697	$10897
5-door 3-seat wagon	12645	10913	11113
Destination charge	450	450	450

Standard equipment:

2.5-liter TBI 4-cylinder engine, 3-speed automatic transmission, power steering, cloth front bench seat with center armrest, split folding second seat, rear shoulder belts, AM/FM radio, bodyside moldings, day/night mirror, left remote and right manual mirrors, intermittent wipers, tinted glass, 185/75R14 tires.

Optional equipment:

3.1-liter V-6	660	561	594
4-speed automatic transmission (V-6 req.) .	200	170	180
Air conditioning	805	684	725
55/45 front seat	133	113	120
Preferred Group 1	921	783	829
Air conditioning, Exterior Molding Pkg., auxiliary lighting, floormats.			
Preferred Group 2	1710	1454	1539
Group 1 plus power locks, cruise control, tilt steering column, roof rack, gauge package with trip odometer, remote liftgate release.			
Preferred Group 3	2259	1920	2033
Group 2 plus AM/FM cassette, power windows, Cargo Security Pkg., deluxe rear compartment decor, remote mirrors.			

	Retail Price	Dealer Invoice	Low Price
Eurosport Base Group	1895	1611	1706
3.1-liter V-6, 4-speed automatic transmission, air conditioning.			
Eurosport Group 1	2011	1709	1810
Base Group plus Exterior Molding Pkg., auxiliary lighting, floormats.			
Eurosport Group 2	2800	2380	2520
Group 1 plus power locks, cruise control, tilt steering column, roof rack, gauge package with trip odometer, remote liftgate release.			
Eurosport Group 3	3349	2847	3014
Group 2 plus AM/FM cassette, power windows, Cargo Security Pkg., deluxe rear compartment decor, remote mirrors.			
Rear defogger	160	136	144
Power locks	215	183	194
Power driver's seat	270	230	243
Power seatback recliners	110	94	99
Inflatable rear shock absorbers	64	54	58
185/75R14 white-stripe tires	68	58	61
Sport wheel covers	65	55	59
Alloy wheels	195	166	176
Rear wiper/washer	125	106	113
AM/FM cassette	140	119	126
California emissions pkg.	100	85	90

Pontiac 6000

	Retail Price	Dealer Invoice	Low Price
LE 4-door notchback	$12149	$10485	$10685
LE 5-door wagon	15309	13212	13412
S/E 4-door notchback	16909	14592	14792
S/E 5-door wagon	18509	15973	16173
Destination charge	450	450	450

Standard equipment:

LE: 2.5-liter TBI 4-cylinder engine, 3-speed automatic transmission (4-door; wagon has 3.1-liter PFI V-6 and 4-speed automatic transmission), power steering, air conditioning (wagon), AM/FM radio, tinted glass, cloth front bench seat with armrest, split folding second seat (wagon), rear defogger (wagon), rear shoulder belts, 185/75R14 SBR tires. **S/E** adds: 3.1-liter PFI V-6, 4-speed automatic transmission, air conditioning, tachometer, trip odometer, voltmeter, coolant temperature and oil pressure gauges, intermittent wipers, power windows and locks, AM/FM cassette, rear defogger, luggage rack (wagon), cloth reclining bucket seats, leather-wrapped steering wheel, sport suspension, Electronic Ride Control (wagon), 195/70R15 Goodyear Eagle GT+4 tires on alloy wheels.

Prices are accurate at time of printing; subject to manufacturer's change.

Optional equipment:	Retail Price	Dealer Invoice	Low Price
3.1-liter V-6, LE 4-door	660	561	594
4-speed automatic transmission, LE 4-door .	200	170	180
Requires V-6 and Pkg. 1SC or 1SD.			
All Wheel Drive Pkg., SE 4-door	3635	3090	3272
Includes anti-lock brakes, 3-speed automatic transmission, automatic level control, specific fog lamps, rear spoiler.			
Air conditioning, LE 4-door	805	684	725
Option Pkg. 1SB, LE 4-door	995	846	896
LE wagon	190	162	171
Air conditioning (std. wagon), tilt steering column, intermittent wipers.			
Option Pkg. 1SC, LE 4-door	1190	1012	1071
LE wagon	385	327	347
Pkg. 1SB plus cruise control.			
Option Pkg. 1SD, LE 4-door	2058	1749	1852
LE wagon	1243	1057	1119
Pkg. 1SC plus power windows and locks, remote tailgate release (wagon), power driver's seat, reading lamps.			
Option Pkg. 1SB, S/E 4-door	343	292	309
S/E wagon	293	249	264
Remote decklid release (4-door), power driver's seat, reading lamps.			
Value Option Pkg. (VOP) R6A, LE	412	350	371
45/55 split seat, AM/FM cassette, alloy wheels.			
Value Option Pkg. R6B, LE 4-door	413	351	372
LE wagon	528	449	475
LE w/Pkg. 1SD	198	168	178
AM/FM cassette, 45/55 split seat, power locks.			
Rear defogger, LE 4-door	160	136	144
Power locks, LE 4-door	215	183	194
LE wagon	255	217	230
Power windows, LE	310	264	279
AM/FM cassette, LE	140	119	126
AM/FM cassette w/EQ, S/E 4-door	350	298	315
S/E wagon	315	268	284
Includes steering wheel controls.			
AM/FM radio w/CD player & EQ, S/E 4-door .	536	456	482
S/E wagon	501	426	451
45/55 seat, LE	133	113	120
Custom interior trim, LE	483	411	435
LE w/VOP	350	298	315
45/55 seat, power recliners, gauges.			
185/75R14 WSW tires, LE	68	58	61
14″ alloy wheels, LE	265	225	239
Simulated woodgrain siding, LE wagon . . .	295	251	266
Two-tone paint	115	98	104
Warranty enhancements for New York . . .	65	55	59
California emissions pkg.	100	85	90

Chevrolet Corsica/Beretta

Chevrolet Beretta GTZ

Chevy's strong-selling front-wheel-drive compacts get more power, while the Beretta gains a convertible model. Corsica and Beretta are built on the same platform, but differ in exterior styling, interior furnishings, and chassis components. The Corsica is available as a 4-door notchback sedan or a 5-door hatchback; the Beretta as a 2-door coupe or a convertible. The new convertible will hit the showrooms in the spring of 1990 with a manual-folding top and a heated glass backlight. Chevy says the roof bar that arcs over the passenger area is not designed to protect occupants in a rollover, but helps reduce body shake, improve window sealing, and cut top-down wind draft into the cabin. It also allows the convertible to use an interior dome lamp and retain the Beretta coupe's door handles and shoulder-belt anchors. Also new is the Beretta GTZ. It replaces the GTU as the sportiest Beretta and sees Chevy's first use of the Quad 4, a dual-cam, 16-valve 2.3-liter 4-cylinder engine developed by Oldsmobile. The GTZ uses the High Output Quad 4, rated at 180 horsepower, and available only with manual transmission. The sporty Corsica LTZ continues as a notchback only. Supplanting a 2.0-liter 4-cylinder as the standard engine in the base Beretta and Corsica is a 2.2-liter four. Horsepower jumps from 90 to 95. The available V-6 jumps from 2.8 liters to 3.1 and bumps horsepower from 130 to 135. The V-6 is optional on base Corsicas and Berettas, and standard on all others except the GTZ. A new molded, non-metallic tank increases fuel capacity from 13.6 gallons to 15.6 on all models. Beretta is appealing as a sporty car with decent road manners and an attractive price. The GTZ takes performance a step forward. Corsica lacks any outstanding features, but is generally competent and offers enough value for the money to make it worth a look. It stacks up well against the Ford Tempo and costs less than imports such as the Toyota Camry.

Specifications	2-door notchback	2-door conv.	4-door notchback	5-door hatchback
Wheelbase, in.	103.4	103.4	103.4	103.4
Overall length, in.	187.2	187.2	183.4	183.4
Overall width, in.	68.2	68.2	68.2	68.2
Overall height, in.	52.9	52.9	53.8	53.8
Turn diameter, ft.	37.8	37.8	37.8	37.8
Curb weight, lbs.	2637	2745	2635	2704
Cargo vol., cu. ft.	13.5	NA	13.5	39.1
Fuel capacity, gals.	15.6	15.6	15.6	15.6
Seating capacity	5	5	5	5
Front headroom, in.	38.0	NA	38.1	38.1
Front shoulder room, in. . .	55.3	NA	55.4	55.4
Front legroom, max., in. . .	43.4	NA	43.4	43.4
Rear headroom, in.	36.6	NA	37.4	37.4
Rear shoulder room, in. . .	55.1	NA	55.6	55.6
Rear legroom, min., in. . .	34.6	NA	35.0	35.0

Powertrain layout: transverse front engine/front-wheel drive.

Engines	ohv I-4	ohv V-6	dohc I-4
Size, liters/cu. in.	2.2/133	3.1/191	2.3/138
Fuel delivery	TBI	PFI	PFI
Horsepower @ rpm	95 @ 5200	135 @ 4200	180 @ 6200
Torque (lbs./ft.) @ rpm	120 @ 3200	180 @ 3600	160 @ 5200
Availability	S[1]	S[2]	S[3]

EPA city/highway mpg

5-speed OD manual	24/34	19/28	22/31
3-speed automatic	24/31	20/27	

1. Corsica LT, base Beretta.   2. Corsica LTZ, Beretta GT and conv.   3. Beretta GTZ.

CONSUMER GUIDE®

Prices

Chevrolet Corsica	Retail Price	Dealer Invoice	Low Price
LT 4-door notchback	$9495	$8479	$8679
LT 5-door hatchback	9895	8836	9036
LTZ 4-door notchback	12795	11426	11626
Destination charge	425	425	425

Standard equipment:

LT: 2.2-liter TBI 4-cylinder engine, 5-speed manual transmission, power steering, cloth reclining front bucket seats, 4-way driver's seat, door pockets, rear shoulder belts, left remote and right manual mirrors, AM/FM radio, 185/75R14 tires; hatchback has folding rear seat, sliding package tray, cargo cover. **LTZ** adds: 3.1-liter PFI V-6, FE3 sport suspension, luggage rack, sport steering wheel, sport front seats, 60/40 split rear seatback with center armrest, gauge package with tachometer, overhead console, 205/60R15 tires on alloy wheels.

Optional equipment:

3.1-liter V-6, LT	685	582	617
3-speed automatic transmission	540	459	486
Air conditioning	780	663	702
Custom cloth CL bucket seats, LT 4-door .	425	361	383
LT 5-door	275	234	248
Preferred Group 1, LT	232	197	209
Tinted glass, intermittent wipers, floormats, map lamps with consolette.			
Preferred Group 2, LT	1342	1141	1208
Group 1 plus air conditioning, cruise control, tilt steering column.			
Preferred Group 3, LT	2042	1736	1838
Group 2 plus AM/FM cassette, power windows and locks, remote decklid release.			
Preferred Group 1, LTZ	363	309	327
Cruise control, tilt steering column, floormats.			
Preferred Pkg. 2, LTZ	1063	904	957
Group 1 plus AM/FM cassette, power windows and locks, remote decklid release.			
AM/FM cassette	140	119	126
AM/FM cassette w/EQ	290	247	261
Sound system prices are for base models; prices vary with option package content.			
Floor console	60	51	54
Rear defogger	160	136	144
Power locks	215	183	194

Prices are accurate at time of printing; subject to manufacturer's change.

	Retail Price	Dealer Invoice	Low Price
Gauge pkg., LT	139	118	125

Tachometer, coolant temperature and oil pressure gauges, voltmeter, trip odometer.

	Retail Price	Dealer Invoice	Low Price
185/75R14 white-stripe tires, LT	68	58	61
Styled steel wheels, LT	56	48	50
Two-tone paint	123	105	111
Decklid luggage carrier, LT	115	98	104
California emissions pkg.	100	85	90

Chevrolet Beretta

	Retail Price	Dealer Invoice	Low Price
2-door notchback	$10320	$9216	$9416
GT 2-door notchback	12500	11163	11363
GTZ 2-door notchback	13750	12279	12479
2-door convertible	NA	NA	NA
Destination charge	425	425	425

Standard equipment:

2.2-liter TBI 4-cylinder engine, 5-speed manual transmission, power steering, cloth reclining front bucket seats, console with storage armrest, rear shoulder belts, tachometer, coolant temperature and oil pressure gauges, voltmeter, trip odometer, left remote and right manual mirrors, AM/FM radio, console, tinted glass, F41 sport suspension, 195/70R14. **GT** adds: 3.1-liter PFI V-6, air conditioning, FE3 sport suspension, sport steering wheel, 60/40 split folding rear seatback, custom cloth trim, overhead consolette, remote decklid release, 205/60R15 Goodyear tires on styled steel wheels. **GTZ** adds: 2.3-liter DOHC 16-valve PFI Quad 4 engine, FE7 performance suspension, air conditioning, front air dam with fog lights, rear spoiler, leather-wrapped steering wheel, 205/55R16 Goodyear Eagle GT + 4 tires on alloy wheels. **Convertible** has base equipment plus 3.1-liter V-6, FE3 sport suspension, 205/55R16 tires on alloy wheels.

Optional equipment:

	Retail Price	Dealer Invoice	Low Price
3.1-liter V-6, base	685	582	617
3-speed automatic transmission	540	459	486
Air conditioning, base	780	663	702
Preferred Group 1, base	112	95	101

Intermittent wipers, floormats, map lights, consolette.

	Retail Price	Dealer Invoice	Low Price
Preferred Group 2, base	1222	1039	1100

Group 1 plus air conditioning, cruise control, tilt steering column.

	Retail Price	Dealer Invoice	Low Price
Preferred Group 3, base	1817	1544	1635

Group 2 plus AM/FM cassette, power windows and locks, remote decklid release.

	Retail Price	Dealer Invoice	Low Price
Preferred Group 1, GT	442	376	398

Cruise control, tilt steering column, intermittent wipers, floormats, map lights, consolette.

	Retail Price	Dealer Invoice	Low Price
Preferred Group 2, GT	1037	881	933

Group 1 plus AM/FM cassette, power windows and locks, remote decklid release.

	Retail Price	Dealer Invoice	Low Price
Preferred Group 1, GTZ	363	309	327

Cruise control, tilt steering column, floormats.

	Retail Price	Dealer Invoice	Low Price
Preferred Group 2, GTZ	958	814	862

Group 1 plus AM/FM cassette, power windows and locks, remote decklid release.

	Retail Price	Dealer Invoice	Low Price
Rear defogger	160	136	144
Power locks	175	149	158
Electronic instruments	156	133	140
Removable sunroof	350	298	315
Alloy wheels	210	179	189
AM/FM cassette	140	119	126
AM/FM cassette w/EQ	290	247	261

Sound system prices are for base models; prices vary with option package content.

Chevrolet Corvette

Chevrolet Corvette ZR-1

The ultra-high performance ZR-1 debuts with a Lotus-designed 32-valve, dual-overhead-cam, 5.7-liter V-8 rated at 380 horsepower. Available in the coupe body style only, the ZR-1 gets a wider rear body to accommodate back tires

Prices are accurate at time of printing; subject to manufacturer's change.

that are wider than the standard 'Vette's. The only other external mark of a ZR-1 is a convex tail with square taillamps in place of the standard car's concave panel and round lights. Standard on the ZR-1 is the new FX3 adjustable suspension, which also is optionally available on standard 'Vette coupes with manual transmission. The base 'Vette's 5.7-liter engine, known as the L98, gets a five more horsepower, to 245, and five more pounds/feet of torque, to 340. Standard on all Corvettes is a 6-speed manual transmission; a 4-speed overdrive automatic is optional on L98 cars only. Among new standard items are 17-inch alloy

Specifications

	3-door hatchback	2-door conv.
Wheelbase, in.	96.2	96.2
Overall length, in.	176.5	176.5
Overall width, in.	71.0[1]	71.0
Overall height, in.	46.7	46.4
Turn diameter, ft.	40.0	40.0
Curb weight, lbs.	3223[2]	3263
Cargo vol., cu. ft.	17.9	6.6
Fuel capacity, gals.	20.0	20.0
Seating capacity	2	2
Front headroom, in.	36.4	36.4
Front shoulder room, in.	54.1	54.1
Front legroom, max., in.	42.6	42.6
Rear headroom, in.	—	—
Rear shoulder room, in.	—	—
Rear legroom, min., in.	—	—

1. ZR-1, 74.0.   2. ZR-1, 3465.

Powertrain layout: longitudinal front engine/rear-wheel drive.

Engines

	ohv V-8	dohc V-8
Size, liters/cu. in.	5.7/350	5.7/350
Fuel delivery	PFI	PFI
Horsepower @ rpm	245 @ 4000	380 @ 6200
Torque (lbs./ft.) @ rpm	340 @ 3200	370 @ 4500
Availability	S	S[1]

EPA city/highway mpg

6-speed OD manual	16/25	16/25
4-speed OD automatic	16/24	

1. ZR-1.

wheels and an engine oil cooler. All '90 'Vettes get a new interior with a driver's-side airbag mounted in the steering-wheel. The new dashboard uses a combination of digital and analog gauges in place of previously all-digital instrumentation. The seats, door panels, and center console are new and the windshield wiper switch is moved from the door panel to the turn-signal stalk. Corvette's cabin now is much more appealing and functional. The ZR-1 is among the world's fastest production cars and seems to minimize Corvette's bad habit of juddering over rough pavement so that the tires lose traction. Corvette remains a car of limited dimension, but it delivers thrilling performance so long as the road is smooth and dry.

Prices

Chevrolet Corvette	Retail Price	Dealer Invoice	Low Price
3-door hatchback	$31979	$26958	$27358
2-door convertible	37264	31414	31814
ZR-1 3-door hatchback	58995	NA	NA
Destination charge	500	500	500

Standard equipment:

5.7-liter PFI V-8, 6-speed manual or 4-speed automatic transmission, power steering, 4-wheel disc brakes, anti-lock braking system, driver's-side airbag, Pass Key theft deterrent system, air conditioning, AM/FM cassette, power antenna, cruise control, rear defogger, leather-wrapped steering wheel, tinted glass, heated power mirrors, fog lamps, power windows and locks, intermittent wipers, 275/40ZR17 Goodyear Eagle GT tires on alloy wheels **ZR-1** adds: DOHC 32-valve engine, FX3 Selective Ride Control.

Optional equipment:

Leather seats	425	353	374
Leather sport seats	1050	872	924
Preferred Group 1	1273	1057	1120
Automatic climate control, Delco-Bose Gold audio system, power driver's seat.			
CD player	396	329	348
Automatic climate control	180	149	158
Performance axle ratio	22	18	19
Luggage rack, convertible	140	116	123
Engine oil cooler	110	91	97

Prices are accurate at time of printing; subject to manufacturer's change.

	Retail Price	Dealer Invoice	Low Price
Z51 Performance Handling Pkg.	460	382	405
Includes engine oil cooler and HD brakes.			
FX3 Selective Ride Pkg.	1695	1407	1492
Single removable roof panel	615	510	541
Dual removable roof panels	915	759	805
Removable hardtop, convertible	1995	1656	1756
Power seats, each	270	224	238
Engine block heater	20	17	18
California emissions pkg.	100	83	88

Chevrolet Lumina

Chevrolet Lumina

A coupe joins the 4-door Lumina sedan in Chevy's new front-drive intermediate troupe. Introduced in the late spring of 1989 as an early 1990 model, the Lumina sedan was the first 4-door from the General Motors design that in 1988 produced the Buick Regal, Oldsmobile Cutlass Supreme, and Pontiac Grand Prix coupes. Both Luminas are 6-passenger cars available in base guise and in sportier Euro trim. A 2.5-liter 4-cylinder engine is standard; a 3.1-liter V-6 is optional and standard in the Euro. The coupe and sedan share the same 107.5-inch wheelbase, but the coupe's body is about one inch longer than the sedan's, at 198.4 inches. The wheelbase of the Lumina 4-door is three inches longer than that of the sedan it replaces, the Celeb-

Specifications

	2-door notchback	4-door notchback
Wheelbase, in.	107.5	107.5
Overall length, in.	198.4	197.6
Overall width, in.	71.1	71.0
Overall height, in.	53.3	53.6
Turn diameter, ft.	39.0	39.0
Curb weight, lbs.	3042	3122
Cargo vol., cu. ft.	15.5	15.7
Fuel capacity, gals.	17.1	17.1
Seating capacity	6	6
Front headroom, in.	37.6	38.8
Front shoulder room, in.	57.5	58.2
Front legroom, max., in.	42.4	42.4
Rear headroom, in.	37.2	38.1
Rear shoulder room, in.	56.9	56.2
Rear legroom, min., in.	34.8	36.9

Powertrain layout: transverse front engine/front-wheel drive.

Engines

	ohv I-4	ohv V-6
Size, liters/cu. in.	2.5/151	3.1/191
Fuel delivery	TBI	PFI
Horsepower @ rpm	110 @ 5200	135 @ 4400
Torque (lbs./ft.) @ rpm	135 @ 3200	180 @ 3600
Availability	S	O[1]

EPA city/highway mpg

3-speed automatic	21/27	19/27
4-speed OD automatic		19/30

1. Standard, Euro.

rity. The Lumina coupe is intended to replace the slightly larger rear-drive Monte Carlo, which was discontinued in 1988. The Euro has blackout exterior trim, larger tires, a sport suspension, and air conditioning standard. Features common to all Luminas include 4-wheel disc brakes, power steering, and an all-independent suspension. Judging Lumina's value means comparing it to the pace-setter in this class, the Ford Taurus, which is entering its fifth model year. Lumina's cabin doesn't feel any bigger than the Taurus's, though it is significantly airier, thanks to more glass area. And while a Lumina with the 3.1 V-6 has adequate power, the Taurus has a superior over-the-road

Prices are accurate at time of printing; subject to manufacturer's change.

feel, with better suspension control over bumps and a less ponderous feel around town. Plus, Taurus's ergonomics are better. Lumina is an advance over the Celebrity and Monte Carlo, but Chevy has failed to produce a new mid-size standard-bearer.

Prices

Chevrolet Lumina	Retail Price	Dealer Invoice	Low Price
2-door notchback	$12140	$10477	$10677
4-door notchback	12340	10649	10849
Euro 2-door notchback	14040	12117	12317
Euro 4-door notchback	14240	12289	12489
Destination charge	455	455	455

Standard equipment:

2.5-liter TBI 4-cylinder engine, 3-speed automatic transmission, 4-wheel disc brakes, power steering, front bench seat with reclining seatbacks, AM/FM radio, visor mirrors, tinted glass, left remote and right manual mirrors, intermittent wipers, 197/75R14 tires. **Euro** adds: 3.1-liter PFI V-6, air conditioning, decklid spoiler, 195/70R15 tires.

Optional equipment:

3.1-liter V-6, base	660	561	594
4-speed automatic transmission (V-6 req.)	200	170	180
Air conditioning, base	805	684	725
Custom cloth bucket seats w/console	299	254	269
Custom cloth 60/40 seat	199	169	179
Cloth 60/40 seat	159	135	143
Preferred Group 1, base	1180	1003	1062
Air conditioning, cruise control, tilt steering column, floormats.			
Preferred Group 2, base 2-door	1665	1415	1499
Base 4-door	1770	1505	1593
Group 1 plus power windows and locks, remote decklid release, remote mirrors.			
Preferred Group 1, Euro	475	404	428
Cruise control, tilt steering column, gauge package with tachometer, floormats.			
Preferred Group 2, Euro 2-door	1100	935	990
Euro 4-door	1205	1024	1085
Group 1 plus AM/FM cassette, power windows and locks, remote decklid release, remote mirrors.			
Rear defogger	160	136	144

	Retail Price	Dealer Invoice	Low Price
Power locks, 2-doors	175	149	158
4-doors	215	183	194
AM/FM cassette	140	119	126
Power driver's seat	270	230	243
Rear spoiler delete (credit)	(128)	(109)	(109)
195/75R14 white-stripe tires, base	72	61	65
215/60R16 tires, Euro	76	65	68
Alloy wheels	250	213	225

Chevrolet Lumina APV

Chevrolet Lumina APV

The APV, for "All Purpose Vehicle," is Chevrolet's version of the space-age-looking new front-drive minivan from General Motors. Pontiac and Oldsmobile get copies as well, but only Chevy offers a cargo version in addition to its passenger model. Available in base and CL trim levels, the APV offers five different seating configurations, accommodating between two and seven passengers. The only powertrain is a 3.1-liter V-6 mounted transversely and accessible only through the front hood. A 3-speed automatic is the only transmission. The APV has two front doors, a sliding right-side door, and a one-piece rear liftgate. The APV is built of fiberglass-like composite exterior panels bonded to a steel frame. Its 109.8-inch wheelbase is shorter than that of the rear-drive Chevy Astro van and the front-drive Dodge Caravan/Plymouth Voyager, but the APV's overall length of about 193 inches is longer than any of these. The APV's sloped snout puts nearly two feet of dash shelf between the driver and the base of the massive windshield. The front of the vehicle is invisible from the driver's vantage and the initial impression is that you're steering from one of the rear seats. The effect overshadows some APV attributes. Its all-independent suspension helps it ride and handle much like a large family car. Storage bins abound and there's no engine hump to hinder passage to the rear. The modular seating allows for a variety of passenger and cargo configurations. The body is impervious to rust and resists dings. Once up to freeway speed, it settles

Specifications

	4-door van
Wheelbase, in.	109.8
Overall length, in.	193.9
Overall width, in.	74.2
Overall height, in.	65.5
Turn diameter, ft.	38.0
Curb weight, lbs.	3505
Cargo vol., cu. ft.	104.6
Fuel capacity, gals.	20.0
Seating capacity	7
Front headroom, in.	40.2
Front shoulder room, in.	53.5
Front legroom, max., in.	40.7
Rear headroom, in.	38.6
Rear shoulder room, in.	61.6
Rear legroom, min., in.	33.7

Powertrain layout: transverse front engine/front-wheel drive.

Engines

	ohv V-6
Size, liters/cu. in.	3.1/191
Fuel delivery	TBI
Horsepower @ rpm	120 @ 4200
Torque (lbs./ft.) @ rpm	170 @ 2200
Availability	S

EPA city/highway mpg

3-speed automatic	18/23

into a quiet canter that's ideal for long trips. The 3500-pound APV's major shortfall is a lack of power in merging or passing maneuvers, especially with the air conditioner on and passengers and luggage aboard. Chevy's new mini-van is priced to compete with the class-leading Dodge Caravan/Plymouth Voyager and Mazda MPV. The APV's avant-garde nose and underpowered V-6, however, are drawbacks.

Prices

Chevrolet Lumina APV	Retail Price	Dealer Invoice	Low Price
Base van	$13995	$12498	—
CL van	15745	14060	—
Destination charge	500	500	500

Low price not available at time of publication.

Standard equipment:

3.1-liter TBI V-6, 3-speed automatic transmission, power steering, reclining front bucket seats, 3-passenger middle seat, tinted glass, left remote and right manual mirrors, rear wiper/washer, 205/70R14 tires. **CL** adds: air conditioning, tilt steering column, individual seats, misc. lights.

Optional equipment:

Air conditioning, base	805	684	—
6-passenger seating	510	434	—
Includes two front bucket seats and four modular rear seats.			
7-passenger seating, base	660	561	—
CL	425	361	—
Includes two front bucket seats and five modular rear seats.			
Load leveling suspension	170	145	—
Preferred Group 1, base	1000	850	—
Air conditioning, tilt steering column, auxiliary lighting.			
Preferred Group 2, base w/5-pass. seating	1895	1611	—
Base w/6- or 7-pass. seating	1910	1624	—
Group 1 plus AM/FM cassette, power windows and locks, cruise control, remote mirrors, floormats.			
Preferred Group 1, CL w/5-pass. seating .	895	761	—
CL w/7-pass. seating	910	774	—
AM/FM cassette, power windows and locks, cruise control, remote mirrors, floormats.			
AM/FM cassette	140	119	—

Prices are accurate at time of printing; subject to manufacturer's change.

	Retail Price	Dealer Invoice	Low Price
AM/FM radio w/CD player	396	337	—

Sound system prices are for base models; prices vary with option package content.

Rear defogger	160	136	—
Deep tinted glass	245	208	—
Power locks	255	217	—
Power driver's seat	270	230	—
195/70R15 tires	62	53	—
Alloy wheels	265	225	—

Chrysler Imperial/ New Yorker Fifth Avenue

Chrysler Imperial

Chrysler returns full-bore to the domestic luxury market with a pair of new front-drive cars based on the New Yorker. Resurrected for the occasion is the Imperial badge, last used in 1983 on a rear-drive "bustleback" coupe. The 1982-89 Fifth Avenue was built on the same rear-drive chassis as the previous Imperial. For '90, the Imperial becomes the corporation's flagship sedan, with the Fifth Avenue its slightly less plush sibling. Both new models are full-size, 6-passenger, 4-door sedans. They use the New Yorker platform that was introduced for 1988, but with the wheelbase

Specifications

	Imperial 4-door notchback	Fifth Avenue 4-door notchback
Wheelbase, in.	109.3	109.3
Overall length, in.	203.0	198.6
Overall width, in.	68.9	68.9
Overall height, in.	56.3	55.9
Turn diameter, ft.	42.1	42.1
Curb weight, lbs.	3570	3452
Cargo vol., cu. ft.	16.7	16.5
Fuel capacity, gals.	16.0	16.0
Seating capacity	6	6
Front headroom, in.	38.4	38.4
Front shoulder room, in.	55.9	56.2
Front legroom, max., in.	43.0	43.0
Rear headroom, in.	55.7	55.7
Rear shoulder room, in.	37.9	37.9
Rear legroom, min., in.	41.7	41.7

Powertrain layout: transverse front engine/front-wheel drive.

Engines

	ohv V-6
Size, liters/cu. in.	3.3/201
Fuel delivery	PFI
Horsepower @ rpm	147 @ 4800
Torque (lbs./ft.) @ rpm	183 @ 3600
Availability	S

EPA city/highway mpg

4-speed OD automatic	18/25

stretched five inches, to 109.3. At 203 inches, the Imperial's body is four inches longer than the Fifth Avenue's, and almost 10 inches longer than the New Yorker's. The Imperial and Fifth Avenue share the same interior dimensions; their main advantage over the New Yorker is three more inches of rear leg room. Like the New Yorker, they're powered by Chrysler's new 147-horsepower 3.3-liter V-6 mated to a 4-speed automatic transmission. A lengthy list of luxury equipment is standard on both the Imperial and Fifth Avenue. Anti-lock brakes are standard on the Imperial, optional on the Fifth Avenue. A driver's-side airbag is standard on both. The new Fifth Avenue leaves us unenthusiastic. The 3.3 V-6 sounds gruff and provides only adequate

Prices are accurate at time of printing; subject to manufacturer's change.

acceleration. The ride isn't very absorbent and cornering ability is subpar even for an opulent barge. The Fifth Avenue doesn't feel as solid as such rivals as the Buick Electra Park Avenue or Lincoln Continental, and though it has more rear leg room than those cars, it has nearly three inches less shoulder room than the Buick and two less than the Lincoln. Except for more rear leg room, the Fifth Avenue/Imperial offers nothing of substance that isn't available for less money in the regular New Yorker.

Prices

Chrysler Imperial	Retail Price	Dealer Invoice	Low Price
4-door notchback	$25495	$21691	—
Destination charge	550	550	550

Low price not available at time of publication.

Standard equipment:

3.3-liter PFI V-6, 4-speed automatic transmission, anti-lock 4-wheel disc brakes, power steering, driver's-side airbag, rear shoulder belts, automatic temperature control air conditioning, leather/cloth 50/50 power bench seat with 2-position memory, power windows and locks, automatic load leveling suspension, cruise control, heated power mirrors with 2-position memory, Chrysler Infinity I AM/FM cassette with power antenna, rear defogger, tilt steering column, leather-wrapped steering wheel, headlamp delay, coolant temperature and oil pressure gauges, voltmeter, trip odometer, illuminated entry, remote fuel door and decklid releases, tinted glass, floormats, cornering lights, lighted visor mirrors, landau vinyl roof, wire wheel covers, 195/75R14 WSW tires.

Optional equipment:

Electronic Features Pkg.	1572	1336	—

Overhead console with Vehicle Information Center, electronic instruments, automatic day/night mirror, Infinity II AM/FM cassette with EQ, security alarm.

Security alarm	146	124	—
Electronically controlled air suspension	628	534	—
Mark Cross leather	354	301	—
Pearl/clearcoat paint	75	64	—
Conventional spare tire	NC	NC	NC
California emissions pkg.	NC	NC	NC

Chrysler New Yorker Fifth Avenue

	Retail Price	Dealer Invoice	Low Price
4-door notchback	$20860	$18006	—
Destination charge	550	550	550

Low price not available at time of publication.

Standard equipment:

3.3-liter PFI V-6, 4-speed automatic transmission, power steering, driver's-side airbag, rear shoulder belts, automatic temperature control air conditioning, 50/50 cloth bench seat with power driver's side and center armrest, power windows and locks, cruise control, AM/FM radio, heated power mirrors, rear defogger, coolant temperature and oil pressure gauges, voltmeter, trip odometer, remote fuel door and decklid releases, tilt steering column, leather-wrapped steering wheel, automatic rear load leveling, tinted glass, intermittent wipers, cornering lights, visor mirrors, landau vinyl roof, 195/75R14 WSW tires.

Optional equipment:

Anti-lock 4-wheel disc brakes	926	787	—
Luxury Equipment Pkg.	1563	1329	—
Bodyside molding, illuminated entry, floormats, headlamp delay, lighted visor mirrors, power antenna, power decklid pulldown, heated power mirrors with 2-position memory, power seats with 2-position memory, security alarm, undercoating, wire wheel covers.			
Mark Cross Edition	2129	1810	—
Luxury Pkg. plus leather interior.			
Interior Illumination Pkg.	192	163	—
Illuminated entry, lighted visor mirrors.			
Electronic Features Pkg.	1216	1034	—
Overhead console with Vehicle Information Center, electronic instrument cluster, automatic day/night mirror.			
Power decklid pulldown	80	68	—
AM/FM cassette w/Infinity speakers	482	410	—
AM/FM cassette w/Infinity speakers & EQ .	692	588	—
Requires Luxury or Mark Cross Pkg.			
Security alarm	146	124	—
Conventional spare tire	83	71	—
Alloy wheels	49	42	—
Requires Luxury or Mark Cross Pkg.			
Wire wheel covers	224	190	—
Pearl/clearcoat paint	75	64	—
California emissions pkg.	100	85	—

Prices are accurate at time of printing; subject to manufacturer's change.

Chrysler LeBaron

Chrysler LeBaron Coupe GTC

The world's best-selling convertible and its coupe cousin are available for the first time with V-6 power and are treated to a new interior design, while the LeBaron name has been extended to a 4-door sedan based on the Dodge Spirit/Plymouth Acclaim. For '90, a Mitsubishi-made 3.0-liter V-6 is standard or optional on all coupes and convertibles except the performance-oriented GTC models. GTCs come standard with Chrysler's 2.2-liter turbocharged 4-cylinder, this year known as the VNT (Variable Nozzle Turbo) Turbo IV, which uses pivoting turbo vanes to sharpen throttle response. Also available for the first time is a 4-speed automatic transmission only with the V-6. The VNT Turbo IV comes only with Chrysler's new 5-speed manual transmission. New on the GTC for '90 is an electronically variable suspension that allows the driver to alter shock absorber damping. Rear shoulder belts are now standard on the coupe; a driver's-side airbag is standard on all LeBarons. The A-body LeBaron Sedan will reach showrooms in early 1990. It replaces the K-car-derived LeBaron sedan that was retired for the '89 model year. This front-wheel-drive, 6-passenger 4-door has the Mitsubishi 3.0 V-6 mated to a 4-speed automatic as its only powertrain. The V-6 is a welcome alternative to the base 4-cylinder and the raucous turbo engines, while the shift action of the new 5-speed is a quantum leap ahead of the previous one's. The new LeBaron interior is far more user-friendly than the old, supplanting the severe angles of the previous dashboard with rounded forms that places controls closer to the driver. The new 4-door is a quiet and competent luxury compact that's a worthy first rung on the Chrysler-sedan ladder.

Specifications

	2-door notchback	2-door conv.	4-door notchback
Wheelbase, in.	100.3	100.3	103.3
Overall length, in.	184.9	184.9	182.7
Overall width, in.	68.5	68.5	68.1
Overall height, in.	51.0	52.3	53.7
Turn diameter, ft.	38.1	38.1	37.6
Curb weight, lbs.	2810	2929	2854
Cargo vol., cu. ft.	14.0	10.3	14.4
Fuel capacity, gals.	14.0	14.0	16.0
Seating capacity	5	4	6
Front headroom, in.	37.6	38.3	38.4
Front shoulder room, in.	55.9	55.9	53.9
Front legroom, max., in.	42.4	42.4	41.9
Rear headroom, in.	36.3	37.0	37.9
Rear shoulder room, in.	56.3	45.7	54.2
Rear legroom, min., in.	33.0	33.0	38.3

Powertrain layout: transverse front engine/front-wheel drive.

Engines	ohc I-4	Turbo ohc I-4	Turbo ohc I-4	ohc V-6
Size, liters/cu. in.	2.5/153	2.5/153	2.2/135	3.0/181
Fuel delivery	TBI	PFI	PFI	PFI
Horsepower @ rpm	100 @ 4800	150 @ 4800	174 @ 5200	141 @ 5000
Torque (lbs./ft.) @ rpm	135 @ 2800	180 @ 2000	210 @ 2400	171 @ 2800
Availability	S	O	S[1]	S[2]

EPA city/highway mpg

5-speed OD manual		21/29	20/28	19/28
3-speed automatic	22/27	19/23		
4-speed OD automatic				19/26

1. GTC. 2. Premium and GT coupe and convertible; LeBaron Sedan.

Prices

Chrysler LeBaron Coupe/Convertible

	Retail Price	Dealer Invoice	Low Price
Highline (HL) 2-door notchback	$12495	$11046	$11246
Premium (PR) 2-door notchback	16415	14456	14656

Prices are accurate at time of printing; subject to manufacturer's change.

	Retail Price	Dealer Invoice	Low Price
GT 2-door notchback	15678	13815	14015
GTC 2-door notchback	17811	15671	15871
Highline 2-door convertible	14995	13221	13421
Premium 2-door convertible	19595	17223	17423
GT 2-door convertible	17757	15624	15824
GTC 2-door convertible	20052	17620	17820
Destination charge	465	465	465

Standard equipment:

Highline: 2.5-liter TBI 4-cylinder engine, 3-speed automatic transmission, power steering, 4-wheel disc brakes, driver's-side airbag, rear shoulder belts, cloth reclining front bucket seats, coolant temperature and oil pressure gauges, voltmeter, trip odometer, mini trip computer, AM/FM radio, power windows, intermittent wipers, console with storage, remote fuel door and decklid releases, tinted glass, remote mirrors, visor mirrors, 195/70R14 tires; convertible has power top. **Premium** adds: 3.0-liter PFI V-6, 4-speed automatic transmission, power locks, 60/40 folding rear seat (coupe), leather-wrapped steering wheel, overhead console (coupe), floormats, electronic instruments, cornering lights, heated power mirrors, rear defogger, 205/60R15 touring tires; convertible has illuminated entry, lighted visor mirrors, cruise control, tilt steering column, AM/FM cassette with Infinity speakers and power antenna, undercoating. **GT** adds to Highline: 3.0-liter PFI V-6, 5-speed manual transmission, sport handling suspension, air conditioning, rear defogger, power locks, heated power mirrors, AM/FM cassette with Infinity speakers and power antenna, floormats, cruise control, tilt steering column, leather-wrapped steering wheel, undercoating, 205/60R15 performance tires on alloy wheels. **GTC** adds: 2.2-liter intercooled Turbo IV PFI 4-cylinder engine, HD transmission and brakes, performance suspension, overhead console, illuminated entry, decklid luggage rack, lighted visor mirrors, 205/55R16 tires.

Optional equipment:

2.5-liter turbo engine, HL	680	578	612
3.0-liter V-6, HL	680	578	612
2.5-liter turbo engine, GT & GTC	NC	NC	NC
5-speed manual transmission, HL w/3.0 (credit)	(536)	(456)	(456)
3-speed automatic transmission, GT	536	456	482
GTC	NC	NC	NC
GTC includes 2.5-liter turbo engine instead of Turbo IV.			
4-speed automatic transmission, GT w/3.0	627	533	564
HL w/3.0	91	77	82
Air conditioning, HL	805	684	725

	Retail Price	Dealer Invoice	Low Price
Popular Equipment Pkg., HL cpe	1263	1074	1137
HL coupe w/Deluxe Convenience	933	793	840
HL convertible	1073	912	966

Air conditioning, rear defogger, floormats, cruise control, tilt steering column, undercoating.

Luxury Equipment Pkg., HL coupe	2280	1938	2052
HL coupe w/Power Convenience	1999	1699	1799
PR coupe	825	701	743

Popular Pkg. plus illuminated entry, lighted visor mirrors, overhead console, power locks, heated power mirrors, power driver's seat, leather-wrapped steering wheel.

Deluxe Convenience Pkg., HL & PR	330	281	297

Cruise control, tilt steering column; standard on Premium convertible.

Light Pkg., HL & PR	192	163	173

Illuminated entry, lighted visor mirrors; standard on Premium convertible.

Power Convenience Pkg., HL	311	264	280

Power locks, heated power mirrors.

Overhead console, GT	268	228	241
Rear defogger, HL coupe	160	136	144
Electronic instruments, HL	299	254	269

Requires Popular Pkg.

Delete electronic instruments, PR	NC	NC	NC
Vehicle Info Center, PR convertible & GTC .	676	575	608
PR coupe	527	448	474
Leather power driver's seat, PR & GT coupes	962	818	866
PR & GT convertibles	1212	1030	1091
Leather power enthusiast seat, GTC coupe .	627	533	564
Power driver's seat, convertibles exc. GTC .	270	230	243

HL requires Power Convenience Pkg.

8-way power driver's seat, PR & GT convertibles	335	285	302

Requires leather trim.

AM/FM cassette, HL	152	129	137
AM/FM cassette, PR coupe	552	469	497
AM/FM cassette w/EQ, HL & PR coupes . .	762	648	686
PR & GTC convertibles, GTC coupe . . .	210	179	189

Convertibles require Popular Pkg.; coupes require Popular or Luxury Pkg.

Security alarm, PR & GTC	146	124	131
Removable sunroof, HL & GT coupes . . .	396	337	356
PR & GTC coupes	222	189	200
Sport handling suspension, HL	57	48	51
195/70R14 WSW touring tires, HL	72	61	65
205/60R15 WSW touring tires, PR	76	65	68
Alloy wheels & sport suspension, HL . . .	627	533	564
PR	530	451	477
Alloy wheels, HL	322	274	290

Prices are accurate at time of printing; subject to manufacturer's change.

	Retail Price	Dealer Invoice	Low Price
Two-tone paint, HL coupe	226	192	203
California emissions pkg.	100	85	90

Chrysler LeBaron Sedan

4-door notchback	$15995	$14091	—
Destination charge	440	440	440

Low price not available at time of publication.

Standard equipment:

3.0-liter PFI V-6, 4-speed automatic transmission, power steering, driver's-side airbag, air conditioning, 50/50 reclining front bench seat, driver's-seat lumbar support adjustment, rear defogger, tinted glass, trip odometer, coolant temperature and oil pressure gauges, voltmeter, message center, remote OS mirrors, lighted visor mirrors, AM/FM cassette, rear shoulder belts, landau vinyl roof, cruise control, tilt steering column, remote fuel door and decklid releases, intermittent wipers, 195/70R14 WSW tires.

Optional equipment:

Power Equipment Discount Pkg.	573	487	—
Power windows and locks, heated power mirrors.			
Luxury Equipment Discount Pkg.	1772	1506	—
Power Equipment Pkg. plus leather interior, power driver's seat, leather-wrapped steering wheel, wire wheel covers, Infinity I AM/FM cassette.			
Power locks	225	191	—
Infinity I AM/FM cassette	300	255	—
Infinity II AM/FM cassette w/EQ	510	434	—
w/Luxury Pkg.	210	179	—
Power driver's seat	270	230	—
Wire wheel covers	224	190	—
Pearl coat/clearcoat paint	75	64	—
Conventional spare tire	93	79	—
California emissions pkg.	100	85	—

Chrysler New Yorker

The Landau continues as the full-zoot companion to the base New Yorker, which for '90 looses some standard features and gains a new name, Salon. The big mechanical change is the introduction of the Chrysler-made 3.3-liter

Chrysler New Yorker Salon

V-6 as the standard engine in place of a Mitsubishi-made 3.0-liter V-6. The 3.3 has 147 horsepower, six more than the Mitsubishi. Added to last year's long list of Landau standard equipment is a one-touch driver power window, among other items. The Salon basically is a stripped Landau. Its trim is akin to that of the similar front-drive Dodge Dynasty LE and relegates to the options list such luxury touches as power windows and air conditioning. Both the Landau and Salon get a driver's-side airbag as standard for '90. Optional equipment common to both includes 4-wheel disc brakes with an anti-lock feature in place of the standard front disc/rear drum brakes. Exclusive to the Salon options list is a road-handling suspension. These are conservative, smooth, quiet, and unexciting cars. There's adequate power for most situations and around-town handling is competent, but these cars succumb to tire-squealing and excessive body lean at the first hint of spirited cornering. The soft suspension filters out most bumps and the available anti-lock brakes are a big plus. The interior seats five adults in comfort, the dashboard is generally well laid out, and trunk space is ample. As for the Salon, the Dynasty is Dodge's biggest-selling car, so there obviously is a market for such a package. Comparing a similarly equipped Salon to a Dynasty LE, however, buyers will find the one with the Chrysler label about $2000 more expensive.

Prices are accurate at time of printing; subject to manufacturer's change.

Specifications

	4-door notchback
Wheelbase, in.	104.3
Overall length, in.	193.6
Overall width, in.	68.5
Overall height, in.	54.8
Turn diameter, ft.	40.4
Curb weight, lbs.	3066
Cargo vol., cu. ft.	16.5
Fuel capacity, gals.	16.0
Seating capacity	6
Front headroom, in.	38.3
Front shoulder room, in.	56.0
Front legroom, max., in.	41.9
Rear headroom, in.	37.8
Rear shoulder room, in.	55.7
Rear legroom, min., in.	38.9

Powertrain layout: transverse front engine/front-wheel drive.

Engines

	ohv V-6
Size, liters/cu. in.	3.3/201
Fuel delivery	PFI
Horsepower @ rpm	147 @ 4800
Torque (lbs./ft.) @ rpm	183 @ 3600
Availability	S

EPA city/highway mpg

4-speed OD automatic	19/26

Prices

Chrysler New Yorker	Retail Price	Dealer Invoice	Low Price
Salon 4-door notchback	$16342	$14141	$14541
Landau 4-door notchback	18795	16226	16626
Destination charge	520	520	520

Standard equipment:

Salon: 3.3-liter PFI V-6, 4-speed automatic transmission, power steering, driver's-side airbag, rear shoulder belts, 50/50 cloth front bench seat with seatback pockets, AM/FM radio, intermittent wipers, rear defogger, remote fuel door and decklid releases, coolant temperature and oil pressure gauges, voltmeter, trip odometer, remote mirrors, tinted glass, visor mirrors, 195/75R14 WSW tires. **Landau** adds: air conditioning, power windows and mirrors, cornering lamps, landau vinyl roof, automatic rear load leveling.

Optional equipment:

	Retail Price	Dealer Invoice	Low Price
Anti-lock 4-wheel disc brakes	926	787	833
Air conditioning, Salon	805	684	725
Popular Equipment Pkg., Salon	1549	1317	1394
Air conditioning, power windows and locks, floormats, heated power mirrors, cruise control, tilt steering column, undercoating.			
Luxury Equipment Pkg., Salon	2766	2351	2489
Popular Pkg. plus Interior Illumination Pkg., automatic day/night mirror, leather-wrapped steering wheel, power seats, security alarm, wire wheel covers.			
Interior Illumination Pkg., Salon	192	163	173
Illuminated entry, lighted visor mirrors; requires Popular Pkg.			
Deluxe Convenience Pkg.	330	281	297
Cruise control, tilt steering column.			
Power Accessories Pkg.	155	132	140
Power decklid pulldown, power antenna; requires Luxury Pkg.			
Luxury Equipment Pkg., Landau	1699	1444	1529
Power locks, floormats, headlamp delay system, illuminated entry, lighted visor mirrors, bodyside moldings, power seats, cruise control, tilt steering column, undercoating, wire wheel covers.			
Mark Cross Edition, Landau	2324	1975	2092
Luxury Pkg. plus leather upholstery, leather-wrapped steering wheel.			
Electronic Features Pkg., Landau	1216	1034	1094
Overhead console with Vehicle Information Center, automatic day/night mirror, electronic instruments.			
Power locks	305	259	275
AM/FM cassette, Salon	152	129	137
w/seek/scan, Landau	254	216	229
Infinity I AM/FM cassette	482	410	434
Infinity II AM/FM cassette	692	588	623
Requires Luxury Pkg.			
Security alarm	146	124	131
Salon requires Popular Pkg.; Landau requires power locks.			
Power driver's seat	270	230	243
Salon requires Popular Pkg.			
Memory power seats	368	313	331
Requires Luxury Pkg.			
Power sunroof	776	660	698
Salon requires Luxury Pkg.			
Road handling suspension, Salon	57	48	51
Requires Popular Pkg.; not available with automatic rear load leveling.			
Automatic rear load leveling, Salon	190	162	171
Requires Popular or Luxury Pkg.			

Prices are accurate at time of printing; subject to manufacturer's change.

	Retail Price	Dealer Invoice	Low Price
Conventional spare tire	83	71	75
Wire wheel covers	224	190	202
Alloy wheels	273	232	246
w/Luxury Pkg. or Mark Cross	49	42	44
Salon without Luxury Pkg. requires Popular Pkg.			
Pearl/clearcoat paint	75	64	68
California emissions pkg.	100	85	90

Dodge/Plymouth Colt

Dodge Colt GT

Chrysler tones down the performance of its nimble captive import for '90 by deleting the 3-door's optional turbocharged engine. The 5-door Colt wagon continues in front- and 4-wheel drive versions with only minor trim changes. Sold in identical forms under the Dodge and Plymouth nameplates, these front-drive subcompacts are made by Chrysler's Japanese partner, Mitsubishi. The current-generation 3-door debuted last year. It returns in three trim levels: base; GL (which replaces last year's E as the mid-level Colt); and GT. Gone is last year's optional 135-horsepower dual-cam 1.6-liter turbo 4-cylinder. This year's top engine is essentially the same 1.6, but without the turbocharger. It's available on the Colt GT and is rated at 113 horsepower. An 81-horsepower 1.5-liter four remains the standard engine on all Colt 3-door models. The 1.5 also is

Specifications

	3-door hatchback	5-door wagon
Wheelbase, in.	93.9	93.9
Overall length, in.	158.7	169.3
Overall width, in.	65.7	64.4
Overall height, in.	51.9	56.1
Turn diameter, ft.	30.2	32.5
Curb weight, lbs.	2194	2568
Cargo vol., cu. ft.	34.7	60.4
Fuel capacity, gals.	13.2	12.4
Seating capacity	5	5
Front headroom, in.	38.3	37.7
Front shoulder room, in.	53.5	52.8
Front legroom, max., in.	41.9	40.6
Rear headroom, in.	36.9	38.0
Rear shoulder room, in.	52.1	52.6
Rear legroom, min., in.	32.5	34.1

Powertrain layout: transverse front engine/front-wheel drive or automatic 4WD.

Engines

	ohc I-4	dohc I-4	ohc I-4
Size, liters/cu. in.	1.5/90	1.6/97	1.8/107
Fuel delivery	PFI	PFI	PFI
Horsepower @ rpm	81 @ 5500[1]	113 @ 6500	87 @ 5000
Torque (lbs./ft.) @ rpm	91 @ 3000	99 @ 5000	102 @ 3000
Availability	S	O[2]	S

EPA city/highway mpg

4-speed OD manual	31/36		
5-speed OD manual	28/34	23/28	23/28
3-speed automatic	27/29		
4-speed OD automatic		23/28	

1. 75 @ 5500/87 lbs/ft @ 2500, DL Wagon FWD. 2. Colt GT.

used in the front-drive wagon, but it's rated at 75 horsepower. Transmission choices have broadened and an automatic is now available on all except the base Colt and the 4WD wagon. The 4WD wagon has a center differential with a viscous coupling that automatically engages to send enough power to the rear wheels to maintain traction. Its only powertrain is an 87-horsepower 1.8-liter 4-cylinder mated to a 5-speed manual. Both Colt body styles, and especially the 4WD wagon, are sleepers that are well worth

Prices are accurate at time of printing; subject to manufacturer's change.

checking out. The base hatchback has a pleasing, no-nonsense manner while the GT model with the 1.6 engine is slick and quick. The 3-door provides decent space for four adults, though rear headroom is at a premium. There's better room all around in the wagon, plus the available security of no-fuss 4WD.

Prices

Dodge/Plymouth Colt	Retail Price	Dealer Invoice	Low Price
3-door hatchback	$6851	$6269	$6569
GL 3-door hatchback	7909	7189	7489
GT 3-door hatchback	9121	7935	8235
Destination charge	285	285	285

Standard equipment:

1.5-liter PFI 4-cylinder engine, 4-speed manual transmission, vinyl reclining front bucket seats, remote fuel door release, coolant temperature gauge, trip odometer, rear shoulder belts, 155/80R13 tires. **GL** adds: 5-speed manual transmission, cloth and vinyl upholstery, cigarette lighter, rear defogger, remote OS mirrors, tachometer, intermittent wipers. **GT** adds: velour upholstery, assist grip, wheel covers, 175/70R13 tires.

Optional equipment:

3-speed automatic transmission (NA base)	499	414	449
4-speed automatic transmission, GT	673	559	606
Requires Pkg. IFD or IFE.			
Air conditioning	739	613	665
Option Pkg. IFB, base	63	52	57
Tinted glass.			
Option Pkg. IFC, base	66	55	59
Rear defogger.			
Option Pkg. IFD, base	180	149	162
Rear defogger, tinted glass, rear shelf panel.			
Option Pkg. IFE, base	456	378	410
Pkg. IFD plus AM/FM radio.			
Option Pkg. IFB, GL	196	163	176
Tinted glass, rear wiper/washer.			
Option Pkg. IFD, GL	734	609	661
AM/FM radio, rear shelf panel, rear wiper/washer, wheel trim rings, bodyside graphics, spoiler.			
Option Pkg. IFE, GL	649	539	584
Power steering, AM/FM radio, rear shelf panel, tinted glass.			

CONSUMER GUIDE®

	Retail Price	Dealer Invoice	Low Price
Option Pkg. IFF, GL	868	720	781
Pkg. IFE plus rear wiper/washer, wheel covers.			
Option Pkg. IFG, GL	1035	859	932
Pkg. IFE plus cassette player.			
Option Pkg. IFJ, GL	1056	876	950
Power steering, AM/FM radio, rear shelf panel, tinted glass, rear wiper/ washer, wheel trim rings, bodyside graphics, spoiler.			
Option Pkg. IFA, GT	622	516	560
AM/FM radio, power steering, tinted glass.			
Option Pkg. IFB, GT	1036	860	932
Pkg. IFA plus cassette player, power mirrors, digital clock, rear wiper/ washer.			
Option Pkg. IFC, GT	1433	1189	1290
Power steering, AM/FM radio, tinted glass, digital clock, GT Sport Appearance Pkg (front air dam and rear spoiler, sill extensions, power mirrors, rear wiper/washer, alloy wheels).			
Option Pkg. 1FD, GT	1977	1641	1779
AM/FM cassette, tinted glass, GT Performance Pkg. (1.6-liter DOHC 16-valve engine, 4-wheel disc brakes, power steering, sport suspension, tilt/ telescopic steering column, driver's foot rest, digital clock, upgraded seat trim, 195/60HR14 tires, wheel trim rings).			
Option Pkg. IFE, GT	3159	2622	2843
Pkg. IFD plus power windows, cruise control, GT Sport Appearance Pkg.			
Wheel trim rings, GL	55	46	50
Floormats	28	23	25

Dodge/Plymouth Colt DL Wagon

	Retail Price	Dealer Invoice	Low Price
5-door wagon, 2WD	$9316	$8105	$8405
5-door wagon, 4WD	11145	9696	9996
Destination charge	285	285	285

Standard equipment:

1.5-liter PFI 4-cylinder engine, 5-speed manual transmission, cloth reclining front bucket seats, rear defogger, remote fuel door release, coolant temperature gauge, trip odometer, remote OS mirrors, rear wiper/washer, 175/70R13 tires. **4WD** adds: 1.8-liter engine, automatic full-time 4WD, 185/70R14 tires.

Optional equipment:

	Retail Price	Dealer Invoice	Low Price
3-speed automatic transmission, 2WD . . .	499	414	449
Air conditioning	739	613	665
Option Pkg. IFB, 2WD	595	494	536
4WD	336	279	302
Power steering, AM/FM radio, tinted glass.			

Prices are accurate at time of printing; subject to manufacturer's change.

	Retail Price	Dealer Invoice	Low Price
Option Pkg. IFC, 2WD	768	637	691
4WD	509	422	458

Pkg. IFB plus variable intermittent wipers, power mirrors, digital clock, driver's seat height control.

	Retail Price	Dealer Invoice	Low Price
Option Pkg. IFD, 2WD	1019	846	917
4WD	760	631	684

Power steering, AM/FM radio, driver's seat height control, Custom Pkg. (upgraded interior trim, digital clock, power mirrors, intermittent wipers, tinted glass, remote fuel door and liftgate releases, right visor mirror, cargo area light, rear heat ducts, dual horns, maintenance-free battery).

	Retail Price	Dealer Invoice	Low Price
Option Pkg. IFE, 2WD	1481	1229	1333
4WD	1222	1014	1100

Power steering, AM/FM cassette, driver's seat height control, alloy wheels, Custom Pkg.

	Retail Price	Dealer Invoice	Low Price
Luggage rack	128	106	115
Floormats	28	23	25
Two-tone paint	157	130	141

Dodge/Plymouth Colt Vista

Dodge Colt Vista

The 4-wheel drive version of the Vista for 1990 gets a viscous coupling system that automatically engages 4WD when the driving conditions warrant. This replaces the previous on-demand 4WD system, in which the driver had to press a dashboard button to activate all-wheel power. Otherwise, these 7-passenger front-drive and 4WD wagons

Specifications

	5-door wagon	4WD 5-door wagon
Wheelbase, in.	103.3	103.5
Overall length, in.	176.6	176.6
Overall width, in.	64.8	64.8
Overall height, in.	57.3	59.4
Turn diameter, ft.	34.8	34.8
Curb weight, lbs.	2667	2965
Cargo vol., cu. ft.	63.9	63.9
Fuel capacity, gals.	13.2	14.5
Seating capacity	7	7
Front headroom, in.	38.3	38.3
Front shoulder room, in.	53.1	53.1
Front legroom, max., in.	38.8	38.8
Rear headroom, in.	38.3	38.3
Rear shoulder room, in.	53.2	53.2
Rear legroom, min., in.	36.5	36.5

Powertrain layout: transverse front engine/front-wheel drive or automatic 4WD.

Engines

	ohc I-4
Size, liters/cu. in.	2.0/122
Fuel delivery	PFI
Horsepower @ rpm	96 @ 5000
Torque (lbs./ft.) @ rpm	113 @ 3500
Availability	S

EPA city/highway mpg

5-speed OD manual	23/29
3-speed automatic	22/23

continue with only trim changes. Vista is made by Chrysler's Japanese partner, Mitsubishi. The only engine offered is a 96-horsepower 2.0-liter 4-cylinder engine. The front-drive version comes standard with a 5-speed manual transmission; a 3-speed automatic is optional. The 4WD model comes only with a 5-speed manual. Colt Vista is one of the more versatile wagons on the market. With the 3-place middle seat and 2-position back seat folded forward, a carpeted cargo area of 64 cubic feet is formed. Fold the seats backward and their cushions form a single or double bed. The rear seat is better suited to children than adults,

Prices are accurate at time of printing; subject to manufacturer's change.

and there isn't much room for climbing in or out of either rear seating position. Vista's main drawback is a lack of engine power, however. With 96 horsepower for nearly 2700 pounds of curb weight on the front-drive model (and nearly 3000 on the 4WD model), you don't have much in reserve, especially with four or five people aboard and particularly with automatic transmission. Still, the utility of a 7-passenger cabin in a vehicle of such modest exterior dimensions is appealing.

Prices

Dodge/Plymouth Colt Vista	Retail Price	Dealer Invoice	Low Price
5-door wagon, 2WD	$11941	$10150	$10450
5-door wagon, 4WD	13167	11192	11492
Destination charge	285	285	285

Standard equipment:

2.0-liter PFI 4-cylinder engine, 5-speed manual transmission, cloth and vinyl reclining front bucket seats, rear defogger, remote fuel door release, coolant temperature gauge, trip odometer, tinted glass, remote OS mirrors, rear shoulder belts, variable intermittent wipers, 165/80R13 tires. **4WD** adds: automatic full-time 4WD, 185/70R14 tires.

Optional equipment:

3-speed automatic transmission, 2WD . . .	499	414	449
Air conditioning	739	613	665
Option Pkg. IFA, 2WD	687	570	618
4WD	428	355	385
Power steering, AM/FM radio, rear wiper/washer.			
Option Pkg. IFB, 2WD	1303	1081	1173
4WD	1044	867	940
Pkg. A plus cruise control, power windows and locks.			
Option Pkg. IFC, 2WD	951	789	856
4WD	612	508	551
Power steering, AM/FM radio, Custom Pkg. (digital clock, velour seats, upgraded interior trim, remote liftgate release, misc. lights, power mirrors, visor mirror, tachometer, wheel covers (2WD), 185/70R13 tires (2WD), tape stripes).			
Option Pkg. IFD, 2WD	2006	1665	1805
4WD	1386	1150	1247
Power steering, AM/FM cassette, cruise control, power windows and locks, Custom Pkg., alloy wheels (2WD).			

	Retail Price	Dealer Invoice	Low Price
Option Pkg. IFE, 2WD	870	722	783
Power steering, AM/FM radio, cruise control, rear wiper/washer.			
Option Pkg. IFE, 4WD	1915	1589	1724
AM/FM cassette, cruise control, power windows and locks, limited-slip differential, alloy wheels, Custom Pkg.			
Option Pkg. IFF, 4WD	611	507	550
AM/FM radio, cruise control, rear wiper/washer.			
Option Pkg. IFG, 4WD	830	689	747
AM/FM radio, limited-slip differential, Custom Pkg.			
Luggage rack	128	106	115
Floormats	28	23	25
Two-tone paint, w/Custom Pkg.	252	209	227
w/o Custom Pkg.	305	253	275

Dodge Daytona

Dodge Daytona ES

Dodge's front-drive sports coupe gets a new engine and a new interior for 1990. Available for the first time is a V-6 engine, the 141-horsepower 3.0-liter made by Mitsubishi. It's optional on the base and ES Daytonas and is available with Chrysler's new 5-speed manual transmission or 4-speed automatic. Standard in the Daytona Shelby model and optional with the C/S Competition Package for 1990

Prices are accurate at time of printing; subject to manufacturer's change.

is Chrysler's 2.2-liter 4-cylinder with new variable-nozzle turbocharging (VNT). VNT uses pivoting vanes inside the turbocharger to reduce turbo lag and improve throttle response. The 174-horsepower VNT turbo is available only with a 5-speed manual transmission. A naturally aspirated 100-horsepower 2.5-liter four remains standard on base and ES Daytonas. A 150-horsepower turbocharged 2.5 is standard on the ES Turbo and is fitted to Shelbys when they're ordered with the 3-speed automatic. Shelbys get slight exterior trim changes for '90, and are available for

Specifications

	3-door hatchback
Wheelbase, in.	97.0
Overall length, in.	179.2
Overall width, in.	69.3
Overall height, in.	50.1
Turn diameter, ft.	34.3
Curb weight, lbs.	2751
Cargo vol., cu. ft.	33.0
Fuel capacity, gals.	14.0
Seating capacity	4
Front headroom, in.	37.1
Front shoulder room, in.	55.9
Front legroom, max., in.	42.4
Rear headroom, in.	34.3
Rear shoulder room, in.	53.6
Rear legroom, min., in.	30.0

Powertrain layout: transverse front engine/front-wheel drive.

Engines	ohc I-4	Turbo ohc I-4	Turbo ohc I-4	ohc V-6
Size, liters/cu. in.	2.5/153	2.5/153	2.2/135	3.0/181
Fuel delivery	TBI	PFI	PFI	PFI
Horsepower @ rpm	100 @ 4800	150 @ 4800	174 @ 5200	141 @ 5000
Torque (lbs./ft.) @ rpm	135 @ 2800	180 @ 2000	210 @ 2400	171 @ 2800
Availability	S	O	S[1]	O
EPA city/highway mpg				
5-speed OD manual	24/32	20/29	20/28	19/27
3-speed automatic	22/27	19/23		
4-speed OD automatic				19/26

1. Daytona Shelby.

the first time with Chrysler's electronic variable suspension. This allows the driver to manually select firm, normal, or soft shock-absorber damping via console switches. All Daytonas get a revamped interior, highlighted by a new dashboard. A new steering wheel houses an airbag and rear shoulder belts are now standard. The 1990 changes increase Daytona's appeal. The VNT turbo does indeed improve throttle response and the smooth V-6 is a welcome addition that mates well with automatic transmission for the most refined Daytona yet. Chrysler's new 5-speed manual shifts as well as the best front-drive gearboxes, while the new interior design gives the cabin a much needed modernization.

Prices

Dodge Daytona	Retail Price	Dealer Invoice	Low Price
3-door hatchback	$9745	$8848	$9070
ES 3-door hatchback	10995	9961	10222
ES Turbo 3-door hatchback	12895	11652	11974
Shelby 3-door hatchback	14057	12686	13045
Destination charge	454	454	454

Standard equipment:

2.5-liter TBI 4-cylinder engine, 5-speed manual transmission, power steering, driver's-side airbag, rear shoulder belts, reclining front bucket seats, split folding rear seat, tinted glass, intermittent wipers, console with armrest and storage, rear defogger, remote fuel door and hatch releases, tachometer, coolant temperature and oil pressure gauges, voltmeter, trip odometer, remote mirrors, visor mirrors, AM/FM radio, 185/70R14 all-season tires. **ES** adds: fog lights, sill extensions, rear spoiler, tonneau cover, 205/60R15 all-season tires on Eurocast alloy wheels. **ES Turbo** adds: 2.5-liter Turbo I PFI engine, misc. lights, AM/FM cassette with Infinity speakers, enthusiast seats, performance handling suspension, tilt steering column, leather-wrapped steering wheel. **Shelby** adds: 2.2-liter intercooled Turbo II engine, maximum performance suspension, 205/55VR16 unidirectional tires on "pumper" alloy wheels.

Optional equipment:

3.0-liter V-6, base & ES	680	578	612
3-speed automatic transmission	536	456	482
4-speed automatic transmission	627	533	564
Requires 3.0-liter V-6.			

Prices are accurate at time of printing; subject to manufacturer's change.

	Retail Price	Dealer Invoice	Low Price
4-wheel disc brakes, ES	179	152	161

Requires V-6 Pkg. or V-6 Performance Pkg.

	Retail Price	Dealer Invoice	Low Price
Popular Equipment Pkg., base	1054	896	949
ES	1004	853	904
ES Turbo & Shelby	1346	1144	1211

Base & ES: air conditioning, front floormats, misc. lights, heated power mirrors. ES Turbo and Shelby add: power windows and locks, cruise control, tilt steering column.

Popular Equipment Pkg. w/o A/C, base ..	349	297	314

Floormats, misc. lights, heated power mirrors, tilt steering column.

Value Pkg., base	347	295	312

Power locks, cruise control, AM/FM cassette.

C/S Performance Pkg., base	1502	1277	1352

2.5-liter turbo engine, 4-wheel disc brakes, rear spoiler, performance handling suspension, 205/60R15 all-season performance tires on Eurocast alloy wheels.

C/S Competition Pkg., base	2702	2297	2432

2.2-liter intercooled Turbo IV engine, 4-wheel disc brakes, rear spoiler, tilt steering column, maximum-performance suspension, 225/50VR15 unidirectional tires on alloy wheels.

V-6 Pkg., ES	769	654	692

3.0-liter V-6, 4-wheel disc brakes.

V-6 Performance Pkg., ES	2185	1857	1967
ES w/Power Convenience Pkg.	1725	1466	1553

3.0-liter V-6 with tuned exhaust, 4-wheel disc brakes, performance handling suspension, wheelhouse carpet, power windows and locks, cloth enthusiast seats, door pockets, leather-wrapped steering wheel, AM/FM cassette with Infinity speakers.

Premium Light Pkg., base & ES	192	163	173

Illuminated entry, lighted visor mirrors.

Overhead Convenience Pkg., ES Turbo & Shelby	376	320	338

Overhead console with compass and outside temperature readout, lighted visor mirrors.

Security Pkg., ES Turbo & Shelby	222	189	200

Anti-theft security system, illuminated entry; requires Popular Pkg.

Power Convenience Pkg., base & ES	240	204	216

Power windows and locks.

Automatic Transmission Pkg., Shelby ...	NC	NC	NC
Shelby w/Popular Equipment (credit) ..	(195)	(166)	(166)

2.5-liter Turbo I engine, 3-speed automatic transmission, cruise control.

Overhead console, ES	260	221	234
AM/FM cassette, base & ES	152	129	137
AM/FM cassette w/Infinity speakers,			
base & ES	483	411	435
Base w/Value Pkg.	331	281	298

	Retail Price	Dealer Invoice	Low Price
AM/FM cassette w/EQ & Infinity speakers, base & ES	692	588	623
Base w/Value Pkg.	540	459	486
ES w/V-6 Performance Pkg.	210	179	189
ES Turbo & Shelby	210	179	189
Power driver's seat, base & ES	270	230	243
Power enthusiast seat, ES, ES Turbo & Shelby	335	285	302
w/leather, ES Turbo & Shelby	974	828	877
ES requires V-6 Performance Pkg.; ES Turbo and Shelby require Popular Pkg.			
Cruise control, base & ES	195	166	176
Rear window sun louver	210	179	189
Removable sunroof	397	337	357
Requires Popular Pkg.			
Conventional spare tire, base	83	71	75
ES & ES Turbo w/Eurocast wheels	237	201	213
Rear wiper/washer	126	107	113
Styled steel wheels, base	100	85	90
Alloy wheels, base	322	274	290

Dodge Dynasty

Dodge Dynasty LE

Dynasty is Chrysler Motors' best-selling car and it's back
for a third model year with a larger optional V-6 engine
and a standard driver's-side airbag. This front-drive, 6-
passenger 4-door sedan is Dodge's version of the car

Chrysler sells as the New Yorker. Dynasty is available in base and upscale LE trim. Chrysler's new 3.3-liter V-6 is now optional on the LE in place of a 3.0-liter V-6. The 3.0, built by Chrysler's Japanese partner, Mitsubishi, is optional on the base Dynasty in place of its standard 2.5-liter four. A new steering wheel accommodates the airbag and the cruise control switches move from the turn-signal stalk to the steering wheel. Among other changes for '90: double-sided keys that can be inserted either side up; and side marker lights that flash with the turn signals. New options on the LE model include an automatic day/night mirror and leather upholstery. Four-wheel anti-lock disc brakes

Specifications

	4-door notchback
Wheelbase, in.	104.3
Overall length, in.	192.0
Overall width, in.	68.5
Overall height, in.	54.8
Turn diameter, ft.	40.4
Curb weight, lbs.	2992
Cargo vol., cu. ft.	16.5
Fuel capacity, gals.	16.0
Seating capacity	6
Front headroom, in.	38.3
Front shoulder room, in.	56.4
Front legroom, max., in.	41.9
Rear headroom, in.	37.8
Rear shoulder room, in.	55.9
Rear legroom, min., in.	38.0

Powertrain layout: transverse front engine/front-wheel drive.

Engines

	ohc I-4	ohc V-6	ohv V-6
Size, liters/cu. in.	2.5/153	3.0/181	3.3/201
Fuel delivery	TBI	PFI	PFI
Horsepower @ rpm	100 @ 4800	141 @ 5000	147 @ 4800
Torque (lbs./ft.) @ rpm	135 @ 2800	171 @ 2800	183 @ 3600
Availability	S	O[1]	O

EPA city/highway mpg

3-speed automatic	22/27		
4-speed OD automatic		20/26	19/26

1. Standard on Dynasty LE.

(ABS) are optional again in place of the standard front disc/rear drum setup. Other than ABS—an important safety feature that we recommend—there's nothing technically interesting about the Dynasty. The styling is purposely middle-of-the-road, but evidently, right on target. This is a well-designed family sedan with room for six adults (with a little squeezing), a big trunk, and decent acceleration with one of the V-6s. The ride is comfortable, but take it easy around corners: the body leans heavily in turns and the soft all-season tires roll onto their sidewalls, squealing in protest. Dynasty is one of the cheapest cars available with both an airbag and anti-lock brakes.

Prices

Dodge Dynasty	Retail Price	Dealer Invoice	Low Price
4-door notchback	$12295	$11246	$12745
LE 4-door notchback	14395	12436	14845
Destination charge	520	520	520

Standard equipment:

2.5-liter TBI 4-cylinder engine, 3-speed automatic transmission, power steering, driver's-side airbag, rear shoulder belts, bench seat, cloth upholstery, headlamps-on tone, front cup holder, rear defogger, trip odometer, voltmeter, coolant temperature and oil pressure gauges, intermittent wipers, tinted glass, dual remote mirrors, visor mirrors, bodyside moldings, AM/FM ST ET, remote decklid and fuel filler releases, P195/75R14 SBR tires. **LE** adds: 3.0-liter PFI V-6, 4-speed automatic transmission, 50/50 bench seat, leather-wrapped steering wheel, upgraded wheel covers.

Optional equipment:

3.0-liter V-6, base	680	578	612
3.3-liter V-6, LE	100	85	90
4-speed automatic transmission, base	91	77	82
Requires 3.0-liter V-6.			
Anti-lock brakes	926	787	833
Not available with 4-cylinder engine.			
Air conditioning	805	684	725
Popular Equipment Pkg., base	1203	1023	1083
LE	1574	1338	1417

Base: air conditioning, power locks, floormats, cruise control, tilt steering column, undercoating. LE adds: 3.3-liter V-6, power windows, heated power mirrors.

Prices are accurate at time of printing; subject to manufacturer's change.

	Retail Price	Dealer Invoice	Low Price
Luxury Equipment Pkg., LE	2791	2372	2512
Popular Pkg., Interior Illumination Pkg., Power Convenience Pkg., Deluxe Convenience Pkg., automatic day/night mirror, power front seats, security alarm, leather-wrapped steering wheel, wire wheel covers.			
Deluxe Convenience Pkg., LE.........	330	281	297
Cruise control, tilt steering column.			
Power Convenience Pkg., base	356	303	320
Power windows and mirrors; requires Popular Pkg.			
Interior Illumination Pkg.	192	163	173
Illuminated entry, lighted visor mirrors; base requires Popular Pkg.			
Power Accessories Pkg., LE	155	132	140
Power decklid pulldown, power antenna; requires Luxury Pkg.			
Power locks	305	259	275
AM/FM cassette	152	129	137
Infinity I AM/FM cassette	482	410	434
Requires Popular Pkg.			
Infinity II AM/FM cassette w/EQ, LE	692	588	623
Requires Luxury Pkg.			
Memory power seats, LE	368	313	331
Requires Luxury Pkg.			
Power driver's seat, LE	270	230	243
Requires Popular Pkg.			
Security alarm	146	124	131
Requires Popular Pkg.			
Power sunroof, LE	776	660	698
Requires Popular Pkg.			
Road handling suspension, LE	57	48	51
Requires Popular Pkg.			
Automatic rear load leveling	190	162	171
LE requires Popular or Luxury Pkg.			
Wire wheel covers	224	190	202
Requires Popular Pkg.			
Alloy wheels, LE	273	232	246
LE w/Luxury Pkg.	49	42	44
Requires Popular Pkg.			

Dodge Shadow/ Plymouth Sundance

These front-drive twins get a standard driver's-side airbag and a restyled instrument panel for '90. They share 3- and 5-door hatchback body styles and most mechanicals, but the Dodge is marketed as the sportier car. To that end,

Dodge Shadow ES

Shadow is available for '90 with a 2.2-liter 4-cylinder engine that uses Chrysler's variable nozzle turbocharging (VNT), which reduces turbo lag for quicker throttle response. The VNT 2.2 is available on Shadows in sporty ES trim and on 3-door models with the optional Competition Package. The VNT engine comes only with a 5-speed manual transmission. Other engines are shared by the two lines and are unchanged: naturally aspirated 2.2- and 2.5-liter fours and a turbo 2.5. Each is available with a standard 5-speed manual or optional 3-speed automatic. The addition of the airbag brings a new steering wheel that incorporates the optional cruise control buttons. Both Shadow and Sundance get a revamped instrument cluster and newly available Infinity audio system. Shadow ES, which has 4-wheel disc brakes and performance tires on alloy wheels, also gets slight revisions to its front and rear fascias, ground-effects body panels, and bodyside tape graphics. We consider these cars subcompacts based on their wheelbase, overall length, and limited rear-seat leg room. There's plenty of head room all around in a nicely packaged interior, though. Luggage space is adequate with the rear seatback up, generous with it folded down. Handling is competent, the ride stable. The base engine is listless. The turbos are quicker but more raucous, though a VNT Shadow is a sneaky-fast budget hot rod. A good compromise is the naturally aspirated 2.5. Chrysler's improved 5-speed manual is now a worthwhile alternative to the 3-speed automatic transmission.

Prices are accurate at time of printing; subject to manufacturer's change.

Specifications

	3-door hatchback	5-door hatchback
Wheelbase, in.	97.0	97.0
Overall length, in.	171.7	171.7
Overall width, in.	67.3	67.3
Overall height, in.	52.6	52.6
Turn diameter, ft.	34.0	34.0
Curb weight, lbs.	2606	2642
Cargo vol., cu. ft.	33.3	33.3
Fuel capacity, gals.	14.0	14.0
Seating capacity	5	5
Front headroom, in.	38.3	38.3
Front shoulder room, in.	54.4	54.7
Front legroom, max., in.	41.5	41.5
Rear headroom, in.	37.4	37.4
Rear shoulder room, in.	52.5	54.5
Rear legroom, min., in.	34.0	34.0

Powertrain layout: transverse front engine/front-wheel drive.

Engines	ohc I-4	ohc I-4	Turbo ohc I-4	Turbo ohc I-4
Size, liters/cu. in.	2.2/135	2.5/153	2.5/153	2.2/135
Fuel delivery	TBI	TBI	PFI	PFI
Horsepower @ rpm	93 @ 4800	100 @ 4800	150 @ 4800	174 @ 5200
Torque (lbs./ft.) @ rpm	122 @ 3200	$35 @ 2800	180 @ 2000	210 @ 2400
Availability	S	O	O	O

EPA city/highway mpg

5-speed OD manual	24/31	24/32	21/29	20/28
3-speed automatic	23/28	22/27	20/23	

Prices

Dodge Shadow	Retail Price	Dealer Invoice	Low Price
3-door hatchback	$8785	$8032	$8203
5-door hatchback	8985	8212	8389
Destination charge	440	440	440

Standard equipment:

2.2-liter TBI 4-cylinder engine, 5-speed manual transmission, power steering and brakes, reclining front bucket seats, cloth upholstery, driver's-side airbag, rear shoulder belts, one-piece folding rear seatback, removable shelf panel, dual remote mirrors, intermittent wipers, trip odometer, tachometer, coolant temperature gauge, voltmeter, optical horn, mini console with storage bin, remote liftgate release, bodyside moldings, AM/FM radio, 185/70R14 SBR tires.

Optional equipment:

	Retail Price	Dealer Invoice	Low Price
2.5-liter engine	280	238	252
3-speed automatic transmission	536	456	482
Competition Pkg.	2558	2174	2302

2.2-liter intercooled Turbo IV PFI engine, 4-wheel disc brakes, remote hatch release, message center, remote mirrors, performance front seats, 60/40 split rear seat, spoiler, sport suspension, 195/60HR15 all-season performance tires on alloy wheels.

	Retail Price	Dealer Invoice	Low Price
Air conditioning	775	659	698
4-wheel disc brakes	179	152	161
Rear defogger	160	136	144
Power locks, 3-door	175	149	158
5-door	215	183	194
Power windows, 3-door	230	196	207
5-door	295	251	266
Power mirrors	56	48	50
AM/FM cassette	201	171	181
AM/FM cassette w/Infinity speakers	422	359	380
Cruise control	195	166	176
Tilt steering column	135	115	122
Removable sunroof	372	316	335
Tinted glass	105	89	95
Conventional spare tire, 14″	83	71	75
w/turbo engine	101	86	91
15″, ES	209	178	188
Alloy wheels	403	343	363
Floormats	45	38	41
Pearl/clearcoat paint	75	64	68
California emissions pkg.	100	85	90

Note: ES Pkg. and other equipment is available in Customer Preferred Packages. Space limitations prevent listing these packages.

Plymouth Sundance

3-door hatchback	$8845	$8086	$8286
5-door hatchback	9045	8265	8465
Destination charge	440	440	440

Standard equipment:

2.2-liter TBI 4-cylinder engine, 5-speed manual transmission, power steering, driver's-side airbag, cloth reclining front bucket seats, split folding rear seatback, tachometer, coolant temperature gauge, voltmeter, trip odometer,

Prices are accurate at time of printing; subject to manufacturer's change.

intermittent wipers, remote liftgate release, remote mirrors, visor mirrors, bodyside moldings, AM/FM radio, removable shelf panel, 185/70R14 SBR tires.

Optional equipment:	Retail Price	Dealer Invoice	Low Price
2.5-liter engine	280	238	252
3-speed automatic transmission	536	456	482
Air conditioning	775	659	698
Requires tinted glass.			
Tinted glass	105	89	95
4-wheel disc brakes	179	152	161
Rear defogger	160	136	144
Power locks, 3-door	175	149	158
5-door	215	183	194
Power windows, 3-door	230	196	207
5-door	295	251	266
Requires power locks and mirrors.			
Power mirrors	56	48	50
AM/FM cassette	201	171	181
Cruise control	195	166	176
Requires tilt steering column.			
Tilt steering column	135	115	122
Sunroof	372	316	335
Conventional spare tire	83	71	75
w/turbo	101	86	91
w/RS Pkg.	180	153	162
Alloy wheels w/conventional spare	403	343	363
w/o conventional spare	322	274	290
Pearl/clearcoat paint	75	64	68
Floormats	45	38	41
California emissions pkg.	100	85	90

Note: RS Pkg. and other equipment is available in Customer Preferred Packages. Space limitation prevent listing these packages.

Eagle Premier/Dodge Monaco

Dodge has scheduled a January 1990 introduction for Monaco, its version of Chrysler's international-flavored sedan. Monaco will differ from Premier only in interior and exterior trim. Four-wheel disc brakes are now standard on all models and a floor-mounted shift lever for the automatic transmission replaces a column-mounted lever.

Eagle Premier ES Limited

Specifications

	4-door notchback
Wheelbase, in.	106.0
Overall length, in.	192.8
Overall width, in.	70.0
Overall height, in.	54.7
Turn diameter, ft.	35.9
Curb weight, lbs.	3083
Cargo vol., cu. ft.	17.0
Fuel capacity, gals.	17.0
Seating capacity	5
Front headroom, in.	38.5
Front shoulder room, in.	57.8
Front legroom, max., in.	43.8
Rear headroom, in.	37.5
Rear shoulder room, in.	56.9
Rear legroom, min., in.	39.4

Powertrain layout: longitudinal front engine/front-wheel drive.

Engines

	ohc V-6
Size, liters/cu. in.	3.0/180
Fuel delivery	PFI
Horsepower @ rpm	150 @ 5000
Torque (lbs./ft.) @ rpm	171 @ 3600
Availability	S

EPA city/highway mpg

4-speed OD automatic	17/26

Prices are accurate at time of printing; subject to manufacturer's change.

Chrysler inherited this front-drive 4-door in its acquisition of American Motors. Premier was designed jointly by American Motors and Renault; it was styled in Italy and it is built in Canada. The only engine is a Renault-built 3.0-liter V-6; a 2.5-liter 4-cylinder offered previously has been dropped. The Monaco—a name last used in 1978, on a mid-size, rear-drive sedan—will have trim levels mirroring the Premier LX and ES, but will not replicate the sporty Premier ES Limited (Monaco prices weren't available). A stainless-steel exhaust system and rear shoulder belts are now standard on all Premiers. The ES gets 205/60R15 all-season tires as standard, and a compact disc player is a new option for all models. This is one of the best driving, most efficiently designed sedans in the Chrysler stable. The smooth V-6 is teamed with a precise-shifting automatic transmission. The ride is firm, but pliant and well controlled. Inside, there are supportive seats and plenty of room for five in an airy cabin. The trunk is roomy. The floor-mounted automatic shift lever eliminates an awkward serpentine column stalk, but Premier and Monaco are still saddled with illogically engineered headlamp, wiper, and climate-system controls. Slow sales mean Premier should be available at big discounts.

Prices

Eagle Premier	Retail Price	Dealer Invoice	Low Price
LX 4-door notchback	$15350	$13248	$13448
ES 4-door notchback	17845	15368	15568
ES Limited 4-door notchback	20284	17441	17641
Destination charge	465	465	465

Standard equipment:

3.0-liter PFI V-6, 4-speed automatic transmission, power steering, 4-wheel disc brakes, 45/45 front seat, tachometer, coolant temperature and oil pressure gauges, voltmeter, trip odometer, AM/FM radio, rear shoulder belts, leather-wrapped steering wheel, tinted glass, intermittent wipers, remote mirrors, center console with armrest, rear defogger, floormats, 195/70R14 tires. **ES** adds: air conditioning, AM/FM cassette with eight Jensen speakers, trip computer, vehicle maintenance monitor, lighted visor mirrors, 205/60R15 tires on alloy wheels. **ES Limited** adds: leather upholstery, monochrome exterior treatment, cruise control, tilt steering column, premium audio system with EQ, power antenna, power locks, remote keyless entry, illuminated entry, power windows, remote fuel door and decklid releases, power front seats, 205/60HR15 tires with full-size spare.

Optional equipment:	Retail Price	Dealer Invoice	Low Price
Air conditioning, LX	860	731	774
Popular Option Group, LX	1387	1179	1248
Air conditioning, cruise control, tilt steering column.			
Luxury Option Group, LX	2316	1969	2084
Popular Group plus power mirrors, lighted visor mirrors, premium audio system, power antenna, power windows.			
Popular Option Group, ES	652	554	587
Cruise control, tilt steering column, Power Lock Group.			
Luxury Option Group, ES	1087	924	978
Popular Group plus power windows, premium audio system, power antenna.			
45/45 leather & vinyl seats, ES	566	481	509
Requires power seats.			
Power seats	540	459	486
Convenience Group, LX & ES	330	255	270
Cruise control, tilt steering column.			
Electronic Information Pkg., LX			
Trip computer, vehicle maintenance monitor.			
Power Lock Group, LX & ES	437	371	393
Power locks with remote keyless entry, remote fuel door and decklid releases, illuminated entry.			
Power windows	305	259	275
Requires Power Lock Group.			
AM/FM cassette, LX	234	199	211
Premium audio system, LX	532	452	479
ES	130	111	117
AM/FM cassette with EQ, power amp and eight Accusound by Jensen speakers.			
Premium audio system w/CD player, LX . .	806	685	725
ES	404	343	364
ES Limited	274	233	247
Power glass sunroof	776	660	698
Lace-style alloy wheels, LX	466	396	419
ES	295	251	266

Eagle Summit

This imported front-drive subcompact is the entry-level car in Chrysler's Eagle line. Built by Mitsubishi, Chrysler's Japanese partner, Summit is a 4-door sedan derived from the same design as the 3-door hatchback Dodge and

Prices are accurate at time of printing; subject to manufacturer's change.

Eagle Summit LX

Plymouth dealers sell as the Colt. Mitsubishi dealers sell both body styles as the Mirage. Summit was introduced for 1989, and the lineup gets juggled for '90. Added is a base sedan with manual steering and a budget-oriented interior. This base sedan, along with the carried-over mid-level DL and luxury-oriented LX models, is powered by an 81-horsepower 1.5-liter 4-cylinder engine. Also new to the roster is the performance-oriented ES Sport. Its standard features include a sport suspension, 4-wheel disc brakes, sports bucket seats, monochromatic exterior trim, and 195/60R14 tires (other Summits have 13-inch tires). The ES is powered by a dual-cam, 16-valve 1.6-liter four. The 1.6 is available on the Summit LX as part of the DOHC Package. The Summit is a pleasant example of the contemporary Japanese subcompact. Storage bins and pockets are placed thoughtfully throughout Summit's airy cabin. Front-seat room is fine for a subcompact, though rear-seat head room is scarce for those over 5-foot-10. Power is adequate with the 1.5 engine, though automatic transmission saps a lot of verve. Road manners are competent and the absorbent ride is especially pleasing. The small tires on the base and DL models have unimpressive roadholding ability, which discourages aggressive driving. Summit is a well-rounded subcompact that doesn't reach the high level of refinement or assembly quality enjoyed by such rivals as the Honda Civic and Toyota Corolla, but Eagle dealers are more likely to bargain on price.

Specifications

	4-door notchback
Wheelbase, in.	96.7
Overall length, in.	170.1
Overall width, in.	65.7
Overall height, in.	52.8
Turn diameter, ft.	30.8
Curb weight, lbs.	2271
Cargo vol., cu. ft.	10.3
Fuel capacity, gals.	13.2
Seating capacity	5
Front headroom, in.	39.1
Front shoulder room, in.	53.5
Front legroom, max., in.	41.9
Rear headroom, in.	37.5
Rear shoulder room, in.	53.1
Rear legroom, min., in.	34.3

Powertrain layout: transverse front engine/front-wheel drive.

Engines

	ohc I-4	dohc I-4
Size, liters/cu. in.	1.5/90	1.6/97
Fuel delivery	PFI	PFI
Horsepower @ rpm	81 @ 5500	113 @ 6500
Torque (lbs./ft.) @ rpm	91 @ 3000	99 @ 5000
Availability	S	S[1]

EPA city/highway mpg

	ohc I-4	dohc I-4
5-speed OD manual	28/34	23/28
3-speed automatic	27/29	
4-speed OD automatic		23/28

1. Summit ES.

Prices

Eagle Summit	Retail Price	Dealer Invoice	Low Price
4-door notchback	$8895	$8264	$8464
DL 4-door notchback	9456	8541	8741
LX 4-door notchback	10408	9388	9588
ES 4-door notchback	11257	10144	10344
Destination charge	295	295	295

Standard equipment:

1.5-liter PFI 4-cylinder engine, 5-speed manual transmission, cloth reclining front bucket seats, coolant temperature gauge, trip odometer, remote mir-

Prices are accurate at time of printing; subject to manufacturer's change.

rors, rear shoulder belts, center console with storage, 155/80R13 tires on styled steel wheels. **DL** adds: intermittent wipers, upgraded carpet, remote fuel door and decklid releases, rear defogger, tinted glass. **LX** adds: power steering, tachometer, velour upholstery, driver's-seat height adjustment, split folding rear seat, tilt/telescopic steering column, visor mirrors, rear heat ducts, 175/70R13 tires. **ES** adds: 1.6-liter DOHC 16-valve engine, 4-wheel disc brakes, sport seats, sport suspension, 195/60R14 tires.

Optional equipment:	Retail Price	Dealer Invoice	Low Price
3-speed automatic transmission, w/1.5 ..	505	429	455
4-speed automatic transmission, w/1.6 ..	682	580	614
Air conditioning	748	636	673
Pkg. IFF, base	130	111	117
Rear defogger, tinted glass.			
Pkg. IFG, base	434	369	391
Pkg. IFF plus AM/FM radio.			
Pkg. IFH, base	696	592	626
Pkg. IFG plus power steering.			
Pkg. IFB, DL	621	528	559
Power steering, digital clock, AM/FM radio.			
Pkg. IFC, DL	839	713	755
Pkg. IFB plus AM/FM cassette, power mirrors.			
Pkg. IFD, DL	1135	965	1022
Pkg. IFC plus alloy wheels.			
Pkg. IFA, LX	353	300	318
Power mirrors, AM/FM radio.			
Pkg. IFB, LX	962	818	866
Pkg. IFA plus AM/FM cassette, power windows and locks.			
Pkg. IFC, LX	1234	1049	1111
Pkg. IFB plus alloy wheels.			
DOHC Pkg. IFD, LX	1319	1121	1187
1.6-liter DOHC 16-valve engine, power mirrors, AM/FM cassette, 195/60R14 tires.			
DOHC Pkg. IFE, LX	1970	1675	1773
Pkg. IFD plus power windows and locks, cruise control, variable intermittent wipers.			
DOHC Pkg. IFF, LX	2242	1906	2018
Pkg. IFE plus alloy wheels.			
Pkg. IFA, ES	365	310	329
Power mirrors, AM/FM radio.			
Pkg. IFB, ES	1017	864	915
Pkg. IFA plus AM/FM cassette, cruise control, variable intermittent wipers, alloy wheels.			
Pkg. IFC, ES	1729	1470	1556
Pkg. IFB plus premium audio system with cassette, power windows and locks.			
Decklid luggage rack	94	80	85

Ford Aerostar

Ford Aerostar

Optional 4-wheel drive, a larger available engine, and standard anti-lock rear brakes highlight changes to Ford's rear-drive minivan. Aerostar has standard seating for five and optional seating for seven. An extended-length model joined the line in '89. It retains the 118.9-inch wheelbase of the regular models, but adds 15.4 inches to the rear cargo area for a 28-cubic-foot boost in luggage volume. It also gains one inch of leg room for the middle seats and two inches for the rear seats. For '90, both standard and extended-length models will be available with the new 4WD system, which is permanently engaged. Under normal conditions, one-third of the engine's torque is sent to the front wheels and two-thirds to the rear, but a center differential locks in a 50-50 split if wheel slip is detected. The new V-6 displaces 4.0 liters and is optional on 2WD extended-length Aerostars and standard on the 4WD version. The 4.0 is teamed only with a new heavy-duty 4-speed automatic transmission. Aerostar comes standard with a 3.0-liter V-6; a 5-speed manual is standard with this engine and a 4-speed automatic is optional. Among other changes, a locking storage compartment is included under the front passenger seat when captain's chairs are fitted. Aerostar's allure is enhanced with 4WD and the new V-6, but its ride and handling are still quite truck-like compared to the Dodge Caravan/Plymouth Voyager and Mazda MPV. Aerostar is good for heavy-duty hauling and trailer towing, but it may not be as comfortable for family duty as the Chrysler or Mazda rivals. We give Aerostar a slight edge over the similarly truck-like Chevrolet Astro/GMC Safari, which also gets an extended-length/4WD combination for '90.

Specifications

	4-door van	4-door van
Wheelbase, in.	118.9	118.9
Overall length, in.	174.9	190.3
Overall width, in.	61.5	61.5
Overall height, in.	71.7	72.0
Turn diameter, ft.	39.8	39.8
Curb weight, lbs.	3359	3502
Cargo vol., cu. ft.	139.3	167.7
Fuel capacity, gals.	21.0	21.0
Seating capacity	7	7
Front headroom, in.	39.5	39.5
Front shoulder room, in.	60.0	60.0
Front legroom, max., in.	41.4	41.4
Rear headroom, in.	38.1	38.3
Rear shoulder room, in.	NA	NA
Rear legroom, min., in.	37.9	38.8

Powertrain layout: longitudinal front engine/rear-wheel drive or permanent 4-wheel drive.

Engines

	ohv V-6	ohv V-6
Size, liters/cu. in.	3.0/182	4.0/245
Fuel delivery	PFI	PFI
Horsepower @ rpm	145 @ 4800	155 @ 4200
Torque (lbs./ft.) @ rpm	165 @ 3600	220 @ 2400
Availability	S	S[1]

EPA city/highway mpg

5-speed OD manual	17/22	
4-speed OD automatic	16/22	NA

1. Standard Aerostar 4WD; optional, Aerostar Extended Length 2WD.

Prices

Ford Aerostar	Retail Price	Dealer Invoice	Low Price
RL van	$12469	$11212	$11552
EL van	13216	11869	12237

	Retail Price	Dealer Invoice	Low Price
4WD RL van	14669	13148	13569
4WD EL van	15416	13805	14254
Destination charge	475	475	475

RL and EL denote regular-length and extended-length models.

Standard equipment:

XL: 3.0-liter PFI V-6, 5-speed manual transmission, power steering, anti-lock rear brakes, front bucket seats, 3-passenger middle seat, remote fuel door release, tinted glass, dual outside mirrors, visor mirrors, AM radio, 215/70R14SL tires.

Optional equipment:

	Retail Price	Dealer Invoice	Low Price
4.0-liter V-6, 2WD EL	316	268	284
4-speed automatic transmission, RL	623	530	561
Limited-slip axle	248	210	223
Air conditioning	846	719	761
High-capacity A/C w/auxiliary heater, base .	1422	1209	1280
w/any Preferred Pkg.	576	489	518
XL Plus Pkg. 401A	2080	1768	1872

Air conditioning, 7-passenger seating with two captain's chairs, privacy glass, cruise control, tilt steering column, rear wiper/washer.

Xl Plus 4WD Special Value Pkg. 402A ...	3405	2894	3065

Pkg. 401A plus rear defogger, Exterior Appearance Group, AM/FM cassette.

XLT Pkg. 403A	3100	2635	2790

Pkg. 401A plus premium wheel covers, door pockets, rear grab handle, Light Group, upgraded interior trim, dual-note horn, leather-wrapped steering wheel, AM/FM cassette.

XLT Plus Pkg. 404A	4476	3804	4028

Pkg. 403A plus Electronics Group, luggage rack, Power Convenience Group.

Eddie Bauer Pkg. 405A	6697	5692	6027

Pkg. 404A plus high-capacity air conditioning with auxiliary heater, two rear seats fold into a bed, floor console, forged alloy wheels, two-tone paint, floormats.

WSW tires	72	61	65
7-pass. seating w/front bucket seats	296	252	266
Captain's chairs	517	440	465
7-pass. seating w/captain's chairs & seat/bed	1405	1194	1265
w/Pkg. 401 or 402	539	458	485
7-passenger seating w/2 captain's chairs .	866	736	779
w/4 captain's chairs, XLT	585	498	527
w/4 captain's chairs, Eddie Bauer	NC	NC	NC
Floor console	174	148	157

Prices are accurate at time of printing; subject to manufacturer's change.

	Retail Price	Dealer Invoice	Low Price
Rear defogger, base	224	191	202
XL Plus	166	141	149
Electronics Group, base or w/Pkg. 401	1027	873	924
w/Pkg. 402 or 403	745	633	671
Overhead console (includes trip computer, automatic day/night mirror, map lights), electronic instruments, Super Sound System with EQ.			
Exterior Appearance Group, base	857	729	771
w/Pkg. 401	268	228	241
w/Pkg. 403 or 404	189	161	170
Privacy glass, two-tone paint, rear wiper/washer, swing-lock A-pillar mirrors, styled wheel covers.			
Light Group	159	135	143
Luggage rack	141	120	127
Swing-lock A-pillar mirrors	52	45	47
Bodyside molding, base	63	54	57
XLT or Eddie Bauer	35	30	32
Power Convenience Group	501	426	451
Power windows, locks and mirrors.			
Cruise control & tilt steering column	296	252	266
Trailer Towing Pkg.	282	239	254
Rear wiper/washer, w/rear defogger	139	118	125
w/o rear defogger	198	168	178
Forged alloy wheels, base	326	277	293
w/XLT or Exterior Appearance Group	287	244	258
AM/FM radio	211	179	190
AM/FM cassette	313	266	282
Engine block heater	33	28	30
California emissions pkg.	99	84	89

Ford Escort

America's best-selling car returns with few changes as Ford gears up to introduce an all-new 1991 model in the spring of '90. For 1990, rear shoulder belts become standard; as before, motorized front shoulder belts with manual lap belts meet the federal passive-restraint requirement. The optional polycast wheels have a slightly different appearance, and the premium sound system and heavy duty alternator are now available only as part of the LX and GT Special Value Packages. Escort is a front-drive subcompact available as a 3- and 5-door hatchback and a 5-door wagon. Pony and LX models are powered by a 90-horsepower 1.9-

Ford Escort

Specifications

	3-door hatchback	5-door hatchback	5-door wagon
Wheelbase, in.	94.2	94.2	94.2
Overall length, in.	169.4	169.4	169.4
Overall width, in.	65.9	65.9	65.9
Overall height, in.	53.7	53.7	53.4
Turn diameter, ft.	35.7	35.7	35.7
Curb weight, lbs.	2242	2310	2313
Cargo vol., cu. ft.	38.8	38.8	58.8
Fuel capacity, gals.	13.0	13.0	13.0
Seating capacity	5	5	5
Front headroom, in.	38.1	38.1	38.1
Front shoulder room, in.	51.3	51.3	51.3
Front legroom, max., in.	41.5	41.5	41.5
Rear headroom, in.	37.1	37.1	38.2
Rear shoulder room, in.	51.5	51.4	51.4
Rear legroom, min., in.	35.1	35.1	35.1

Powertrain layout: transverse front engine/front-wheel drive.

Engines

	ohc I-4	ohc I-4
Size, liters/cu. in.	1.9/114	1.9/114
Fuel delivery	TBI	PFI
Horsepower @ rpm	90 @ 4600	110 @ 5400
Torque (lbs./ft.) @ rpm	106 @ 3400	115 @ 4200
Availability	S	S[1]

EPA city/highway mpg

4-speed OD manual	32/42	
5-speed OD manual	27/36	24/30
3-speed automatic	27/31	

1. GT.

Prices are accurate at time of printing; subject to manufacturer's change.

liter 4-cylinder engine. The GT's 1.9 produces 110 horsepower. The 1991 Escort will be based on the Mazda 323 chassis and running gear, but the styling and interior design will be by Ford. The '91 Escort will be available as a 3- and a 5-door hatchback, as well as a 5-door wagon. A new Mercury Tracer will be built from the same design. Today's Escort dates to the '81 model year and while it remains average in most ways, it's a pretty good value by virtue of its fairly low price and long warranties. Escort is still priced higher than the even more archaic Dodge Omni/ Plymouth Horizon subcompacts, but expect Ford dealers to start offering heavy discounts. Like the Omni/Horizon, Escort shows its age in an interior that's cramped compared to newer Japanese designs and in a control layout that isn't as convenient. The 90-horsepower engine is merely adequate with the 5-speed manual, and inadequate with automatic transmission. As for the Escort GT, it is stylish, but promises more performance than it delivers. There are several newer Japanese small cars with more to offer than Escort, but they're also more expensive, so don't cross this Ford off your list.

Prices

Ford Escort	Retail Price	Dealer Invoice	Low Price
Pony 3-door hatchback	$7402	$6879	$7079
LX 3-door hatchback	7806	7090	7290
LX 5-door hatchback	8136	7384	7584
LX 5-door wagon	8737	7919	8119
GT 3-door hatchback	9844	8904	9104
Destination charge	340	340	340

Standard equipment:

Pony: 1.9-liter TBI 4-cylinder engine, 4-speed manual transmission, cloth and vinyl reclining front bucket seats, folding rear seat, rear lap/shoulder belts, removable cargo cover, 175/70R14 tires. **LX adds:** AM radio, full cloth upholstery, door pockets; wagon has 5-speed manual transmission and retractable cargo cover. **GT adds:** PFI engine, 5-speed manual transmission, handling suspension, sport seats, remote fuel door and liftgate releases, power mirrors, tachometer, coolant temperature gauge, trip odometer, visor mirrors, overhead console with digital clock and stopwatch, map lights, center console with graphic monitor and folding armrest, AM/FM radio, split folding rear seatback, 195/60HR15 tires on alloy wheels.

Optional equipment:	Retail Price	Dealer Invoice	Low Price
5-speed manual transmission, LX hatchbacks	76	64	68
3-speed automatic transmission,			
LX hatchbacks & Pony	539	458	485
LX wagon	463	394	417
Power steering, Pony & LX	235	200	212
Air conditioning	744	632	670
Special Value Pkg. 320A, LX hatchbacks .	562	478	506
LX wagon	486	414	437

5-speed manual transmission, power steering, overhead console with clock, rear defogger, tinted glass, Instrumentation Group, Light/Security Group, power mirrors, wide bodyside moldings, AM/FM radio, power steering, luxury wheel covers, intermittent wipers.

Special Value Pkg. 321A, LX hatchbacks .	965	820	869
LX wagon	889	756	800

Pkg. 320A but with 3-speed automatic transmission.

Special Value Pkg. 330A, GT	878	747	790

Air conditioning, rear defogger, tinted glass, Light/Security Group, AM/FM cassette, cruise control, tilt steering column, intermittent wipers.

Overhead console w/clock	82	69	74
Rear defogger	160	136	144
Tinted glass	105	89	95
Instrumentation Group	87	74	78
Light/Security Group, LX	78	66	70
GT	67	57	60
Luggage rack	115	97	104
Power mirrors	98	83	88
Wide bodyside moldings	50	43	45
AM radio, Pony	54	46	49
AM/FM radio, Pony	206	175	185
LX	152	130	137
AM/FM cassette, Pony	361	307	325
LX	307	261	276
GT	155	132	140
Premium sound system	138	117	124
Cruise control	201	171	181
Split folding rear seat	50	43	45
Tilt steering column	135	115	122
Luxury wheel covers	71	60	64
Vinyl trim	37	31	33
Polycast wheels	193	164	174
Intermittent wipers	55	47	50
Rear wiper/washer	126	107	113
HD battery	27	23	24
Clearcoat paint, LX	91	78	82
Clearcoat two-tone paint, GT	183	155	165
Two-tone paint	91	78	82

Prices are accurate at time of printing; subject to manufacturer's change.

Ford Festiva

Ford Festiva

This subcompact now comes standard with a 5-speed manual transmission and a fuel-injected engine, while power steering is offered for the first time. Festiva is a front-drive 3-door hatchback designed by Mazda, which is owned partly by Ford Motor Co. It's built for Ford in South Korea by Kia Motors and comes in L, L Plus, and LX trim. Standard on all for '90 are a fuel- injected 1.3-liter 4-cylinder engine and a 5-speed manual transmission. Previously, the L and L Plus came with a carbureted engine and a 4-speed manual, while only the L Plus was available with automatic. This year, the automatic is offered on all three trim levels and power steering can now be ordered on L Plus and LX models. Cosmetic changes include a new grille and taillamps. A rear wiper/washer, standard on LX, is newly optional on L and L Plus. Inside, motorized front shoulder belts replace manual belts, while rear shoulder belts are now standard. Front seat cushions are larger and the AM radio has been dropped in favor of an AM/FM stereo unit as standard on the L Plus. Among cars sold in the U.S., only the Suzuki-built Geo Metro weighs less than Festiva's 1713 pounds. In most respects, Festiva is competent and efficient, though a little harsh mechanically. Low base prices make it a decent entry-level buy and high gas mileage compensates some for the mediocre performance and lack of refinement. Cabin space is decent for the car's size, though the rear seat is no place for adults on long trips and cargo room is at a premium, even with the rear seat-back folded. A tall body, forward weight bias, and skinny 12-inch tires encourage the body to roll and the nose to plow in corners. Ride comfort is pretty good, though, all things considered.

Specifications

	3-door hatchback
Wheelbase, in.	90.2
Overall length, in.	140.5
Overall width, in.	63.2
Overall height, in.	55.3
Turn diameter, ft.	28.9
Curb weight, lbs.	1713
Cargo vol., cu. ft.	26.5
Fuel capacity, gals.	10.0
Seating capacity	4
Front headroom, in.	38.8
Front shoulder room, in.	51.9
Front legroom, max., in.	40.6
Rear headroom, in.	37.7
Rear shoulder room, in.	50.9
Rear legroom, min., in.	35.7

Powertrain layout: transverse front engine/front-wheel drive.

Engines

	ohc I-4
Size, liters/cu. in.	1.3/81
Fuel delivery	PFI
Horsepower @ rpm	63 @ 5000
Torque (lbs./ft.) @ rpm	73 @ 3000
Availability	S

EPA city/highway mpg

5-speed OD manual	35/41
3-speed automatic	31/33

Prices

Ford Festiva	Retail Price	Dealer Invoice	Low Price
L 3-door hatchback	$6319	$5877	$6077
L Plus 3-door hatchback	7111	6613	6813

Prices are accurate at time of printing; subject to manufacturer's change.

	Retail Price	Dealer Invoice	Low Price
LX 3-door hatchback	7750	7208	7408
Destination charge	260	260	260

Standard equipment:

L: 1.3-liter PFI 4-cylinder engine, 5-speed manual transmission, cloth and vinyl reclining bucket seats, one-piece folding rear seat, coolant temperature gauge, locking fuel door, rear shoulder belts, 145SR12 tires. **L Plus** adds: wide bodyside moldings, door pockets, tachometer and trip odometer, rear defogger, AM/FM radio, 165/70R12 tires. **LX** adds: power mirrors, intermittent wipers, rear wiper/washer, cargo cover, tilt steering column, soft-feel steering wheel, upgraded seats with see-through head restraints, split folding rear seat, upgraded sound insulation.

Optional equipment:

3-speed automatic transmission	515	437	464
Power steering	235	200	212
Air conditioning, L Plus	849	721	764
LX	744	632	670
Rear defogger	267	227	240
Rear wiper/washer	126	107	113
AM/FM radio	245	208	221
AM/FM cassette, L	400	340	360
L Plus & LX	155	132	140
Alloy wheels, L Plus	421	358	379
LX	396	337	356
Flip-up sunroof	243	206	219
Sport Appearance Pkg.	317	270	285

Ford LTD Crown Victoria/ Mercury Grand Marquis

These traditional full-size, rear-drive sedans and wagons weigh in with a driver's-side airbag, a new dashboard, and other revisions. Grand Marquis is a slightly plusher version of the LTD Crown Victoria. They share a 5.0-liter fuel-injected V-8 and 4-speed overdrive automatic transmission as the sole powertrain. The sedans seat six, while the wagons have 8-passenger capacity with the optional dual rear-facing seats. The airbag is contained in a new steering wheel, and a tilt steering column is now standard across

Ford LTD Crown Victoria

Specifications

	4-door notchback	5-door wagon
Wheelbase, in.	114.3	114.3
Overall length, in.	211.0	215.7
Overall width, in.	77.5	79.3
Overall height, in.	55.6	56.5
Turn diameter, ft.	39.1	39.1
Curb weight, lbs.	3821	3978
Cargo vol., cu. ft.	21.0	90.4
Fuel capacity, gals.	18.0	18.0
Seating capacity	6	8
Front headroom, in.	38.3	39.2
Front shoulder room, in.	61.6	61.6
Front legroom, max., in.	42.5	42.5
Rear headroom, in.	37.2	39.1
Rear shoulder room, in.	61.6	61.6
Rear legroom, min., in.	39.7	38.6

Powertrain layout: longitudinal front engine/rear-wheel drive.

Engines

	ohv V-8
Size, liters/cu. in.	5.0/302
Fuel delivery	PFI
Horsepower @ rpm	150 @ 3200
Torque (lbs./ft.) @ rpm	270 @ 2000
Availability	S

EPA city/highway mpg

4-speed OD automatic	17/24

Prices are accurate at time of printing; subject to manufacturer's change.

the board. All models also get a new instrument panel with revised graphics, modified climate controls, and a larger glovebox, among other changes. Front speakers have been moved from the dashboard to the door panels, eliminating the map pockets. Rear shoulder belts are now standard on all models, and the LTD's front full bench seat retires in favor of a split bench with folding armrests and reclining backrests. Power windows and mirrors are standard instead of optional on the Ford, and pivoting front vent windows and the Tripminder computer, previously optional, are no longer available. The Crown Vic and Grand Marquis are among the few cars still using body-on-frame construction. They appeared on their current platform in 1978, underwent a facelift in '88, and will get a major restyling in 1991. They'll retain their full-size, rear-drive layout, though. That means you'll continue to get true 6-passenger seating, ample cargo room, and the ability to tow hefty trailers (up to 5000 pounds when properly equipped). We hope the '91 revamp will include measures to improve the abysmal fuel economy, loose handling, and floaty ride on the open road.

Prices

Ford LTD Crown Victoria	Retail Price	Dealer Invoice	Low Price
4-door notchback	$17257	$14924	$15124
LX 4-door notchback	17894	15465	15665
5-door wagon	17668	15273	15473
Country Squire 5-door wagon	17921	15488	15688
LX 5-door wagon	18418	15911	16111
LX Country Squire 5-door wagon	18671	16125	16325
Destination charge	510	510	510

Standard equipment:

5.0-liter PFI V-8, 4-speed automatic transmission, power steering, driver's-side airbag, reclining cloth and vinyl split bench seat with center armrests, air conditioning, power windows, power mirrors, AM/FM radio, coolant temperature gauge, trip odometer, Autolamp system, automatic parking brake release, tinted glass, intermittent wipers, tilt steering column, right visor mirror, 215/70R15 tires; wagon has luggage rack, 3-way tailgate with power window, simulated woodgrain (Country Squire). **LX** adds: Light Group, lighted visor mirrors, upgraded upholstery, rear armrest (except wagon), seatback pockets, dual facing rear seats (wagon).

Optional equipment:

	Retail Price	Dealer Invoice	Low Price
Traction-Lok axle	100	85	90
Automatic temperature control A/C	226	193	203
w/Pkg., 112A, 113A, 131A or 133A . . .	66	56	59
Preferred Pkg. 112A, LX 4-door	468	398	421
Bumper guards, rear defogger, cruise control, Power Lock Group, AM/FM cassette.			
Preferred Pkg. 113A, LX 4-door	926	787	833
Pkg. 112A plus power driver's seat, alloy wheels, cornering lamps, illuminated entry, leather-wrapped steering wheel.			
Preferred Pkg. 114A, LX 4-door	1582	1344	1424
Pkg. 113A plus floormats, automatic temperature control, high-level audio system, power antenna, power front seats.			
Preferred Pkg. 131A, wagons exc. LX . . .	1020	867	918
Bumper guards, rear defogger, cruise control, Power Lock Group, AM/FM cassette, power driver's seat, dual facing rear seats.			
Preferred Pkg. 133A, LX wagons	861	732	775
Pkg. 131A plus alloy wheels, HD battery, cornering lamps, floormats, illuminated entry, leather-wrapped steering wheel.			
Preferred Pkg. 134A, LX wagons	1224	1040	1102
Pkg. 133A plus automatic temperature control, high-level audio system, power antenna, power front seats.			
Front cornering lamps	68	58	61
Rear defogger	160	136	144
Illuminated entry	82	69	74
Light Group	59	50	53
Power Lock Group, 4-doors	265	225	239
Wagons	280	238	252
Bodyside moldings	66	56	59
High-level audio system	490	417	441
w/Pkg. 112A, 113A, 131A or 133A	335	285	302
AM/FM cassette	155	132	140
AM/FM delete (credit)	(206)	(175)	(175)
Premium sound system	168	143	151
Power antenna	82	69	74
Power seats, each	280	238	252
Dual facing rear seats, wagons	173	147	156
Cruise control	201	171	181
Leather-wrapped steering wheel	63	54	57
Automatic load-leveling suspension	195	166	176
HD/handling suspension	26	22	23
HD Trailer Towing Pkg.	405	344	365
w/Pkg. 133A or 134A	378	321	340
Delete vinyl roof (credit)	(200)	(170)	(170)
Wire wheel covers	228	194	205
Alloy wheels	440	374	396
Insta-Clear heated windshield	250	213	225

Prices are accurate at time of printing; subject to manufacturer's change.

	Retail Price	Dealer Invoice	Low Price
Brougham half vinyl roof treatment	665	565	599
All-vinyl seat trim	37	31	33
Duraweave vinyl seat trim	96	82	86
Leather seat trim	489	416	440
HD battery	27	23	24
Bumper guards	62	53	56
Floormats	43	36	39
Engine block heater	20	17	18
Clearcoat paint	230	196	207
Two-tone paint/tape treatment	122	104	110
California emissions pkg.	100	85	90

Mercury Grand Marquis

	Retail Price	Dealer Invoice	Low Price
GS 4-door notchback	$17784	$15391	$16183
LS 4-door notchback	18284	15816	16634
Colony Park GS 5-door wagon	18504	16002	16832
Colony Park LS 5-door wagon	19076	16488	17348
Destination charge	510	510	510

Standard equipment:

GS: 5.0-liter PFI V-8 engine, 4-speed automatic transmission, power steering, driver's-side airbag, rear shoulder belts, air conditioning, tinted glass, reclining front seats, cloth trim (vinyl on wagon), power windows, intermittent wipers, tilt steering column, digital clock, coolant temperature gauge, trip odometer, Autolamp system, padded half vinyl roof, right visor mirror, AM/FM radio, power 3-way tailgate (wagon), lockable storage compartments (wagon), simulated woodgrain exterior applique (wagon), 215/70R15 WSW SBR tires. **LS** adds: rear armrest (4-door), front seatback map pockets, Light Group.

Optional equipment:

	Retail Price	Dealer Invoice	Low Price
Traction-Lok axle	100	85	90
Preferred Pkg. 156A, GS 4-door	1024	870	922
Pkg. 157A w/alloy wheels, GS 4-door . . .	1300	1104	1170
w/wire wheel covers	1088	924	979
Pkg. 172A, LS 4-door	1326	1125	1193
Pkg. 192A, GS wagon	1196	1016	1076
LS wagon	1150	977	1035
Pkg. 193A, GS wagon	1473	1251	1326
LS wagon	1339	1138	1205
Conventional spare tire	85	73	77
Automatic climate control	226	225	239
w/rear defogger	66	56	59
Rear defogger	160	136	144

	Retail Price	Dealer Invoice	Low Price
Insta-Clear heated windshield	250	213	225
HD battery	27	23	24
Power Lock Group	265	225	239
Power decklid release	50	43	45
Power seats, each	280	238	252
AM/FM cassette	155	132	140
High Level Audio System	490	417	441
w/Pkg. 157 or 172	335	285	302
w/Pkg. 193	167	142	150
Premium sound system	168	143	151
Power antenna	82	69	74
AM/FM delete (credit)	(206)	(175)	(175)
Cornering lamps	68	58	61
Bodyside moldings, wagons	66	56	59
Two-tone paint	159	135	143
Formal coach vinyl roof	665	565	599
Clearcoat paint	230	196	207
Front bumper guards	38	32	34
Rear bumper guards	24	21	22
Leather-wrapped steering wheel	63	54	57
Floormats	43	46	39
Cruise control	201	171	181
Illuminated entry	82	69	74
Light Group	46	39	41
Lighted visor mirrors	109	92	98
Automatic load leveling	195	166	176
Handling/HD suspension	26	22	23
Trailer Tow III Pkg.	405	332	365
Inboard-facing rear seats, wagons	173	147	156
Cloth seat trim, GS wagon	54	46	49
Vinyl seat trim, GS 4-door	37	31	33
Leather seat trim, LS	489	416	440
Wire wheel covers	228	194	205
Turbine-spoke alloy wheels	440	374	396
w/Pkg. having wire wheel covers	212	180	191
California emissions pkg.	100	85	90

Ford Mustang

Mustang gallops into 1990 with a driver's-side airbag and rear shoulder belts, but without a tilt steering column and console armrest. The same basic front-engine, rear-drive platform introduced in the fall of 1978 continues in three

Prices are accurate at time of printing; subject to manufacturer's change.

Ford Mustang LX 5.0L Sport

trim levels, LX, LX 5.0L Sport, and GT. The LX comes standard with a 2.3-liter 4-cylinder engine and is available as a 2-door coupe, 3-door hatchback, or 2-door convertible. The GT has a 5.0-liter V-8 in either the hatchback or convertible body style. The GT's V-8, beefed-up suspension, and wider tires—but not its body spoilers and air dams—are standard on the LX 5.0L Sport, which is available in all three body styles. All models are available with a 5-speed manual transmission or a 4-speed overdrive automatic. For '90, map pockets have been added to the door panels, and LX models feature a driver's "dead pedal" footrest previously exclusive to the GT. New options include a Power Equipment Group, leather interior trim for GT and LX 5.0L hatchbacks, and clearcoat paint. The 2.3-liter four is too weak for this 2800-pound car, so if you want a Mustang, get the V-8. We realize an aging, high-powered, rear-drive car with a small interior, a rough ride, and a formidable thirst for fuel isn't everyone's cup of tea. But for performance-minded buyers on a budget, few other mounts deliver this much bang for the buck. A V-8 convertible is loads of fun and, like the GT, will develop collector value. With this level of performance, we'd prefer a suspension that didn't jiggle and jounce over rough pavement. And 130-mph cars should have all-disc, anti-lock brakes instead of the Mustang's mediocre front-disc/rear-drum setup. But this is the best of a vanishing breed. Check with your insurance agent before you buy, however: A V-8 Mustang can be costly to insure.

Specifications

	2-door notchback	3-door hatchback	2-door conv.
Wheelbase, in.	100.5	100.5	100.5
Overall length, in.	179.6	179.6	179.6
Overall width, in.	68.3	68.3	68.3
Overall height, in.	52.1	52.1	52.1
Turn diameter, ft.	37.4	37.4	37.4
Curb weight, lbs.	2759	2824	2960
Cargo vol., cu. ft.	10.0	30.0	6.4
Fuel capacity, gals.	15.4	15.4	15.4
Seating capacity	4	4	4
Front headroom, in.	37.0	37.0	37.6
Front shoulder room, in.	55.5	55.5	55.5
Front legroom, max., in.	41.7	41.7	41.7
Rear headroom, in.	35.9	35.7	37.0
Rear shoulder room, in.	54.3	54.3	48.9
Rear legroom, min., in.	30.7	30.7	30.7

Powertrain layout: longitudinal front engine/rear-wheel drive.

Engines

	ohc I-4	ohv V-8
Size, liters/cu. in.	2.3/140	5.0/302
Fuel delivery	PFI	PFI
Horsepower @ rpm	88 @ 4000	225 @ 4200
Torque (lbs./ft.) @ rpm	132 @ 2600	300 @ 3200
Availability	S[1]	S[2]

EPA city/highway mpg

5-speed OD manual	23/29	17/24
4-speed OD automatic	21/27	17/25

1. LX   2. GT, LX 5.0L.

Prices

Ford Mustang	Retail Price	Dealer Invoice	Low Price
LX 2-door notchback	$9456	$8618	$8818
LX 3-door hatchback	9962	9068	9268
LX 2-door convertible	15141	13677	13877

Prices are accurate at time of printing; subject to manufacturer's change.

	Retail Price	Dealer Invoice	Low Price
LX 5.0L Sport 2-door notchback	12164	11028	11228
LX 5.0L Sport 3-door hatchback	13007	11778	11978
LX 5.0L Sport 2-door convertible	18183	16384	16584
GT 3-door hatchback	13986	12650	12850
GT 2-door convertible	18805	16938	17138
Destination charge	405	405	405

Standard equipment:

LX: 2.3-liter PFI 4-cylinder engine, 5-speed manual transmission, power steering, driver's-side airbag, rear shoulder belts, cloth reclining bucket seats, tinted glass, tachometer, trip odometer, coolant temperature and oil pressure gauges, voltmeter, intermittent wipers, remote mirrors, door pockets, cargo area cover (3-door), AM/FM radio, 195/70R14 tires. **LX 5.0L Sport** adds: 5.0-liter PFI V-8, Traction-Lok axle, articulated sport seats (hatchback and convertible), 215/65R15 Goodyear Eagle GT+4 tires on alloy wheels. **GT** adds: power windows and locks, remote hatch release, tilt steering column, fog lights, driver's foot rest, pivoting map light. **Convertibles** have power top, power windows and locks, remote decklid release, luggage rack, footwell lights, 225/60VR15 unidirectional tires.

Optional equipment:

4-speed automatic transmission	563	479	507
Custom Equipment Group, LX 2.3	917	780	825
LX 2.3 conv.	817	695	735
Air conditioning, lighted visor mirrors.			
Preferred Pkg. 240A, LX 2.3	NC	NC	NC
Power Equipment Group (power windows and locks, power mirrors), AM/FM cassette, cruise control.			
Preferred Pkg. 245A/249A, V-8s exc. conv. .	1061	902	955
V-8 conv.	524	446	472
Power Equipment Group (power windows and locks, power mirrors), AM/FM cassette, cruise control, air conditioning, lighted visor mirrors, premium sound system.			
Rear defogger	160	136	144
Flip-up sunroof	355	302	320
Wire wheel covers	193	164	174
Premium sound system	168	143	151
Leather articulated sport seats	489	416	440
Vinyl seat trim	37	31	33
Clearcoat paint	91	78	82
WSW tires, LX 2.3	82	69	74
California emissions pkg.	100	85	90

Ford Probe

Ford Probe GL

This front-drive sports coupe gets several important changes. LX models now have a V-6 engine and 4-wheel disc brakes as standard, while anti-lock brakes are a new option. The GT keeps its turbocharged 4-cylinder engine, but an automatic transmission is now optionally available. And all models get subtle exterior alterations. Probe shares its chassis and most mechanical components with Mazda's MX-6 coupe; both are built at Mazda's plant in Flat Rock, Michigan. Ford styled the Probe's hatchback exterior and interior, however. Base GL models use a Mazda-built 2.2-liter 12-valve 4-cylinder engine. Probe GT comes with a turbocharged and intercooled version of the 2.2. The LX's Ford-made 3.0-liter V-6—the same engine used in the Taurus—is not available on other Probes. All models have a 5-speed manual transmission as standard and a 4-speed automatic as optional; the GT was previously offered only with the manual. For '90, all Probes sport new front and rear fascias and taillamps, while the GT is fitted with new bodyside cladding and restyled alloy wheels. Rear shoulder belts are standard, and the front shoulder belts now are motorized. LX and GT also ride on wider tires, and their options list now includes leather upholstery. The new V-6 engine gives Probe a leg up on the similar MX-6. The V-6 blesses the LX with far more power than the 4-cylinder

GL and adds a sense of refinement absent from the turbocharged GT. The GT suffers from excessive torque steer (the front end pulls to one side) in hard acceleration. The GL's handling is unexceptional for the class; the LX is a little more sporting; and the GT has outstanding handling, though at the expense of ride quality.

Specifications

	3-door hatchback
Wheelbase, in.	99.0
Overall length, in.	177.0
Overall width, in.	57.3
Overall height, in.	51.8
Turn diameter, ft.	34.8
Curb weight, lbs.	2731
Cargo vol., cu. ft.	41.9
Fuel capacity, gals.	15.1
Seating capacity	4
Front headroom, in.	37.3
Front shoulder room, in.	54.7
Front legroom, max., in.	42.5
Rear headroom, in.	35.0
Rear shoulder room, in.	53.7
Rear legroom, min., in.	29.9

Powertrain layout: transverse front engine/front-wheel drive.

Engines	ohc I-4	Turbo ohc I-4	ohv V-6
Size, liters/cu. in.	2.2/133	2.2/133	3.0/182
Fuel delivery	PFI	PFI	PFI
Horsepower @ rpm	110 @ 4700	145 @ 4300	140 @ 4800
Torque (lbs./ft.) @ rpm	130 @ 3000	190 @ 3500	160 @ 3000
Availability	S	S[1]	S[2]
EPA city/highway mpg			
5-speed OD manual	24/30	21/27	19/26
4-speed OD automatic	21/28	19/25	19/26

1. Probe GT. 2. Probe LX.

Prices

Ford Probe	Retail Price	Dealer Invoice	Low Price
GL 3-door hatchback	$11470	$10420	$10620
LX 3-door hatchback	13008	11789	11989

	Retail Price	Dealer Invoice	Low Price
GT 3-door hatchback	14726	13318	13518
Destination charge	295	295	295

Standard equipment:

GL: 2.2-liter PFI 4-cylinder engine, 5-speed manual transmission, power steering, cloth reclining front bucket seats with driver's seat height adjustment, rear shoulder belts, tachometer, coolant temperature and oil pressure gauges, ammeter, AM/FM radio, tinted backlight and quarter windows, cargo cover, full console with storage, split folding rear seatbacks, right visor mirror, digital clock, 185/70R14 tires. **LX** adds: 3.0-liter PFI V-6, 4-wheel disc brakes, remote fuel door and liftgate releases, intermittent wipers, rear defogger, full tinted glass, tilt steering column and instrument cluster, power mirrors, overhead console with map light, leather-wrapped steering wheel and shift knob, upgraded carpet and upholstery, door pockets, left visor mirror, folding armrest, driver's seat lumbar and side bolster adjustments, 195/70R14 tires. **GT** adds: 2.2-liter turbocharged engine, performance suspension with automatic adjustment, passenger lumbar support adjustment, fog lights, 205/60VR15 tires on alloy wheels.

Optional equipment:

4-speed automatic transmission	732	622	659
Air conditioning, GL	937	796	843
GL w/Pkg. 251A, LX & GT	817	695	735
Electronic air conditioning, LX & GT	1000	850	900
Anti-lock brakes, LX & GT	924	786	832
Preferred Pkg. 251A, GL	179	152	161

Tinted glass, tilt steering column and instrument cluster, rear defogger, Convenience Group.

Preferred Pkg. 253A, LX	2182	1854	1964

Electronic instruments with vehicle maintenance monitor, electronically controlled air conditioning, illuminated entry, power driver's seat, trip computer, rear wiper/washer, walk-in passenger seat, power windows and locks, cruise control, AM/FM cassette with premium sound and power antenna, cargo tiedown net.

Preferred Pkg. 261A, GT	2889	2455	2600

Anti-lock brakes, electronically controlled air conditioning, illuminated entry, power driver's seat, trip computer, vehicle maintenance monitor, rear wiper/washer, walk-in passenger seat, power windows and locks, cruise control, AM/FM cassette with premium sound and power antenna, lighted visor mirrors, cargo tiedown net.

Cruise control, LX & GT	201	171	181
Power locks, LX & GT	176	149	158

Requires power windows.

Power windows, LX & GT	251	214	226

Requires power locks.

Prices are accurate at time of printing; subject to manufacturer's change.

	Retail Price	Dealer Invoice	Low Price
AM/FM cassette	368	313	331
Includes premium sound and power antenna.			
AM/FM cassette w/CD player	1077	915	969
LX w/Pkg. 253A, GT w/Pkg. 261A	709	602	638
Rear defogger, GL	160	136	144
Leather seating surface trim	489	416	440
Flip-up sunroof, LX & GT	355	302	320
Alloy wheels, GL	313	266	282
LX	376	319	338
Engine block heater	20	17	18

Ford Taurus/Mercury Sable

Ford Taurus LX

These popular front-drive intermediates receive a standard driver's-side airbag, a new instrument panel, and newly optional anti-lock brakes (ABS). ABS is available only on sedans, and replaces the rear drums with discs. Sable is a slightly plusher version of the Taurus. Both are available in 4-door sedan or 5-door wagon body styles. They share 3.0- and 3.8-liter V-6 engines. Exclusive to the base Taurus, however, is its standard 2.5-liter 4-cylinder, while the Taurus SHO has sole use of a Yamaha-built 24-valve, twin-cam 3.0 V-6. The SHO comes only with a 5-speed manual

Specifications

	4-door notchback	5-door wagon
Wheelbase, in.	106.0	106.0
Overall length, in.	188.4	191.9
Overall width, in.	70.8	70.8
Overall height, in.	54.6	55.4
Turn diameter, ft.	38.1	38.1
Curb weight, lbs.	2956	3244
Cargo vol., cu. ft.	18.5	81.0
Fuel capacity, gals.	16.0	16.0
Seating capacity	6	8
Front headroom, in.	38.3	38.6
Front shoulder room, in.	57.7	57.5
Front legroom, max., in.	41.7	41.7
Rear headroom, in.	37.6	38.4
Rear shoulder room, in.	57.5	57.5
Rear legroom, min., in.	37.5	36.6

Powertrain layout: transverse front engine/front-wheel drive.

Engines	ohv I-4	ohv V-6	ohv V-6	dohc V-6
Size, liters/cu. in.	2.5/153	3.0/182	3.8/232	3.0/182
Fuel delivery	TBI	PFI	PFI	PFI
Horsepower @ rpm	90 @ 4400	140 @ 4800	140 @ 3800	220 @ 6200
Torque (lbs./ft.) @ rpm	130 @ 2600	160 @ 3000	215 @ 2200	200 @ 4800
Availability	S[1]	S[2]	O[3]	S[4]

EPA city/highway mpg

5-speed OD manual				18/27
3-speed automatic	21/27			
4-speed OD automatic		21/29	19/28	

1. Taurus L and GL 4-doors. 2. Taurus L, GL wagons and LX 4-door; all Sables.
3. Taurus GL models, and LX 4-door, all Sables; std., Taurus LX wagon. 4. Taurus SHO.

transmission and is the only Taurus or Sable not equipped with an automatic transmission. The SHO also gets standard 4-wheel disc brakes for '90. New to the line this year is variable-assist power steering: The Sable gets it when the optional 3.8 six is ordered; the Taurus when the optional automatic climate system is specified. The new dashboard is similar on both cars. The basic layout is unchanged, but there are slightly reworked controls, a slide-out cup and coin holder, an illuminated headlamp switch, and a glovebox twice the size of the previous one. Taurus and

Prices are accurate at time of printing; subject to manufacturer's change.

Sable debuted in 1985 as '86 models. They brought aerodynamic styling to mainstream America and introduced domestic family car buyers to a taut ride, responsive steering, and composed cornering. This year's models add to those virtues with the standard airbag and optional ABS. We favor the 3.8 V-6 for its added torque, but could live with the 3.0 and its slightly better fuel mileage. The Taurus' base 2.5-liter 4-cylinder is underpowered. The SHO is very fast, but you're forced to accept its balky-shifting manual transmission. Upon initial exposure to the new sedans from GM—the Chevrolet Lumina, Oldsmobile Cutlass Supreme, Buick Regal, and Pontiac Grand Prix—it appears they have failed to surpass the all-around utility and roadworthiness of their primary targets, Taurus and Sable.

Prices

Ford Taurus	Retail Price	Dealer Invoice	Low Price
L 4-door notchback	$12640	$10970	$11170
L 5-door wagon	14272	12357	12557
GL 4-door notchback	13113	11372	11572
GL 5-door wagon	14722	12740	12940
SHO 4-door notchback	21633	18614	18814
LX 4-door notchback	16180	13979	14179
LX 5-door wagon	17771	15331	15531
Destination charge	455	455	455

Standard equipment:

L: 2.5-liter TBI 4-cylinder engine, 3-speed automatic transmission (wagon has 3.0-liter PFI V-6 and 4-speed automatic), power steering, driver's-side airbag, tilt steering column, power mirrors, cloth reclining split bench seat, rear shoulder belts, 60/40 folding rear seatbacks (wagon), cargo tiedowns (wagon), intermittent wipers, trip odometer, coolant temperature gauge, AM/FM radio, tinted glass, luggage rack (wagon), 195/70R14 SBR tires. **GL** adds: split bench or bucket seats with console and recliners, seatback pockets, rear armrest, rear head restraints (4-door), cargo net (4-door). **LX** adds: 3.0-liter V-6 (4-door; wagon has 3.8-liter V-6), air conditioning, power windows and locks, power lumbar support, diagnostic alert lights, remote fuel door and decklid/liftgate releases, Light Group, automatic parking brake release, lower bodyside cladding, cornering lights, upgraded door panels, lighted visor mirrors, 205/70R14 SBR tires. **SHO** adds: 3.0-liter DOHC 24-valve PFI V-6, 5-speed manual transmission, 4-wheel disc brakes, handling suspension, dual exhausts, sport seats with power lumbar, 8000-rpm tachometer, 140-mph speedometer, fog lamps, special bodyside cladding, wheel spats, rear defogger, cruise control, leather-wrapped steering wheel, 215/65R15 performance tires on alloy wheels.

Optional equipment:

	Retail Price	Dealer Invoice	Low Price
3.0L V-6 & 4-speed auto trans, L & GL 4-doors	721	613	649
3.8L V-6, GL wagon & LX 4-door	555	472	500
GL 4-door	1276	1085	1148
Anti-lock braking system	985	838	887
Preferred Pkg. 204A, GL 4-door	1765	1501	1589
GL wagon	1715	1458	1544

Air conditioning, cruise control, remote fuel door and decklid releases, Light Group, rear defogger, rocker panel moldings, paint stripe, power windows and locks, AM/FM cassette, power driver's seat, finned wheel covers.

Preferred Pkg. 207A, LX	786	667	707

Cruise control, rear defogger, paint stripe, AM/FM cassette with premium sound system, alloy wheels, Autolamp system, floormats, illuminated entry, leather-wrapped steering wheel.

Preferred Pkg. 208A, LX 4-door	3317	2819	2985
LX wagon	1777	1509	1599

Pkg. 207A plus 3.8-liter V-6, anti-lock braking system, speed-sensitive power steering, high-level audio system, electronic instruments, keyless entry, power antenna, power front seats.

Preferred Pkg. 211A, SHO	533	452	480

Autolamp system, floormats, illuminated entry, high-level audio system.

Preferred Pkg. 212A, SHO	2432	2067	2189

Pkg. 211A plus automatic air conditioning, keyless entry, power antenna, Ford JBL Audio System, power front seats, leather seat trim, power moonroof.

Automatic air conditioning	1000	850	900
SHO, LX or GL w/204A	193	164	174
Manual air conditioning	817	695	735
Autolamp system	73	62	66
Cargo area cover, wagons	66	56	59
Cornering lamps	68	58	61
Rear defogger	160	136	144
Remote fuel door and decklid releases	91	78	82
Remote fuel door release, wagons	41	35	37
Extended range fuel tank	46	39	41
Illuminated entry	82	69	74
Diagnostic instrument cluster	89	76	80
Electronic instruments, LX	239	203	215
GL	351	299	316

Prices are accurate at time of printing; subject to manufacturer's change.

	Retail Price	Dealer Invoice	Low Price
Keyless entry	218	186	196
w/Pkg. 207A or 211A	137	116	123
Light Group	59	50	53
Picnic table load floor extension, wagons	66	56	59
Power locks	215	182	194
Lighted visor mirrors	100	85	90
Rocker panel moldings	55	47	50
Power moonroof	741	630	667
Automatic parking brake release	12	10	11
CD player	491	418	442
High-level audio system	490	417	441
GL w/Pkg. 204A, SHO	335	285	302
LX w/Pkg. 207A	167	142	150
AM/FM cassette	155	132	140
Premium sound system	168	143	151
Power antenna	82	69	74
Ford JBL Audio System	488	415	439
Rear facing third seat	155	132	140
Power seats, each	280	238	252
Cruise control	201	171	181
Leather-wrapped steering wheel	63	54	57
HD suspension	26	22	23
Speed-sensitive steering	104	88	94
Rear wiper/washer	126	107	113
Finned wheel covers	65	55	59
Alloy wheels, GL	279	237	251
LX or GL w/Pkg. 204A	215	182	194
Styled road wheels, GL	193	164	174
LX or GL w/Pkg. 204A	128	109	115
Black alloy wheels, SHO	24	21	22
Power windows	306	260	275
Insta-Clear heated windshield	250	213	225
Bucket seats	NC	NC	NC
Leather seat trim, LX & SHO	489	416	440
GL	593	504	534
Vinyl seat trim, L	51	44	46
GL	37	31	33
205/70R14 WSW tires	82	69	74
205/65R15 tires	65	55	59
Conventional spare tire	73	62	66
HD battery	27	23	24
Engine block heater	20	17	18
Floormats	43	36	39
Clearcoat paint	188	160	169
Paint stripe	61	52	55
California emissions pkg.	100	85	90

Mercury Sable

	Retail Price	Dealer Invoice	Low Price
GS 4-door notchback	$15065	$13043	$13711
LS 4-door notchback	16067	13895	14616
GS 5-door wagon	16010	13846	14564
LS 5-door wagon	17038	14720	15492
Destination charge	455	455	455

Standard equipment:

GS: 3.0-liter PFI V-6 engine, 4-speed automatic transmission, power steering, driver's-side airbag, air conditioning, 50/50 cloth reclining front seats with armrests, 60/40 split rear seatback (wagons), rear shoulder belts, tinted glass, digital clock, intermittent wipers, tilt steering column, tachometer, coolant temperature gauge, trip odometer, coin and cup holders, tiedown hooks (wagon), front cornering lamps, power mirrors, luggage rack (wagon), AM/FM radio, front door pockets, rear armrest (except wagons), covered package tray storage bin (4- doors), visor mirrors, 205/70R14 all-season SBR tires. **LS** adds: power windows, automatic parking brake release, warning lights, Light Group, bodyside cladding, remote fuel door and liftgate releases, upgraded upholstery, power front lumbar support adjustments, front seatback map pockets, lighted visor mirrors.

Optional equipment:

Anti-lock brakes, 4-doors	985	838	887
3.8-liter V-6	555	472	500
Preferred Pkg. 450A, 4-door	773	657	696
Wagon	723	615	651
Preferred Pkg. 451A, 4-door	1099	934	989
Wagon	1049	892	944
Preferred Pkg. 461A	917	779	825
Preferred Pkg. 462A	1719	1462	1547
Variable-assist power steering	104	88	94
Automatic air conditioning	193	164	174
Autolamp system	73	62	66
Lighted visor mirrors, GS	100	85	90
Electronic instrument cluster	351	299	316
Insta-Clear heated windshield	250	213	225
Keyless entry	218	186	196
Power moonroof	741	630	667
Rear defogger	160	136	144
Cruise control	201	171	181
Luxury Touring Pkg., LS 4-door	2015	1653	1814
Anti-lock brakes, moonroof, leather bucket seats.			
Light Group, GS	59	50	53
HD battery	27	23	24
HD suspension	26	22	23

Prices are accurate at time of printing; subject to manufacturer's change.

	Retail Price	Dealer Invoice	Low Price
Extended-range fuel tank	46	39	41
Power Lock Group, GS 4-door	306	260	275
GS wagon	256	218	230
LS 4-door	215	182	194
Power seats, each	280	238	252
Power windows	306	260	275
AM/FM cassette	155	132	140
AM/FM radio delete (credit)	(206)	(175)	(175)
Premium sound system	168	143	151
High Level Audio System	490	417	441
w/Pkg. 451	335	285	302
w/Pkg. 461	167	142	150
JBL sound system	488	415	439
CD player	491	418	442
Power antenna	82	69	74
Clearcoat paint	188	160	169
Bodyside accent stripes	61	52	55
Floormats	43	36	39
Leather-wrapped steering wheel	63	54	57
Leather seat trim	489	416	440
All-vinyl trim	37	31	33
Picnic tray, wagons	66	56	59
Rear-facing third seat, wagons	155	132	140
Rear wiper/washer, wagons	126	107	113
Cargo area cover, wagons	66	56	59
205/70R14 WSW tires	82	69	74
205/65R15 tires	65	55	59
205/65R15 WSW tires	146	124	131
Conventional spare tire	73	62	66
Alloy wheels	224	191	202
Polycast wheels	138	117	124
California emissions pkg	100	85	90

Ford Tempo/Mercury Topaz

These compact twins are little changed for 1990. Floor mats and footwell and trunk lights are made standard. Tempo's polycast wheels are restyled, and both cars get rear shoulder belts. A front center armrest has joined the Tempo GL options list, and the sport instrument cluster is now available only as part of GL Special Value packages. On Topaz, 2-way head restraints replace the 4-way design used previously on some models, and wire wheel covers

Ford Tempo

have been dropped from the options list. Both cars come as 2- or 4-door sedans; the 4-door models are optionally available with a part-time, on-demand 4-wheel drive system not for use on dry pavement. The 98-horsepower 2.3-liter 4-cylinder standard on the Tempo GL and Topaz GS and LS is supplanted by a 100-horsepower version on the other models and those equipped with 4WD. A 5-speed manual transmission is standard and a 3-speed automatic is optional in all models except the 4WD, which has the automatic standard. A driver's-side airbag is an $815 stand-alone option on base models (it's $690 on the base models as part of an extra-equipment package) and a $622 stand-alone option on other models. Motorized automatic front shoulder belts are standard on all models. Performance is barely adequate with either engine, which struggle to muster passing power. Passenger room, trunk space, ride, and handling fail to rise above average in the compact field. Still, prices are attractive, the styling is contemporary, and the dashboard design is one of the best in an American-built car. Another nice feature is the available driver's-side airbag. Except for their easy-to-use 4WD system, neither Tempo nor Topaz can compete with Japanese rivals in sophistication, but they beat most of them on sticker price.

Prices are accurate at time of printing; subject to manufacturer's change.

Specifications

	2-door notchback	4-door notchback
Wheelbase, in.	99.9	99.9
Overall length, in.	176.7	177.0
Overall width, in.	68.3	68.3
Overall height, in.	52.8	52.9
Turn diameter, ft.	38.7	38.7
Curb weight, lbs.	2462[1]	2515[2]
Cargo vol., cu. ft.	13.2	13.2
Fuel capacity, gals.	15.9[3]	15.9[3]
Seating capacity	5	5
Front headroom, in.	37.5	37.5
Front shoulder room, in.	53.9	53.9
Front legroom, max., in.	41.5	41.5
Rear headroom, in.	36.8	36.9
Rear shoulder room, in.	54.0	53.3
Rear legroom, min., in.	36.0	36.0

1. 2667 with 4WD   2. 2720 with 4WD   3. 14.2 with 4WD.

Powertrain layout: transverse front engine/front-wheel drive or on-demand 4WD.

Engines

	ohv I-4	ohv I-4
Size, liters/cu. in.	2.3/141	2.3/141
Fuel delivery	PFI	PFI
Horsepower @ rpm	98 @ 4400	100 @ 4400
Torque (lbs./ft.) @ rpm	124 @ 2200	130 @ 2600
Availability	S	S[1]

EPA city/highway mpg

5-speed OD manual	23/33	21/28
3-speed automatic	22/26	22/26

1. Tempo GLS, Topaz XR5 and LTS, and 4WD models.

Prices

Ford Tempo (preliminary)	Retail Price	Dealer Invoice	Low Price
GL 2-door notchback	$9483	$8605	$8805
GL 4-door notchback	9633	8739	8939
GLS 2-door notchback	10300	9333	9533
GLS 4-door notchback	10448	9464	9664
LX 4-door notchback	10605	9604	9804
All Wheel Drive 4-door notchback	11331	10251	10451
Destination charge	425	425	425

Standard equipment:

GL: 2.3-liter PFI 4-cylinder engine, 5-speed manual transmission, power steering, cloth reclining front bucket seats, rear shoulder belts, AM/FM radio, coolant temperature gauge, tinted glass, intermittent wipers, door pockets, 185/70R14 tires. **GLS** adds: high-output engine, Light Group, tachometer and trip odometer, leather-wrapped steering wheel, AM/FM cassette, power mirrors, sport seats, luggage tiedown, front center armrest, performance tires on alloy wheels. **LX** adds to GL: illuminated entry, power locks, remote fuel door and decklid releases, Light Group, power mirrors, tachometer and trip odometer, tilt steering column, front center armrest, upgraded upholstery, seatback pockets, polycast wheels. **All Wheel Drive** adds to GL: high-output engine, 3-speed automatic transmission, part-time 4-wheel drive, tachometer and trip odometer, Light Group, power mirrors, polycast wheels.

Optional equipment:	Retail Price	Dealer Invoice	Low Price
3-speed automatic transmission	539	458	485
Air conditioning	807	686	726
Supplemental airbag restraint system,			
GL 4-door	815	692	734
GL 4-door w/226A, LX	690	587	621
Requires automatic transmission.			
Preferred Pkg. 226A, GL 2-door	486	414	437
GL 4-door	538	458	484
Air conditioning, rear defogger, Light Group, Power Lock Group, power mirrors, tilt steering column.			
Preferred Pkg. 229A, GLS 2-door	1267	1078	1140
GLS 4-door	1319	1122	1187
Air conditioning, Power Lock Group, tilt steering column, power driver's seat, premium sound system, cruise control.			
Preferred Pkg. 233A, LX	911	774	820
3-speed automatic transmission, air conditioning, rear defogger, decklid luggage rack.			
Preferred Pkg. 232A, AWD	378	322	340
Rear defogger, Power Lock Group, tilt steering column, power windows.			
Front center armrest, GL	55	47	50
Rear defogger	150	128	135
Sport instrument cluster, GL	87	74	78
Light Group, GL	38	32	34
Decklid luggage rack	115	97	104
Power Lock Group (std. LX), 2-doors . . .	246	209	221
4-doors	298	253	268
Power locks, remote decklid and fuel door releases.			
Power mirrors, GL	121	103	109
AM/FM cassette (std. LX)	137	116	123
Premium sound system	138	117	124
Power driver's seat	261	222	235

Prices are accurate at time of printing; subject to manufacturer's change.

	Retail Price	Dealer Invoice	Low Price
Cruise control	191	163	172
Sports Appearance Group, GLS	1178	1001	1060
Tilt steering column (std. LX)	124	106	112
Polycast wheels, GL	193	164	174
Power windows, 4-doors	306	260	275
All vinyl seat trim	37	31	33
WSW tires (NA GLS)	82	69	74
Clearcoat metallic paint	91	78	82
Lower accent paint treatment	159	135	143
California emissions pkg.	100	85	90

Mercury Topaz

	Retail Price	Dealer Invoice	Low Price
GS 2-door notchback	$10007	$9080	$9311
GS 4-door notchback	10164	9220	9456
XR5 2-door notchback	11006	9969	10232
LS 4-door notchback	11543	10447	10727
LTS 4-door notchback	12567	11359	11671
Destination charge	430	430	430

Standard equipment:

GS: 2.3-liter PFI 4-cylinder engine, 5-speed manual transmission, power steering, reclining cloth and vinyl front bucket seats, motorized front shoulder belts, manual lap belts, rear shoulder belts, tachometer, coolant temperature gauge, trip odometer, tinted glass, intermittent wipers, AM/FM radio, diagnostic alert module, door pockets, map lights, floormats, 185/70R14 tires. **LS** adds: tilt steering column, power windows and locks, cruise control, all-cloth upholstery, rear defogger, remote decklid and fuel door releases, Light Group, cargo net, headlamps-on tone, front armrest, console cassette storage, touring suspension, performance tires. **XR5** adds to GS: high-output engine, 3.73 final drive ratio, performance suspension, leather-wrapped steering wheel, tilt steering column, sport seats with power lumbar, Light Group, cargo net, front armrest, remote decklid and fuel door releases, performance tires on alloy wheels. **LTS** adds to LS: high-output engine, 3.73 final drive ratio, performance suspension, air conditioning, cruise control, sport seats with power lumbar, cargo net, performance tires on alloy wheels.

Optional equipment:

3-speed automatic transmission	563	479	507
Driver's side airbag, GS	815	692	734
GS w/Pkg. 361 or 363	690	587	621
LS, LTS	622	529	560

	Retail Price	Dealer Invoice	Low Price
Air conditioning	817	695	735
All Wheel Drive, GS	1490	1267	1341
GS w/Pkg. 363	927	788	834
LTS	1380	1173	1242
LS	1478	1256	1330
LS w/Pkg. 365	915	777	824
Special Value Pkg. 361A, GS	485	413	437
Special Value Pkg. 363A, GS	848	722	763
Special Value Pkg. 362A, GS	1228	1044	1105
Special Value Pkg. 371A, XR5	456	388	410
Special Value Pkg. 365A, LS	NC	NC	NC
Comfort/Convenience Group, GS	173	147	156
Folding armrest, Light Group, remote fuel door and decklid releases.			
Rear defogger	160	136	144
Power Lock Group, GS 2-door	267	227	240
XR5	187	159	168
GS 4-door	307	261	276
GS 2-door w/Comfort/Convenience	187	159	168
GS 4-door w/Comfort/Convenience	227	193	204
Clearcoat paint	91	78	82
Cruise control	201	171	181
Tilt steering column	135	115	122
Polycast wheels	193	164	174
Decklid luggage rack	115	97	104
Power windows, 4-doors	306	260	275
Power driver's seat	280	238	252
AM/FM cassette, GS	137	116	123
AM/FM delete (credit), GS	(245)	(208)	(208)
AM/FM cassette delete (credit), XR5, LS & LTS	(400)	(340)	(340)
Premium sound system	138	117	124
Vinyl seat trim	37	31	33
California emissions pkg.	100	85	90

Ford Thunderbird/ Mercury Cougar

After a clean-sheet redesign for 1989, these mid-size coupes slip into 1990 with only minor changes. Thunderbird gets two new option packages: a Power Equipment Group and a Luxury Group. Cougar's head restraints are now contoured, and items included in the Luxury Lamp Group are

Prices are accurate at time of printing; subject to manufacturer's change.

Ford Thunderbird

now available individually. The Mercury's Luxury Light Group has been dropped, but its components return as separate options. Cougar's rear window is more vertical than the fastback Thunderbird's, but the styling is otherwise similar. They are shorter, wider, and lower than the models they replaced, yet ride on a wheelbase that is nine inches longer. Every cabin measurement was increased in the revamp, which brought an all-independent suspension but retained a rear-drive layout. Powertrains are unchanged for '90. A 3.8-liter V-6 coupled to a 4-speed automatic transmission is the only choice on the base and LX T-Birds and on the Cougar LS. A supercharged version of the 3.8 powers the Thunderbird Super Coupe and Cougar XR7. This engine is available with a 5-speed manual gearbox. Next year, Ford is expected to offer a V-8 5.0-liter as an option on all but the SC and XR7, which will keep the supercharged V-6. The SC and XR7 come standard with 4-wheel anti-lock disc brakes; these brakes are optional on base and LX models in place of their standard front discs/rear drums. The Cougar and Thunderbird are improved over their predecessors, and we like them better than the rival Pontiac Grand Prix/Chevrolet Lumina/Oldsmobile Cutlass Supreme/Buick Regal coupes. But the T-Bird and Cougar remain too heavy, a burden that dulls their handling and overwhelms the ability of the base V-6 to deliver acceptable acceleration. The supercharged versions are faster, but fuel mileage is poor and the manual transmission is a chore to shift. The V-8 will help, but we yearn for a lighter, more efficiently sized bird and cat.

Specifications

	2-door notchback
Wheelbase, in.	113.0
Overall length, in.	198.7
Overall width, in.	72.7
Overall height, in.	52.7
Turn diameter, ft.	34.9
Curb weight, lbs.	3581
Cargo vol., cu. ft.	14.7
Fuel capacity, gals.	19.0
Seating capacity	5
Front headroom, in.	38.1
Front shoulder room, in.	59.1
Front legroom, max., in.	42.5
Rear headroom, in.	37.5
Rear shoulder room, in.	59.1
Rear legroom, min., in.	35.8

Powertrain layout: longitudinal front engine/rear-wheel drive.

Engines	ohv V-6	Supercharged ohv V-6
Size, liters/cu. in.	3.8/232	3.8/232
Fuel delivery	PFI	PFI
Horsepower @ rpm	140 @ 3800	210 @ 4000
Torque (lbs./ft.) @ rpm	215 @ 2400	315 @ 2600
Availability	S	S[1]

EPA city/highway mpg

5-speed OD manual		17/24
4-speed OD automatic	19/27	17/23

1. Super Coupe, Cougar XR7.

Prices

Ford Thunderbird	Retail Price	Dealer Invoice	Low Price
2-door notchback	$14980	$12997	$13197
LX 2-door notchback	17263	14938	15138
Super Coupe 2-door notchback	20390	17596	17796
Destination charge	460	460	460

Prices are accurate at time of printing; subject to manufacturer's change.

Standard equipment:

3.8-liter PFI V-6, 4-speed automatic transmission, power steering, air conditioning, cloth reclining front bucket seats, rear shoulder belts, tinted glass, power windows, intermittent wipers, left remote mirror, full-length console with armrest and storage bin, coolant temperature gauge, trip odometer, visor mirrors, AM/FM radio, 205/70R15 all-season tires. **LX** adds: power driver's seat, illuminated entry, remote fuel door and decklid releases, power locks, cruise control, tilt steering column, maintenance monitor, power mirrors, folding rear armrest, electronic instruments, Light Convenience Group, lighted visor mirrors, AM/FM cassette, leather-wrapped steering wheel, tilt steering column, instrument panel storage compartment. **Super Coupe** adds to base: supercharged engine with dual exhaust, 5-speed manual transmission, 4-wheel disc brakes, anti-lock braking system, handling suspension, articulated sport seats, lower bodyside cladding, fog lights, analog instruments with tachometer, soft-feel steering wheel, remote fuel door release, maintenance monitor, power mirrors, folding rear armrest, Light Group, instrument panel storage compartment, 225/60VR16 tires on alloy wheels.

Optional equipment:	Retail Price	Dealer Invoice	Low Price
4-speed automatic transmission, SC	563	479	507
Anti-lock brakes, base & LX	1085	923	977
Traction-Lok axle, base & LX	100	85	90
Preferred Pkg. 151B, base	613	523	552
AM/FM cassette, rear defogger, power passenger seat, cruise control, tilt steering column, power mirrors, styled wheel covers.			
Preferred Pkg. 155B, LX	805	681	725
Rear defogger, power passenger seat, keyless entry, AM/FM cassette with premium sound, power antenna, front floormats, Autolamp Group, cornering lamps, alloy wheels.			
Preferred Group 157B, SC	NC	NC	NC
AM/FM cassette, rear defogger, power passenger seat, Power Lock Group, cruise control, tilt steering column.			
Anti-theft system	183	155	165
Autolamp Group, base & SC	176	149	158
Includes auto dim feature and automatic day/night mirror.			
Cornering lamps, base & SC	68	58	61
Keyless entry, base & SC	219	185	197
Base & SC w/illuminated entry	137	116	123
Light Convenience Group, base	146	124	131
SC	100	85	90
Front reading light, instrument panel courtesy light, engine compartment light, lighted visor mirrors.			
Power Lock Group	237	201	213
Power locks, remote decklid release.			
Front floormats	33	28	30

	Retail Price	Dealer Invoice	Low Price
Power moonroof, SC	841	715	757
LX, base or SC w/Light Convenience Group	741	630	667
AM/FM cassette, base & SC	155	132	140
AM/FM cassette w/premium sound, base & SC	460	391	414
Base w/151B, SC w/157B	305	259	275
Ford JBL audio system	488	415	439
CD player	491	418	442
Power antenna	82	69	74
Leather seating surfaces, LX	489	416	440
SC	622	529	560
Rear defogger	160	136	144
Power passenger seat	280	238	252
Vehicle maintenance monitor, base	89	76	80
Cold Weather Group	205	174	185
SC w/automatic	178	152	160
All models w/Preferred Pkg.	45	38	41
SC w/automatic & Pkg. 157B	18	16	16
Engine block heater, HD battery and alternator, rear defogger.			
Wire wheel covers, base	228	194	205
Base w/151B	143	121	129
LX w/155B & 205/70R15 WSW tires . .	NC	NC	NC
215/70R15 tires on alloy wheels, base . . .	299	254	269
Base w/151B	214	181	193
205/70R15 tires, base & LX	73	62	66
225/60R16 Eagle GT+4 tires, SC	73	62	66
Conventional spare tire, base & LX	73	62	66
Clearcoat paint	188	160	169
California emissions pkg.	100	85	90

Mercury Cougar

	Retail Price	Dealer Invoice	Low Price
LS 2-door notchback	$15816	$13699	$14398
XR7 2-door notchback	20213	17437	18366
Destination charge	460	460	460

Standard equipment:

LS: 3.8-liter PFI V-6, 4-speed automatic transmission, power steering and brakes, air conditioning, cloth reclining front bucket seats, tinted glass, intermittent wipers, electronic instruments (tachometer, coolant temperature, oil pressure, voltmeter, trip computer, service interval reminder), power windows and mirrors, visor mirrors, AM/FM radio, motorized front shoulder belts with manual lap belts, rear lap/shoulder belts, 205/70R15 tires. **XR7** adds: supercharged engine with dual exhaust, 5-speed manual transmission, handling suspension, Traction-Lok axle, sport seats with power lumbar and side bolsters, analog instruments (tachometer, coolant temperature, oil pres-

Prices are accurate at time of printing; subject to manufacturer's change.

sure, boost/vacuum), Diagnostic Maintenance Monitor, 225/60VR16 tires on alloy wheels.

Optional equipment:	Retail Price	Dealer Invoice	Low Price
4-speed automatic transmission, XR7 . . .	563	479	507
Performance Traction-Lok axle, LS	100	85	90
Required with anti-lock brakes.			
Anti-lock braking system, LS	985	838	887
Preferred Pkg. 261A	NC	NC	NC
Preferred Pkg. 262A	1070	909	963
w/clearcoat paint instead of lighted visor			
mirrors	1158	984	1042
Preferred Pkg. 263A	2030	1724	1827
Preferred Pkg. 265A	NC	NC	NC
Preferred Pkg. 266A	977	828	879
WSW tires, LS	73	62	66
225/60VR16 Eagle GT + 4 tires, XR7 . . .	73	62	66
Conventional spare tire, LS	73	62	66
Radial spoke wheels covers, LS	228	194	205
w/Pkg. 261	143	121	129
Alloy wheels, LS	299	254	269
LS w/Pkg. 261	214	181	193
Styled sport wheel covers, LS	85	73	77
Power Lock Group	237	201	213
Diagnostic maintenance monitor, LS	89	76	80
Power moonroof	741	630	667
Power seats, each	280	238	252
AM/FM cassette	155	132	140
AM/FM cassette w/High Level Audio	460	391	414
w/Pkg. 262 or 265	305	259	275
JBL sound system	488	415	439
CD player	491	418	442
Power antenna	82	69	74
AM/FM delete (credit)	(245)	(208)	(208)
Clearcoat metallic paint	188	160	169
Leather trim	489	416	440
Split fold-down rear seat	133	113	120
Cold Weather Group, LS, XR7 5-speed . .	205	174	185
XR7 automatic	178	152	160
w/Pkg. 261, 262 or 263	45	38	41
XR7 5-speed w/Pkg. 265 or 266	45	38	41
XR7 automatic w/Pkg. 265 or 266	18	16	16
Rear defogger	160	136	144
Light Group	46	39	41
Lighted visor mirrors	100	85	90
Illuminated entry	82	69	74
Luxury Lamp Group	244	207	220

CONSUMER GUIDE®

	Retail Price	Dealer Invoice	Low Price
Headlamp Convenience Group	176	149	158
Cornerning lamps	68	58	61
Keyless entry	219	185	197
w/Pkg. 262, 263 or 266	137	226	123
Cruise control	201	171	181
Tilt steering column	135	115	122
Leather-wrapped steering wheel	63	54	57
Front floormats	33	28	30
Anti-theft alarm system	183	155	165
California emissions pkg.	100	85	90

Geo Metro

Geo Metro

Changes in trim and standard equipment mark this front-drive minicompact. Metro is currently offered in 3- and 5-door hatchback body styles, but a convertible version is scheduled to hit the showrooms later in the year. A stripper 3-door holds the title of U.S. fuel-economy leader and gets the XFi designation for '90. The XFi is available only as a 3-door and is rated by the EPA at 53 mpg city/58 mpg highway. One step up from the XFi is the base Metro, followed by the plusher LSi. All are powered by a 55-horse-

Prices are accurate at time of printing; subject to manufacturer's change.

power 1.0-liter 3-cylinder engine. A 5-speed manual transmission is standard; a 3-speed automatic is optional on base and LSi models. New for '90 on base and LSi Metros are full wheel covers, black body-side moldings, and intermittent wipers. The LSi tag brings a remote trunk release and new interior fabrics. The convertible is to hit dealer showrooms in the spring as a late 1990 model. Chevrolet had released no other information on the convertible at publication time. Metro is built for General Motors by Suzuki in Japan. GM sells it under its Geo-brand collection of "captive imports" through Chevrolet dealers. Metro's main virtue is high fuel economy. It will carry four adults,

Specifications

	3-door hatchback	5-door hatchback
Wheelbase, in.	89.2	93.2
Overall length, in.	146.3	150.4
Overall width, in.	62.0	62.7
Overall height, in.	53.4	53.5
Turn diameter, ft.	30.2	31.5
Curb weight, lbs.	1591	1640
Cargo vol., cu. ft.	29.1	31.4
Fuel capacity, gals.	10.6	10.6
Seating capacity	4	4
Front headroom, in.	37.8	38.8
Front shoulder room, in.	51.6	51.6
Front legroom, max., in.	42.5	42.5
Rear headroom, in.	36.6	38.0
Rear shoulder room, in.	50.5	50.6
Rear legroom, min., in.	29.8	32.6

Powertrain layout: transverse front engine/front-wheel drive.

Engines

	ohc I-3
Size, liters/cu. in.	1.0/61
Fuel delivery	TBI
Horsepower @ rpm	55 @ 5700
Torque (lbs./ft.) @ rpm	58 @ 3300
Availability	S

EPA city/highway mpg

5-speed OD manual	53/58
3-speed automatic	37/40

but is best as a commuter car for no more than two. With the 5-speed manual, Metro is lively in the lower gears and easily keeps pace with traffic. Mileage and acceleration do not suffer unduly with the automatic transmission. Excessive engine noise and inadequate sound insulation turn the tiny cabin into an audio penalty box, however. The short wheelbase and light curb weight make for a bouncy, jarring ride, and don't inspire confidence in terms of occupant protection in the event of a collision.

Prices

Geo Metro	Retail Price	Dealer Invoice	Low Price
XFi 3-door hatchback	$5995	$5755	$5855
3-door hatchback	6695	6159	6359
5-door hatchback	6995	6435	6635
LSi 3-door hatchback	7495	6895	7095
LSi 5-door hatchback	7795	7171	7371
Destination charge	255	255	255

Standard equipment:

XFi & base: 1.0-liter TBI 3-cylinder engine, 5-speed manual transmission, cloth and vinyl reclining front bucket seats, one-piece folding rear seatback, rear shoulder belts, intermittent wipers, left door pocket, 145/80R13 tires. **LSi** adds: composite headlamps, full cloth upholstery, trip odometer, door pockets, split folding rear seatback, wheel covers, remote hatch release, rear defogger.

Optional equipment:

Air conditioning	670	590	603
XFi Preferred Group 2	150	132	135
Rear defogger.			
Base Preferred Group 2	576	507	518
AM/FM radio, rear defogger, rear wiper/washer.			
Base Preferred Group 3	465	409	419
3-speed automatic transmission.			
Base Preferred Group 4	1041	916	937
3-speed automatic transmission, AM/FM radio, rear defogger, rear wiper/washer.			
LSi Preferred Group 2	451	397	406
AM/FM radio, rear defogger, rear wiper/washer, console.			
LSi Preferred Group 3	465	409	419
3-speed automatic transmission, rear defogger.			

Prices are accurate at time of printing; subject to manufacturer's change.

	Retail Price	Dealer Invoice	Low Price
LSi Preferred Group 4	916	806	824
3-speed automatic transmission, AM/FM radio, rear defogger, rear wiper/ washer, console.			
Left remote & right manual mirrors	20	18	18
AM/FM radio	301	265	271
AM/FM cassette	441	388	397
Sound system prices are for base models; prices vary with option package content.			
Console	25	22	23
Floormats	25	22	23
Bodyside moldings	50	44	45
Mud guards	30	26	27
Sport stripe, base	50	44	45
XFi	100	88	90

Geo Storm and
Isuzu Impulse/Stylus

Geo Storm GSi

Chevrolet dealers introduced the Isuzu-built Geo Storm during the fall and by the spring of 1990 Isuzu dealers will add a pair of new passenger cars built from the same design. Isuzu is partly owned by General Motors. Storm is a sporty front-drive hatchback that comes two ways: The base model uses a 95-horsepower 1.6-liter 4-cylinder engine while the GSi uses a dual-cam, 125-horsepower version of that engine. A 5-speed manual transmission is standard on both; a 3-speed automatic is optional on the base car and a 4-speed automatic is optional on the GSi. Isuzu's versions are a sporty 2 + 2 hatchback called Impulse and a subcompact 4-door sedan called Stylus. They share Storm's front-drive chassis and engines, but Impulse also is available as a high-performance coupe with a 160-horsepower turbocharged engine and permanently engaged 4-wheel-drive

Specifications

	3-door hatchback	4-door notchback
Wheelbase, in.	96.5	96.5
Overall length, in.	166.0	165.1
Overall width, in.	66.7	66.1
Overall height, in.	51.1	54.0
Turn diameter, ft.	32.2	32.2
Curb weight, lbs.	2282[1]	2261
Cargo vol., cu. ft.	21.8	11.4
Fuel capacity, gals.	12.4	12.4
Seating capacity	4	5
Front headroom, in.	37.5	39.0
Front shoulder room, in.	53.3	53.6
Front legroom, max., in.	43.8	43.3
Rear headroom, in.	31.9	37.9
Rear shoulder room, in.	51.2	52.8
Rear legroom, min., in.	30.4	31.9

1. 2714 lbs., 4WD.

Powertrain layout: transverse front engine/front-wheel drive or permanent 4WD (Impulse RS).

Engines	ohc I-4	dohc I-4	Turbo dohc I-4
Size, liters/cu. in.	1.6/98	1.6/98	1.6/98
Fuel delivery	PFI	PFI	PFI
Horsepower @ rpm	95 @ 5800	125 @ 6800	160 @ 6600
Torque (lbs./ft.) @ rpm	97 @ 3400	102 @ 4600	150 @ 4800
Availability	S[1]	S[2]	S[3]
EPA city/highway mpg			
5-speed OD manual	32/37	26/34	22/28
3-speed automatic	27/32		
4-speed OD automatic		24/32	

1. Base Storm, Stylus S.   2. Storm GSi, Impulse/Stylus XS.   3. Impulse RS.

Prices are accurate at time of printing; subject to manufacturer's change.

system. All Storm, Impulse, and Stylus models have a driver's-side airbag as standard equipment. Standard equipment on the base Impulse XS includes a sport suspension tuned by Lotus, the British car company owned by GM; 4-wheel disc brakes; and 185/60HR14 tires. The Impulse XS and Stylus XS use the 125-horsepower engine. The base 4-door sedan, the Stylus S, has the 95-horsepower engine. We have not driven the new Impulse or Stylus, nor were prices available at publication time. We've driven both Storm models and found them to be nimble and entertaining, at least with the manual transmission, though they suffer from too much engine noise. Storm has supportive, low-mounted front bucket seats that contribute to a sports-car atmosphere, while the rear seat is so small it's virtually useless for carrying people. The base prices aren't dirt cheap, but there are only a few options to increase the cost. Storm is worth looking at for sporty, economical transport.

Prices

Geo Storm	Retail Price	Dealer Invoice	Low Price
3-door hatchback	$10390	$9351	—
GSi 3-door hatchback	11650	10485	—
Destination charge	315	315	315

Low prices not available at time of publication.

Standard equipment:

1.6-liter 12-valve PFI 4-cylinder engine, 5-speed manual transmission, power steering, driver's-side airbag, cloth and vinyl reclining front bucket seats, one-piece folding rear seatback, AM/FM radio, rear defogger, remote mirrors, tachometer, tinted glass, door pockets, visor mirror, remote hatch release. **GSi** adds: DOHC 16-valve engine, sport suspension, faster steering ratio, contoured front seats with bolsters, rocker extensions, rear spoiler, oil pressure gauge, V-rated tires.

Optional equipment:

Air conditioning	690	587	—
Preferred Group 2, base	545	463	—
3-speed automatic transmission.			
Preferred Group 2, GSi	745	633	—
4-speed automatic transmission.			

	Retail Price	Dealer Invoice	Low Price
AM/FM cassette	140	119	—
California emissions pkg.	70	60	—
Floormats	30	26	—

Honda Accord

Honda Accord EX

A new Accord went on sale in October riding a 4.7-inch longer wheelbase, making it a mid-sized car. While primary targets remain Japanese compacts such as the Toyota Camry, Honda also mentions the mid-size Ford Taurus as one of the new Accord's rivals. The most obvious styling change is at the front, where flush-mounted, exposed headlamps replace the hidden headlamps of the previous model. Two body styles are offered, a 4-door notchback sedan and a 2-door notchback coupe. The 3-door hatchback, part of the roster since Accord debuted for 1976, has been discontinued. Next year, a 5-door station wagon conceived, designed, and built in the U.S. will join the lineup. The new Accord still has front-wheel drive and a transverse-mounted 4-cylinder engine. The engine is a new, fuel-injected 2.2-liter that replaces a pair of 2.0-liter fours. The new 2.2 produces 125 horsepower in the base DX and mid-level LX models and 130 horsepower in the top-shelf EX (which replaces last year's LXi). A dual exhaust manifold on the EX boosts horsepower by five. Two transmissions are available, a standard 5-speed manual and a 4-speed automatic with Normal and Sport shift modes. All models have motorized front shoulder belts with manual lap belts. The new Accord's longer wheelbase provides generous rear-seat leg room. Cargo room has also increased; the trunk on both body styles is deep, wide at the rear, and easy to load, thanks to a bumper-height opening. The new engines are quieter and smoother; the new automatic transmission

Specifications

	2-door notchback	4-door notchback
Wheelbase, in.	107.1	107.1
Overall length, in.	184.8	184.8
Overall width, in.	67.9	67.9
Overall height, in.	53.9	54.7
Turn diameter, ft.	36.1	36.1
Curb weight, lbs.	2738	2773
Cargo vol., cu. ft.	14.4	14.4
Fuel capacity, gals.	17.0	17.0
Seating capacity	5	5
Front headroom, in.	38.8	38.9
Front shoulder room, in.	54.9	54.8
Front legroom, max., in.	42.9	42.6
Rear headroom, in.	36.5	37.5
Rear shoulder room, in.	54.3	54.8
Rear legroom, min., in.	32.3	34.3

Powertrain layout: transverse front engine/front-wheel drive.

Engines

	ohc I-4	ohc I-4
Size, liters/cu. in.	2.2/132	2.2/132
Fuel delivery	PFI	PFI
Horsepower @ rpm	125 @ 5200	130 @ 5200
Torque (lbs./ft.) @ rpm	137 @ 4000	142 @ 4000
Availability	S[1]	S[2]

EPA city/highway mpg

5-speed OD manual	24/30	24/30
4-speed OD automatic	22/28	22/28

1. DX, LX   2. EX.

has smoother shift quality; and wind noise has been reduced. Since Honda intends to compete with Taurus and other mid-size cars, the lack of a V-6 engine and anti-lock brakes are major omissions. However, the new Accord's spacious interior, greater refinement, solid construction, improved dynamic qualities, and impressive overall quality make it a fine choice. Prices are $700-$800 higher this year, not a huge jump considering the larger dimensions. As with the previous generation, the mid-level LX models, at about $15,000 to $16,000, offer the most value.

Prices

Honda Accord	Retail Price	Dealer Invoice	Low Price
DX 2-door notchback, 5-speed	$12145	$10201	$10900
DX 2-door notchback, automatic	12895	10831	10574
LX 2-door notchback, 5-speed	14695	12343	13189
LX 2-door notchback, automatic	15445	12973	13862
EX 2-door notchback, 5-speed	16395	13771	14715
EX 2-door notchback, automatic	17145	14401	15388
DX 4-door notchback, 5-speed	12345	10369	11080
DX 4-door notchback, automatic	13095	10999	11753
LX 4-door notchback, 5-speed	14895	12511	13369
LX 4-door notchback, automatic	15645	13141	14042
EX 4-door notchback, 5-speed	16595	13939	14895
EX 4-door notchback, automatic	17345	14569	15568
Destination charge	245	245	245

Standard equipment:

DX: 2.2-liter SOHC 16-valve PFI 4-cylinder engine, 5-speed manual or 4-speed automatic transmission, power steering, cloth reclining front bucket seats, folding rear seatback, tachometer, coolant temperature gauge, trip odometer, tinted glass, tilt steering column, intermittent wipers, rear defogger, remote fuel door and decklid releases, door pockets, rear shoulder belts, 185/70R14 tires. **LX adds:** air conditioning, cruise control, power windows and locks, power mirrors, AM/FM cassette, rear armrest, beverage holder. **EX adds:** driver's seat lumbar support adjuster, front spoiler, power sunroof, sport suspension, 195/60R15 Michelin MXV3 tires on alloy wheels.

OPTIONS are available as dealer-installed accessories.

Prices are accurate at time of printing; subject to manufacturer's change.

Honda Civic

Honda Civic Si

A new EX 4-door with a 108-horsepower engine has been added, while all versions of the subcompact Civic have new instrument panels with larger gauges. The EX 4-door, which supplants the LX as the top-of-the-line model, uses the same 1.6-liter 4-cylinder engine as the sporty Civic Si hatchback. All hatchbacks and 4-door models have new front and rear bumpers for 1990, and new taillamps. The DX 4-door also gains a fold-down rear seatback. This year's lineup includes the base Civic Hatchback, with a 70-horsepower 1.5-liter engine; DX hatchback and 4-door sedan, and the LX 4-door, with a 92-horsepower 1.5-liter engine; and the EX 4-door and Si hatchback with the 108-horsepower 1.6-liter engine. All have front-wheel drive. The 5-door wagon again comes two ways: front-wheel drive with the 92-horsepower engine and 4-wheel drive with the 108-horsepower engine. The 4WD system engages automatically, sending power to the rear wheels as needed to maintain traction. The base Hatchback and Si come only with manual transmissions; a 4-speed automatic is available on all other Civics. Civic ranks at the top of the subcompact class because of its overall quality, high refinement, and good resale value. The fact that it's also enjoyable to drive puts it a couple of more notches higher above most rivals. A Civic Si or EX with the 5-speed manual transmission displays the frisky eagerness of a sports car. An LX or DX with the 5-speed is no slouch either (11.5 seconds to 60 mph in our test). With automatic transmission you'll lose a little acceleration. You'll pay more for a Civic, but you'll get your money's worth.

Specifications

	3-door hatchback	4-door notchback	5-door wagon
Wheelbase, in.	98.4	98.4	98.4
Overall length, in.	157.1	168.8	161.7
Overall width, in.	66.3	66.7	66.1
Overall height, in.	52.5	53.5	56.1
Turn diameter, ft.	32.4	32.4	32.2
Curb weight, lbs.	2127	2262	2335[1]
Cargo vol., cu. ft.	25.0	12.0	60.3
Fuel capacity, gals.	11.9	11.9	11.9
Seating capacity	5	5	5
Front headroom, in.	38.2	38.5	39.4
Front shoulder room, in.	53.5	53.5	53.5
Front legroom, max., in.	43.3	43.1	41.2
Rear headroom, in.	36.6	37.4	38.0
Rear shoulder room, in.	53.2	53.0	53.5
Rear legroom, min., in.	30.4	32.0	33.2

1. 2628 lbs., 4WD Wagon.

Powertrain layout: transverse front engine/front-wheel drive or automatic 4WD (Wagon).

Engines

	ohc I-4	ohc I-4	ohc I-4
Size, liters/cu. in.	1.5/91	1.5/91	1.6/97
Fuel delivery	TBI	TBI	PFI
Horsepower @ rpm	70 @ 5500	92 @ 6000	108 @ 6000
Torque (lbs./ft.) @ rpm	83 @ 3000	89 @ 4500	100 @ 5000
Availability	S[1]	S[2]	S[3]

EPA city/highway mpg

4-speed OD manual	33/37		
5-speed OD manual		31/34	28/32
6-speed OD manual			24/26
4-speed OD automatic		28/33	25/29

1. Hatchback   2. DX, LX, 2WD Wagon   3. Si, EX, 4WD Wagon.

Prices

Honda Civic	Retail Price	Dealer Invoice	Low Price
3-door hatchback, 4-speed	$6635	$5971	$6271
DX 3-door hatchback, 5-speed	8695	7390	7640

Prices are accurate at time of printing; subject to manufacturer's change.

	Retail Price	Dealer Invoice	Low Price
DX 3-door hatchback, automatic	9575	8138	8388
Si 3-door hatchback, 5-speed	10245	8708	8958
DX 4-door notchback, 5-speed	9440	8024	8324
DX 4-door notchback, automatic	10370	8814	9114
LX 4-door notchback, 5-speed	10450	8882	9182
LX 4-door notchback, automatic	11150	9477	9777
EX 4-door notchback, 5-speed	11145	9473	9773
EX 4-door notchback, automatic	11845	10068	10368
2WD 5-door wagon, 5-speed	10325	8776	9076
2WD 5-door wagon, automatic	11370	9664	9964
4WD 5-door wagon, 6-speed	12410	10548	10848
4WD 5-door wagon, automatic	13140	11169	11469
Destination charge	245	245	245

Dealer invoice and low price not available at time of publication.

Standard equipment:

1.5-liter TBI 16-valve 70-bhp 4-cylinder engine, 4-speed manual transmission, reclining front bucket seats, 50/50 split folding rear seatback, rear shoulder belts, remote fuel door and hatch releases, tinted glass, rear defogger, 165/70R13 tires. **DX** adds: 92-bhp engine, 5-speed manual or 4-speed automatic transmission, power steering (with automatic transmission), rear wiper/washer (hatchback), tilt steering column, cargo cover (hatchback), intermittent wipers, 175/70R14 tires. **Si** adds: 108-bhp PFI engine, dual manual mirrors, power moonroof, digital clock, tachometer, sport seats, 185/60R14 tires. **LX** adds to DX 4-door: power mirrors, power windows and locks, cruise control, digital clock, tachometer. **EX** adds: 108-bhp PFI engine, upgraded interior trim, 175/65HR14 tires. **2WD wagon** has DX equipment plus digital clock, tachometer; **4WD wagon** has 108-bhp PFI engine, 6-speed manual or 4-speed automatic transmission, permanent 4WD.

OPTIONS are available as dealer-installed accessories.

Honda CRX

New bumpers and a new instrument panel are the major changes for the CRX, Honda's front-drive, 2-seat hatchback. The new bumpers are complemented by new front turn signals and taillamps. Inside, the instrument panel retains the basic layout of the previous design, but has larger gauges. The CRX Si gains rear disc brakes this year (in

Honda CRX Si

place of drum brakes) and new alloy wheels. The Si is powered by a 108-horsepower 1.6-liter 4-cylinder engine and comes only with a 5-speed manual transmission. The base CRX HF ("high fuel economy") has a 62-horsepower 1.5-liter and also comes only with a 5-speed manual; the HF earns EPA estimates of 49 mpg city and 52 highway. The mid-level CRX comes with a 92-horsepower 1.5-liter engine and a choice of 5-speed manual or 4-speed automatic transmissions. Two-seaters are supposed to be fun to drive, and the CRX certainly is, but they aren't supposed to be practical, and the CRX is that, too. The seats go back far enough for tall people to stretch their legs and the cargo area is big enough for a twosome's luggage. Where the CRX is really practical is in fuel economy; we averaged 29 mpg with a hot-shot Si last year from urban commuting. We would expect well into the 30s on the highway, and into the 40s with the miserly HF model. A mid-level CRX with the 5-speed manual or an Si are the logical choices if brisk acceleration is your priority. You'll lose some zip with the automatic transmission. CRX's petite size and low center of gravity help it take corners with remarkable agility, but the ride can be quite harsh on rough surfaces, especially in the Si model, and the interior is bombarded by engine, wind, and road noise. However, for high times at low cost, this is one little car that should keep you smiling most of the time.

Prices are accurate at time of printing; subject to manufacturer's change.

Specifications

	3-door hatchback
Wheelbase, in.	90.6
Overall length, in.	148.5
Overall width, in.	65.9
Overall height, in.	50.1
Turn diameter, ft.	30.4
Curb weight, lbs.	1967
Cargo vol., cu. ft.	23.2
Fuel capacity, gals.	11.9[1]
Seating capacity	2
Front headroom, in.	37.0
Front shoulder room, in.	53.5
Front legroom, max., in.	40.8
Rear headroom, in.	—
Rear shoulder room, in.	—
Rear legroom, min., in.	—

1. 10.6 gals., HF.

Powertrain layout: transverse front engine/front-wheel drive.

Engines	ohc I-4	ohc I-4	ohc I-4
Size, liters/cu. in.	1.5/91	1.5/91	1.6/97
Fuel delivery	PFI	TBI	PFI
Horsepower @ rpm	62 @ 4500	92 @ 6000	108 @ 6000
Torque (lbs./ft.) @ rpm	90 @ 2000	89 @ 4500	100 @ 5000
Availability	S[1]	S[2]	S[3]

EPA city/highway mpg			
5-speed OD manual	49/52	32/35	28/33
4-speed OD automatic		29/35	

1. HF   2. CRX   3. Si.

Prices

Honda CRX	Retail Price	Dealer Invoice	Low Price
HF 3-door hatchback, 5-speed	$9145	$7773	$8073
3-door hatchback, 5-speed	9410	7999	8296
3-door hatchback, automatic	10010	8509	8808
Si 3-door hatchback, 5-speed	11130	9461	9760
Destination charge	245	245	245

Standard equipment:

HF: 1.5-liter 8-valve PFI 4-cylinder engine, 5-speed manual transmission, reclining front bucket seats, left remote mirror, tinted glass, tachometer, coolant temperature gauge, trip odometer, intermittent wipers, rear defogger, remote fuel door and hatch releases, bodyside moldings, 165/70R13 tires. **CRX** adds: 1.5-liter SOHC 16-valve PFI engine, tilt steering column, dual remote mirrors, rear wiper/washer, cargo cover. **Si** adds: 1.6-liter engine, 4-wheel disc brakes, sport suspension, power sunroof, front spoiler, 185/60HR14 tires on alloy wheels.

OPTIONS are available as dealer-installed accessories.

Honda Prelude

1989 Honda Prelude Si

The 1990 Prelude sports coupe won't arrive until early spring, when a slightly larger engine and minor cosmetic changes will be introduced. Until then, Honda dealers will be selling 1989 models. Details on the 1990 models and prices weren't available, but changes will include minor styling revisions, a slightly larger engine with small increases in horsepower and torque, and the addition of antilock brakes. Carryover 1989 models are the base S, powered by a 104-horsepower 2.0-liter 4-cylinder with two single-barrel carburetors, and the Si, with a 135-horsepower 2.0-liter engine with dual-overhead cams and multi-point fuel injection. The Si 4WS has the 135-horsepower engine and Honda's mechanical 4-wheel-steering system. With 4WS, the rear wheels steer a few degrees right or left, depending on steering-wheel angle, to improve handling and maneuverability. With 4WS, Prelude's turning diameter is 31.5 feet; without 4WS, it's 34.8. Prelude was redesigned for 1988 and hasn't been a hot seller lately, so you should be able to negotiate a good deal. Prelude has suffered partly because of its conservative styling compared to flashier rivals such as the Nissan 240SX, Mitsubishi Eclipse, and Toyota Celica. Underneath the skin, though, Prelude has a well-designed front-drive chassis that provides competent handling without a punishing ride, strong brakes, and

1989 Specifications

	2-door notchback
Wheelbase, in.	101.0
Overall length, in.	175.6
Overall width, in.	67.3
Overall height, in.	49.2
Turn diameter, ft.	34.8[1]
Curb weight, lbs.	2571
Cargo vol., cu. ft.	11.0
Fuel capacity, gals.	15.9
Seating capacity	4
Front headroom, in.	36.9
Front shoulder room, in.	53.1
Front legroom, max., in.	43.1
Rear headroom, in.	34.1
Rear shoulder room, in.	51.1
Rear legroom, min., in.	27.1

1. 31.5 ft., Si 4WS.

Powertrain layout: transverse front engine/front-wheel drive.

Engines	ohc I-4	dohc I-4
Size, liters/cu. in.	2.0/119	2.0/119
Fuel delivery	2 × 1 bbl.	PFI
Horsepower @ rpm	104 @ 5800	135 @ 6200
Torque (lbs./ft.) @ rpm	111 @ 4000	127 @ 4500
Availability	S[1]	S[2]

EPA city/highway mpg		
5-speed OD manual	23/38	23/26
4-speed OD automatic	20/26	21/26

1. S   2. Si.

high-revving engines that deliver brisk acceleration. While 4WS improves Prelude's maneuverability, it doesn't do enough in routine driving to justify a $1485 price premium above the Si model. You can save even more on a base S model, though you'll lose some acceleration and standard features. Prelude isn't the most exciting sports coupe around, but it should be one of the most reliable and have good resale value.

Prices

Honda Prelude (1989 prices)	Retail Price	Dealer Invoice	Low Price
S 2-door notchback, 5-speed	$13945	$11713	$12213
S 2-door notchback, automatic	14670	12322	12822
Si 2-door notchback, 5-speed	16965	14250	14750
Si 2-door notchback, automatic	17690	14859	15359
Si 4WS 2-door notchback, 5-speed	18450	15498	15998
Si 4WS 2-door notchback, automatic	19175	16107	16607
Destination charge	245	245	245

Standard equipment:

S: 2.0-liter 12-valve carbureted 4-cylinder engine, 5-speed manual or 4-speed automatic transmission, power steering, 4-wheel disc brakes, cloth reclining front bucket seats, tilt steering column, console, AM/FM cassette, power antenna, tachometer, coolant temperature gauge, trip odometer, intermittent wipers, 185/70HR13 tires. **Si** adds: DOHC 16-valve PFI engine, air conditioning, cruise control, adjustable lumbar support and side bolsters, diversity antenna, 195/60HR14 tires. **Si 4WS** adds: 4-wheel steering, power door locks, bronze tinted glass, alloy wheels.

OPTIONS are available as dealer-installed accessories.

Hyundai Excel/Mitsubishi Precis

A new Hyundai Excel and nearly identical Mitsubishi Precis arrived for 1990. Like the old Excel/Precis, the new one is built in Korea from a front-drive design derived from the Mitsubishi Mirage (Mitsubishi owns part of Hyundai). Styling is wholly Hyundai's work and deliberately resembles that of the larger Sonata. Excel models dwindle from

Prices are accurate at time of printing; subject to manufacturer's change

Hyundai Excel

eight to six: base and sporty GS 3-door hatchbacks, GL 5-door hatchback, and a notchback 4-door in base, GL and top-shelf GLS trim. The Precis line shrinks from six models and two body styles to just a pair of 3-door hatchbacks, in base and RS trim. Interior volume gains three cubic feet, but other dimensions are little changed. Excel and Precis still uses a 1.5-liter 4-cylinder Mitsubishi-designed engine, but it now has 81-horsepower (instead of 68) and multi-point fuel injection (instead of a carburetor). Base models come with a 4-speed overdrive manual transmission, others with a 5-speed manual or new 4-speed overdrive automatic. Later this year, Hyundai will introduce a sports coupe based on the Excel, but with a more potent engine. Though it's hardly grown at all, the new Excel/Precis is a more mature small car: quieter, smoother-riding, and happier with automatic transmission than the first-generation model. Economy is still a plus, but performance remains only adequate with either transmission (0-60 mph: nearly 15 seconds with automatic, about 12 with manual). Hyundai still has much to learn about taming road noise, which borders on excessive even for a low-end car. Interior room remains adequate for four, five if you must. The new Excel/Precis is a good choice for those who value rock-bottom price over other considerations.

Specifications

	3-door hatchback	5-door hatchback	4-door notchback
Wheelbase, in.	93.9	93.9	93.9
Overall length, in.	161.4	161.4	163.3
Overall width, in.	63.2	63.2	63.2
Overall height, in.	54.5	54.5	54.5
Turn diameter, ft.	30.2	30.2	30.2
Curb weight, lbs.	2040	NA	2185
Cargo vol., cu. ft.	37.9	37.9	11.4
Fuel capacity, gals.	11.9	11.9	11.9
Seating capacity	5	5	5
Front headroom, in.	37.8	37.8	37.8
Front shoulder room, in.	52.2	52.2	52.2
Front legroom, max., in.	41.7	41.7	41.7
Rear headroom, in.	37.6	37.6	37.6
Rear shoulder room, in.	52.2	52.2	52.2
Rear legroom, min., in.	33.1	33.1	33.1

Powertrain layout: transverse front engine/front-wheel drive.

Engines

	ohc I-4
Size, liters/cu. in.	1.5/90
Fuel delivery	PFI
Horsepower @ rpm	81 @ 5500
Torque (lbs./ft.) @ rpm	91 @ 3000
Availability	S

EPA city/highway mpg

4-speed OD manual	29/33
5-speed OD manual	29/36
4-speed OD automatic	28/32

Prices

Hyundai Excel	Retail Price	Dealer Invoice	Low Price
3-door hatchback, 4-speed	$5899	$5386	$5686
3-door hatchback, automatic	6474	5909	6209
GS 3-door hatchback, 5-speed	6999	6159	6459
GS 3-door hatchback, automatic	7499	6599	6899
GL 5-door hatchback, 5-speed	7599	6687	6987
GL 5-door hatchback, automatic	8099	7127	7427
4-door notchback, 4-speed	6999	6369	6669
4-door notchback, automatic	7574	6892	7192
GL 4-door notchback, 5-speed	7879	6934	7234
GL 4-door notchback, automatic	8379	7374	7674

Prices are accurate at time of printing; subject to manufacturer's change

	Retail Price	Dealer Invoice	Low Price
GLS 4-door notchback, 5-speed	8479	7207	7507
GLS 4-door notchback, automatic	8979	7647	7947
Destination charge	295	295	295

Standard equipment:

1.5-liter PFI 4-cylinder engine, 4-speed manual transmission, cloth-insert reclining front bucket seats, 60/40 split rear seat (hatchbacks), rear defogger, trip odometer, center console, locking fuel door, variable intermittent wipers, cargo cover, rear shoulder belts, 155/80R13 tires. **GS** adds: 5-speed manual or 4-speed automatic transmission, sport seats with driver's-side lumbar support and cushion height adjustments, upgraded upholstery, wheel covers, 175/70R13 tires. **GL** adds to base: digital clock, remote OS mirrors, tinted glass, rear wiper/washer (5-door), door pockets, remote fuel door and decklid/hatch releases, wheel covers, upgraded upholstery, right visor mirror, console with cassette storage, 60/40 split rear seat, rear heat ducts. **GLS** adds: AM/FM cassette, upgraded carpet, windshield sunshade band, 6-way driver's seat, tilt steering column, storage tray under passenger seat.

Optional equipment:

	Retail	Dealer	Low
Air conditioning	755	606	664
Power steering, GS & GLS	260	221	235
Power Steering/Tilt Wheel Pkg., GL	335	285	302
Alloy wheels, GS & GLS	250	200	220
Alloy Wheel Pkg., GS & GLS	325	260	285
Includes 175/70R13 tires.			
Console armrest, GL, GS & GLS	99	59	77
Excel Option Pkg.(NA base)	180	144	158
Right OS mirror, tinted glass, bodyside moldings.			
AM/FM cassette, GL & GS	295	221	252
Hi-Power AM/FM cassette, GL & GS	440	330	376
GLS	145	109	124
Power sunroof (NA base)	415	332	364
Rear spoiler, GS	50	40	44
Security system (NA base)	185	111	144

Mitsubishi Precis (1989 prices)

	Retail	Dealer	Low
3-door hatchback, 4-speed	$5499	$5004	$5123
RS 3-door hatchback, 5-speed	6699	5895	6143
LS 3-door hatchback, 5-speed	7349	6246	6632
LS 3-door hatchback, automatic	7839	6668	7077
LS 5-door hatchback, 5-speed	7599	6459	6858
LS 5-door hatchback, automatic	8089	6881	7302
Destination charge	265	265	265

Standard equipment:

1.5-liter 2bbl. 4-cylinder engine, 4-speed manual transmission, power brakes, vinyl reclining front bucket seats, folding rear seatbacks, cargo cover, variable intermittent wipers, rear defogger, rear heat ducts, trip odometer, coolant temperature gauge, low fuel and door/hatch ajar warning lights, locking fuel door, 155/80R13 all-season tires with full-size spare. **RS** adds: 5-speed manual transmission, cloth trim, upgraded door panels with map pockets, console, analog clock, wide bodyside moldings, remote fuel door and hatch releases, rear wiper/washer, dual remote mirrors, tinted glass. **LS** adds: 5-speed manual or 3-speed automatic transmission, tachometer, digital clock, upgraded steering wheel, storage tray under front passenger seat (5-door), right visor mirror, AM/FM ST ET cassette, dark upper windshield band, roll-down rear windows (5-door), wheel covers, 175/70R13 all-season tires.

Optional equipment:	Retail Price	Dealer Invoice	Low Price
Air conditioning (NA base)	735	588	662
AM/FM ST ET cassette, base & RS	295	206	251
High Power, LS	135	88	112
High Power, RS	430	280	355
Passive restraint, LS 5-door	75	64	70
Alloy Wheel Pkg., LS	295	221	258
Power steering, LS	260	221	241
Power sunroof, LS	395	316	356
Floormats	51	31	41

Hyundai Sonata

The Korean-built Sonata arrived last spring as Hyundai's compact entry and has been a slow seller so far. For 1990, Hyundai banks on several new options to bolster Sonata's appeal. Heading the list is a Hyundai-built 3.0-liter V-6 engine, copied from Japanese partner Mitsubishi. The 142-horsepower V-6 is identical to the one used in the Mitsubishi Sigma. It teams only with a 4-speed overdrive automatic transmission with Normal and Power shift ranges. A 116-horsepower 2.4-liter 4-cylinder remains standard. Included with the V-6 option are a larger fuel tank (17.2 vs. 15.8 gallons) and 195/70R14 tires. The front-drive Sonata comes as a 4-door sedan with choice of standard and plusher GLS trim. The V-6 is optional for both, as is a new 15-inch wheel/tire package with cast aluminum rims

Hyundai Sonata GLS

Specifications

	4-door notchback
Wheelbase, in.	104.3
Overall length, in.	184.3
Overall width, in.	68.9
Overall height, in.	55.4
Turn diameter, ft.	NA
Curb weight, lbs.	2717[1]
Cargo vol., cu. ft.	14.0
Fuel capacity, gals.	15.8[2]
Seating capacity	5
Front headroom, in.	38.5
Front shoulder room, in.	57.0
Front legroom, max., in.	42.4
Rear headroom, in.	37.4
Rear shoulder room, in.	56.5
Rear legroom, min., in.	37.5

1. Base model; 2926 lbs., GLS V6   2. 17.2 gals. with V-6.

Powertrain layout: transverse front engine/front-wheel drive.

Engines	ohc I-4	ohc V-6
Size, liters/cu. in.	2.4/143	3.0/181
Fuel delivery	PFI	PFI
Horsepower @ rpm	116 @ 4500	142 @ 5000
Torque (lbs./ft.) @ rpm	142 @ 3500	168 @ 2500
Availability	S	O

EPA city/highway mpg

5-speed OD manual	21/28	
4-speed OD automatic	21/26	18/24

wearing H-rated 205/60 all-season rubber. Also new are a leather interior option for the GLS and two acoustically tuned Polk Audio sound systems, including a premium setup for the GLS with 12 speakers, and a compact disc player. Motorized front shoulder belts are standard this year. The new V-6 engine doesn't drastically change Sonata. Against a 4-cylinder/automatic GLS, the V-6 version is only 0.7-second faster 0-60 mph (10.1 seconds vs. 10.8 in our tests), though the V-6 has stronger, faster response for highway passing. Sonata appeals for its roomy interior, attractively low prices, and lots of standard features.

Prices

Hyundai Sonata	Retail Price	Dealer Invoice	Low Price
4-door notchback, 5-speed	$9999	$8699	$9121
4-door notchback, automatic	10694	9366	9785
GLS 4-door notchback, 5-speed	12349	10497	11144
GLS 4-door notchback, automatic	13044	11164	11809
4-door notchback w/V-6, automatic	11389	9957	10413
GLS 4-door notchback w/V-6, automatic . .	13739	11755	12436
Destination charge	295	295	295

Standard equipment:

2.4-liter PFI 4-cylinder engine, 5-speed manual or 4-speed automatic transmission, power steering, tachometer, trip odometer, tilt steering column, rear shoulder belts, reclining front bucket seats, remote fuel door and decklid releases, rear defogger, door pockets, remote OS mirrors, tinted glass, variable intermittent wipers, visor mirror, 185/70R14 Michelin EP-X tires. **GLS** adds: power windows and locks, cruise control, power mirrors, AM/FM cassette with power antenna, 6-way driver's seat, 60/40 split rear seat with storage armrest, upgraded upholstery and carpet, voltmeter, oil pressure gauge, windshield sunshade band, underseat storage tray, lighted visor mirror, seatback pockets, full wheel covers. **V-6** models add: 3.0-liter PFI V-6, 4-speed automatic transmission, larger fuel tank, 195/70R14 tires.

Optional equipment:

Air conditioning	780	624	685
Alloy Wheel Pkg., 4-cyl.	390	312	342
Includes 195/70R14 tires.			
High Performance Alloy Wheel Pkg., V-6 .	450	360	395
Includes 205/60R15 tires.			
Leather Pkg., GLS	575	489	519

Prices are accurate at time of printing; subject to manufacturer's change

	Retail Price	Dealer Invoice	Low Price
Power Pkg., base	795	636	698
Power windows and locks, power mirrors, power antenna, cruise control.			
AM/FM cassette, base	335	251	286
Deluxe AM/FM cassette, base	450	338	384
GLS	115	87	99
Hyundai/Polk Audio sound system, base ..	795	636	698
GLS	460	385	412
Premium Hyundai/Polk system, GLS V-6 .	390	312	342
CD player, GLS	600	480	527
Remote keyless entry	125	75	98
Power glass sunroof	475	380	417
Wind deflector for sunroof	49	22	35
Security system	185	111	144
Two-tone paint, GLS	150	120	132
Floormats	60	36	47
Door edge guards	37	22	29

Infiniti M30

Infiniti M30

The entry-level model from Nissan's new Infiniti Division, the $23,500 M30 coupe is essentially an Americanized version of the Japanese-market Nissan Leopard, which dates from early 1986. A convertible goes on sale around the first

Specifications

	2-door notchback
Wheelbase, in.	103.0
Overall length, in.	188.8
Overall width, in.	66.5
Overall height, in.	54.3
Turn diameter, ft.	32.2
Curb weight, lbs.	3333
Cargo vol., cu. ft.	11.6
Fuel capacity, gals.	17.2
Seating capacity	4
Front headroom, in.	36.8
Front shoulder room, in.	53.6
Front legroom, max., in.	42.2
Rear headroom, in.	35.7
Rear shoulder room, in.	50.3
Rear legroom, min., in.	30.2

Powertrain layout: longitudinal front engine/rear-wheel drive.

Engines

	ohc V-6
Size, liters/cu. in.	3.0/181
Fuel delivery	PFI
Horsepower @ rpm	162 @ 5200
Torque (lbs./ft.) @ rpm	180 @ 3600
Availability	S

EPA city/highway mpg

4-speed OD automatic	19/25

of the year (price to be announced). Nissan admits that an M30 replacement will bow in about two years, following release of a mid-size V-6 sports sedan for 1991 to round out the Infiniti line. The rear-drive M30 comes with anti-lock brakes (ABS) and a driver's-side airbag standard. Power comes from a 162-horsepower 3.0-liter V-6, also used in the Nissan Maxima. It teams exclusively with a 4-speed over-drive automatic transmission. A standard feature inherited from the Maxima is "Sonar Suspension II," which uses an ultrasonic sensor mounted beneath the radiator to "read" road surfaces and adjust shock absorber damping to suit. A cockpit switch allows choosing soft, medium, or firm damping modes. The M30 is marketed as a fully equipped "one-price" car. Options are limited to a cellular telephone

Prices are accurate at time of printing; subject to manufacturer's change.

and a compact disc player/changer, both dealer installed. The M30 strikes us as a pleasant but unexceptional mid-size luxury coupe. From its angular styling to the tight cockpit and trunk space, this is a car of Nissan's past, and not state-of-the-art. Seating is strictly for four. There are attractions, though. The 3.0-liter V-6 provides brisk acceleration (Nissan claims 9.7 seconds 0-60 mph) and the smooth, responsive automatic transmission suits it well. While the M30 doesn't strike us as a great buy among premium coupes, it comes with Infiniti's 4-year/60,000-mile bumper-to-bumper warranty and 24-hour roadside service with free loaner cars.

Prices

Infiniti M30	Retail Price	Dealer Invoice	Low Price
2-door notchback	$23500	$18800	—
Destination charge	350	350	350

Low price not available at time of publication.

Standard equipment:

3.0-liter PFI V-6, 4-speed automatic transmission, 4-wheel disc brakes, anti-lock braking system, power steering, limited-slip differential, driver's-side airbag, cruise control, automatic climate control, Nissan/Bose AM/FM cassette with power antenna, leather upholstery, power sunroof, tinted glass, power windows and locks, power driver's seat, tilt steering column, power mirrors, remote fuel door and decklid releases, intermittent wipers, front and rear folding armrests, theft deterrent system, 215/60HR15 tires on alloy wheels.

Infiniti Q45

Infiniti, Nissan's new luxury division, opened for business November 8 with about 50 dealers selling two models. The Q45 is the Infiniti flagship. Like the Lexus LS 400, the Q45 is a rear-drive notchback sedan that aims at premium European and domestic cars. The Q45 packs an aluminum 4.5 liter, dual-cam V-8 with four valves per cylinder and 278 horsepower. Like most every other rival, it comes with

Infiniti Q45

a 4-speed automatic transmission and an anti-lock braking system. The one major option is "Super HICAS," Nissan's 4-wheel-steering system, part of an optional Touring Package that includes forged alloy wheels (versus cast alloy) and a rear spoiler. Otherwise, the Q45 is a "one-price" car with most everything standard, including a driver's-side airbag. Dealer-installed options number only two: cellular telephone and a trunk-mounted compact disc player/changer. At $38,000, the Q45 comes in quite a bit less than most European competitors but $3000 above the LS 400, though some of its standard features are optional on the Lexus. The Q45 feels more like a European sedan than the LS 400 does. The quiet, silky, and responsive powertrain gives the Q45 high refinement and good off-the-line pickup —provided you put your foot down. Like Mercedes' automatic, the Q45's starts in second gear at anything less than 3/4 throttle; only tromping on the pedal persuades the transmission's electronic control to give you first. Nissan claims 7.5 seconds for the 0-60-mph dash. In ride, the big Infiniti isn't quite as smooth as the LS 400 or Jaguar XJ6, but easily equals the BMW 7-Series and the aging Mercedes SEL. Handling and braking are top notch. Rear leg and shoulder room are unexceptional for a car this large, and rear-seat width is just sufficient for three grownups. The Q45 is a good BMW and Mercedes alternative, especially at its price, though we think Nissan hasn't reached quite as far as Toyota has with the Lexus LS 400. A full road test may change our minds. We encourage you to try both new Japanese luxury sedans.

Specifications

	4-door notchback
Wheelbase, in.	113.2
Overall length, in.	199.8
Overall width, in.	71.9
Overall height, in.	56.3
Turn diameter, ft.	37.3
Curb weight, lbs.	3950
Cargo vol., cu. ft.	14.8
Fuel capacity, gals.	22.5
Seating capacity	5
Front headroom, in.	38.2
Front shoulder room, in.	58.3
Front legroom, max., in.	43.9
Rear headroom, in.	36.3
Rear shoulder room, in.	57.5
Rear legroom, min., in.	32.0

Powertrain layout: longitudinal front engine/rear-wheel drive.

Engines	dohc V-8
Size, liters/cu. in.	4.5/274
Fuel delivery	PFI
Horsepower @ rpm	278 @ 6000
Torque (lbs./ft.) @ rpm	292 @ 4000
Availability	S

EPA city/highway mpg	
4-speed OD automatic	16/22

Prices

Infiniti Q45	Retail Price	Dealer Invoice	Low Price
4-door notchback	$38000	$30500	—
Destination charge	350	350	350

Low price not available at time of publication.

Standard equipment:

4.5-liter DOHC 32-valve V-8, 4-speed automatic transmission, 4-wheel disc brakes, anti-lock braking system, power steering, limited-slip differential, driver's-side airbag, cruise control, automatic climate control, leather reclining front bucket seats (wool is available at no charge), Nissan/Bose AM/FM cassette, power antenna, power sunroof, tinted glass, power windows and locks, power driver's seat with 2-position memory (memory includes tilt/telescopic steering column), power passenger seat, heated power mirrors, remote fuel door and decklid releases, intermittent wipers, front and rear folding armrests, theft deterrent system, 215/65R15 tires on alloy wheels.

Optional equipment:	Retail Price	Dealer Invoice	Low Price
Touring Pkg.	2500	2000	—

Super HICAS 4-wheel steering, rear spoiler, forged alloy wheels.

Note: Cellular telephone and CD changer are available as dealer-installed accessories; prices may vary.

Lexus ES 250

Lexus ES 250

The entry-level Lexus is the ES 250, a 4-door sedan based on the Toyota Camry's front-drive platform and powered by the 2.5-liter V-6 that's optional in Camry. This year the dual-cam V-6 gains a knock-control system and three horsepower, to 156. The ES 250 is available with either a 5-speed manual or a 4-speed automatic transmission with electronic shift controls. While the ES 250's chassis has the same 102.4-inch wheelbase as Camry, the Lexus version has firmer springs and shock absorbers, a rear stabilizer bar and thicker front stabilizer, and 4-wheel disc brakes with anti-lock control standard. Exterior styling is different than Camry's and body panels are made of corrosion-resistant Excelite steel. Inside, standard features include a driver's-side airbag, air conditioning, power windows and locks, and maple wood trim. Lexus predicted the ES 250 would account for 40 percent of its sales this year, but early

Specifications

	4-door notchback
Wheelbase, in.	102.4
Overall length, in.	183.0
Overall width, in.	66.9
Overall height, in.	53.1
Turn diameter, ft.	36.0
Curb weight, lbs.	3163
Cargo vol., cu. ft.	13.1
Fuel capacity, gals.	15.9
Seating capacity	5
Front headroom, in.	37.8
Front shoulder room, in.	53.9
Front legroom, max., in.	42.9
Rear headroom, in.	36.6
Rear shoulder room, in.	53.3
Rear legroom, min., in.	32.2

Powertrain layout: transverse front engine/front-wheel drive.

Engines

	dohc V-6
Size, liters/cu. in.	2.5/153
Fuel delivery	PFI
Horsepower @ rpm	156 @ 5600
Torque (lbs./ft.) @ rpm	160 @ 4400
Availability	S

EPA city/highway mpg

5-speed OD manual	19/26
4-speed OD automatic	19/25

figures showed it was running at less than 20 percent. Against nearly all "sport sedans" under $30,000 the ES 250 scores well in the performance areas, but whenever the ES 250 is compared to the Lexus LS 400, it always comes out second best, except in price. Base price is $21,050, which is the low end of the Acura Legend line, about $2000 more than a Nissan Maxima SE, and a few grand below a BMW 3-Series. The ES 250 has a sporty, European feel, with a stable, well-controlled high-speed ride, though the steering is too light at all speeds. You can buy a Camry LE with the V-6, ABS, leather seats, and fancy stereo for less than $20,000, but you don't get the ES 250's airbag, superior ride and handling ability, and longer warranty coverage. For under $25,000, there are several other good cars to consider, such as the Maxima, Legend, and the Infiniti M30.

Prices

Lexus ES 250	Retail Price	Dealer Invoice	Low Price
4-door notchback, 5-speed	$21050	$17261	—
4-door notchback, automatic	21800	17876	—
Destination charge	350	350	350

Low price not available at time of publication.

Standard equipment:

2.5-liter PFI V-6, 5-speed manual or 4-speed automatic transmission, anti-lock 4-wheel disc brakes, power steering, driver's-side airbag, air conditioning, cruise control, power windows and locks, AM/FM cassette, cloth reclining front bucket seats, folding rear seatback, bird's-eye maple trim, theft deterrent system, 195/60R15 tires on alloy wheels.

Optional equipment:

Leather Pkg.	950	760	—
Requires power driver's seat.			
Power driver's seat	250	200	—
Moonroof	700	560	—
CD player	700	525	—

Prices are accurate at time of printing; subject to manufacturer's change.

Lexus LS 400

Lexus LS 400

Toyota joins the luxury-car league for 1990 with its new Lexus Division. Among targets is Nissan's new Infiniti Division. The Lexus flagship is the $35,000 LS 400, a 4-door notchback sedan. A sports coupe will be added for 1991. About 70 dealers in major markets were in operation for the September 1 launch; 85 were supposed to be in business by January 1990. The LS 400 is a rear-drive sedan powered by a 250-horsepower 4.0-liter V-8. The V-8 mates with a 4-speed automatic transmission with electronic shift controls. Body features include corrosion-resistant Excelite II exterior panels, a 5-coat paint finish, and plastic-lined inner panels for better sound insulation. Standard equipment includes anti-lock disc brakes and a driver's-side airbag. An optional traction-control system uses the anti-lock brake sensors to detect wheel slip. If one or both of the rear wheels slip, power is momentarily retarded until traction is restored. Two suspensions are offered: a standard coil-spring system and an optional air suspension. The air suspension automatically adjusts spring and damping rates, and the ride height. The LS 400 is perhaps the quietest car we've driven. The engine is nearly silent at idle and not much louder underway; road and wind noise are low even at 80 mph. The 4.0-liter V-8 is incredibly smooth, from idle up to more than 6000 rpm. You never feel vibration or harshness, just more power building as you press on the accelerator. The LS 400 rides with reassuring stability at high speed and easily absorbs tar strips and other bumps. The optional traction-control system works nearly instantly on slippery surfaces to get the LS 400 going when other rear-drive cars are spinning their wheels. Our main gripes are over rear-seat room. There's ample leg room in back, but little room under the front seats for feet. The folding rear armrest bulges into the center passenger's lower back, effectively making this a 4-passenger sedan. While the base price for the LS 400 is $35,000, with all the extras the price can climb over

Specifications

	4-door notchback
Wheelbase, in.	110.8
Overall length, in.	196.7
Overall width, in.	71.7
Overall height, in.	55.3
Turn diameter, ft.	36.1
Curb weight, lbs.	3755
Cargo vol., cu. ft.	14.2
Fuel capacity, gals.	22.5
Seating capacity	5
Front headroom, in.	38.6
Front shoulder room, in.	57.1
Front legroom, max., in.	43.8
Rear headroom, in.	36.8
Rear shoulder room, in.	56.3
Rear legroom, min., in.	34.3

Powertrain layout: longitudinal front engine/rear-wheel drive.

Engines

	dohc V-8
Size, liters/cu. in.	4.0/242
Fuel delivery	PFI
Horsepower @ rpm	250 @ 5600
Torque (lbs./ft.) @ rpm	260 @ 4400
Availability	S

EPA city/highway mpg

4-speed OD automatic	18/23

Prices are accurate at time of printing; subject to manufacturer's change.

$43,000. That's still cheaper than most BMW or Mercedes models. The LS 400 is an extremely rewarding car that is virtually vice free, but we also encourage you to try the Infiniti Q45 for comparison.

Prices

Lexus LS 400	Retail Price	Dealer Invoice	Low Price
4-door notchback	$35000	$28000	—
w/Luxury Features Group	39400	31425	—
Destination charge	350	350	350

Low price not available at time of publication.

Standard equipment:

4.0-liter DOHC 32-valve PFI V-8, 4-speed automatic transmission, anti-lock braking system, 4-wheel disc brakes, power steering, driver's-side airbag, automatic climate control, cloth reclining front bucket seats, power windows and locks, cruise control, power mirrors, tachometer, trip odometer, coolant temperature gauge, tilt/telescopic steering column, AM/FM cassette, intermittent wipers, toolkit, first aid kit, 205/65R15 tires on alloy wheels. **Luxury Features Group Pkg.** adds: remote entry, Leather Pkg., moonroof, Lexus/Nakamichi audio system with CD changer.

Optional equipment:

Remote entry	200	160	—
Leather Pkg.	1400	1120	—
Moonroof	900	720	—
Traction control & heated front seats	1600	1280	—

Lexus LS 400

	Retail Price	Dealer Invoice	Low Price
Electronic air suspension	1500	1200	—
Requires Leather Pkg., moonroof and memory system.			
Memory system	800	640	—
Lexus/Nakamichi audio system	1000	750	—
Requires CD changer.			
Remote 6-CD auto-changer	900	675	—

Lincoln Continental

Lincoln Continental Signature

The luxury sedan that introduced Lincoln buyers to front-wheel drive and V-6 power in 1988 coasts into 1990 with minor trim and equipment changes. The grille features bolder vertical bars, the hood wears a new ornament, and the taillamps are slightly revised. An automatic power antenna also is standard, eliminating the dashboard-mounted rocker switch. New styled alloy wheels are optional, while the wire wheel covers have been dropped. As before, Continental is available in base and Signature Series versions, both powered by a 140-horsepower 3.8-liter V-6 coupled to a 4-speed automatic transmission. Airbags are standard for both the driver and front-seat passenger. The driver's-side airbag is contained in the steering wheel hub; the passenger's is loaded above the glove compartment. Continental's chassis has a computer-controlled

Prices are accurate at time of printing; subject to manufacturer's change.

damping system designed to maintain a smooth ride by adjusting in fractions of a second to changes in the road surface. Its power steering has speed-sensitive and variable-effort assist. Four-wheel anti-lock disc brakes are standard. Performance is adequate with the V-6, but a car in this class needs more power. Ford reportedly is working on a 4.6-liter V-8 for the '91 model. The well-appointed cabin accommodates five adults comfortably, and one more with some squeezing. Continental cruises quietly and rides softly, though its suspension is a touch floaty at high speeds, and the nose dives excessively under even moderate braking. Continental has a lot going for it, but the Cadillac Fleetwood and De Ville are formidable rivals by virtue of their V-8 performance and roomier interiors.

Specifications

	4-door notchback
Wheelbase, in.	109.0
Overall length, in.	205.1
Overall width, in.	72.7
Overall height, in.	55.6
Turn diameter, ft.	38.0
Curb weight, lbs.	3663
Cargo vol., cu. ft.	19.0
Fuel capacity, gals.	18.6
Seating capacity	6
Front headroom, in.	38.7
Front shoulder room, in.	57.5
Front legroom, max., in.	41.7
Rear headroom, in.	38.4
Rear shoulder room, in.	57.4
Rear legroom, min., in.	39.2

Powertrain layout: transverse front engine/front-wheel drive.

Engines

	ohv V-6
Size, liters/cu. in.	3.8/232
Fuel delivery	PFI
Horsepower @ rpm	140 @ 3800
Torque (lbs./ft.) @ rpm	215 @ 2200
Availability	S

EPA city/highway mpg

4-speed OD automatic	18/25

Prices

Lincoln Continental	Retail Price	Dealer Invoice	Low Price
4-door notchback	$29258	$25008	$25208
Signature Series 4-door notchback	31181	26623	26823
Destination charge	550	550	550

Standard equipment:

3.8-liter PFI V-6 engine, 4-speed automatic transmission, power steering, 4-wheel anti-lock disc brakes, dual front airbags, automatic climate control, 50/50 front seats with recliners, leather upholstery (cloth is available at no cost), folding front and rear armrests, rear shoulder belts, cruise control, automatic parking brake release, AM/FM cassette, tinted glass, heated power mirrors, rear defogger, remote fuel door and decklid releases, power windows and locks, intermittent wipers, tilt steering column, right visor mirror, electronic instruments with coolant temperature, oil pressure and voltage gauges, trip computer, service interval reminder, digital clock, vinyl bodyside moldings, bright rocker panel moldings, cornering lamps, 205/70R15 tires. **Signature** adds: power recliners, power passenger seat, power decklid pulldown, Autolamp system, automatic headlamp dimmer, upgraded upholstery, lighted visor mirrors, alloy wheels.

Optional equipment:

Keyless illuminated entry, base	225	189	200
Anti-theft alarm system	225	189	200
Power moonroof	1420	1193	1264
Memory seat with power lumbar	301	253	268
Cellular phone	926	778	824
Leather-wrapped steering wheel, base . . .	120	101	107
Ford JBL audio system	525	441	467
CD player	617	519	549
Insta-Clear windshield	253	213	225
Comfort/Convenience Group, base	819	688	729
Power decklid pulldown, power passenger seat, lighted visor mirrors, Headlamp Convenience Group (automatic dimmer, Autolamp system), rear floormats, power passenger recliner.			
Overhead console group	236	198	210
Digital compass, electrochromic day/night mirror.			
Styled alloy wheels, base	556	467	495
Geometric alloy wheels, base	556	467	495
Signature	NC	NC	NC
California emissions pkg.	100	84	89

Prices are accurate at time of printing; subject to manufacturer's change.

Lincoln Mark VII

Lincoln Mark VII LSC

Lincoln's luxury 2-door coupe enters 1990 with a revised grille, a new dashboard, and a standard driver's-side airbag. The rear-drive Mark VII continues in two models: the sporty LSC and the luxury Bill Blass Designer Series. Both use a 225-horsepower 5.0-liter V-8 coupled to a 4-speed overdrive automatic transmission. For '90, the sporty LSC version gets standard BBS alloy wheels and revised seats. Rear shoulder belts have been added on both models, and the front head restraints are smaller to improve visibility. The new dash places the audio controls higher for easier use, but the optional compact-disc player now replaces rather than supplements the cassette deck. Puncture-sealant tires are dropped from the options list. Mark VII's V-8 has the muscle for brisk takeoffs, though you have to wait out the transmission's tendency toward tardy downshifts before the engine's abundant passing power is tapped. In normal braking, the pedal is spongy and the front end dips noticeably, but in emergencies the standard anti-lock system stops this heavy coupe with fine control. The LSC corners flatly and has a stable highway ride, but it also suffers some impact harshness that isn't felt in the Bill Blass model with its softer suspension and smaller tires. There's spacious seating for two in front. Rear-seat leg room is ample for adults, but there's not much head room, and the center driveline hump discourages squeezing three

                 CONSUMER GUIDE®

people into the back. Usable trunk space is small for a car this size. On balance, the Mark VII has much to offer, including a reasonable price for the luxury-coupe class. Still, don't decide without first trying the Acura Legend Coupe and the Cadillac Eldorado, both of which have front-wheel drive.

Specifications

	2-door notchback
Wheelbase, in.	108.5
Overall length, in.	202.8
Overall width, in.	70.9
Overall height, in.	54.2
Turn diameter, ft.	40.1
Curb weight, lbs.	3779
Cargo vol., cu. ft.	14.2
Fuel capacity, gals.	22.1
Seating capacity	5
Front headroom, in.	37.8
Front shoulder room, in.	56.0
Front legroom, max., in.	42.0
Rear headroom, in.	37.1
Rear shoulder room, in.	57.8
Rear legroom, min., in.	36.9

Powertrain layout: longitudinal front engine/rear-wheel drive.

Engines

	ohv V-8
Size, liters/cu. in.	5.0/302
Fuel delivery	PFI
Horsepower @ rpm	225 @ 4200
Torque (lbs./ft.) @ rpm	300 @ 3200
Availability	S

EPA city/highway mpg

4-speed OD automatic	17/24

Prices

Lincoln Mark VII	Retail Price	Dealer Invoice	Low Price
Bill Blass 2-door notchback	$29246	$24971	$25171
LSC 2-door notchback	29468	25258	25458
Destination charge	555	555	555

Prices are accurate at time of printing; subject to manufacturer's change.

Standard equipment:

LSC: 5.0-liter PFI V-8, 4-speed automatic transmission, power steering, 4-wheel disc brakes, anti-lock braking system, driver's-side airbag, rear shoulder belts, electronic air suspension with automatic level control, automatic climate control, overhead console with warning lights and reading lamps, power decklid release, rear defogger, power windows and locks, remote fuel door release, tinted glass, automatic headlamp dimmer, Autolamp system, illuminated entry, analog instruments including tachometer and coolant temperature gauge, heated power mirrors, AM/FM cassette, power seats, cruise control, tilt steering column, intermittent wipers, full-length console with lockable compartment, leather interior trim including steering wheel, shift knob, and console, handling suspension, P225/60R16 tires on aluminum wheels. **Bill Blass** has electronic instrument cluster, prairie mist metallic clearcoat paint, bodyside and decklid paint stripes, choice of leather, UltraSuede or cloth/leather seat trim, P215/70R15 tires on wire-spoke aluminum wheels.

Optional equipment:	Retail Price	Dealer Invoice	Low Price
Traction-Lok axle	101	86	90
Anti-theft alarm system	225	189	200
Power moonroof	1420	1193	1264
Cellular phone	849	713	756
AM/FM radio w/CD player	299	251	266
Automatic day/night mirror	89	75	79
Ford JBL audio system	525	441	467
Engine block heater	26	22	23
California emissions pkg.	100	84	89

Lincoln Town Car

Lincoln's best-selling model receives its first major redesign since it was introduced under the Town Car label for 1980. The V-8 engine and rear-drive platform of the original Town Car are retained, but the previous car's sharply squared-off body gives way to rounded corners patterned after those on the smaller Continental. Base, mid-level Signature Series, and top-shelf Cartier Designer Series are offered. The size and weight are virtually identical to the earlier Town Car's, but the '90 model is far more aerodynamic. Anti-lock brakes are a new option, while the revamped interior incorporates front airbags on both the driver and passenger side. Also new are the instrument

Lincoln Town Car

Specifications

	4-door notchback
Wheelbase, in.	117.4
Overall length, in.	220.2
Overall width, in.	78.1
Overall height, in.	56.7
Turn diameter, ft.	40.0
Curb weight, lbs.	4025
Cargo vol., cu. ft.	22.0
Fuel capacity, gals.	18.0
Seating capacity	6
Front headroom, in.	39.0
Front shoulder room, in.	62.0
Front legroom, max., in.	42.5
Rear headroom, in.	38.1
Rear shoulder room, in.	62.0
Rear legroom, min., in.	42.8

Powertrain layout: longitudinal front engine/rear-wheel drive.

Engines

	ohv V-8
Size, liters/cu. in.	5.0/302
Fuel delivery	PFI
Horsepower @ rpm	150 @ 3200
Torque (lbs./ft.) @ rpm	270 @ 2000
Availability	S

EPA city/highway mpg

4-speed OD automatic	17/24

Prices are accurate at time of printing; subject to manufacturer's change.

panel, seat design, rear shoulder belts, automatic power antenna, and a remote fuel-door release. The power steering is now speed sensitive, and the rear suspension is self-leveling via air springs. The 5.0-liter V-8 carries over as before, except that on Cartier models it exhales through dual exhausts for slightly higher power output. The new Town car is every bit as imposing as its predecessor, but not nearly as ponderous. The interior is airy and far more contemporary, the seats are firmer, and the new dashboard is easier to use. The cabin is still quite traditional in its shiny surfaces and imitation wood, but we laud the dual airbags. The rear seat is cavernous and comfortable. Isolation from the road is nearly complete, yet firmer steering and a recalibrated suspension provide just enough feedback to avoid the numb, floaty feel of the previous Town Car and the current Cadillac Brougham. Power is adequate, though the 150-horsepower V-8 is close to being overmatched by the 4100-pound curb weight. The '91 Town Car reportedly will be the first Ford product with the new 4.6-liter V-8, which should produce about 180 horsepower. Also expect a traction-control system for '91.

Prices

Lincoln Town Car	Retail Price	Dealer Invoice	Low Price
4-door notchback	$27986	$23908	$24908
Signature 4-door notchback	30721	26205	27205
Cartier 4-door notchback	32809	27958	28958
Destination charge	555	555	555

Standard equipment:

5.0-liter PFI V-8, 4-speed automatic transmission, speed-sensitive power steering, dual front airbags, automatic climate control, cloth reclining front split bench seat with folding center armrests, power driver's seat, folding rear armrest, power windows and locks, heated power mirrors, tinted glass, intermittent wipers, cruise control, tilt steering column, AM/FM cassette with power antenna, electronic instruments with coolant temperature gauge, front and rear reading lights, lighted right visor mirror, rear shoulder belts, remote fuel door and decklid releases, rear defogger, cornering lights, automatic parking brake release, 215/70R15 tires. **Signature** adds: power passenger seat, lighted visor mirrors, leather-wrapped steering wheel, power decklid pulldown, automatic headlamp dimmer, Autolamp system, door pockets, keyless illuminated entry, floormats. **Cartier** adds: dual exhaust, Ford JBL audio system, cloth and supple leather upholstery (supple leather is available at no extra cost), memory power seats with power recliners and lumbar support.

Optional equipment:

	Retail Price	Dealer Invoice	Low Price
Anti-lock braking system	936	786	833
Traction-Lok axle	101	85	90
Keyless illuminated entry, base	225	189	200
Anti-theft alarm system	225	189	200
Power moonroof	1420	1193	1264
Programmable memory seat, base & Signature	502	422	447
Cellular phone	849	713	756
Leather-wrapped steering wheel, base	120	101	107
AM/FM radio w/CD player	299	251	266
Ford JBL audio system, base & Signature	525	441	467
Electrochromic day/night mirror	99	83	88
Insta-Clear windshield	253	213	225
Base requires Comfort/Convenience Group.			
Leather seat trim, Signature	509	427	453
Base	570	479	507
Comfort/Convenience Group, base	694	583	618
Power decklid pulldown, lighted left visor mirror, Headlamp Convenience Group (automatic dimmer, Autolamp system), power passenger seat, floormats.			
Dual exhaust	83	70	74
Class III Trailer Tow Pkg.	417	351	371
High altitude	335	281	298
Geometric spoke alloy wheels, base	556	467	495
Signature	NC	NC	NC
Turbine spoke alloy wheels, base	556	467	495
California emissions pkg.	100	84	89

Mazda Miata

Built in Japan but conceived at Mazda's U.S. headquarters in California, Miata is the 2-seat roadster that became the star of the automotive world when it debuted last summer. Some Mazda dealers were getting as much as $5000 over Miata's suggested retail price of $13,800 because so many eager buyers were waiting in line for this new sports car. And, some of those who bought Miatas turned around and sold them at an even greater profit. Only 40,000 Miatas

Prices are accurate at time of printing; subject to manufacturer's change.

Mazda Miata

are scheduled to be sent to the U.S. during calendar 1990, though if high demand continues then Mazda might increase the allotment. The rear-drive Miata comes with a 116-horsepower, dual-cam 1.6-liter engine and a 5-speed manual transmission. An automatic transmission is planned for the future. Standard features include 4-wheel disc brakes, a driver's-side airbag, and a manual folding top that can be raised or lowered by one person from inside the car. Power steering and a removable hardtop that weighs about 40 pounds are optional. Miata is great fun to drive; if only you could buy it for suggested retail price. Our biggest complaint about Miata so far is that high demand and dealer greed have driven selling prices sky high. When it comes to driving the Miata, we have lots of good things to say. We timed a Miata at 8.6 seconds 0-60 mph, which is certainly quick. With one test car we averaged 29 mpg in an even city/highway driving mix, and in another we averaged nearly 27 mpg in city/suburban commuting. The cockpit is low and not that wide, but never feels cramped, while the clean, simple dashboard has easy-to-read analog gauges and handy controls. Miata is a great entry-level sports car—everything you ever liked about British roadsters, with none of the hassle.

Specifications

	2-door conv.
Wheelbase, in.	89.2
Overall length, in.	155.4
Overall width, in.	65.9
Overall height, in.	48.2
Turn diameter, ft.	30.6
Curb weight, lbs.	2182
Cargo vol., cu. ft.	3.6
Fuel capacity, gals.	11.9
Seating capacity	2
Front headroom, in.	37.1
Front shoulder room, in.	50.4
Front legroom, max., in.	42.7
Rear headroom, in.	—
Rear shoulder room, in.	—
Rear legroom, min., in.	—

Powertrain layout: longitudinal front engine/rear-wheel drive.

Engines

	dohc I-4
Size, liters/cu. in.	1.6/97
Fuel delivery	PFI
Horsepower @ rpm	116 @ 6500
Torque (lbs./ft.) @ rpm	100 @ 5500
Availability	S

EPA city/highway mpg

5-speed OD manual	25/30

Prices

Mazda Miata	Retail Price	Dealer Invoice	Low Price
2-door convertible	$13800	$11963	$13800
Destination charge	269	269	269

Standard equipment:

1.6-liter DOHC 16-valve PFI 4-cylinder engine, 5-speed manual transmission, 4-wheel disc brakes, driver's-side airbag, cloth reclining front bucket seats, tachometer, coolant temperature gauge, trip odometer, intermittent wipers, 185/60R14 tires.

Prices are accurate at time of printing; subject to manufacturer's change.

Optional equipment:

	Retail Price	Dealer Invoice	Low Price
Air Conditioning	795	635	795
Detachable hardtop	1100	891	1100
Requires Option Pkg. A or B.			
Option Pkg. A	1145	962	1145
Power steering, alloy wheels, leather-wrapped steering wheel, AM/FM cassette.			
Option Pkg. B	1730	1453	1730
Pkg. A plus power windows, cruise control, headrest speakers.			
Limited-slip differential	250	200	250
CD player	600	480	600
Requires Option Pkg. A or B.			
Floormats	59	41	59

Mazda MPV

Mazda MPV 4WD

Rear anti-lock brakes are standard on all MPV models and the 4-wheel-drive version is available with a new 5-speed manual transmission as the major changes this year on Mazda's minivan. The rear-drive MPV ("Multi-Purpose Vehicle") was introduced first and was followed by the 4WD model, which for 1989 came only with a 150-horsepower 3.0-liter V-6 engine and 4-speed automatic transmission.

Specifications

	4-door van
Wheelbase, in.	110.4
Overall length, in.	175.8
Overall width, in.	71.9
Overall height, in.	68.1
Turn diameter, ft.	36.1[1]
Curb weight, lbs.	3459[2]
Cargo vol., cu. ft.	37.5
Fuel capacity, gals.	15.9[3]
Seating capacity	7
Front headroom, in.	40.0
Front shoulder room, in.	57.5
Front legroom, max., in.	40.6
Rear headroom, in.	39.0
Rear shoulder room, in.	57.5
Rear legroom, min., in.	34.8

1. 39.6, 4WD   2. 3920 lbs., 4WD   3. 19.6 gals., V-6; 19.8 gals., 4WD.

Powertrain layout: longitudinal front engine/rear-wheel drive or on-demand 4WD.

Engines

	ohc I-4	ohc V-6
Size, liters/cu. in.	2.6/159	3.0/180
Fuel delivery	PFI	PFI
Horsepower @ rpm	121 @ 4600	150 @ 5000
Torque (lbs./ft.) @ rpm	149 @ 3500	165 @ 4000
Availability	S	O

EPA city/highway mpg

5-speed OD manual	20/24	18/22
4-speed OD automatic	19/24	17/22

This year, a 5-speed manual is standard on the 4WD MPV and the automatic is optional. The 4WD system is the on-demand type that can be engaged by an interior switch. A 121-horsepower 2.6-liter 4-cylinder is standard on the rear-drive MPV and the V-6 is optional. MPV is unique among minivans for its swing-out rear side door; other compact vans have a sliding side door. The MPV's rear door is a one-piece liftgate. Seats for five are standard (two front buckets and a removable 3-place bench) and seats for seven are optional (two front buckets, a removable 2-place middle bench, and a folding 3-place rear bench). The MPV differs

Prices are accurate at time of printing; subject to manufacturer's change.

from other Japanese-made minivans in that it was designed primarily as a passenger vehicle, not as a cargo vehicle. It shows; the MPV is the most car-like minivan since the front-drive Dodge Caravan/Plymouth Voyager. The MPV is slightly shorter than the standard-size Caravan/Voyager and has a similar low profile. The compact dimensions aid parking and maneuverability, and the MPV matches the Chrysler minivans in overall driving ease. We averaged 12.4 seconds to 60 mph with a V-6/automatic. The 4-cylinder engine will be some two seconds slower to 60 mph and have less snap for highway passing. The MPV lives up to its name by combining station-wagon comfort and driving ease with minivan versatility in a compact package. The MPV is the best Japanese minivan so far and the best alternative to the Chrysler minivans.

Prices

Mazda MPV	Retail Price	Dealer Invoice	Low Price
Wagon, 2-row seating, 2.6, 5-speed	$13699	$11876	$12376
Wagon, 2-row seating, 2.6, automatic . . .	14399	12478	12978
Wagon, 3-row seating, 2.6, 5-speed	14944	12947	13447
Wagon, 3-row seating, 2.6, automatic . . .	15644	13549	14049
Wagon, 3-row seating, 3.0, automatic . . .	16394	14194	14694
4WD wagon, 3-row seating, 3.0, 5-speed .	18894	16344	16844
4WD wagon, 3-row seating, 3.0, automatic .	19394	16774	17274
Destination charge	319	319	319

Standard equipment:

2.6-liter PFI 4-cylinder or 3.0-liter PFI 6-cylinder engine, 5-speed manual or 4-speed automatic transmission, anti-lock rear brakes, power steering, cloth reclining front bucket seats, 3-passenger middle seat (with 2-row seating), 2-passenger middle and 3-passenger rear seats (with 3-row seating), power mirrors, tachometer, coolant temperature gauge, trip odometer, tilt steering column, intermittent wipers, illuminated entry, rear wiper/washer, tinted glass, AM/FM cassette, lighted visor mirrors, floormats, remote fuel door release, 205/70R14 all-season SBR tires. **4WD** adds: selectable full-time 4WD.

Optional equipment:

Single air conditioning	849	696	773
Dual air conditioning (3.0 req.)	1497	1228	1363

	Retail Price	Dealer Invoice	Low Price
Cold Pkg.	298	256	277
HD battery, larger windshield washer solvent reservoir, rear heater.			
Option Pkg. A	995	826	911
Power windows and locks, cruise control, privacy glass; not available with 2-row seating or 4WD.			
Option Pkg. B, 2WD	1635	1465	1550
Pkg. A plus alloy wheels, color-keyed trim, electronic heater mode control.			
Option Pkg. C, 4WD	1185	984	1085
Color-keyed trim, electronic heater mode control.			
CD player (3.0/auto req.)	699	559	629
Two-tone paint	251	206	229
Towing Pkg., 2WD w/3.0	498	428	463
4WD automatic	398	342	370
Transmission oil cooler, HD radiator and fan, conventional spare, automatic load leveling (2WD).			
Floormats, w/2-row seating	59	42	51
w/3.0	84	59	72

Mazda RX-7

Mazda RX-7 Turbo

Mazda's rotary-powered sports car was mechanically and cosmetically revised when it arrived late in the 1989 model year, so for 1990 there is only one change of note: A driver's-side airbag is standard on the convertible. Other models continue with motorized front shoulder belts to satisfy the federal passive-restraint requirement. Last spring's revisions included 14 more horsepower for the naturally aspirated twin-rotor engine and 18 more for the turbocharged version. At the same time, the 4-speed automatic transmission gained electronic shift controls and a gear hold feature, plus it became available on the convertible. The 1990 RX-7 lineup includes GTU, GTU S, GXL, Turbo, and convertible models, all with rear-wheel drive. All but the Turbo use the 160-horsepower naturally aspirated rotary engine. The Turbo is rated at 200 horsepower. The GXL is available in 2-seat and 2+2 configurations; the others are 2-seaters.

Specifications	3-door hatchback	2+2 3-door hatchback	2-door conv.
Wheelbase, in.	95.7	95.7	95.7
Overall length, in.	169.9	169.9	169.9
Overall width, in.	66.5	66.5	66.5
Overall height, in.	49.8	49.8	49.8
Turn diameter, ft.	32.2	32.2	32.2
Curb weight, lbs.	2800	2888	3045
Cargo vol., cu. ft.	6.5	6.5	4.1
Fuel capacity, gals.	18.5	18.5	18.5
Seating capacity	2	4	2
Front headroom, in.	37.2	37.2	36.3
Front shoulder room, in.	52.8	52.8	52.8
Front legroom, max., in.	43.7	43.7	43.7
Rear headroom, in.	—	33.0	—
Rear shoulder room, in.	—	NA	—
Rear legroom, min., in.	—	NA	—

Powertrain layout: longitudinal front engine/rear-wheel drive.

Engines	2-rotor Wankel	Turbo 2-rotor Wankel
Size, liters/cu. in.	1.3/80	1.3/80
Fuel delivery	PFI	PFI
Horsepower @ rpm	160 @ 7000	200 @ 6500
Torque (lbs./ft.) @ rpm	140 @ 4000	196 @ 3500
Availability	S	S
EPA city/highway mpg		
5-speed OD manual	17/25	16/24
4-speed OD automatic	17/23	

All models have 4-wheel disc brakes, while the Turbo also has a standard anti-lock system. Mazda's rotary engines provide thrilling acceleration, at least with the 5-speed manual. The lack of low-end torque is a handicap with automatic transmission. We tested a GXL with automatic that needed 10.4 seconds to reach 60 mph—mediocre when cars that cost half as much can be quicker. You'll get much more enjoyment from an RX-7 with the 5-speed manual, which makes better use of the rotary's high-revving character. As with most sports cars, the RX-7 has a firm suspension that makes the ride rough. There's compensation in sharp, responsive, agile handling. RX-7 prices have climbed considerably the past few years, but you might be able to get a good deal on one now.

Prices

Mazda RX-7	Retail Price	Dealer Invoice	Low Price
GTU 3-door hatchback	$17880	$15512	$16262
GTU S 3-door hatchback	20180	17295	18045
2-door convertible	26530	22427	23177
GXL 3-door hatchback	22330	18899	19649
GXL 2 + 2 3-door hatchback	22830	19319	20069
Turbo 3-door hatchback	26530	22427	23177
Destination charge	269	269	269

Standard equipment:

GTU: 1.3-liter PFI rotary engine, 5-speed manual transmission, 4-wheel disc brakes, power steering, cloth reclining front bucket seats, theft deterrent system, AM/FM cassette with power diversity antenna, full console with storage, rear defogger, remote fuel door and hatch releases, tinted glass, power mirrors, intermittent wipers, 205/60VR15 SBR tires on alloy wheels. **GTU S** adds: limited-slip differential, front air dam with fog lights, sill extensions, 205/55VR16 tires. **GXL** adds to GTU: air conditioning, fog lights, cargo cover, cruise control, power windows and locks, graphic equalizer, door pockets, tilt steering column, driver's seat cushion angle and lumbar support adjustments, leather-wrapped steering wheel and shift knob, rear wiper/washer. **Turbo** deletes tilt steering column and adds: turbocharged, intercooled engine, anti-lock braking system, air dam with fog lights, sill extensions, auto adjusting suspension, 205/55VR16 tires. **Convertible** adds to GTU: power top, driver's-side airbag, CD player, leather upholstery, cruise control, power windows and locks, fog lights, door pockets, leather-wrapped steering wheel and shift knob, tilt steering column.

Prices are accurate at time of printing; subject to manufacturer's change.

Optional equipment:

	Retail Price	Dealer Invoice	Low Price
4-speed automatic transmission	750	638	661
Available on GTU, convertible and GXL 2-seater.			
Air conditioning, GTU, GTU S & conv. . . .	859	688	737
Graphic equalizer, GTU	219	175	188
CD player, GXL & Turbo	875	705	752
Power sunroof, GTU	650	553	573
Leather seats, GXL 2-seater	850	680	729
Turbo	1000	800	857
Armrest lid, conv.	55	42	46
Floormats	59	41	48

Mazda 323/Protege

Mazda Protege LX

The subcompact 323 has been redesigned, offering a choice of two body styles, three engines, and two distinct model series. The 3-door hatchback is still called 323, while the 4-door sedan is called 323 Protege. Mazda touts Protege as roomier than competitors such as the Honda Civic, Nissan Sentra, and Toyota Corolla. Though they have similar front styling, Protege and the hatchback share none of their sheetmetal. Protege has a 98.4-inch wheelbase, nearly four inches longer than last year's 323 sedan and nearly two inches longer than the new hatchback's. The base Protege SE is powered by a 103-horsepower 1.8-liter

4-cylinder engine. The LX uses a 125-horsepower 1.8 with dual camshafts. Hatchbacks come in base and SE trim, both with an 82-horsepower 1.6-liter 4-cylinder carried over from the previous 323. All models have front-wheel drive; a 4-wheel-drive sedan, with a permanently engaged 4WD system and the 103-horsepower engine, is scheduled to be added at mid-year in all states but California. Not returning from last year's roster are the sporty GTX 4WD hatchback and the 132-horsepower turbocharged 1.6-liter that

Specifications

	323 3-door hatchback	Protege 4-door notchback
Wheelbase, in.	96.5	98.4
Overall length, in.	163.6	171.5
Overall width, in.	65.7	65.9
Overall height, in.	54.3	54.1
Turn diameter, ft.	31.5	32.2
Curb weight, lbs.	2238	2359[1]
Cargo vol., cu. ft.	15.8	12.8
Fuel capacity, gals.	13.2	14.5[2]
Seating capacity	5	5
Front headroom, in.	38.6	38.4
Front shoulder room, in.	53.6	53.4
Front legroom, max., in.	42.2	42.2
Rear headroom, in.	37.6	37.1
Rear shoulder room, in.	53.4	53.7
Rear legroom, min., in.	34.2	34.6

1. 2634 lbs., 4WD   2. 15.9 gals., 4WD.

Powertrain layout: transverse front engine/front-wheel drive or permanent 4WD.

Engines

	ohc I-4	ohc I-4	dohc I-4
Size, liters/cu. in.	1.6/97	1.8/112	1.8/112
Fuel delivery	PFI	PFI	PFI
Horsepower @ rpm	82 @ 5000	103 @ 5500	125 @ 6500
Torque (lbs./ft.) @ rpm	92 @ 5000	111 @ 4000	114 @ 4500
Availability	S[1]	S[2]	S[3]

EPA city/highway mpg

5-speed OD manual	29/37	28/36	25/30
4-speed OD automatic	26/33	24/31	23/29

1. 323   2. Protege SE and 4WD.   3. Protege LX.

Prices are accurate at time of printing; subject to manufacturer's change.

came with it. The basic design for the 323/Protege will be used for the 1991 Ford Escort and Mercury Tracer, which will go on sale next spring. Mazda will supply most mechanical components, while Ford will do its own styling. Ford owns an equity interest in Mazda. The new 323 and Protege have spacious interiors with ample front head room and generous leg room. In the back seat, there's plenty of leg room, thanks to this year's longer wheelbase. Our early impressions of the Protege 4-door and the 323 hatchback are that they're well-designed, roomy small cars with above-average performance.

Prices

Mazda 323/Protege	Retail Price	Dealer Invoice	Low Price
323 3-door hatchback	$6599	$6121	$6321
323 SE 3-door hatchback	8329	7498	7698
Protege SE 4-door notchback	9339	8313	8613
Protege LX 4-door notchback	10349	9099	9399
Protege 4WD 4-door notchback	NA	NA	NA
Destination charge	269	269	269

Standard equipment:

323: 1.6-liter PFI 4-cylinder engine, 5-speed manual transmission, rear defogger, center console, coolant temperature gauge, trip odometer, 155SR13 tires. **323 SE** adds: tinted glass, cloth upholstery, upgraded interior trim, 175/70SR13 tires. **Protege SE** has: 1.8-liter SOHC 16-valve 4-cylinder engine, 5-speed manual transmission, cloth reclining front bucket seats, coolant temperature gauge, trip odometer, tinted glass, dual outside mirrors, 175/70SR13 tires. **4WD** adds: power steering, intermittent wipers, 185/65R14 tires. **LX** adds: DOHC 16-valve engine, 4-wheel disc brakes, tachometer, power mirrors, tilt steering column, upgraded upholstery, 185/60R14 tires.

Optional equipment:

4-speed automatic transmission	700	630	633
Air conditioning	785	630	674
Power steering, 323, Protege SE	250	213	220
AM/FM cassette, Protege	450	342	377
Power sunroof, Protege LX	555	444	476
Alloy wheels, Protege LX	400	320	343
Cruise control, Protege LX	220	176	189
Power windows & locks, Protege LX	300	240	257

Mazda 626/MX-6

Mazda 626 LX

Anti-lock brakes (ABS) are a new option for the LX models of the 626 sedans and the MX-6 sports coupe, which are derived from the same front-drive platform. The optional anti-lock feature includes rear disc brakes in place of the standard drum brakes. Previously, ABS was available only on GT models. The 626 4-door sedan is being built at Mazda's Flat Rock, Michigan, plant, where the MX-6 and similar Ford Probe are built. All 626 Touring Sedan 5-door hatchbacks, and some of the 626 4-doors and MX-6 models are still imported from Japan. All models wear new styling touches for 1990. The 626 has a new grille and taillamps, while the MX-6 has new bumpers, wider body-side moldings, a body-color grille, and new taillamps. Model and engine choices are similar for the 626 and MX-6 lines. DX and LX models are powered by a 110-horsepower 2.2-liter 4-cylinder. GT models use a 145-horsepower turbocharged 2.2. In addition, the MX-6 GT 4WS has Mazda's 4-wheel-steering system. We tested a 626 LX for more than 12,000 miles, averaging nearly 25 mpg overall while regularly getting more than 30 mpg in highway driving. Our test car suffered no mechanical problems, though the driver's front shoulder belt had to be replaced after the motor quit. The 110-horsepower engine provides fairly brisk acceleration and lively passing power, but the automatic transmission shifts harshly and balks at downshifting to furnish more power. The 145-horsepower turbo engine delivers ferocious acceleration, but excessive torque steer as well; the

Prices are accurate at time of printing; subject to manufacturer's change.

front end pulls markedly to one side under hard acceleration. These cars are more appealing to us with the wider availability of anti-lock brakes. If you're interested in the MX-6, also check out the similar Ford Probe.

Specifications

	MX-6 2-door notchback	626 4-door notchback	626 5-door hatchback
Wheelbase, in.	99.0	101.4	101.4
Overall length, in.	177.0	179.3	179.3
Overall width, in.	66.5	66.5	66.5
Overall height, in.	53.5	55.5	54.1
Turn diameter, ft.	35.3[1]	36.0	36.0
Curb weight, lbs.	2560[2]	2610	2710
Cargo vol., cu. ft.	15.4	15.9	22.4
Fuel capacity, gals.	15.9	15.9	15.9
Seating capacity	4	5	5
Front headroom, in.	38.4	39.0	38.7
Front shoulder room, in.	54.9	54.9	54.9
Front legroom, max., in.	43.6	43.7	43.6
Rear headroom, in.	37.8	37.8	37.2
Rear shoulder room, in.	53.3	54.9	54.9
Rear legroom, min., in.	31.8	36.6	32.9

1. 33.5 ft. GT 4WS   2. 2920 lbs., GT 4WS.

Powertrain layout: transverse front engine/front-wheel drive.

Engines

	ohc I-4	Turbo ohc I-4
Size, liters/cu. in.	2.2/133	2.2/133
Fuel delivery	PFI	PFI
Horsepower @ rpm	110 @ 4700	145 @ 4300
Torque (lbs./ft.) @ rpm	130 @ 3000	190 @ 3500
Availability	S	S

EPA city/highway mpg

5-speed OD manual	24/31	21/28
4-speed OD automatic	22/28	19/25

Prices

Mazda 626/MX-6	Retail Price	Dealer Invoice	Low Price
626 DX 4-door notchback	$12459	$10872	$11172
626 LX 4-door notchback	13929	12004	12304
626 LX Touring Sedan 5-door hatchback	14129	12175	12475

	Retail Price	Dealer Invoice	Low Price
626 GT Touring Sedan 5-door hatchback .	15699	13518	13818
MX-6 DX 2-door notchback	12279	10594	10794
MX-6 LX 2-door notchback	13769	11730	11930
MX-6 GT 2-door notchback	16029	13640	13840
MX-6 GT 4WS 2-door notchback	17229	14654	14854
Destination charge	269	269	269

Standard equipment:

DX: 2.2-liter PFI 4-cylinder engine, 5-speed manual transmission, power steering, cloth reclining front bucket seats, AM/FM cassette, tachometer, coolant temperature gauge, tip odometer, tilt steering column, tinted glass, intermittent wipers, center console, rear defogger, remote fuel door and trunk/hatch releases, remote mirrors, 185/70R14 tires. **LX** adds: power windows and locks, cruise control, upgraded audio system with subwoofer, power antenna, map lights, variable intermittent wipers; **Touring Sedan** has removable shelf panel and rear wiper/washer. **GT** adds: turbocharged, intercooled engine, 4-wheel disc brakes, auto adjusting suspension (except MX-6 4WS), graphic equalizer (MX-6), 195/60HR15 tires on alloy wheels.

Optional equipment:

4-speed automatic transmission	720	634	645
Not available on MX-6 4WS.			
Anti-lock brakes, GT	1000	850	881
w/rear disc brakes, LX	1150	977	1013
Air conditioning	810	649	695
Rear spoiler, MX-6 LX	375	300	321
Alloy wheels, LX	400	320	343
Power moonroof, LX & GT	700	560	600
Standard on MX-6 4WS.			
Cruise control, DX	220	176	189
Theft alarm, LX & GT	100	80	86
CD player, 626 LX & GT, MX-6 GT	700	560	600
205/60 tires, MX-6 GT	30	24	26
Armrest, 626 LX & GT	57	44	48
Floormats	59	41	48

Mazda 929

The rear-drive 929, Mazda's flagship sedan, rolls into its third model year in the U.S. with a mild facelift and a sportier model powered by a stronger engine. The new 929 S has a 190-horsepower version of Mazda's 3.0-liter V-6

Prices are accurate at time of printing; subject to manufacturer's change.

Mazda 929 S

with dual camshafts and four valves per cylinder, and it exhales into a dual exhaust system with two catalytic converters. The base 929 returns with last year's 158-horsepower 3.0, with a single camshaft and three valves per cylinder. Both models come only with a 4-speed automatic transmission. The 929 S also has firmer springs and shock absorbers than the base model and standard anti-lock brakes (ABS remains optional on the base). Styling changes are a new grille and bumpers, lower body cladding, and contrasting lower-body paint. Inside, a new steering wheel houses the cruise-control switches and the seats have been redesigned for more lateral support. Gone from last year's options list are the slow-selling Automatic Adjusting Suspension and electronic instrument cluster. The 929 S engine is much livelier starting off and in highway passing than the base engine, which delivers enough power to keep pace with traffic but feels lethargic rather than eager. The 929 S engine is more energetic, responding quickly to the throttle and running smoothly to higher speeds. The 929 S has more cornering power thanks to its firmer suspension and wider tires, without a big penalty in ride quality. The base 929 copes well with sharp bumps and handily absorbs rough roads. The spacious interior provides ample room for up to five adults, while trunk space is more than adequate. The 929 is a functional, comfortable car, but it looks and feels bland compared to rivals such as the Acura Legend and Nissan Maxima SE.

Specifications

	4-door notchback
Wheelbase, in.	106.7
Overall length, in.	193.9
Overall width, in.	67.9
Overall height, in.	54.5
Turn diameter, ft.	35.4
Curb weight, lbs.	3477
Cargo vol., cu. ft.	15.1
Fuel capacity, gals.	18.5
Seating capacity	5
Front headroom, in.	37.8
Front shoulder room, in.	55.2
Front legroom, max., in.	43.3
Rear headroom, in.	37.4
Rear shoulder room, in.	55.2
Rear legroom, min., in.	37.0

Powertrain layout: longitudinal front engine/rear-wheel drive.

Engines

	ohc V-6	dohc V-6
Size, liters/cu. in.	3.0/180	3.0/180
Fuel delivery	PFI	PFI
Horsepower @ rpm	158 @ 5500	190 @ 5600
Torque (lbs./ft.) @ rpm	170 @ 4000	191 @ 4500
Availability	S	S

EPA city/highway mpg

	ohc V-6	dohc V-6
4-speed OD automatic	19/23	18/22

Prices

Mazda 929	Retail Price	Dealer Invoice	Low Price
4-door notchback	$23300	$19474	$19974
S 4-door notchback	24800	20719	21219
Destination charge	269	269	269

Standard equipment:

3.0-liter PFI V-6 engine, 4-speed automatic transmission, power steering, 4-wheel disc brakes, automatic climate control, cloth reclining front bucket seats, power driver's seat, power windows and locks, cruise control, leather-wrapped steering wheel, power mirrors, power moonroof, rear armrest, tachometer, coolant temperature gauge, voltmeter, trip odometer, intermit-

Prices are accurate at time of printing; subject to manufacturer's change.

tent wipers, AM/FM cassette with EQ, 195/65R15 tires on alloy wheels. **S** adds: DOHC 24-valve engine, anti-lock brakes, uprated suspension, 205/60R15 tires.

Optional equipment:	Retail Price	Dealer Invoice	Low Price
Anti-lock brakes, base	1000	850	881
CD player	700	560	600
Leather power seats	880	730	767
Cold Pkg.	250	208	218
All-weather tires, HD battery, semi-concealed wipers, heated driver's seat, larger washer fluid reservoir.			
Armrest lid	79	55	64

Mercedes-Benz S-Class

Mercedes-Benz 500 SL

A new SL roadster is the featured attraction in the S-Class. The new 2-seat SL, which succeeds a design that endured 18 years, comes two ways for 1990: The 300SL (base price $72,500) has a 228-horsepower 3.0-liter inline 6-cylinder engine and the 500SL (base price $83,500) a 322-horsepower 5.0-liter V-8. Both engines have dual overhead cams and four valves per cylinder. Both models come with a removable aluminum hardtop and a power soft top; they are visually the same except for trunk-lid badging. A 5-speed manual transmission is standard on the 300SL; fifth gear has direct drive, not overdrive. A 5-speed overdrive automatic transmission is optional on the 300SL. The V-8-powered 500SL comes only with a 4-speed automatic transmission with a direct-drive top gear. A driver's-side and a passenger-side airbag are standard. The most innovative safety feature is a roll-over bar designed to flip into place behind the seats in 0.3 seconds when needed. Anti-lock brakes are standard on both models. The new Mercedes-Benz SL is much more athletic than its predecessor and, in V-8 form, has a top speed of 155 mph. Elsewhere in the S-Class lineup, all models have a new fuel injection system

Specifications

	SL 2-door conv.	560SEC 2-door notchback	300SE 4-door notchback	SEL 4-door notchback
Wheelbase, in.	99.0	112.2	115.6	121.1
Overall length, in.	176.0	199.2	202.6	208.1
Overall width, in.	71.3	72.0	71.7	71.7
Overall height, in.	50.7	55.0	56.6	56.7
Turn diameter, ft.	35.4	38.1	39.0	40.6
Curb weight, lbs.	3970	3915	3730	3770
Cargo vol., cu. ft.	7.9	14.9	15.2	15.2
Fuel capacity, gals.	23.7	27.1	27.1	27.1
Seating capacity	2	4	5	5
Front headroom, in.	37.1	36.8	37.2	37.3
Front shoulder room, in.	55.4	57.2	56.2	56.2
Front legroom, max., in.	42.4	41.9	41.9	41.9
Rear headroom, in.	—	36.0	36.5	36.6
Rear shoulder room, in.	—	54.2	55.7	55.7
Rear legroom, min., in.	—	30.6	33.4	39.6

Powertrain layout: longitudinal front engine/rear-wheel drive.

Engines

	dohc I-6	ohc V-8	dohc V-8	ohc V-8
Size, liters/cu. in.	3.0/181	4.2/256	5.0/303	5.6/338
Fuel delivery	PFI	PFI	PFI	PFI
Horsepower @ rpm	228 @ 6300	201 @ 5200	322 @ 5500	238 @ 4800
Torque (lbs./ft.) @ rpm	201 @ 4600	228 @ 3600	332 @ 4000	278 @ 3500
Availability	S[1]	S[2]	S[3]	S[4]

EPA city/highway mpg

5-speed manual	15/21			
4-speed automatic		15/18	14/18	13/17
5-speed OD automatic	16/22			

1. 300SL; 300SE and 300 SEL have 177 horsepower and 188 lbs/ft torque.   2. 420SEL.
3. 500SL.   4. 560SEC and 560SEL.

Prices are accurate at time of printing; subject to manufacturer's change.

and a revised stereo system. The V-8 models (420SEL, 560SEL, and 560SEC) have dual front airbags as standard; the 6-cylinder models (300SE and 300SEL) have a driver's side airbag standard and a passenger-side airbag optional. Anti-lock brakes are standard on all. Next spring, the SEL body will be fitted with a 3.5-liter 6-cylinder turbocharged diesel engine to create the 350SDL, the first Mercedes turbodiesel in the U.S. since 1987. New S-Class sedans are planned for 1992. The principal rival for the Mercedes SEL is the BMW 750iL, which uses a V-12 engine. We also suggest you try the Infiniti Q45 and Lexus LS 400.

Prices

Mercedes-Benz S-Class	Retail Price	Dealer Invoice	Low Price
300SE 4-door notchback	$52950	—	—
300SEL 4-door notchback	56800	—	—
420SEL 4-door notchback	62500	—	—
560SEL 4-door notchback	73800	—	—
560SEC 2-door notchback	81500	—	—
300SL 2-door convertible, 5-speed	72500	—	—
300SL 2-door convertible, automatic	73500	—	—
500SL 2-door convertible	83500	—	—
Destination charge	250	250	250
Gas Guzzler Tax, 300SL automatic	500	500	500
300SL 5-speed	650	650	650
300SE, 300SEL	850	850	850
420SEL	1050	1050	1050
560SEC, 500SL	1300	1300	1300
560SEL	1500	1500	1500

Dealer invoice and low price not available at time of publication.

Standard equipment:

300SE, 300SEL: 3.0-liter PFI 6-cylinder engine, 4-speed automatic transmission, power steering, anti-lock 4-wheel disc brakes, Supplemental Restraint System, rear shoulder belts, anti-theft alarm, power windows and locks, automatic climate control, AM/FM cassette, leather power front seats with 2-position memory, power telescopic steering column, leather-wrapped steering wheel and shift knob, rear defogger, cruise control, headlamp wipers and washers, heated power mirrors, outside temperature indicator, tachometer, coolant temperature and oil pressure gauges, lighted visor mirrors, 205/65VR15 tires on alloy wheels. **420SEL** adds: 4.2-liter V-8, passenger-side airbag. **560SEL** and **560SEC** add: 5.6-liter PFI V-8, automatic rear level control, limited-slip differential. **300SL 500SL** has: 3.0-liter DOHC 24-valve 6-cylinder engine, 5-speed manual or 5-speed automatic transmission, power steering, anti-lock 4-wheel disc brakes, driver and passenger airbags, automatic soft top, removable hard top, power seats with 3-position memory, heated power mirrors, electrically adjustable steering column, outside temperature readout, cruise control, AM/FM cassette with power antenna, power windows and locks, infrared keyless entry, anti-theft alarm, automatic climate control, fog lamps, headlamp wipers and washers, rear defogger (for hard top), tachometer, coolant temperature and oil pressure gauges, trip odometer, 225/55VR16 tires on alloy wheels.

Optional equipment:	Retail Price	Dealer Invoice	Low Price
Metallic paint	NC	NC	NC
Passenger-side airbag, 300SE/SEL	615	—	—
Rear-window sunshade (NA SLs)	365	—	—
Power sunroof, 300SE/SEL, 420SEL	NC	NC	NC
Orthopedic front backrests, each	325	—	—
Power rear seat, 300SEL, 420SEL	680	—	—
Four-place seating pkg., 300SEL, 420SEL .	3005	—	—
560SEL	2330	—	—
Heated front seats, all exc. 560SEL/SEC . .	505	—	—
Heated rear seats, 300SE/SEL, 420SEL . .	505	—	—

Mercedes-Benz 190E 2.6

Mercedes-Benz 190E 2.6

The 190D 2.5, Mercedes' only diesel model last year, has been dropped, so the "Baby Benz" line consists of a single model this year, the 190E 2.6 4-door sedan. Mercedes will add two new turbocharged diesel models next spring, in

Prices are accurate at time of printing; subject to manufacturer's change.

the mid-size 300-Class and the larger S-Class. The compact 190E uses a 158-horsepower 2.6-liter 6-cylinder engine and comes with either a 5-speed manual or 4-speed automatic transmission, the only Mercedes sedan that offers that choice. Changes for 1990 are that power front seats are standard instead of optional, the fuel injection system is a new design borrowed from the SL roadster, and the new stereo radio/cassette player has anti-theft coding and a new location—lower in the center of the dashboard so a cassette holder could be built into the area above. The base of the center console has been trimmed to allow more knee room, while the top portion has more wood trim. A driver's-side

Specifications

	4-door notchback
Wheelbase, in.	104.9
Overall length, in.	175.1
Overall width, in.	66.5
Overall height, in.	54.7
Turn diameter, ft.	35.0
Curb weight, lbs.	2955
Cargo vol., cu. ft.	11.7
Fuel capacity, gals.	16.1
Seating capacity	5
Front headroom, in.	36.9
Front shoulder room, in.	53.5
Front legroom, max., in.	41.9
Rear headroom, in.	36.3
Rear shoulder room, in.	53.2
Rear legroom, min., in.	31.1

Powertrain layout: longitudinal front engine/rear-wheel drive.

Engines

	ohc I-6
Size, liters/cu. in.	2.6/159
Fuel delivery	PFI
Horsepower @ rpm	158 @ 5800
Torque (lbs./ft.) @ rpm	162 @ 4600
Availability	S

EPA city/highway mpg

5-speed OD manual	19/27
4-speed automatic	19/23

airbag and anti-lock brakes are standard. Prices on the 190E soared from $23,000 in 1984 to nearly $34,000 in 1988, but they have dropped since then even though more features have been made standard. No wonder: $34,000 for a compact sedan with a cramped rear seat and small trunk was hard to swallow, even for a Mercedes. For less money, you could buy a roomier Acura Legend with similar features—and a lot of people did just that. The 190E has the same high-quality materials, sound engineering, and impeccable fit and finish as other Mercedes; all it lacks is the size to justify its price.

Prices

Mercedes-Benz 190E 2.6	Retail Price	Dealer Invoice	Low Price
4-door notchback, 5-speed	$31600	—	—
4-door notchback, automatic	32500	—	—
Destination charge	250	250	250

Dealer invoice and low price not available at time of publication.

Standard equipment:

2.6-liter PFI 6-cylinder engine, 5-speed manual or 4-speed automatic transmission, power steering, anti-lock 4-wheel disc brakes, Supplemental Restraint System, rear shoulder belts, automatic climate control, power windows and locks, cruise control, intermittent wipers, rear defogger, vinyl reclining power front bucket seats, heated power mirrors, AM/FM cassette, tachometer, coolant temperature and oil pressure gauges, trip odometer, leather-wrapped steering wheel and shift knob, lighted visor mirrors, wide bodyside moldings, 185/65VR15 tires on alloy wheels.

Optional equipment:

Anti-theft alarm system	530	—	—
Rear head restraints	300	—	—
Headlamp wipers & washers	285	—	—
Metallic paint	400	—	—
Power sunroof	NC	NC	NC
Orthopedic front backrests, each	325	—	—
Heated front seats	505	—	—
Reinforced front seat frames, each	25	—	—
Memory driver's seat	415	—	—
Leather upholstery	1460	—	—
Velour upholstery	1440	—	—

Prices are accurate at time of printing; subject to manufacturer's change.

Mercedes-Benz 300

Mercedes-Benz 300E 4Matic

Mercedes' automatic 4-wheel-drive system, available in Europe since 1987, arrives in the U.S. this fall on the 300E sedan and the 300TE station wagon. Called 4Matic, the system automatically engages 4WD for more traction when needed. All the power normally goes to the rear wheels. On slippery surfaces, 4Matic uses the same sensors as the anti-lock brakes to detect wheel slip and determine when to transfer some of the engine torque to the front wheels. The standard anti-lock brake system remains fully operational when 4Matic is engaged. Rear-drive versions of the 300E and 300TE also return this fall. Elsewhere in the mid-size 300 series, the 300CE 2-door coupe gets 40 more horsepower thanks to a new engine: the dual-camshaft 3.0-liter 6-cylinder used in the 300SL roadster. Horsepower is rated at 217 in the 300CE, 11 fewer than in the SL because of a more restrictive catalytic converter. Last year's 260E sedan is now called the 300E 2.6; it uses a 158-horsepower 2.6-liter six. Other 300 models use a 177-horsepower 3.0-liter six with a single camshaft. Next spring, a 2.5-liter 5-cylinder turbocharged diesel engine will be added in a sedan called the 250D. Other changes this fall are that leather upholstery is standard on the 300E and the 300CE gains burl walnut trim throughout the interior and a wood-trimmed storage bin between the rear seats. Other models have new seats and wood trim across the dashboard and doors. Outside, lower-body panels have new protective panels and the mirrors are painted body color. A driver's-side airbag is standard on all models and a passenger-side airbag is optional. Anti-lock brakes are standard across the board. Mercedes is calling in fresh troops to combat the BMW 5-Series sedan, and the new Infiniti Q45 and Lexus LS 400, which are less expensive than the 300 models yet offer V-8 engines. Mercedes' prices jumped substantially during most of the 1980s, but have only crept up the past couple of years because fewer buyers were willing to pay so much money—even for the vaunted 3-pointed star.

Specifications

	300CE 2-door notchback	300E 4-door notchback	300TE 5-door wagon
Wheelbase, in.	106.9	110.2	110.2
Overall length, in.	183.9	187.2	188.2
Overall width, in.	68.5	68.5	68.5
Overall height, in.	55.5	56.9	59.8
Turn diameter, ft.	35.8	36.7	36.7
Curb weight, lbs.	3505	3265	3560
Cargo vol., cu. ft.	14.4	14.6	76.8
Fuel capacity, gals.	20.9	20.9	21.4
Seating capacity	4	5	5
Front headroom, in.	36.0	36.9	37.4
Front shoulder room, in.	55.7	55.9	55.9
Front legroom, max., in.	41.9	41.7	41.7
Rear headroom, in.	35.5	36.9	36.8
Rear shoulder room, in.	50.2	55.7	55.6
Rear legroom, min., in.	29.6	33.5	33.9

Powertrain layout: longitudinal front engine/rear-wheel drive or automatic 4-wheel drive.

Engines

	ohc I-6	ohc I-6	dohc I-6
Size, liters/cu. in.	2.6/159	3.0/181	3.0/181
Fuel delivery	PFI	PFI	PFI
Horsepower @ rpm	158 @ 5800	177 @ 5700	217 @ 6300
Torque (lbs./ft.) @ rpm	162 @ 4600	188 @ 4400	201 @ 4600
Availability	S[1]	S[2]	S[3]

EPA city/highway mpg

4-speed automatic	19/23	17/22	17/21

1. 300E 2.6.   2. 300E and 300TE.   3. 300CE.

Prices are accurate at time of printing; subject to manufacturer's change.

Prices

Mercedes-Benz 300	Retail Price	Dealer Invoice	Low Price
300E 2.6 4-door notchback	$39950	—	—
300E 4-door notchback	45950	—	—
300E 4Matic 4-door notchback	52500	—	—
300CE 2-door notchback	55700	—	—
300TE 5-door wagon	49650	—	—
300TE 4Matic 5-door wagon	56250	—	—
Destination charge	250	250	250
Gas Guzzler Tax, 300CE & 300E 4Matic . .	500	500	500
Wagons	650	650	650

Dealer invoice and low price not available at time of publication.

Standard equipment:

300E 2.6: 2.6-liter PFI 6-cylinder engine, 4-speed automatic transmission, power steering, anti-lock 4-wheel disc brakes, Supplemental Restraint System, cruise control, rear headrests, rear shoulder belts, heated power mirrors, automatic climate control, power windows and locks, rear defogger, tachometer, coolant temperature and oil pressure gauges, trip odometer, intermittent wipers, heated windshield washer fluid reservoir and nozzles, leather-wrapped steering wheel and shift knob, 195/65VR15 SBR tires. **300E** adds: 3.0-liter engine, headlamp wipers and washers, anti-theft alarm system, power telescopic steering column, power front seat, leather upholstery, outside temperature indicator. **300CE** adds DOHC 24-valve engine. **300TE wagon** adds to 300E: automatic level control, roof rack, rear wiper/washer. **4Matic** models have automatic full-time 4WD.

Optional equipment:

Anti-theft alarm system, 300E 2.6	595	—	—
Headlamp wipers & washers, 300E 2.6 . .	285	—	—
Partition net & luggage cover, wagons . . .	435	—	—
Passenger-side airbag (NA 300E 2.6) . . .	615	—	—
Rear reading lamps, 4-doors	80	—	—
Electric rear-window sunshade, 4-doors . .	365	—	—
Power sunroof	NC	NC	NC
Orthopedic front backrests, each	325	—	—
Heated front seats	505	—	—
Memory driver's seat, 300E 2.6	415	—	—
Adjustable steering column, 300E 2.6 . . .	325	—	—
Third rear-facing seat, wagons	1095	—	—
Leather upholstery, 300E 2.6 & wagons . .	1460	—	—
Velour upholstery, 300E 2.6 & wagons . .	1440	—	—
Others	NC	NC	NC

Mercury Capri

Mercury Capri (prototype)

Mercury dealers are scheduled to get a Mazda Miata-fighter in the spring of 1990. The Capri, a front-drive $2+2$ convertible, is set to be introduced then as a 1991 model. Capri is based on the Mazda 323 chassis and styled by Italian designer Giorgetto Giugiaro, but will be built by Ford in Australia. Prices haven't been announced, but Mercury officials predict Capri's base price will be under $12,000 (base price on the hot-selling Miata is $13,800). Mercury also portrays the Capri's front-drive traction and rear-seat space as advantages over the rear-drive, 2-seat Miata. Two series are planned: a base model powered by a 1.6-liter single-cam four with a choice of manual or automatic transmissions, and a high-performance XR2 with a dual-cam, turbocharged 1.6 available only with a 5-speed manual. Both versions will be available with an optional removable hardtop. Specifications and other details weren't available at publication time.

Mercury Tracer

The front-drive subcompact Tracer will not be offered as a 1990 model. High inventories and the need to include passive restraints prompted Ford to stop production with 1989½ versions, which should be available well into the 1990 model year. Only a red stripe (instead of chrome) on

Mercury Tracer

the bodyside moldings and bumpers distinguishes the '89½ Tracer from the '89. In the spring of 1990, a new 1991 model will be introduced, sharing its front-drive platform and powertrains with the '91 Ford Escort. The new Tracer will be based on the Mazda 323 chassis and most mechanical components will be supplied by Mazda, but the exterior styling and interior design will be Mercury's. The current Tracer is built in Mexico, from the previous-generation Mazda 323 design. It comes in 3-and 5-door hatchback and 5-door wagon body styles. All models have folding rear seatbacks that enlarge the cargo hold. The lone engine is an 82-horsepower 1.6-liter 4-cylinder. A 5-speed manual is standard and a 3-speed automatic optional. Mercury markets Tracer as a fully-equipped subcompact, listing only a handful of options. We haven't driven the 1991 Tracer, but we find the current version to be a generally enjoyable subcompact that handles competently, rides fairly well for a small car, and gets good fuel economy. We prefer the standard 5-speed manual because the optional 3-speed automatic has the engine running at a frantic 3300 rpm at 60 mph. With the 5-speed, it runs a more relaxed and hushed 2600 rpm at 60. Tracer is reasonably priced and comes with Ford's competitive warrantics. Leftover 1989½ models are sure to be heavily discounted.

1989 Specifications

	3-door hatchback	5-door hatchback	5-door wagon
Wheelbase, in.	94.7	94.7	94.7
Overall length, in.	162.0	162.0	169.7
Overall width, in.	65.2	65.2	65.2
Overall height, in.	53.0	53.0	53.7
Turn diameter, ft.	30.8	30.8	30.8
Curb weight, lbs.	2158	2185	2233
Cargo vol., cu. ft.	28.9	28.9	57.6
Fuel capacity, gals.	11.9	11.9	11.9
Seating capacity	5	5	5
Front headroom, in.	38.3	38.3	38.2
Front shoulder room, in.	51.9	51.9	51.9
Front legroom, max., in.	41.5	41.5	41.5
Rear headroom, in.	37.0	37.0	37.0
Rear shoulder room, in.	51.9	51.9	51.9
Rear legroom, min., in.	34.7	34.7	34.7

Powertrain layout: transverse front engine/front-wheel drive.

Engines

	ohc I-4
Size, liters/cu. in.	1.6/97
Fuel delivery	PFI
Horsepower @ rpm	82 @ 5000
Torque (lbs./ft.) @ rpm	92 @ 2500
Availability	S

EPA city/highway mpg

5-speed OD manual	28/35
3-speed automatic	26/29

Prices

Mercury Tracer (1989 prices)	Retail Price	Dealer Invoice	Low Price
3-door hatchback	$8556	$7718	$8137
5-door hatchback	9242	8328	8785
5-door wagon	9726	8759	9243
Destination charge	335	335	335

Standard equipment:

1.6-liter PFI 4-cylinder engine, 5-speed manual transmission, tachometer, trip odometer, coolant temperature gauge, digital clock, tinted glass, cloth reclining front bucket seats, driver's seat height and lumbar support adjustments. split folding rear seatback with headrests and recliners, AM/FM ST

Prices are accurate at time of printing; subject to manufacturer's change.

ET, rear defogger, power mirrors, map lights, center console with storage, remote fuel door and liftgate releases, right visor mirror, cargo area cover, P175/70R13 tires on steel wheels (hatchbacks; alloy on wagon), full wheel covers.

Optional equipment:	Retail Price	Dealer Invoice	Low Price
3-speed automatic transmission	415	352	384
Air conditioning	688	585	637
AM/FM ST ET cassette	137	116	127
AM/FM ST ET delete (credit)	(206)	(175)	(175)
Preferred Pkg. 551A	235	200	218
Power steering.			
Sport Pkg., exc. wagon	268	228	248
Two-tone paint, alloy wheels, tape stripe.			
Cruise control	182	154	168
Alloy wheels (std. wagon)	183	155	169
Delete alloy wheels, wagon (credit)	(183)	(155)	(155)

Mitsubishi Eclipse

Mitsubishi Eclipse GSX

The front-drive Eclipse arrived as an early 1990 model and was followed by an all-wheel-drive version last summer. All Eclipses are built at the Diamond-Star Motors plant in Illinois that Mitsubishi operates with Chrysler, which offers a similar mix of front-drive Plymouth Lasers and front- and AWD Eagle Talons. Eclipse models comprise base and GS versions powered by a 1.8-liter 4-cylinder engine with 92 horsepower; GS DOHC with a dual-cam 2.0-liter engine and 135 horsepower; and the GS Turbo and AWD GSX, which use an intercooled, turbocharged 2.0-

liter with 190 horsepower. The GSX all-wheel-drive system is permanently engaged and has a viscous-coupling center differential that apportions power between front and rear wheels as needed for optimum traction. A 5-speed manual transmission is standard across the board and a 4-speed automatic transmission is optional for all but turbocharged Eclipses. We really like this line of sports coupes, especially the GS DOHC and the 4WD GSX. None of these cars cost a bundle, and all but the 1.8-liter models are a ball to

Specifications

	3-door hatchback
Wheelbase, in.	97.2
Overall length, in.	170.5
Overall width, in.	66.5
Overall height, in.	51.4
Turn diameter, ft.	34.1
Curb weight, lbs.	2524[1]
Cargo vol., cu. ft.	10.2
Fuel capacity, gals.	15.9
Seating capacity	4
Front headroom, in.	37.9
Front shoulder room, in.	53.9
Front legroom, max., in.	43.9
Rear headroom, in.	34.1
Rear shoulder room, in.	NA
Rear legroom, min., in.	28.5

1. 3095 lbs., GSX

Powertrain layout: transverse front engine/front-wheel drive or permanent 4WD (GSX).

Engines

	ohc I-4	dohc I-4	Turbo dohc I-4
Size, liters/cu. in.	1.8/107	2.0/122	2.0/122
Fuel delivery	PFI	PFI	PFI
Horsepower @ rpm	92 @ 5000	135 @ 6000	190 @ 6000[1]
Torque (lbs./ft.) @ rpm	105 @ 3500	125 @ 3000	203 @ 3000
Availability	S[2]	S[3]	S[4]
EPA city/highway mpg			
5-speed OD manual	23/32	22/29	22/29
4-speed OD automatic	23/30	22/27	

1. GSX: 195 horsepower.   2. Base, GS 1.8.   3. GS DOHC.   4. GS Turbo, GSX.

Prices are accurate at time of printing; subject to manufacturer's change.

drive. The 1.8-liter base and GS editions don't have enough low-speed power to pull with any gusto, especially with automatic transmission. At the other end of the line, the turbo models deliver ferocious acceleration. Torque steer (sudden pulling to one side in hard acceleration) is a problem in the Turbo but not the all-wheel drive GSX, which spreads the abundant power among all four wheels. Even better, the GSX grips the road like a leech. The 135-horsepower engine is smooth, responsive, and has more low-end power than the 1.8. Eclipse has much to offer, including reasonable prices that run from about $11,000 for the base car to under $18,000 for a loaded GSX.

Prices

Mitsubishi Eclipse	Retail Price	Dealer Invoice	Low Price
3-door hatchback, 5-speed	$10819	$9465	$10142
3-door hatchback, automatic	11469	10033	10751
GS 1.8 3-door hatchback, 5-speed	11839	10302	11071
GS 1.8 3-door hatchback, automatic	12489	10866	11678
GS DOHC 3-door hatchback, 5-speed . . .	12679	11032	11856
GS DOHC 3-door hatchback, automatic . .	13329	11596	12463
GS Turbo 3-door hatchback, 5-speed . . .	14639	12735	13687
GSX 3-door hatchback, 5-speed	16449	14314	15382
Destination charge	285	285	285

Standard equipment:

1.8-liter PFI 4-cylinder engine, 5-speed manual or 4-speed automatic transmission, 4-wheel disc brakes, cloth reclining front bucket seats, folding rear seatback, tilt steering column, map lights, remote fuel door and hatch releases, visor mirrors, rear shoulder belts, tachometer, coolant temperature gauge, dual trip odometers, intermittent wipers, automatic-off headlamp feature, AM/FM radio, tinted glass, remote mirrors, 185/70R14 tires. **GS** adds: power steering, 3-way driver's seat, upgraded door panels, power mirrors, rear defogger, cargo cover, center console with coin and cup holders, AM/FM cassette, full wheel covers. **GS DOHC** adds: 2.0-liter DOHC 16-valve engine, sport suspension, 205/55R16 tires. **GS DOHC Turbo** adds: turbocharged engine, rear wiper/washer, air dam and rear spoiler, sill extensions, alloy wheels. **GSX** adds: permanent 4-wheel drive, cruise control, 6-way driver's seat, driving lamps.

Optional equipment:

Power steering, base	241	198	220
Air conditioning	811	665	738

	Retail Price	Dealer Invoice	Low Price
AM/FM cassette, base	170	139	155
AM/FM cassette w/EQ, exc. base	241	198	220
AM/FM cassette w/CD player, 16V models	628	515	572
Power Pkg., exc. base	366	300	333
Power windows and locks.			
Leather front seating surfaces, GSX	427	350	389
Security alarm, GSX	163	134	149
Alloy wheels, GS DOHC	315	258	287
Rear wiper/washer, base, GS & GS DOHC	129	106	118
Cruise control, exc. GSX	187	153	170
Sunroof	366	300	333
Limited-slip differential, GSX	477	391	434
Rear defogger, base	119	101	110
Wheel covers, base	100	82	91
Floormats	27	22	25

Mitsubishi Galant

Mitsubishi Galant GS

Mitsubishi's front-drive compact sedan returns from its 1989 redesign with no major change save the addition of an all-wheel drive model. Called GSX, the newcomer uses the 135-horsepower 2.0-liter 4-cylinder engine of the sporty front-drive GS model, and is likewise available only with a 5-speed manual transmission. Its permanently engaged all-wheel drive system is the same one used in the Mitsubishi Eclipse GSX. Base and upscale LS Galants continue with a 102-horsepower 2.0-liter. The LS comes only with a 4-speed automatic transmission; a 5-speed manual is standard on the base and the automatic is optional. Automatic transmission is supposed to be available later this year on the GS. Standard on the GS is an electronically controlled suspension with variable-rate air springs and shock absorbers controlled by three driver-selected programs—Soft, Auto, and Sport. An anti-lock braking system (ABS) is optional for GS and GSX. All Galant models have the robust solidity and precise, "well-oiled" feel associated with expensive German brands. All models but the GS

Specifications

	4-door notchback
Wheelbase, in.	102.4
Overall length, in.	183.9
Overall width, in.	66.7
Overall height, in.	53.5
Turn diameter, ft.	34.8
Curb weight, lbs.	2601[1]
Cargo vol., cu. ft.	12.3
Fuel capacity, gals.	15.9
Seating capacity	5
Front headroom, in.	38.6
Front shoulder room, in.	54.7
Front legroom, max., in.	41.9
Rear headroom, in.	37.4
Rear shoulder room, in.	54.4
Rear legroom, min., in.	36.0

1. 2799 lbs., GS.

Powertrain layout: transverse front engine/front-wheel drive or permanent 4WD (GSX).

Engines	ohc I-4	dohc I-4
Size, liters/cu. in.	2.0/122	2.0/122
Fuel delivery	PFI	PFI
Horsepower @ rpm	102 @ 5000	135 @ 6000
Torque (lbs./ft.) @ rpm	116 @ 2500	125 @ 3000
Availability	S	S
EPA city/highway mpg		
5-speed OD manual	23/29	21/27
4-speed OD automatic	22/27	

have a supple suspension that handily absorbs bumps. The GS is annoyingly jittery on anything other than ice-smooth surfaces yet handles little better than the more softly sprung LS. All-wheel drive makes the new GSX an enthusiast's delight. It leans less through tight turns and hangs on tenaciously. Galant's engines have relatively weak low-end torque, which makes for less-than-sparkling performance. With the automatic transmission, the base and LS amble from 0 to 60 mph in 12.5 seconds. The GS and GSX are quicker, but require frequent gear shifts to keep pace with traffic. Even so, Galant is a strong, capable compact with several virtues and no real vices. Give it a look.

Prices

Mitsubishi Galant	Retail Price	Dealer Invoice	Low Price
4-door notchback, 5-speed	$10989	$9904	$10254
4-door notchback, automatic	12389	10535	10885
LS 4-door notchback, automatic	13969	11874	12224
GS 4-door notchback, 5-speed	15669	13320	13670
GSX 4-door notchback, 5-speed	16369	13915	14265
Destination charge	285	285	285

Standard equipment:

2.0-liter PFI 4-cylinder engine, 5-speed manual or 4-speed automatic transmission, power steering, tinted glass, remote mirrors, intermittent wipers, tachometer, dual trip odometers, tilt steering column, cloth reclining front bucket seats, center console, rear defogger, remote fuel door and decklid releases, right visor mirror, 185/70SR14 tires. **LS** adds: 4-speed automatic transmission, power windows and locks, power mirrors, variable intermittent wipers, front map lights, driver's seat height and lumbar support adjustments, velour upholstery, seatback pockets, storage tray beneath right front seat, bilevel center console with armrest, rear center armrest w/trunk passthrough, AM/FM cassette with power antenna, full wheel covers. **GS** adds to base: DOHC 16-valve engine, 4-wheel disc brakes, speed-sensitive power steering, electronically controlled suspension, dark upper windshield band, upgraded upholstery, speed-sensitive intermittent wipers, leather-wrapped steering wheel and shift knob, switchable green/orange instrument illumination, cruise controlo, power windows and locks, power mirrors, front and rear map lights, driver's-seat height adjustment, AM/FM cassette with power antenna, front mud guards, 195/60HR15 tires on alloy wheels. **GSX** adds permanent 4-wheel drive.

Prices are accurate at time of printing; subject to manufacturer's change.

Optional equipment:	Retail Price	Dealer Invoice	Low Price
Anti-lock brakes, GS & GSX	1495	1226	1327
Air conditioning	802	658	712
AM/FM cassette, base	552	386	458
AM/FM cassette w/EQ, LS, GS & GSX . . .	316	221	262
Power sunroof, LS, GS & GSX	685	548	601
Wheel covers, base	78	62	68

Mitsubishi Mirage

Mitsubishi Mirage

The front-drive Mirage sees no major design changes for 1990, but models and equipment are revised to make the line more price-competitive. Last year's "pocket-rocket" Turbo 3-door hatchback is gone. The new order begins with a VL ("Value Leader") 3-door hatchback, followed by a standard 3-door and 4-door notchback sedan. Topping the line are EXE versions of both body styles and a sporty RS 3-door. The VL is available only with a 4-speed manual transmission, the RS with a 5-speed manual. Other models have the 5-speed standard and a 3-speed automatic optional. For now, Mitsubishi's 1.5-liter 4-cylinder engine with 81 horsepower is standard across the board. Early in 1990, Diamond-Star Motors, the Chrysler-Mitsubishi plant in Illinois, begins turning out 4-door Mirages. When that happens, a new GS 4-door powered by a 113-horsepower 1.6-liter engine (a twin to the Mirage-based Eagle Summit LX) will be added. The GS will be the only Mirage available with a 4-speed automatic transmission, now used in the Summit and new Hyundai Excel/Mitsubishi Precis. Though it breaks no new ground, Mirage is a competent, well-rounded small car with some surprising pluses and fewer of the usual small-car minuses. Fuel economy is great; we averaged 37 mpg last year with a manual-transmission 4-door. Handling is nimble, as you would expect. What you don't expect are a comfortable ride and adult-size back-seat space in the 4-door. Choose the hatchback and you'll lose a lot in both cargo room and rear-seat space. The main debit

Specifications

	3-door hatchback	4-door notchback
Wheelbase, in.	93.9	96.7
Overall length, in.	158.7	170.1
Overall width, in.	65.7	65.7
Overall height, in.	52.0	52.8
Turn diameter, ft.	30.2	30.8
Curb weight, lbs.	2238	2271
Cargo vol., cu. ft.	34.7	10.3
Fuel capacity, gals.	13.2	13.2
Seating capacity	5	5
Front headroom, in.	38.3	39.1
Front shoulder room, in.	53.5	53.5
Front legroom, max., in.	41.9	41.9
Rear headroom, in.	36.9	37.5
Rear shoulder room, in.	52.1	53.1
Rear legroom, min., in.	32.5	34.4

Powertrain layout: transverse front engine/front-wheel drive.

Engines

	ohc I-4	dohc I-4
Size, liters/cu. in.	1.5/90	1.6/97
Fuel delivery	PFI	PFI
Horsepower @ rpm	81 @ 5500	113 @ 6500
Torque (lbs./ft.) @ rpm	91 @ 3000	99 @ 5000
Availability	S	S[1]

EPA city/highway mpg

4-speed OD manual	31/36	
5-speed OD manual	28/34	23/28
3-speed automatic	27/29	
4-speed OD automatic		23/28

1. GS only.

Prices are accurate at time of printing; subject to manufacturer's change.

involves performance: There isn't much. Automatic models take some 13 seconds to do 0-60 mph; manual versions are just a little quicker. Still, this year's new price structure makes Mirage a better buy that's worth considering.

Prices

Mitsubishi Mirage	Retail Price	Dealer Invoice	Low Price
VL 3-door hatchback, 4-speed	$6929	$6260	$6560
3-door hatchback, 5-speed	7839	7063	7363
3-door hatchback, automatic	8299	7481	7781
RS 3-door hatchback, 5-speed	8759	7839	8139
EXE 3-door hatchback, 5-speed	8339	7451	7751
EXE 3-door hatchback, automatic	8799	7869	8169
4-door notchback, 5-speed	8559	7711	8011
4-door notchback, automatic	9019	8129	8429
EXE 4-door notchback, 5-speed	9509	8460	8760
EXE 4-door notchback, automatic	9979	8878	9178
Destination charge	285	285	285

Standard equipment:

VL: 1.5-liter PFI 4-cylinder engine, 4-speed manual transmission, reclining front bucket seats, split folding rear seat, center console with storage, rear shoulder belts, coolant temperature gauge, trip odometer, locking fuel door. **Base** adds: 5-speed manual or 3-speed automatic transmission, cloth upholstery, wide bodyside molding, rear defogger, dual outside mirrors (4-door). **RS** adds: carpet, cloth door panels with pockets, driver's foot rest, rear parcel shelf, storage tray under passenger seat, remote fuel door and hatch releases, tinted glass, dual outside mirrors. **EXE** adds: air conditioning, power steering, AM/FM cassette, remote decklid release, full wheel covers, 175/70R13 tires.

Optional equipment:

Air conditioning (std. EXE)	756	620	671
Power steering, base & RS	262	215	233
AM/FM radio w/4 speakers, base	280	196	232
VL	327	229	271
AM/FM cassette w/6 speakers, RS	507	355	420
Dual remote mirrors, base 3-door	32	26	28
Rear defogger, VL & base 4-door	62	53	56
Digital clock, RS	56	45	49
Radio accommodation pkg., VL	47	33	39
Floormats, VL, base & RS	63	41	51
Mud guards, VL, base & RS	74	54	62

Mitsubishi Sigma

Mitsubishi Sigma

This slow-selling compact luxury sedan says *sayonara* after 1990, so noteworthy changes for this final edition are limited to a standard driver's-side airbag, new 4-spoke steering wheel with duplicate audio controls, and modestly revised dashboard. Sigma originated as the 2.6-liter 4-cylinder Galant of 1985. It then became Galant Sigma in a 1988 makeover that brought V-6 power and available anti-lock braking system (ABS). Last year the name was changed to simply Sigma to avoid confusion with the new Galant. Mitsubishi's 3.0-liter V-6 (also offered in a variety of Chrysler products and the Hyundai Sonata) drives the front wheels through a 4-speed automatic transmission with Power and Economy electronic shift programs. ABS remains a separate option and is also combined with electronic auto-leveling air shocks in the extra-cost "Eurotech" package. Not much is known about Sigma's 1991 successor, but Mitsubishi hints it will be an all-wheel-drive sedan that's larger and much costlier than the current model. With 142 horsepower, the 3100-pound Sigma accelerates on par with rivals such as the Acura Legend, Mazda 929, Nissan Maxima, and Toyota Cressida. The V-6 is smooth, quiet, and well matched to the 4-speed automatic. The anti-lock brake system is a costly option, but more worthwhile than the electronically controlled suspension (ECS) it teams with in the even costlier Eurotech Package. We find the ECS more high-tech frill than helpful function.

Sigma's main shortcoming is literally that: an interior that's tight for four adults, let alone five. Balancing the ledger is a full helping of standard luxuries at a starting price just below $18,000.

Specifications

	4-door notchback
Wheelbase, in.	102.4
Overall length, in.	185.8
Overall width, in.	66.7
Overall height, in.	51.6
Turn diameter, ft.	34.8
Curb weight, lbs.	3108
Cargo vol., cu. ft.	12.4
Fuel capacity, gals.	15.9
Seating capacity	5
Front headroom, in.	37.5
Front shoulder room, in.	53.5
Front legroom, max., in.	40.3
Rear headroom, in.	36.7
Rear shoulder room, in.	53.2
Rear legroom, min., in.	36.4

Powertrain layout: transverse front engine/front-wheel drive.

Engines

	ohc V-6
Size, liters/cu. in.	3.0/181
Fuel delivery	PFI
Horsepower @ rpm	142 @ 5000
Torque (lbs./ft.) @ rpm	168 @ 2500
Availability	S

EPA city/highway mpg

4-speed OD automatic	18/22

Prices

Mitsubishi Sigma	Retail Price	Dealer Invoice	Low Price
4-door notchback	$17879	$15200	$15700
Destination charge	285	285	285

Standard equipment:

3.0-liter PFI V-6 engine, 4-speed automatic transmission, power steering, driver's-side airbag, automatic climate control, velour reclining front bucket seats, 8-way adjustable driver's seat, underseat tray, seatback pockets, folding rear seatbacks, rear armrest, door pockets, rear heat ducts, power windows and locks, heated power mirrors, tinted glass with dark upper band, tilt steering column, rear defogger, speed-sensitive intermittent wipers, digital clock, trip odometer, tachometer, coolant temperature gauge, voltmeter, cruise control, AM/FM cassette with EQ, additional audio system switches in steering wheel hub, power antenna, leather-wrapped steering wheel, theft deterrent system, remote fuel door and decklid releases, 195/60HR15 tires on alloy wheels.

Optional equipment:	Retail Price	Dealer Invoice	Low Price
Anti-lock braking system	1495	1226	1327
Eurotech Pkg.	2042	1674	1813
Anti-lock brakes, electronically controlled suspension.			
Power glass sunroof	685	548	601
Leather seats	816	652	716
Floormats	80	52	64

Nissan Axxess

Nissan Axxess XE All-Wheel Drive

Axxess arrived as an early 1990 model to replace the Stanza station wagon. Like its predecessor, Axxess is a tall, compact wagon with two sliding rear side doors and a choice of front- or 4-wheel drive, which Nissan calls all-wheel drive (AWD). Both versions offer a standard 5-speed manual or optional 4-speed automatic transmission linked to a 138-horsepower 2.4-liter 4-cylinder engine. AWD models have a permanently engaged 4WD system. Torque is normally split 50/50 front/rear, but in slippery conditions a center viscous coupling delivers more power to the wheels with the most traction—either fore/aft or side-to-side as conditions demand. Seats for five are standard and an optional 2-place rear seat is available. Base models are called XE and top-line models are called SE; the SE comes only with automatic transmission. The dual sliding side doors and tall liftgate make the Axxess easy to get in or out of

Specifications

	5-door wagon	AWD 5-door wagon
Wheelbase, in.	102.8	102.4
Overall length, in.	171.9	171.9
Overall width, in.	66.5	66.5
Overall height, in.	64.6	64.6
Turn diameter, ft.	34.8	35.4
Curb weight, lbs.	2877	3146
Cargo vol., cu. ft.	35.5	35.5
Fuel capacity, gals.	17.2	15.9
Seating capacity	7	7
Front headroom, in.	39.7	39.7
Front shoulder room, in.	55.4	55.4
Front legroom, max., in.	38.6	38.6
Rear headroom, in.	39.4	39.4
Rear shoulder room, in.	56.6	56.6
Rear legroom, min., in.	36.0	36.0

Powertrain layout: transverse front engine/front-wheel drive or permanent 4WD.

Engines

	ohc I-4
Size, liters/cu. in.	2.4/146
Fuel delivery	PFI
Horsepower @ rpm	138 @ 5600
Torque (lbs./ft.) @ rpm	148 @ 4400
Availability	S

EPA city/highway mpg

5-speed OD manual	21/27
4-speed OD automatic	20/24

and/or load cargo, so Nissan's claim that this is more than just a wagon is apt. Unfortunately, it's not quite a minivan. The optional 5 + 2 seating package is accurately named: The third seat is too narrow and cramped to take anyone larger than small children. The third seat double-folds for extra hauling space, but neither the third nor the second seat can be removed. With automatic transmission, the front-drive Axxess is no slingshot, but provides respectable acceleration: 11.5 seconds to 60 mph. The AWD model is nearly 300 pounds heavier, and it shows in slower acceleration. However, the AWD instantly delivers impressive traction on slippery roads, with no input from the driver required. Axxess is a good choice for those who have outgrown a small sedan or wagon, but don't need a minivan.

Prices

Nissan Axxess	Retail Price	Dealer Invoice	Low Price
XE 5-door wagon, 5-speed	$13949	$12327	$12818
XE 5-door wagon, automatic	14699	12990	13507
XE 4WD 5-door wagon, 5-speed	15749	13918	14472
XE 4WD 5-door wagon, automatic	16499	14581	15161
SE 5-door wagon, automatic	16749	14802	15391
SE 4WD 5-door wagon, automatic	18749	16569	17228
Destination charge	260	260	260

Standard equipment:

XE: 2.4-liter PFI 12-valve 4-cylinder engine, 5-speed manual or 4-speed automatic transmission, power steering, cloth reclining front bucket seats, 3-passenger middle bench seat, motorized front shoulder belts with manual lap belts, outboard lap/shoulder belts for middle seat, power locks, tonneau cover, storage bin under driver's seat, AM/FM ST ET cassette with diversity antenna, intermittent wipers, rear defogger and wiper/washer, remote fuel door and liftgate releases, 195/70R14 all-season M + S tires; All Wheel Drive has permanent 4-wheel drive, viscous limited-slip rear differential. **SE** adds: 4-speed automatic transmission, air conditioning, 7-passenger seating (2WD), sunroof, power windows and mirrors, cruise control, leather-wrapped steering wheel, tinted glass, upgraded upholstery, alloy wheels.

Optional equipment:

5 + 2 Seating Pkg., XE	400	335	359

2-passenger third seat with 3-point seatbelts, 60/40 split folding second seat.

Prices are accurate at time of printing; subject to manufacturer's change.

	Retail Price	Dealer Invoice	Low Price
XE Power Value Option Pkg.	900	795	827
Air conditioning, power front windows, power mirrors, cruise control.			
XE Power/Sunroof Value Option Pkg.	1385	1224	1273
Power Value Pkg. plus power sunroof.			
Luggage rack	140	117	125
Two-tone paint	300	251	269

Nissan Maxima

Nissan Maxima GXE

Maxima was redesigned last year, so this year's changes are minor. On the sporty SE, anti-lock brakes and a sport suspension are now in a $995 SE Sport Package; last year, a similar package cost $1500. Both the SE and luxury GXE are front-drive 4-door sedans with a 160-horsepower 3.0-liter V-6 engine. The SE comes with either a 5-speed manual or 4-speed automatic transmission, the GXE only with the automatic. The GXE has two exclusive option groups. The Luxury Package has power front seats, a power sunroof, and a Nissan-Bose sound system. The Electronic Equipment Package adds a digital instrument cluster with a head-up display that displays the speedometer reading in the lower left corner of the windshield, plus "Sonar Suspension II," which uses a sonar sensor to "read" the road surface and automatically adjust shock-absorber firmness to maintain ride comfort. The electronic suspension also has firm

Specifications

	4-door notchback
Wheelbase, in.	104.3
Overall length, in.	187.6
Overall width, in.	69.3
Overall height, in.	55.1
Turn diameter, ft.	36.7
Curb weight, lbs.	3086
Cargo vol., cu. ft.	14.5
Fuel capacity, gals.	18.5
Seating capacity	5
Front headroom, in.	39.5
Front shoulder room, in.	56.8
Front legroom, max., in.	43.7
Rear headroom, in.	36.9
Rear shoulder room, in.	56.1
Rear legroom, min., in.	33.2

Powertrain layout: transverse front engine/front-wheel drive.

Engines

	ohc V-6
Size, liters/cu. in.	3.0/181
Fuel delivery	PFI
Horsepower @ rpm	160 @ 5200
Torque (lbs./ft.) @ rpm	182 @ 2800
Availability	S

EPA city/highway mpg
5-speed OD manual	20/26
4-speed OD automatic	19/26

and soft settings. The Sonar Suspension bangs over sharp bumps in its firm mode and allows a floaty ride in its soft mode. GXE buyers should also forget the Electronic Equipment Package, whose digital and graphic-display instruments are less readable than the standard analog gauges. Otherwise, Maxima is a capable all-around performer, and in SE trim a close match for the Acura Legend—at a much lower price. We tested an SE with the 5-speed manual that ran 0-60 mph in a brisk 8.9 seconds, slightly slower than a Legend with automatic. A Maxima GXE did the sprint to 60 mph in 9.3 seconds. We prefer the SE because it comes with rear disc brakes (instead of drums) standard and anti-lock brakes optional.

Prices are accurate at time of printing; subject to manufacturer's change.

Prices

Nissan Maxima	Retail Price	Dealer Invoice	Low Price
GXE 4-door notchback, automatic	$17699	$15552	$16220
SE 4-door notchback, 5-speed	18749	16475	17182
SE 4-door notchback, automatic	19679	17292	18035
Destination charge	260	260	260

Standard equipment:

3.0-liter PFI V-6, 4-speed automatic transmission, power steering, air conditioning, power windows and locks with keyless entry, velour reclining front bucket seats, driver's seat height and lumbar adjustments, split folding rear seat, power mirrors, cruise control, tinted glass, AM/FM cassette with diversity antenna, motorized front shoulder belts with manual lap belts, theft deterrent system, tilt steering column, variable intermittent wipers, rear defogger, remote fuel door and decklid releases, illuminated entry, tachometer, dual trip odometers, coolant temperature gauge, digital clock, 195/60R16 tires on alloy wheels. **SE** adds: 5-speed manual or 4-speed automatic transmission, 4-wheel disc brakes, Nissan-Bose audio system, leather-wrapped steering wheel and shift knob, power glass sunroof, fog lights.

Optional equipment:

Luxury Pkg., GXE	1900	1593	1704
Power seats, power sunroof, Nissan-Bose audio system.			
Electronic Equipment Pkg., GXE	1550	1300	1390
Digital instruments, head-up display, automatic temperature control, Nissan Sonar Suspension II, speed-sensitive power steering; requires Luxury Pkg.			
Leather trim	950	797	852
Sport Pkg., SE	995	834	892
Anti-lock brakes, sport suspension.			
Pearlglow paint	350	294	314

Nissan Pulsar NX

The SE model and its dual-camshaft, 125-horsepower 1.8-liter 4-cylinder engine have been dropped from the Pulsar NX lineup. That leaves the XE model with its single-cam, 90-horsepower 1.6-liter 4-cylinder. The front-drive Pulsar is a 3-door hatchback with a removable hatch lid and removable roof panels, making it nearly topless when all three

Nissan Pulsar NX XE

Specifications

	3-door hatchback
Wheelbase, in.	95.7
Overall length, in.	166.5
Overall width, in.	66.1
Overall height, in.	51.0
Turn diameter, ft.	31.5
Curb weight, lbs.	2388
Cargo vol., cu. ft.	17.0
Fuel capacity, gals.	13.2
Seating capacity	4
Front headroom, in.	38.0
Front shoulder room, in.	NA
Front legroom, max., in.	42.0
Rear headroom, in.	33.9
Rear shoulder room, in.	NA
Rear legroom, min., in.	24.5

Powertrain layout: transverse front engine/front-wheel drive.

Engines

	ohc I-4
Size, liters/cu. in.	1.6/97
Fuel delivery	TBI
Horsepower @ rpm	90 @ 6000
Torque (lbs./ft.) @ rpm	96 @ 3200
Availability	S

EPA city/highway mpg

5-speed OD manual	26/34
3-speed automatic	25/31

Prices are accurate at time of printing; subject to manufacturer's change.

pieces are off the car. Two front buckets and a folding 2-place rear seat are standard, giving Pulsar nominal seating for four. A driver's-side airbag, optional last year, is standard this year. Pulsar created a bit of a stir when it debuted for 1987 in its present form, offering nearly open-air motoring in a low-cost, sporty package. However, success is fleeting in the sports coupe market and Pulsar sales have tumbled. That means you should be able to get a good deal on one these days, especially if you find a leftover 1989 model. Grab an '89 SE model if you can, since its 125-horsepower engine provides stronger acceleration. The 90-horsepower XE engine delivers unspectacular performance, especially with automatic transmission, but returns pleasing fuel economy. The automatic is slow to downshift for passing and shifts harshly under hard throttle. Handling is above average, and the ride is compliant for a sporty small car. Inside, the control layout is excellent, but visibility is hampered by the low seating position and thick roof pillars to the rear and over the shoulders. The 2-place rear seat is fine for children and acceptable for adults only on short trips.

Prices

Nissan Pulsar NX	Retail Price	Dealer Invoice	Low Price
XE 3-door hatchback, 5-speed	$12249	$10932	$11308
XE 3-door hatchback, automatic	12789	11414	11806
Destination charge	275	275	275

Standard equipment:

1.6-liter TBI 4-cylinder engine, 5-speed manual or 3-speed automatic transmission, power steering, driver's-side airbag, T-bar roof with removable panels, cloth reclining front bucket seats, folding rear seat, AM/FM radio with diversity antenna, center console, rear defogger, remote fuel door and hatch releases, tinted glass, power mirrors, tilt steering column, tachometer and trip odometer, variable intermittent wipers, wheel covers, 185/70R13 tires.

Optional equipment:

Air conditioning	825	699	743
Fog lights	145	122	130
Pearl glow paint	350	297	316
Vehicle security system	100	85	90

Nissan Sentra

Nissan Sentra XE

The 4-wheel-drive station wagon has been dropped and the E price series has disappeared, so the subcompact Sentra line has been trimmed from 19 models to 11. The 4WD wagon was dropped after two seasons and its role is filled in Nissan's lineup by the Axxess All-Wheel Drive wagon. With the E price series gone, Sentra now comes in Standard trim as a 2-door sedan; XE trim as a 2- and 4-door sedan, 5-door wagon, and 3-door Sport Coupe hatchback. The hatchback also comes in higher-priced SE trim. All 1990 models have front-wheel drive. There was an XE trim level last year, but the 1989 models had more standard equipment and were priced about $1400 higher than the 1990 versions. The Standard 2-door comes with a 4-speed manual transmission; all other Sentras come with a 5-speed manual or extra-cost 3-speed automatic. All use a 90-horsepower 1.6-liter 4-cylinder engine with single-point fuel injection. Some Sentras are built at Nissan's Tennessee assembly plant and some are imported from Japan. Sentra is scheduled to be redesigned for the 1991 model year. With this year's streamlined roster, it's much easier to pick a model that suits your needs and budget. Trouble is, Sentra is no longer priced as an entry level model. The cheapest 4-door sedan is nearly $10,000 with automatic transmission, and over $11,000 with air conditioning and the XE Value Option Package. If you can live without the option package, air conditioning, or automatic transmission, a

Prices are accurate at time of printing; subject to manufacturer's change.

Sentra is a pretty good deal as basic, low-cost transportation. Acceleration and fuel economy also will be better with manual transmission.

Specifications	2-door notchback	3-door hatchback	4-door notchback	5-door wagon
Wheelbase, in.	95.7	95.7	95.7	95.7
Overall length, in.	168.7	166.5	168.7	172.7
Overall width, in.	64.6	65.6	64.6	64.6
Overall height, in.	54.3	52.2	54.3	54.3
Turn diameter, ft.	30.2	30.2	30.2	30.2
Curb weight, lbs.	2156	2304	2208	2301
Cargo vol., cu. ft.	12.0	16.0	12.0	24.0
Fuel capacity, gals.	13.2	13.2	13.2	13.2
Seating capacity	5	4	5	5
Front headroom, in.	38.2	37.0	38.2	38.2
Front shoulder room, in. . .	52.1	52.3	52.1	52.1
Front legroom, max., in. . .	41.8	41.6	41.8	41.8
Rear headroom, in.	36.8	29.2	36.8	39.3
Rear shoulder room, in. . .	51.3	52.1	50.3	52.1
Rear legroom, min., in. . .	31.4	31.4	31.4	31.4

Powertrain layout: transverse front engine/front-wheel drive.

Engines	ohc I-4
Size, liters/cu. in.	1.6/97
Fuel delivery	TBI
Horsepower @ rpm	90 @ 6000
Torque (lbs./ft.) @ rpm	96 @ 3200
Availability	S

EPA city/highway mpg

4-speed OD manual	29/36
5-speed OD manual	28/36
3-speed automatic	26/31

Prices

Nissan Sentra	Retail Price	Dealer Invoice	Low Price
Standard 2-door notchback, 4-speed	$7299	$7003	$7100
XE 2-door notchback, 5-speed	8549	7598	7877
XE 2-door notchback, automatic	9149	8132	8430
XE 4-door notchback, 5-speed	9149	8132	8430
XE 4-door notchback, automatic	9749	8665	8982
XE 5-door wagon, 5-speed	9899	8749	9097

	Retail Price	Dealer Invoice	Low Price
XE 5-door wagon, automatic	10499	9279	9648
XE 3-door hatchback, 5-speed	10999	9720	10107
XE 3-door hatchback, automatic	11924	10538	10957
SE 3-door hatchback, 5-speed	12299	10807	11271
SE 3-door hatchback, automatic	12839	11282	11766
Destination charge	260	260	260

Standard equipment:

Standard: 1.6-liter TBI 4-cylinder engine, 4-speed manual transmission, coolant temperature gauge, rear defogger, reclining front bucket seats, center console, 155/80R13 tires. **XE** adds: 5-speed manual or 3-speed automatic transmission, cloth seats, split folding rear seat (wagon and hatchback), upgraded interior trim, intermittent wipers, left door pocket, trip odometer, tachometer (hatchback), AM/FM radio (hatchback with automatic transmission). **SE** adds: flip-up sunroof, rear wiper/washer, upgraded upholstery, multi-adjustable driver's seat, AM/FM radio with diversity antenna, 185/60R14 tires on alloy wheels.

Optional equipment:

Air conditioning	825	692	740
Two-tone paint, SE	300	251	269
Metallic paint, Standard	100	84	90
XE Value Option Pkg.	600	503	538

AM/FM radio, power steering, wheel covers, remote mirrors, remote fuel door and decklid/hatch release, visor mirrors, 175/70R13 tires.

Power steering & tilt steering column, XE .	300	251	269

Nissan Stanza

The 1990 Stanza is a redesigned compact 4-door that sports a more rounded look, a new engine, and a revamped front-drive chassis. The previous 94-horsepower 2.0-liter 4-cylinder gives way to the 138-horsepower 2.4-liter four used in the 240SX sports coupe and Axxess wagon. It teams with a standard 5-speed manual or optional 4-speed automatic transmission. Model choices comprise a base XE and upscale GXE. Front disc/rear drum brakes are standard, but the GXE can be ordered with an optional all-disc package that includes an anti-locking braking system (ABS)—both firsts for Stanza. A claimed world first for front-drive sedans is the GXE's standard viscous-coupling limited-slip differ-

Prices are accurate at time of printing; subject to manufacturer's change.

Nissan Stanza GXE

Specifications

	4-door notchback
Wheelbase, in.	100.4
Overall length, in.	179.9
Overall width, in.	66.8
Overall height, in.	54.1
Turn diameter, ft.	35.4
Curb weight, lbs.	2788
Cargo vol., cu. ft.	14.0
Fuel capacity, gals.	16.4
Seating capacity	5
Front headroom, in.	38.6
Front shoulder room, in.	54.7
Front legroom, max., in.	42.6
Rear headroom, in.	36.8
Rear shoulder room, in.	53.9
Rear legroom, min., in.	33.6

Powertrain layout: transverse front engine/front-wheel drive.

Engines

	ohc I-4
Size, liters/cu. in.	2.4/146
Fuel delivery	PFI
Horsepower @ rpm	138 @ 5600
Torque (lbs./ft.) @ rpm	148 @ 4400
Availability	S

EPA city/highway mpg

5-speed OD manual	22/29
4-speed OD automatic	21/27

ential. It is designed to increase traction in slippery conditions and in hard cornering. The new Stanza feels much more solid than the old one and delivers spunkier performance. It weighs about the same, yet its engine packs 42 percent more horsepower. We timed a 1990 GXE with automatic in 10.5 seconds to 60 mph—much livelier than the old Stanza and competitive with other compacts. Forget the drag strip stats, though, because the bigger engine's real payoff is swifter, safer passing in the 30-50 mph range. We were also impressed with the stopping distances on our ABS-equipped Stanza: less than 120 feet in 60-mph panic stops. It's great to see ABS ($995 extra) available on a car in this price league. With virtually the same cabin proportions, the new Stanza has no more usable passenger space than its predecessor, so it remains a 4-seater that can be stretched to hold five adults. There's good news on the price front. The 1990 Stanza XE is $749 cheaper than the 1989.

Prices

Nissan Stanza

	Retail Price	Dealer Invoice	Low Price
XE 4-door notchback, 5-speed	$11450	$10119	$10521
XE 4-door notchback, automatic	12250	10826	11257
GXE 4-door notchback, 5-speed	14775	13057	13577
GXE 4-door notchback, automatic	15575	13764	14312
Destination charge	260	260	260

Standard equipment:

XE: 2.4-liter 12-valve PFI 4-cylinder engine, 5-speed manual or 4-speed automatic transmission, power steering, cloth reclining front bucket seats, tinted glass, rear shoulder belts, dual OS mirrors, tilt steering column, rear defogger, coolant temperature gauge, remote fuel door and decklid releases, right visor mirror, console with beverage holders, 195/65R14 tires. **GXE** adds: air conditioning, limited-slip differential, driver's seat lumbar and height adjustments, tachometer, dark upper windshield band, power windows and locks, power mirrors, AM/FM cassette, cruise control, velour upholstery, upgraded interior trim, left visor mirror, map lights, rear center armrest, alloy wheels.

Optional equipment:

Air conditioning, XE	825	692	740
Anti-lock brakes, GXE	995	834	892

Prices are accurate at time of printing; subject to manufacturer's change.

	Retail Price	Dealer Invoice	Low Price
AM/FM cassette, XE	400	335	359
Power Convenience Group, XE	1240	1039	1112

Power windows and locks, power mirrors, velour upholstery, upgraded interior trim, driver's-seat lumbar and height adjustments, tachometer, rear center armrest.

	Retail Price	Dealer Invoice	Low Price
Two-tone paint, GXE	300	251	269
Power glass sunroof, GXE	800	671	718
Alloy wheels, XE	435	365	390

Requires Power Convenience Group.

	Retail Price	Dealer Invoice	Low Price
Cruise control, XE	175	146	157

Not available with 5-speed.

Nissan 240SX

Nissan 240SX SE

Nissan's rear-drive sports coupe was redesigned last year, when it acquired new styling, larger dimensions, and a new engine. For 1990, there's one major change: The Sport Package that was available only on the SE 3-door hatchback last year is now available on the XE 2-door notchback as well. The package includes a sport suspension, alloy wheels, wider tires, front and rear spoilers, and cruise control. A power antenna is a new standard feature on both the SE and XE. Both are powered by a 140-horsepower 2.4-liter 4-cylinder engine and are available with either a 5-speed manual or 4-speed automatic transmission. Four-wheel disc brakes are standard and anti-lock control is optional on the SE. A head-up instrument display is available only on the XE as part of the Power Convenience Group. It projects a digital speedometer reading onto the lower left-hand corner of the windshield. Those who favor rear-wheel drive over front-wheel drive will find the 240SX a rewarding yet undemanding car on twisting roads, especially with the optional Sport package. Too bad the engine doesn't match the capabilities of the suspension. We averaged 10.5 seconds to 60 mph with the 5-speed manual, which is disappointing for a car that looks so sporting. The optional anti-lock brakes are considerably cheaper this year ($995 instead of $1450), but you still have to buy the Sport Package and air conditioning to get them.

Specifications

	2-door notchback	3-door hatchback
Wheelbase, in.	97.4	97.4
Overall length, in.	178.0	178.0
Overall width, in.	66.5	66.5
Overall height, in.	50.8	50.8
Turn diameter, ft.	30.8	30.8
Curb weight, lbs.	2657	2684
Cargo vol., cu. ft.	8.6	14.2
Fuel capacity, gals.	15.9	15.9
Seating capacity	4	4
Front headroom, in.	37.8	37.8
Front shoulder room, in.	52.0	52.0
Front legroom, max., in.	42.0	42.0
Rear headroom, in.	34.5	33.3
Rear shoulder room, in.	52.0	51.8
Rear legroom, min., in.	23.8	23.8

Powertrain layout: longitudinal front engine/rear-wheel drive.

Engines

	ohc I-4
Size, liters/cu. in.	2.4/146
Fuel delivery	PFI
Horsepower @ rpm	140 @ 5600
Torque (lbs./ft.) @ rpm	152 @ 4400
Availability	S

EPA city/highway mpg

5-speed OD manual	20/27
4-speed OD automatic	20/25

Prices are accurate at time of printing; subject to manufacturer's change.

Prices

Nissan 240SX	Retail Price	Dealer Invoice	Low Price
XE 2-door notchback, 5-speed	$13249	$11642	$12142
XE 2-door notchback, automatic	14079	12371	12902
SE 3-door hatchback, 5-speed	13499	11861	12371
SE 3-door hatchback, automatic	14329	12591	13132
Destination charge	260	260	260

Standard equipment:

XE & SE: 2.4-liter PFI 4-cylinder engine, 5-speed manual or 4-speed automatic transmission, power steering, 4-wheel disc brakes, reclining front bucket seats with driver's side lumbar support adjustment, center console with storage, rear shoulder belts, tilt steering column, tachometer, coolant temperature gauge, trip odometer, variable intermittent wipers, tinted glass, dual remote mirrors, AM/FM radio with power diversity antenna, rear defogger, door pockets, remote fuel door and decklid releases, visor mirrors, cargo cover (SE), 195/60R15 tires.

Optional equipment:

Anti-lock brakes, SE	995	834	892
Requires Sport Pkg. and air conditioning.			
Air conditioning	825	692	740
XE Power Convenience Group	1350	1227	1257
Upgraded audio system with cassette and active speakers, head-up display, cruise control, power windows and locks, power mirrors, map lights.			
SE Power Convenience Group	1150	1045	1071
Upgraded audio system with cassette, cruise control, power windows and locks, power mirrors, rear wiper/washer.			
Sport Pkg.	1150	1045	1071
XE: cruise control, sport suspension, front air dam, rear spoiler, leather-wrapped steering wheel and shift knob, 205/60R15 tires on alloy wheels. SE adds seamless-style front seat cloth.			
Power Convenience Group & Sport Pkg., XE	2300	2091	2142
SE	2100	1909	1956
Two-tone paint, XE	300	251	269
Power sunroof, XE	800	671	718
Requires Power Convenience Group or Sport Pkg.			
Flip-up sunroof, SE	450	378	404
Requires Power Convenience Group or Sport Pkg.			

CONSUMER GUIDE®

Nissan 300ZX

Nissan 300ZX

The 1990 300ZX went on sale first as a 2-seater with a 222-horsepower 3.0-liter V-6, and then a 2 + 2 coupe with the same engine joined the lineup. The latest addition is the 300ZX Turbo, with two turbochargers helping its 3.0-liter V-6 pump 300 horsepower with the standard 5-speed manual transmission and 280 with automatic. The turbocharged engine has two intercoolers, four camshafts, and 24 valves. A different turbocharger and intercooler serves each bank of cylinders. Other features unique to the Turbo are intercooler inlets in the front air dam, a rear spoiler, Z-rated tires (for speeds over 149 mph), and Super HICAS, Nissan's 4-wheel steering system. HICAS stands for High Capacity Actively Controlled Steering; the rear wheels first turn slightly in the opposite direction as the fronts, and then in the same direction. Nissan says this improves stability in fast lane changes and provides crisper steering response. To discourage thieves, the vehicle-identification number is etched into the windows and T-tops of 300ZX Turbos. The new 300ZX is more of a sports car than a luxury car, yet it doesn't cheat its occupants out of comfort or convenience. We're impressed by the strong low-end acceleration and prompt, spirited passing response of the base engine, and blown away by the outstanding performance of the turbo. When it comes time to stop, the standard anti-lock brakes do a commendable job. The new Z-car also feels more nimble and zips around tight corners with admirable agility. Now the bad news: Base prices range from $27,300 for the GS 2-seater to $33,800 for the Turbo with automatic. If you can afford this much for a sports car, you'll be rewarded with top-notch performance.

Specifications

	3-door hatchback	2+2 3-door hatchback
Wheelbase, in.	96.5	101.2
Overall length, in.	169.5	178.0
Overall width, in.	70.5	70.9
Overall height, in.	49.2	49.4
Turn diameter, ft.	34.1	35.4
Curb weight, lbs.	3219[1]	3313
Cargo vol., cu. ft.	23.7	NA
Fuel capacity, gals.	18.7	18.7
Seating capacity	2	4
Front headroom, in.	36.8	37.1
Front shoulder room, in.	56.7	56.7
Front legroom, max., in.	43.0	43.0
Rear headroom, in.	—	34.4
Rear shoulder room, in.	—	55.2
Rear legroom, min., in.	—	22.7

1. 3414 lbs., Turbo.

Powertrain layout: longitudinal front engine/rear-wheel drive.

Engines

	dohc V-6	Turbo dohc V-6
Size, liters/cu. in.	3.0/181	3.0/181
Fuel delivery	PFI	PFI
Horsepower @ rpm	222 @ 6400	300 @ [1] 6400
Torque (lbs./ft.) @ rpm	198 @ 4800	283 @ 3600
Availability	S	S

EPA city/highway mpg

5-speed OD manual	18/24	18/24
4-speed OD automatic	19/24	18/24

1. 280 horsepower with automatic transmission.

Prices

Nissan 300ZX	Retail Price	Dealer Invoice	Low Price
GS 3-door hatchback, 5-speed	$27300	$23437	$24750
GS 3-door hatchback, automatic	28100	24124	25475

	Retail Price	Dealer Invoice	Low Price
Turbo 3-door hatchback, 5-speed	33000	28331	29918
Turbo 3-door hatchback, automatic	33800	29017	30642
GS 2+2 3-door hatchback, 5-speed	28500	24467	25838
GS 2+2 3-door hatchback, automatic . . .	29300	25154	26563
Destination charge	260	260	260

Standard equipment:

3.0-liter DOHC 24-valve PFI V-6, 5-speed manual or 4-speed automatic transmission, 4-wheel anti-lock disc brakes, power steering, air conditioning, power windows and locks, power mirrors, cloth reclining front bucket seats, driver's seat height, lumbar and lateral support adjustments, cruise control, tinted glass, T-bar roof, theft-deterrent system, AM/FM cassette with power diversity antenna, variable intermittent wipers, rear defogger and wiper/washer, remote fuel door and hatch releases, tachometer, coolant temperature and oil pressure gauges, leather-wrapped steering wheel and manual shift knob, fog lamps, 225/60R16 tires on alloy wheels. **Turbo** adds: turbocharged, intercooled engine, 4-wheel steering, limited-slip differential, front air dam and rear spoiler, Nissan-Bose audio system, 245/45ZR16 rear tires.

Optional equipment:

Electronic Equipment Pkg., GS	1600	1341	1435
Turbo	900	754	807
Nissan-Bose audio system, automatic temperature control, power driver's seat, heated OS mirrors, illuminated entry.			
Leather Trim Pkg., 2-seater	1000	838	897
2+2	1200	1006	1076
Leather seating surfaces, cargo cover, bronze-tinted glass; requires Electronic Equipment Pkg.			
Nissan-Bose audio system, GS	700	587	628
Pearlglow paint	350	294	314

Oldsmobile Cutlass Ciera/ Buick Century

Ciera and Century received fresh sheetmetal for '89, so changes this year focus on the interiors. Both are again offered in 2-door coupe, 4-door sedan, and 5-door wagon body styles. Century and Ciera debuted for 1982 and are

Prices are accurate at time of printing; subject to manufacturer's change.

Oldsmobile Cutlass Ciera SL

similar to the Chevrolet Celebrity and Pontiac 6000. Cutlass Ciera's lineup has been juggled but these front-drive intermediates otherwise continue with only minor trim changes. For '90, the base Cutlass Ciera coupe has been dropped and mid-level S models has been created for the coupe and sedan. The plush SL coupe is gone, but the SL sedan remains. Century Limited and Cutlass Ciera SL models get a new seat design. Century also gets air conditioning as standard and power seat recliners as a new option. Standard on all Centurys and on Oldsmobile's base and S models is a 2.5-liter 4-cylinder engine, which this year increases from 98 horsepower to 110. A 160-horsepower 3.3-liter V-6 is standard on the Ciera SL and sporty International Series, and optional on other Cieras and Centurys. The 3.3 gives these staid mid-size cars ample power. It's also a fairly quiet engine that should serve Century and Ciera owners better than the weaker, noisier standard four. The base suspensions and narrow standard tires are adequate for gentle, everyday commuting, but spirited cornering sets the front end to plowing and exposes the tires' modest grip. Firmer suspensions are optional and improve cornering ability, but they make the ride harsher and do little to keep the car from bounding dramatically over high-speed dips. Century and Ciera don't handle as well and do not feel as solid as the newer mid-size GM family (Chevrolet Lumina/Olds Cutlass Supreme/Buick Regal/Pontiac Grand Prix). But they're priced lower and are nearly as roomy.

Specifications

	2-door notchback	4-door notchback	5-door wagon
Wheelbase, in.	104.9	104.9	104.9
Overall length, in.	190.3	190.3	194.4
Overall width, in.	69.5	69.5	69.5
Overall height, in.	54.1	54.1	54.5
Turn diameter, ft.	38.5	38.5	38.5
Curb weight, lbs.	2736	2764	2913
Cargo vol., cu. ft.	15.8	15.8	74.4
Fuel capacity, gals.	15.7	15.7	15.7
Seating capacity	6	6	8
Front headroom, in.	38.6	38.6	38.6
Front shoulder room, in.	55.9	56.2	56.2
Front legroom, max., in.	42.1	42.1	42.1
Rear headroom, in.	37.6	38.0	38.9
Rear shoulder room, in.	56.9	56.2	56.2
Rear legroom, min., in.	35.8	35.8	34.7

Powertrain layout: transverse front engine/front-wheel drive.

Engines

	ohv I-4	ohv V-6
Size, liters/cu. in.	2.5/151	3.3/204
Fuel delivery	TBI	PFI
Horsepower @ rpm	110 @ 5200	160 @ 5200
Torque (lbs./ft.) @ rpm	135 @ 3200	185 @ 2000
Availability	S	O[1]

EPA city/highway mpg

3-speed automatic	23/30	20/27
4-speed OD automatic		20/29

1. Std., Ciera SL and I-Series.

Prices

Oldsmobile Cutlass Ciera	Retail Price	Dealer Invoice	Low Price
4-door notchback	$11995	$10592	$10792
S 2-door notchback	12395	10945	11145
S 4-door notchback	12995	11215	11415
Cruiser S 5-door wagon	13395	11560	11760
SL 4-door notchback	14695	12612	12812
Cruiser SL 5-door wagon	15295	13200	13400
I Series 2-door notchback	15995	14124	14324
I Series 4-door notchback	16795	14494	14694
Destination charge	450	450	450

Prices are accurate at time of printing; subject to manufacturer's change.

Standard equipment:

Base & S: 2.5-liter TBI 4-cylinder engine, 3-speed automatic transmission, power steering, front bench seat with folding armrest, rear shoulder belts, tinted glass, door pockets, left remote and right manual mirrors, AM/FM radio, 185/75R14 tires. **SL** adds: 3.3-liter PFI V-6, air conditioning, 55/45 front seat with storage armrest, power driver's seatback recliner, reading lamps, lighted right visor mirror, AM/FM cassette, white-stripe tires. **International Series** adds: 4-speed automatic transmission with floorshift, front bucket seats, front air dam with fog lamps, sill extensions, Driver Information System (trip and service reminders), tachometer, coolant temperature and oil pressure gauges, voltmeter, trip odometer, floormats, tilt steering column, intermittent wipers, remote decklid release, 215/60R14 tires on alloy wheels.

Optional equipment:	Retail Price	Dealer Invoice	Low Price
3.3-liter V-6, base & S	710	604	639
4-speed automatic transmission, S & SL .	200	170	180
Air conditioning, S	805	684	725
Option Pkg. 1SB, base	805	684	725
Air conditioning.			
Option Pkg. 1SC, base	995	846	896
Pkg. 1SB plus tilt steering column, intermittent wipers.			
Option Pkg. 1SD, base	1210	1029	1089
Pkg. 1SC plus power locks.			
Option Pkg. 1SE, base	1505	1279	1355
Pkg. 1SD plus power windows.			
Option Pkg. 1SB, S 2- & 4-door	1040	884	936
S wagon	1124	955	1012
Air conditioning, tilt steering column, intermittent wipers, floormats; wagon includes air deflector and Convenience Group.			
Option Pkg. 1SC, S 2-door	1525	1296	1373
S 4-door	1305	1109	1175
S wagon	1374	1168	1237
Pkg. 1SB plus cruise control, accent stripe (exc. wagon), power windows (2-door), door edge guards, remote mirrors (wagon).			
Option Pkg. 1SD, S 2-door	1801	1531	1621
S 4-door	1916	1629	1724
S wagon	2009	1708	1808
Pkg. 1SC plus Convenience Group, power windows and locks, remote decklid release, power antenna (wagon).			
Option Pkg. 1SE, S 2-door	2372	2016	2135
S 4-door	2487	2114	2238
Pkg. 1SD plus power antenna, molding pkg., power passenger seatback recliner, remote mirrors, power driver's seat.			
Value Option Pkg., S	440	374	396
Rallye instruments, luggage rack, alloy wheels.			

	Retail Price	Dealer Invoice	Low Price
Option Pkg. 1SB, SL 4-door	570	485	513
SL wagon	475	404	428

Tilt steering column, intermittent wipers, cruise control, power passenger seatback recliner (4-door), floormats, accent stripe, door edge guards (4-door).

Option Pkg. 1SC, SL 4-door	1155	982	1040
SL wagon	770	655	693

Wagon: Pkg. 1SB plus power windows. 4-door adds: power locks, power antenna.

Option Pkg. 1SD, SL 4-door	1455	1237	1310
SL wagon	1480	1258	1332

4-door: Pkg. 1SC plus power driver's seat, remote mirrors. Wagon adds: power windows and locks, power antenna, power passenger seatback recliner.

Value Option Pkg., SL 4-door	382	325	344
SL wagon	267	227	240

Rallye instruments, luggage rack (4-door), alloy wheels.

Option Pkg. 1SB, I Series 2-door	975	829	878
I Series 4-door	1080	918	972

Power windows and locks, cruise control, power antenna, power driver's seat, remote mirrors.

Divided bench seat, S 2- & 4-door	253	215	228
S wagon	323	275	291
SL 4-door	275	234	248
Power locks, S 2-door	175	149	158
S 4-door	215	183	194
S wagon	265	225	239
Power windows, S 2-door	230	196	207
S 4-door & wagon	295	251	266
XC Special Edition Pkg., S 2- & 4-door . .	489	416	440
S wagon	604	513	544

Blackout exterior trim, body-color wheel covers, floor console and shifter, leather-wrapped steering wheel, rallye instruments.

Power sunroof, SL 4-door, I Series	775	659	698
Rear defogger	160	136	144
FE3 suspension pkg. (NA wagons), S . . .	505	429	455
SL	447	380	402
Super Stock wheels, S 2- & 4-door	115	98	104
Wire wheel covers, S	283	241	255
SL	215	183	194
Alloy wheels, S	333	283	300
SL	275	234	248
185/75R14 WSW tires, base & S	68	58	61
Rallye instruments, S & SL	142	121	128
AM/FM cassette, base & S	165	140	149
AM/FM cassette w/EQ, SL & I Series . . .	150	128	135

Prices are accurate at time of printing; subject to manufacturer's change.

	Retail Price	Dealer Invoice	Low Price
High-capacity cooling, S & SL	40	34	36
Luggage rack, S & SL	115	98	104
Custom leather trim, I Series	400	340	360
Accent stripe, S	45	38	41
Engine block heater	18	15	16
Front floormats, base	25	21	23
Rear floormats, base	20	17	18
California emissions pkg.	100	85	90

Buick Century

	Retail Price	Dealer Invoice	Low Price
Custom 4-door notchback	$13150	$11348	$11548
Custom 2-door notchback	13250	11435	11635
Custom 5-door wagon	14570	12574	12774
Limited 4-door notchback	14075	12147	12347
Limited 5-door wagon	15455	13338	13538
Destination charge	450	450	450

Standard equipment:

Custom: 2.5-liter TBI 4-cylinder engine, 3-speed automatic transmission, power steering, dual outside mirrors, tinted glass, map lights, instrument panel courtesy lights, cloth split bench seat, AM/FM radio, P185/75R14 all-season SBR tires. **Wagon** adds: split folding rear seatback, two-way tailgate. **Limited and Estate** add: 55/45 notchback cloth seat, armrest with storage, trunk trim (4-door).

Optional equipment:

3.3-liter V-6	710	604	639
4-speed automatic transmission (V-6 req.) .	200	170	180
Popular Pkg. SB, Custom 2-door	410	349	369
Custom 4-door	420	357	378
Custom wagon	535	455	482

Rear defogger, tilt steering column, intermittent wipers, door edge guards, floormats, roof rack (wagon).

Premium Pkg. SC, Custom 2-door	1218	1035	1096
Custom 4-door	1268	1078	1141
Custom wagon	1703	1448	1533

Pkg. SB plus power locks, cruise control, AM/FM cassette, styled steel wheels, 55/45 front seat with storage armrest. Wagon adds: remote tailgate lock release, air deflector, rear-facing third seat.

	Retail Price	Dealer Invoice	Low Price
Luxury Pkg. SD, Custom 2-door	1651	1403	1486
Custom 4-door	1766	1501	1589
Custom wagon	2201	1871	1981

Pkg. SC plus power windows, wire wheel covers, lighted right visor mirror.

	Retail Price	Dealer Invoice	Low Price
Prestige Pkg. SE, Custom 2-door	2124	1805	1912
Custom 4-door	2239	1903	2015
Custom wagon	2624	2230	2362

Pkg. SD plus power mirrors, power driver's seat, power antenna, remote decklid release.

	Retail Price	Dealer Invoice	Low Price
Premium Pkg. SC, Ltd 4-door	945	803	851
Ltd wagon	1125	956	1013

Tilt steering column, rear defogger, intermittent wipers, power locks, cruise control, styled steel wheels, floormats, door edge guards, roof rack and remote tailgate lock release (wagon).

	Retail Price	Dealer Invoice	Low Price
Luxury Pkg. SD, Ltd 4-door	1525	1296	1373
Ltd wagon	2093	1779	1884

Pkg. SC plus wire wheel covers, AM/FM cassette, power windows. Wagon adds: rear window air deflector, rear-facing third seat, lighted right visor mirror, power antenna.

	Retail Price	Dealer Invoice	Low Price
Prestige Pkg. SE, Ltd 4-door	2150	1828	1935
Ltd wagon	2500	2125	2250

Pkg. SD plus power driver's seat, power mirrors, reading lights, premium speakers, lighted right visor mirror, power antenna, remote decklid release.

	Retail Price	Dealer Invoice	Low Price
Cruise control, Custom w/SB	195	166	176
Power locks, Custom 2-door w/SB	175	149	158
Custom 4-door w/SB	215	183	194
AM/FM cassette	140	119	126
Power antenna	75	64	68
Power seatback recliners	110	94	99
Cloth 55/45 seat w/armrest, Custom w/SB	183	156	165
w/Empress cloth, Custom w/SB	551	468	496
w/Empress cloth, Custom w/SC/SD/SE	368	313	331
Leather & vinyl 55/45 seat, Ltd	450	383	405
Wire wheel covers, Custom w/SB	215	183	194
Custom w/SC	100	85	90
Styled steel wheels, Custom w/SB	115	98	104
Alloy wheels, Custom w/SB	270	230	243
Custom & Limited w/SC	155	132	140
Custom & Limited w/SD/SE	55	47	50
Rear wiper/washer, wagons			
Custom w/SB, Limited w/SC	125	106	113
Custom w/SC/SD/SE, Ltd w/SD/SE	85	72	77
Power windows, Custom 2-door w/SB/SC	230	196	207
Custom 4-door w/SB/SC, Ltd 4-door w/SC	295	251	266

Prices are accurate at time of printing; subject to manufacturer's change.

Oldsmobile Cutlass Supreme/ Buick Regal

Oldsmobile Cutlass Supreme I Series

Oldsmobile and Buick get 4-door sedan versions of their mid-size coupes, while the Cutlass Supreme also makes news with a new convertible model. All are built from the same front-drive platform and share the same wheelbase, 4-wheel independent suspension, and standard 4-wheel disc brakes. Only the Regal sedan differs significantly in styling from its coupe counterpart; the 4-door has a smoother nose with a more horizontal grille and a more tapered tail and smaller rear lights. Seating capacity ranges from six to four, depending on model and optional equipment. Both Cutlass and Regal have a 3.1-liter V-6 standard, but a 3.8-liter V-6 is an exclusive option on the Buick for '90. Exclusive to the Cutlass Supreme, meanwhile, are two versions of the 2.3-liter, twin-cam Quad 4 engine. An anti-lock brake system is optional on all Cutlass models and on Limited and GS Regals. A head-up instrument display, which projects the digital speedometer reading and turn signal indicators onto the windshield, is now included in an option package on the Cutlass Supreme I-Series coupe, while the Regal offers optional dual temperature controls for the driver and front-seat passenger. The Cutlass convertible is scheduled for a spring introduction. It seats five and has a power top with a glass backlight. A padded roof bar over the passenger area allows Olds to retain the coupe's door handle and shoulder belt anchor positions. While the roof bar is not designed to provide protection in a rollover, Olds says it helps stiffen the car's body. The Cutlass Supreme sedan hit the showrooms in the fall; the Regal sedan will be available in early 1990. These cars are more appealing as sedans than as coupes. The rear seat is now as accessible as a family car's ought to be. While back-seat room is ample, the seat cushion itself is too small. Opt for one of the V-6 engines. The Quad 4s are high-revving, high-performance engines that feel mismatched to these cars. Overall, these are roomy intermediates that don't leap ahead of the older Ford Taurus.

Specifications	2-door notchback	2-door conv.	4-door notchback
Wheelbase, in.	107.5	107.5	107.5
Overall length, in.	192.3	192.3	192.2
Overall width, in.	71.0	71.0	70.9
Overall height, in.	53.3	54.3	54.8
Turn diameter, ft.	39.0	39.0	39.0
Curb weight, lbs.	3133	3501	3221
Cargo vol., cu. ft.	15.5	12.1	15.5
Fuel capacity, gals.	16.5	16.5	16.5
Seating capacity	6	5	6
Front headroom, in.	37.8	38.5	38.8
Front shoulder room, in.	57.6	57.6	57.4
Front legroom, max., in.	42.3	42.3	42.4
Rear headroom, in.	37.1	38.4	38.4
Rear shoulder room, in.	57.2	56.3	56.6
Rear legroom, min., in.	34.8	34.8	36.2

Powertrain layout: transverse front engine/front-wheel drive.

Engines	ohv V-6	ohv V-6	dohc I-4	dohc I-4
Size, liters/cu. in.	3.1/191	3.8/231	2.3/138	2.3/138
Fuel delivery	PFI	PFI	PFI	PFI
Horsepower @ rpm	135 @ 4400	170 @ 4800	180 @ 6200	160 @ 6200
Torque (lbs./ft.) @ rpm	180 @ 3600	220 @ 3200	160 @ 5200	155 @ 5200
Availability	S[1]	O[2]	S[3]	O[4]

EPA city/highway mpg

5-speed OD manual			22/31	
3-speed automatic				22/29
4-speed OD automatic	19/30	18/27		

1. Regal, Cutlass SL.   2. Regal.   3. Base Cutlass, I Series.   4. Base Cutlass.

Prices are accurate at time of printing; subject to manufacturer's change.

Prices

Oldsmobile Cutlass Supreme	Retail Price	Dealer Invoice	Low Price
2-door notchback	$14495	$12509	$12709
4-door notchback	14595	12595	12795
SL 2-door notchback	16095	13890	14090
SL 4-door notchback	16195	13976	14176
I Series 2-door notchback	17995	13976	14176
I Series 4-door notchback	17995	15530	15730
Destination charge	455	455	455

Standard equipment:

2.3-liter DOHC 16-valve HO Quad 4 engine, 5-speed manual transmission, power steering, 4-wheel disc brakes, air conditioning, front bucket seats, trip odometer, left remote and right manual mirrors, AM/FM radio, rear shoulder belts, tinted glass, 195/75R14 all-season SBR tires. **SL** adds: 3.1-liter PFI V-6, 4-speed automatic transmission, Convenience Group (reading lamps, right visor mirror, misc. lights), AM/FM cassette, remote decklid release, alloy wheels. **International Series** adds: 2.3-liter DOHC 16-valve HO Quad 4, 5-speed manual transmission, FE3 suspension, fast-ratio steering, Driver Information System (trip computer and service reminder), electronic instruments (tachometer, coolant temperature, oil pressure, voltmeter), power locks with remote control, rocker panel extensions, power front bucket seats, rear bucket seats, tilt steering column, intermittent wipers, 215/60R16 tires on alloy wheels.

Optional equipment:

2.3-liter non-HO Quad 4, base	325	276	293
Includes 3-speed automatic transmission.			
3.1-liter V-6, base & I Series	500	425	450
Includes 4-speed automatic transmission.			
Anti-lock brakes	925	786	833
Option Pkg. 1SB, base	627	533	564
Tilt steering column, intermittent wipers, power mirrors, cruise control, Convenience Group, floormats.			
Option Pkg. 1SC, base 2-door	862	733	776
Base 4-door	872	741	785
Pkg. 1SB plus Appearance & Molding Pkg., rear defogger.			
Option Pkg. 1SD, base 2-door	1527	1298	1374
Base 4-door	1642	1396	1478
Pkg. 1SC plus power antenna, Remote Lock Control Pkg., power windows.			
Option Pkg. 1SE, base 2-door	1797	1527	1617
Base 4-door	1912	1625	1721
Pkg. 1SD plus power driver's seat.			

	Retail Price	Dealer Invoice	Low Price
Value Option Pkg., base	320	272	288
Rallye interior, luggage rack.			
Option Pkg. 1SB, SL 2-door	712	605	641
SL 4-door	722	614	650
Cruise control, tilt steering column, floormats, intermittent wipers, Appearance & Molding Pkg., rear defogger, power mirrors.			
Option Pkg. 1SC, SL 2-door	1597	1357	1437
SL 4-door	1712	1455	1541
Pkg. 1SB plus power antenna, Remote Lock Control Pkg., power windows, power driver's seat.			
Option Pkg. 1SD, SL 2-door	2142	1821	1928
SL 4-door	2257	1918	2031
Pkg. 1SC plus automatic climate control, steering wheel touch control, Driver Information System.			
Option Pkg. 1SB, I Series 2-door	670	570	603
I Series 4-door	745	633	671
Cruise control, power windows, rear defogger, Appearance & Molding Pkg.			
Option Pkg. 1SC, I Series 2-door	980	833	882
I Series 4-door	1055	897	950
Pkg. 1SB plus power driver's seat, power antenna.			
Option Pkg. 1SD, I Series 2-door	2200	1870	1980
Pkg. 1SC plus anti-lock brakes, head-up instrument display.			
Easy-entry passenger seat, 2-doors	16	14	14
55/45 front seat, base	NC	NC	NC
Front bucket seats, SL	339	288	305
Power locks, base 2-door	175	149	158
Base 4-door	215	183	194
Power windows, base 2-door	240	204	216
Base 4-door	305	259	275
Power glass sunroof, SL & I Series	650	553	585
Rear defogger	160	136	144
FE3 suspension pkg., base	549	467	494
Alloy wheels, base	343	292	309
AM/FM cassette, base	165	140	149
AM/FM cassette w/EQ, SL	255	217	230
I Series	225	191	203
AM/FM radio w/CD player, SL	399	339	359
I Series	369	314	332
High-capacity cooling equipment	125	106	113
Luggage rack, base & SL	115	98	104
Rallye interior, base	355	302	320
Custom leather trim, SL	490	417	441
I Series	400	340	360
Engine block heater	18	15	16
California emissions pkg.	100	85	90

Prices are accurate at time of printing; subject to manufacturer's change.

CONSUMER GUIDE®

Buick Regal

	Retail Price	Dealer Invoice	Low Price
Custom 2-door notchback	$15200	$13118	$13318
Limited 2-door notchback	15860	13687	13887
Destination charge	455	455	455

Prices for 4-door models not available at time of publication.

Standard equipment:

3.1-liter PFI V-6, 4-speed automatic transmission, power steering, 55/45 cloth front seat with armrest and recliners (bucket seats are available at no charge),tilt steering column, tinted glass, digital speedometer, left remote and right manual mirrors, black lower bodyside moldings, AM/FM radio, automatic front seatbelts, rear shoulder belts, 205/70R14 all-season SBR WSW tires. **Limited** adds: upgraded carpet, bright wide bodyside moldings, 55/45 seat with storage armrest.

Optional equipment:

3.8-liter V-6	395	336	356
Anti-lock braking system, Ltd & GS	925	786	833
Popular Pkg. SB, Custom	306	260	275
Rear defogger, intermittent wipers, door edge guards, white-stripe tires.			
Premium Pkg. SB, Custom	861	732	775
Pkg. SB plus AM/FM cassette, cruise control, power locks, floormats.			
Luxury Pkg. SD, Custom	1574	1338	1417
Pkg. SC plus power windows, power antenna, lighted right visor mirror, wire wheel covers, courtesy and reading lights, remote decklid release.			
Prestige Pkg. SE, Custom	2416	2054	2174
Pkg. SD plus power driver's seat, power mirrors, Concert Sound speakers, steering-wheel-mounted radio controls, electronic instrumentation.			
Premium Pkg. SC, Limited	626	532	563
Rear defogger, AM/FM cassette, intermittent wipers, cruise control, white-stripe tires.			
Luxury Pkg. SD, Limited	1814	1542	1633
Pkg. SC plus power windows and locks, power driver's seat, power antenna, remote decklid release, wire wheel covers, lighted right visor mirror, floormats, door edge guards.			
Prestige Pkg. SE, Limited	2581	2194	2323
Pkg. SD plus power mirrors, Concert Sound speakers, electronic instrumentation, steering-wheel-mounted radio controls, dual air conditioning controls, upgraded radio (includes AM stereo, EQ and tape search/repeat).			
Gran Sport Premium Pkg. SM	1624	1380	1462
Gran Touring Pkg., Gran Sport exterior trim, cloth reclining seats, floorshift, AM/FM cassette, cruise control, rear defogger, intermittent wipers, floormats.			

	Retail Price	Dealer Invoice	Low Price
Gran Sport Prestige Pkg. SF	2969	2524	2672

Pkg. SM plus power windows and locks, electronic instrumentation, front reading/courtesy lights, power mirrors, power antenna, power driver's seat, Concert Sound speakers, remote decklid release, lighted right visor mirror.

	Retail Price	Dealer Invoice	Low Price
Gran Touring Pkg., w/SC	531	451	478
w/SD	271	230	244
w/SE	175	149	158

Gran Touring suspension, leather-wrapped steering wheel (exc. w/SE), 215/60R16 tires on alloy wheels.

	Retail Price	Dealer Invoice	Low Price
Cruise control, Custom w/SB	195	166	176
Power locks	175	149	158
Electronic instrumentation, Ltd w/SD	299	254	269

Tachometer, coolant temperature and oil pressure gauges, voltmeter, trip odometer, low fuel indicator.

	Retail Price	Dealer Invoice	Low Price
Remote keyless entry, Ltd & GS	125	106	113

Requires SE or SF.

	Retail Price	Dealer Invoice	Low Price
Decklid luggage rack	115	98	104
AM/FM cassette, Custom w/SB	140	119	126
AM/FM cassette w/EQ & AM stereo	150	128	135

Available on Custom w/SE and Gran Sport.

	Retail Price	Dealer Invoice	Low Price
CD player, Custom w/SE, GS	274	233	247
Ltd w/SE	124	105	112
Power antenna	75	64	68
Power glass sunroof	650	553	585
Steering-wheel-mounted radio controls, GS .	29	25	26
Leather/vinyl 55/45 seat, Ltd	450	383	405
Leather/vinyl bucket seats, Ltd & GS	450	383	405
Four Seater Pkg., GS	409	348	368

Cloth bucket seats, floorshift, rear bucket seats with head restraints.

	Retail Price	Dealer Invoice	Low Price
Styled steel wheels, w/SB/SC	115	98	104
Wire wheel covers, w/SB/SC	215	183	194
Alloy wheels (14"), w/SB/SC	270	230	243
Alloy wheels w/205/70R15 tires, w/SB/SC .	244	207	220
w/SD/SE	29	25	26
Power windows, w/SB/SC/SD	240	204	216
California emissions pkg.	100	85	90

Oldsmobile Silhouette

The Silhouette minivan is from the General Motors design that also spawned the '90 Pontiac Trans Sport and Chevrolet Lumina APV. Drive is to the front wheels via a 3-speed automatic transmission and a 3.1-liter V-6 mounted trans-

Prices are accurate at time of printing; subject to manufacturer's change.

Oldsmobile Silhouette

versely in the nose. Silhouette's body is made of fiberglass and composite material bonded and bolted to a metal frame. Olds' unique grille, wheel design, and exterior graphics differentiate Silhouette from its Pontiac and Chevy stablemates. Inside, 7-passenger seating—optional on the base models of the other GM vans—is standard on Silhouette, with seven bucket seats in a 2-3-2 layout. One of the middle buckets can be deleted as a credit option. In keeping with its upmarket image, Silhouette is alone among the GM minivans in offering leather upholstery as an option. Silhouette's 21st-Century shape is bait for shoppers who might otherwise eschew minivans as too utilitarian. But they'll first have to get acclimated to the driving position. Silhouette's 17.25-square-foot windshield slants a severe 66 degrees. The driver must peer out over more than two feet of dashboard shelf, beyond which the sheetmetal is invisible. Boxier minivans like the Dodge Caravan/Plymouth Voyager and Mazda MPV are less daunting to drive, though Silhouette's removable lightweight bucket seats (34 pounds each) help its versatility. The Olds rides, steers, maneuvers, and tracks down the highway much like a mid-size front-drive GM car. With only 120 horsepower, however, the 3650-pound van feels underpowered, especially when loaded with passengers and vacation luggage and with the air conditioner running.

Specifications

	4-door van
Wheelbase, in.	109.8
Overall length, in.	194.2
Overall width, in.	73.9
Overall height, in.	65.2
Turn diameter, ft.	42.5
Curb weight, lbs.	3648
Cargo vol., cu. ft.	111.2
Fuel capacity, gals.	20.0
Seating capacity	7
Front headroom, in.	40.2
Front shoulder room, in.	53.5
Front legroom, max., in.	40.7
Rear headroom, in.	38.6
Rear shoulder room, in.	61.6
Rear legroom, min., in.	33.7

Powertrain layout: transverse front engine/front-wheel drive.

Engines

	ohv V-6
Size, liters/cu. in.	3.1/191
Fuel delivery	TBI
Horsepower @ rpm	120 @ 4200
Torque (lbs./ft.) @ rpm	175 @ 2200
Availability	S

EPA city/highway mpg

3-speed automatic	18/23

Prices

Oldsmobile Silhouette	Retail Price	Dealer Invoice	Low Price
4-door van	$17195	$15355	—
Destination charge	500	500	500

Low price not available at time of publication.

Standard equipment:

3.1-liter TBI V-6, 3-speed automatic transmission, power steering, air conditioning, seven bucket seats, tilt steering column, AM/FM radio, tachometer, coolant temperature and oil pressure gauges, voltmeter, trip odometer, map lights, rear defogger, dual remote mirrors, intermittent wipers, rear wiper/washer, floormats, 205/70R14 tires on alloy wheels.

Prices are accurate at time of printing; subject to manufacturer's change.

Optional equipment:

	Retail Price	Dealer Invoice	Low Price
Option Pkg. 1SB	450	383	—
Power locks, cruise control.			
Option Pkg. 1SC	960	816	—
Pkg. 1SB plus power windows, power driver's seat.			
Value Option Pkg.	540	459	—
Custom leather trim, AM/FM cassette.			
6-passenger modular seating (credit)	(110)	(94)	(94)
Rear defogger	160	136	—
FE3 touring suspension	232	197	—
AM/FM cassette	140	119	—
AM/FM radio w/CD player	396	337	—
Custom leather trim	650	553	—
Includes 6-passenger seating.			
Engine block heater	18	15	—
California emissions pkg.	100	85	—

Oldsmobile Toronado/Trofeo

Oldsmobile Trofeo

Every body panel except the hood is new for '90 on Oldsmobile's front-drive personal-luxury coupes. The changes add 12.4 inches to the overall length, a stretch designed to recapture some of the big-car brashness lost in the Toro's 1986 downsizing. Interior space is unaltered, though the trunk gains 2.5 cubic feet. The controversial video Visual Information Center, added as an option last year, has been dropped from the Toronado's options list, but remains available on the sportier Trofeo. Toronados with bucket seats now get analog gauges; digital instruments are fitted to those with the optional 55/45 front bench seat and accompanying column shift lever. Also newly standard this year on both Toronado and Trofeo are a driver's-side air bag, a larger glovebox, illuminated power window switches, and an auto-down driver's window. Trofeo's optional Visual Information Center is a small video screen mounted in the center of the dashboard. Interrupt the appropriate light beam with a finger and the screen allows you to manage the stereo and climate systems, as well as operate the trip computer. Traditional switches are used in the standard dashboard. The Trofeo shares its 3.8-liter V-6 with the Toronado. Cars like these value image over hard-core driving satisfaction. Still, Toronado and Trofeo deliver all that most

Specifications

	2-door notchback
Wheelbase, in.	108.0
Overall length, in.	200.3
Overall width, in.	72.8
Overall height, in.	53.0
Turn diameter, ft.	39.4
Curb weight, lbs.	3462
Cargo vol., cu. ft.	15.8
Fuel capacity, gals.	18.0
Seating capacity	6
Front headroom, in.	37.8
Front shoulder room, in.	58.3
Front legroom, max., in.	43.0
Rear headroom, in.	37.8
Rear shoulder room, in.	57.5
Rear legroom, min., in.	35.7

Powertrain layout: transverse front engine/front-wheel drive.

Engines

	ohv V-6
Size, liters/cu. in.	3.8/231
Fuel delivery	PFI
Horsepower @ rpm	165 @ 5200
Torque (lbs./ft.) @ rpm	210 @ 2000
Availability	S

EPA city/highway mpg

4-speed OD automatic	18/27

Prices are accurate at time of printing; subject to manufacturer's change

of its owners will ask of it. Acceleration is brisk, handling competent. Trofeo's suspension is stiffer, but neither model rides roughly. The cabin is filled with convenience features and offers fine room in front, though rear-seat space is modest. Don't opt for the Visual Information Center: It complicates rather than simplifies stereo and climate-system controls, and costs a whopping $1295.

Prices

Oldsmobile Toronado/Trofeo	Retail Price	Dealer Invoice	Low Price
Toronado 2-door notchback	$21995	$18982	$19182
Trofeo 2-door notchback	24995	21571	21771
Destination charge	550	550	550

Standard equipment:

3.8-liter PFI V-6, 4-speed automatic transmission, power steering, 4-wheel disc brakes, driver's-side airbag, reclining front bucket seats, power driver's seat, automatic climate control, power windows and locks, power mirrors (heated left), cruise control, rear defogger, tachometer, AM/FM cassette, leather-wrapped steering wheel, tilt steering column, tinted glass, floormats, remote decklid release, Twilight Sentinel, anti-theft security system, intermittent wipers, 205/75R15 tires on alloy wheels. **Trofeo** adds: anti-lock brakes, FE3 suspension, automatic power locks, fog lights, cornering lamps, remote fuel door release, lighted visor mirrors, power decklid pulldown, 215/60R16 tires.

Optional equipment:

Anti-lock brakes, Toronado	925	786	833
Option Pkg. 1SB, Toronado	739	628	665
Power passenger seat, Illumination Pkg., lighted visor mirrors, power decklid pulldown, automatic day/night mirror, Remote Lock Control Pkg.			
Value Option Pkg., Toronado	460	391	414
Glamour metallic paint, custom leather trim.			
Divided bench seat, Toronado	NC	NC	NC
Power sunroof	1230	1046	1107
Two-tone paint, Toronado	101	86	91
FE3 suspension pkg., Toronado	126	107	113
205/75R15 tires, Toronado	76	65	68
Delco/Bose music system	703	598	633
AM/FM cassette w/EQ	120	102	108
AM/FM radio w/CD player	516	439	464
Mobile telephone	995	846	896

	Retail Price	Dealer Invoice	Low Price
Visual Information Center	1295	1101	1166
Glamour metallic paint, Toronado	210	179	189
Custom leather trim, Toronado	400	340	360
Engine block heater	18	15	16
California emissions pkg.	100	85	90

Plymouth Acclaim/Dodge Spirit

Plymouth Acclaim LE

A standard driver's-side airbag and wider availability of a
V-6 engine highlight these front-drive compacts for '90. A
Mitsubishi-made 3.0-liter V-6 mated to Chrysler's 4-speed
automatic transmission is now optional on all models. That
powertrain had been exclusive to the top-rung versions for
1989, but mechanical problems with the new automatic
delayed those models—and thus the V-6 engine—until late
in the model year. Base and mid-line LE models of both
cars retain a 2.5-liter 4-cylinder engine as standard and a
turbocharged 2.5 as optional. An optional Acclaim Rallye
Sport package is among other additions for '90. Introduced
for the '89 model year, Spirit and Acclaim are 4-door sedans
that retain the front-drive layout and conservative, upright
styling of the Dodge Aires and Plymouth Reliant, the K-
cars they replaced. They're about three inches longer in
wheelbase and overall length than the K-cars, and have
2.6 inches more rear leg room. The Plymouth is tailored
for family transportation, while the Dodge tilts toward the
sporty. They soundly beat the K-cars in ride, handling,

Prices are accurate at time of printing; subject to manufacturer's change.

power, and quality feel. Neither achieves the Honda Accord-like polish that Chrysler officials say was their goal, but they are comfortable, competent, and competitive with foreign and domestic rivals. The cabin is airy, the trunk roomy. Performance is best with the V-6. The turbo 2.5 feels marginally quicker than the V-6, but the turbo is louder and coarser. The base engine provides adequate pickup. A loaded Acclaim or Spirit with the V-6 and other extras will be less than $15,000, while a basic 4-cylinder model runs about $12,500.

Specifications

	4-door notchback
Wheelbase, in.	103.3
Overall length, in.	181.2
Overall width, in.	68.1
Overall height, in.	53.5
Turn diameter, ft.	37.6
Curb weight, lbs.	2854
Cargo vol., cu. ft.	14.4
Fuel capacity, gals.	16.0
Seating capacity	6
Front headroom, in.	38.4
Front shoulder room, in.	54.3
Front legroom, max., in.	41.9
Rear headroom, in.	37.9
Rear shoulder room, in.	55.0
Rear legroom, min., in.	38.3

Powertrain layout: transverse front engine/front-wheel drive.

Engines	ohc I-4	Turbo ohc I-4	ohc V-6
Size, liters/cu. in.	2.5/153	2.5/153	3.0/181
Fuel delivery	TBI	PFI	PFI
Horsepower @ rpm	100 @ 4800	150 @ 4800	141 @ 5000
Torque (lbs./ft.) @ rpm	135 @ 2800	180 @ 2000	171 @ 2800
Availability	S	O[1]	O[2]

EPA city/highway mpg

5-speed OD manual	24/32	21/29	
3-speed automatic	22/27	19/23	
4-speed OD automatic			19/26

1. Standard, Spirit ES.   2. Standard, Acclaim LX.

Prices

Plymouth Acclaim

	Retail Price	Dealer Invoice	Low Price
4-door notchback	$10395	$9298	$9498
LE 4-door notchback	11875	10600	10800
LX 4-door notchback	13865	12351	12551
Destination charge	440	440	440

Standard equipment:

2.5-liter TBI 4-cylinder engine, 5-speed manual transmission, power steering, driver's-side airbag, cloth reclining front bucket seats, coolant temperature gauge, voltmeter, trip odometer, intermittent wipers, AM/FM radio, remote fuel door and decklid releases, 185/70R14 tires. **LE** adds: cruise control, tilt steering column, driver's seat lumbar support adjustment, lighted visor mirrors, rear defogger, message center, 55/45 folding rear seat, armrest with dual cupholders, 195/70R14 tires. **LX** adds: 3.0-liter PFI V-6, 4-speed automatic transmission, sport suspension, decklid luggage rack, trip computer, AM/FM cassette, leather-wrapped steering wheel, 205/60R15 tires on alloy wheels.

Optional equipment:

2.5-liter turbo engine, base & LE	680	578	612
3.0-liter V-6, base & LE	680	578	612
3-speed automatic transmission, base & LE	536	456	482
4-speed automatic transmission, base & LE	627	533	564
Air conditioning, LE & LX	805	684	725
Super Discount Pkg. A, base	1100	935	990

Air conditioning, rear defogger, floormats, tinted glass, time-delay ignition switch light, four speakers, cruise control, tilt steering column.

Super Discount Pkg. B, base	1403	1193	1263

Pkg. A plus power windows and locks, heated power mirrors.

Super Discount Pkg. C, LE & LX	913	776	822

Air conditioning, power windows and locks, heated power mirrors.

Popular Equipment Discount Pkg., base	934	794	841

Air conditioning, rear defogger, tinted glass, four speakers.

Premium Equipment Discount Pkg., base	293	249	264
Base w/Super Discount or Deluxe Convenience	285	242	257

Front bucket seats, 55/45 folding rear seat, console armrest, premium body sound insulation, misc. lights, message center.

Deluxe Convenience Pkg., base	336	286	302

Floormats, time-delay ignition switch light, cruise control, tilt steering column.

Power Equipment Discount Pkg.	573	487	516

Power windows and locks, heated power mirrors.

Prices are accurate at time of printing; subject to manufacturer's change.

	Retail Price	Dealer Invoice	Low Price
Rallye Sport Pkg., base	159	135	143
Base w/Premium Pkg. & bench seat	90	77	81
Console armrest (with bucket seats), tachometer, oil pressure gauge.			
Rear defogger, base	160	136	144
Power locks	225	191	203
AM/FM cassette, base	201	171	181
Base w/Super Discount or Popular Pkg., LE	152	129	137
AM/FM cassette w/Infinity speakers, base &			
LE	422	359	380
LX	270	230	243
Base requires Popular Pkg.			
AM/FM cassette w/Infinity speakers & EQ,			
LE	632	537	569
LX	480	408	432
Power driver's seat	270	230	243
Base requires Popular Pkg.			
Front bench seat, base	100	85	90
w/55/45 folding rear seat	60	51	54
Premium front bench seat w/55/45 folding			
rear, LE & LX	60	51	54
Pop-up glass sunroof	397	337	357
Base requires Popular Pkg.			
195/70R14 touring tires, base	30	26	27
195/75R14 WSW touring tires, base	102	87	92
Conventional spare tire	83	71	75
195/70R14, base & LE	93	79	84
Alloy wheels, base & LE	322	274	290

Dodge Spirit

	Retail Price	Dealer Invoice	Low Price
4-door notchback	$10495	$9386	$9698
LE 4-door notchback	11905	10626	10991
ES 4-door notchback	13205	11770	12183
Destination charge	440	440	440

Standard equipment:

2.5-liter TBI 4-cylinder engine, 5-speed manual transmission, power steering, driver's-side airbag, rear shoulder belts, cloth reclining front bucket seats, visor mirrors, AM/FM radio, remote fuel filler and decklid releases, 195/70R14 all-season SBR tires. **LE** adds: fog lamps, tinted glass, driver's seat lumbar support adjustment, split folding rear seatback, dual remote mirrors, rear defogger, cruise control, tilt steering column, message center. **ES** adds: 2.5-liter turbo engine, 4-wheel disc brakes, AM/FM cassette, lighted visor mirrors, sill extensions, front air dam with fog lights, trip computer, 205/60R14 Goodyear Eagle GT all-season tires on alloy wheels.

Optional equipment:	Retail Price	Dealer Invoice	Low Price
2.5-liter turbo engine, base & LE	680	578	612
Base requires Popular Pkg.			
3.0-liter V-6, base & LE	680	578	612
ES	NC	NC	NC
3-speed automatic transmission	536	456	482
4-speed automatic transmission	627	533	564
Air conditioning, LE & ES	805	684	725
Super Discount Pkg. A, base	1100	935	990
Air conditioning, rear defogger, floormats, tinted glass, time-delay ignition switch light, cruise control, tilt steering column.			
Super Discount Pkg. B, base	1403	1193	1263
Pkg. A plus heated power windows and locks, heated power mirrors.			
Super Discount Pkg. C, LE & ES	913	776	822
Air conditioning, power windows and locks, heated power mirrors.			
Popular Equipment Pkg.	934	794	841
Air conditioning, rear defogger, tinted glass.			
Premium Equipment Pkg., base	293	249	264
Base w/Super Discount or Deluxe			
Convenience	285	242	257
Front bucket seats, split folding rear seat, front center armrest, premium sound insulation, misc. lights, message center.			
Deluxe Convenience Pkg., base	336	286	302
Floormats, time-delay ignition switch light, cruise control, tilt steering column.			
Power Equipment Pkg.	573	487	516
Power windows and locks, heated power mirrors.			
Rear defogger, base	160	136	144
Power locks	225	191	203
AM/FM cassette, base	201	171	181
Base w/Super Discount or Popular Pkg.,			
LE	152	129	137
AM/FM cassette w/Infinity speakers, base &			
LE	422	359	380
ES	270	230	243
Base requires Popular Pkg.			
AM/FM cassette w/Infinity speakers & EQ,			
LE	632	537	569
ES	480	408	432
Power driver's seat	270	230	243
Base requires Popular Pkg.			
Bench seats, base	100	85	90
Not available with manual transmission.			
Front bench & 55/45 folding rear seat . . .	60	51	54
Base requires Premium Pkg.			
Pop-up sunroof	397	337	357
Base requires Popular Pkg.			

Prices are accurate at time of printing; subject to manufacturer's change.

	Retail Price	Dealer Invoice	Low Price
195/70R14 all-season touring tires, base .	72	61	65
205/60R15 all-season tires, base & LE . . .	164	139	148
Requires alloy wheels.			
Alloy wheels, base & LE	322	274	290
Requires 205/60R15 tires.			

Plymouth Horizon/Dodge Omni

Plymouth Horizon

America's first domestically produced front-wheel-drive subcompacts enter their 13th model year with a standard driver's-side airbag and new interior touches. Horizon and Omni are identical in price, specification, and equipment. Chrysler added the "America" suffix to the cars' names in 1987 when a cost-cutting program consolidated the lines into a single trim level with limited options. The tag has been dropped for '90, but the aim of a basic package with few options remains. A new instrument panel with revised climate-control ducts, a new steering wheel incorporating the airbag, rear-seat shoulder belts, and a new outside mirror are the changes. A 2.2-liter 4-cylinder engine mated to a standard 5-speed manual or an optional 3-speed automatic remains the only powertrain choice. Horizon and Omni are aged subcompacts with a cramped interior and an ungainly driving position, but remain well worth considering. Reinforcing their appeal is the driver's-side airbag, which makes them the least expensive cars offered in the U.S. with this important safety feature as standard equipment. The 2.2-liter engine delivers good performance with the 5-speed manual and, unlike most rivals, isn't underpowered with the optional automatic or with the air conditioner running. Fuel economy isn't bad, either.

Specifications

	5-door hatchback
Wheelbase, in.	99.1
Overall length, in.	163.2
Overall width, in.	66.8
Overall height, in.	53.0
Turn diameter, ft.	35.5
Curb weight, lbs.	2296
Cargo vol., cu. ft.	33.0
Fuel capacity, gals.	13.0
Seating capacity	5
Front headroom, in.	38.1
Front shoulder room, in.	51.7
Front legroom, max., in.	42.1
Rear headroom, in.	36.9
Rear shoulder room, in.	51.5
Rear legroom, min., in.	33.3

Powertrain layout: transverse front engine/front-wheel drive.

Engines

	ohc I-4
Size, liters/cu. in.	2.2/135
Fuel delivery	TBI
Horsepower @ rpm	93 @ 4800
Torque (lbs./ft.) @ rpm	122 @ 3200
Availability	S

EPA city/highway mpg

5-speed OD manual	25/34
3-speed automatic	25/30

Prices

Plymouth Horizon/Dodge Omni	Retail Price	Dealer Invoice	Low Price
5-door hatchback	$6995	$6465	$6685
Destination charge	363	363	363

Standard equipment:

2.2-liter 4-cylinder TBI engine, 5-speed manual transmission, driver's-side airbag, rear shoulder belts, rear defogger, rear wiper/washer, trip odometer,

Prices are accurate at time of printing; subject to manufacturer's change.

tachometer, coolant temperature, oil pressure and voltage gauges, luggage compartment light, black bodyside moldings, left remote mirror, right visor mirror, folding shelf panel, intermittent wipers, cloth and vinyl upholstery, P165/80R13 tires on styled steel wheels.

Optional equipment:	Retail Price	Dealer Invoice	Low Price
Air conditioning	775	659	698
Requires Transmission Discount Pkg.			
Basic Equipment Automatic Transmission Pkg.	776	660	698
3-speed automatic transmission, power steering.			
Manual Transmission Discount Pkg.	764	649	688
Power steering, AM/FM radio, highback reclining front seats, trunk dress-up, floormats, remote mirrors, rallye wheels.			
Automatic Transmission Discount Pkg.	1250	1063	1125
Manual Transmission Discount Pkg. plus 3-speed automatic transmission.			
Rear defogger	160	136	144
Tinted glass	105	89	95
AM/FM cassette	152	129	137
Requires Transmission Discount Pkg.			
Conventional spare tire	73	62	66
165/80R13 WSW tires	63	54	57
California emissions pkg.	100	85	90

Plymouth Laser/Eagle Talon

Plymouth Laser RS

These 2 + 2 sports coupes are built in Illinois by Diamond-Star Motors, a joint venture between Chrysler and its Japanese partner, Mitsubishi. Diamond-Star also builds the same car for sale as the Mitsubishi Eclipse. They're all front-drive hatchbacks, though Talon and Eclipse are available with permanent 4-wheel drive. A Mitsubishi Galant chassis forms their foundation and all use Mitsubishi engines and transmissions. A 1.8-liter 4-cylinder is standard on the base Laser and the slightly better-equipped Laser RS. A 16-valve, twin-cam 2.0-liter is optional on the Laser RS and standard on the base Talon. A turbocharged version of the 2.0 is standard on the Laser RS Turbo and on the Talon TSi. Talon TSi AWD has the turbo engine and permanent 4WD system. Engine power is normally split 50-50 between the front and rear axles, though the system is

---

Specifications

	3-door hatchback
Wheelbase, in.	97.2
Overall length, in.	170.5
Overall width, in.	66.5
Overall height, in.	51.4
Turn diameter, ft.	34.0
Curb weight, lbs.	2524
Cargo vol., cu. ft.	10.2
Fuel capacity, gals.	15.9
Seating capacity	4
Front headroom, in.	37.9
Front shoulder room, in.	53.9
Front legroom, max., in.	42.5
Rear headroom, in.	34.1
Rear shoulder room, in.	53.1
Rear legroom, min., in.	28.5

Powertrain layout: transverse front engine/front-wheel drive or permanent 4WD.

Engines	ohc I-4	dohc I-4	Turbo dohc I-4
Size, liters/cu. in.	1.8/107	2.0/122	2.0/122
Fuel delivery	PFI	PFI	PFI
Horsepower @ rpm	92 @ 5000	135 @ 6000	190 @ 6000
Torque (lbs./ft.) @ rpm	107 @ 3500	125 @ 5000	203 @ 5000
Availability	S[1]	O[2]	S[3]

EPA city/highway mpg

	ohc I-4	dohc I-4	Turbo dohc I-4
5-speed OD manual	23/32	22/29	22/29
4-speed OD automatic	23/30	22/27	

1. Base Laser, RS.   2. Laser RS; std., Talon   3. Laser RS Turbo, Talon TSi.

Prices are accurate at time of printing; subject to manufacturer's change.

capable of sending all the power to either the front or rear if conditions demand. A 5-speed manual transmission is standard on all models, and a 4-speed automatic is optional on all but the turbocharged versions. These are fine handling coupes with smooth engines and a genuine sports-car driving environment. The naturally aspirated 2.0 and 5-speed manual make the most appealing package. Laser's base engine is tepid with automatic transmission, and the front-drive turbo cars can be a handful to control under hard throttle in certain circumstances. The Talon TSi AWD has outstanding power and traction, and is one of the best high-performance buys in the U.S. Among the drawbacks: visibility from the driver's seat is hurt by a high beltline and thick rear pillars; the back seat is tiny; and the cargo hold is small even by sports-coupe standards.

Prices

Plymouth Laser	Retail Price	Dealer Invoice	Low Price
3-door hatchback	$10855	$9975	$10375
RS 3-door hatchback	11900	10885	11285
RS Turbo 3-door hatchback	13905	12691	13091
Destination charge	454	454	454

Standard equipment:

1.8-liter PFI 4-cylinder engine, 5-speed manual transmission, cloth and vinyl reclining front bucket seats, one-piece folding rear seat, tachometer, coolant temperature and oil pressure gauges, trip odometer, rear shoulder belts, tinted glass, variable intermittent wipers, remote fuel door and hatch releases, visor mirrors, remote mirrors, AM/FM radio, tilt steering column, 185/70R14 all-season tires. **RS** adds: power steering, power mirrors, AM/FM cassette, full cloth upholstery, driver's seat lumbar support adjustment, cargo cover, wheelcovers. **RS Turbo** adds: 2.0-liter DOHC 16-valve turbocharged engine, performance suspension, 205/55VR16 all-season performance tires.

Optional equipment:

2.0-liter DOHC engine, RS	873	742	786
4-speed automatic transmission, base & RS	682	580	614
Air conditioning	802	682	722
Base requires Popular Pkg.			

	Retail Price	Dealer Invoice	Low Price
Basic Equipment Pkg., RS	732	622	659

Air conditioning, console cupholder, floormats, AM/FM radio with EQ and six speakers, cruise control, power windows and locks, rear wiper/washer.

Popular Equipment Pkg., base	609	518	548

Base: power steering, console cupholder, rear defogger, floormats, cargo cover, wheelcovers.

Popular Equipment Pkg., RS & RS Turbo .	1398	1188	1258

Air conditioning, console cupholder, floormats, AM/FM cassette with EQ, cruise control, rear wiper/washer.

Deluxe Equipment Pkg., base	1767	1502	1590

Air conditioning, power steering, console cupholder, rear defogger, floormats, AM/FM cassette, cruise control, cargo cover, wheelcovers.

Deluxe Equipment Pkg., RS & RS Turbo .	1776	1510	1598

Air conditioning, console cupholder, floormats, AM/FM cassette with EQ, cruise control, power windows and locks, rear wiper/washer.

Deluxe Pkg. w/CD player, RS & RS Turbo .	2190	1862	1971
Rear defogger, base	150	128	135
AM/FM cassette, base	170	145	153

Requires Popular Pkg.

AM/FM cassette w/EQ, RS & RS Turbo . .	242	206	218

RS requires Basic Pkg.

Removable glass sunroof	378	321	340
Alloy wheels, RS & RS Turbo	321	273	289
California emissions pkg.	103	88	93

Eagle Talon

	Retail Price	Dealer Invoice	Low Price
3-door hatchback	$12995	$11807	$12401
TSi 3-door hatchback	14753	13305	14029
TSi AWD 3-door hatchback	16437	14804	15621
Destination charge	454	454	454

Standard equipment:

2.0-liter DOHC 16-valve PFI 4-cylinder engine, 5-speed manual transmission, 4-wheel disc brakes, reclining front bucket seats, driver's seat adjustable lumbar support, one-piece folding rear seat, center console with storage, rear defogger, tilt steering column, intermittent wipers, tinted glass, tachometer, coolant temperature and oil pressure gauges, voltmeter, power mirrors, AM/FM radio, remote fuel door and hatch releases, rear shoulder belts, front floormats, map lights, visor mirrors, cargo cover, 205/55R16 tires on alloy wheels. **TSi** adds: intercooled turbocharged engine, driving lamps, turbo boost gauge, leather-wrapped steering wheel and shift knob, performance seats with adjustable thigh and lateral support, 205/55VR16 tires. **TSi AWD** adds: permanent 4-wheel drive, split folding rear seat, sport suspension.

Prices are accurate at time of printing; subject to manufacturer's change.

Optional equipment:

	Retail Price	Dealer Invoice	Low Price
4-speed automatic transmission, base . . .	682	580	614
Air conditioning	802	682	722
Popular Equipment Group	1495	1271	1346
Air conditioning, cruise control, power windows and locks, rear wiper/washer.			
Luxury Equipment Group, base & TSi . . .	2021	1718	1819
TSi AWD	2186	1858	1967
Popular Group plus premium audio system and alloy wheels, security alarm (TSi AWD).			
Leather seat facings, TSi & TSi AWD	430	366	387
Premium audio system, base & TSi	242	206	218
w/security alarm, TSi AWD	407	346	366
AM/FM cassette with EQ and six speakers.			
Premium audio system w/CD player, base & TSi	656	558	590
TSi AWD (includes security alarm)	821	698	739
All models w/Luxury Group	414	352	373
Alloy wheels	284	241	256

Plymouth Voyager/ Dodge Caravan/ Chrysler Town & Country

Plymouth Grand Voyager LE

Chrysler packs a long-wheelbase example of its hot-selling minivan with luxury features and a new V-6 engine to create the Town & Country. This version of the front-drive Dodge Caravan/Plymouth Voyager comes in a single trim level with a list of standard features that includes a leather interior and front and rear air conditioning. It shares its 190-inch body and 119-inch wheelbase with the Grand versions of Voyager and Caravan. Standard-size Voyagers and Caravans come in base, SE, and LE trim in a 176-inch-long body on a 112-inch wheelbase. Extended-length models and

Specifications	4-door van	4-door van
Wheelbase, in.	112.0	119.1
Overall length, in.	175.9	190.5
Overall width, in.	72.0	72.0
Overall height, in.	64.8	64.8
Turn diameter, ft.	41.0	43.0
Curb weight, lbs.	3100	3255
Cargo vol., cu. ft.	125.0	150.0
Fuel capacity, gals.	20.0	20.0
Seating capacity	7	7
Front headroom, in.	39.9	39.9
Front shoulder room, in.	58.4	58.4
Front legroom, max., in.	38.2	38.2
Rear headroom, in.	38.5	38.3
Rear shoulder room, in.	61.3	61.3
Rear legroom, min., in.	37.6	37.8

Powertrain layout: transverse front engine/front-wheel drive.

Engines	ohc I-4	Turbo ohc I-4	ohc V-6	ohv V-6
Size, liters/cu. in.	2.5/153	2.5/153	3.0/181	3.3/201
Fuel delivery	TBI	PFI	PFI	PFI
Horsepower @ rpm	100 @ 4800	150 @ 4800	142 @ 5000	150 @ 4800
Torque (lbs./ft.) @ rpm	135 @ 2800	180 @ 2000	173 @ 2800	185 @ 3600
Availability	S	O	O	S[1]
EPA city/highway mpg				
5-speed OD manual	22/28	18/26		
3-speed automatic	21/23	19/23	19/24	
4-speed OD automatic			19/24	18/24

1. Grand Voyager/Caravan, Town & Country.

Prices are accurate at time of printing; subject to manufacturer's change.

the regular-length LE have seats for seven standard. Other regular-length models have seats for five standard and seats for seven as an option. The long-wheelbase models come standard with Chrysler's new 3.3-liter V-6 engine and have exclusive rights to it in 1990. Regular-length Voyagers and Caravans come with a 2.5-liter 4-cylinder engine standard. Two engines are optional: a 3.0-liter V-6 made by Mitsubishi and Chrysler's 2.5-liter turbocharged four. Also for '90, the standard 15-gallon fuel tank is replaced by a 20-gallon unit, and a sport road wheel package with 205/70R15 tires is a new option. The new 3.3 is quicker than the 3.0, but sounds gruffer than the smooth-running Japanese engine. Either of the sixes is still a better choice than either of the fours, however. The base 2.5 is underpowered, while the turbocharged 2.5's turbo lag and coarse nature is ill suited to these vehicles. Chrysler has done little to alter the character of its minivans for '90.

Prices

Plymouth Voyager/ Dodge Caravan	Retail Price	Dealer Invoice	Low Price
Base SWB 4-door van	$11995	$10756	$11376
SE SWB 4-door van	12675	11354	12015
LE SWB 4-door van	16125	14390	15258
Caravan ES SWB 4-door van	17350	15468	16409
Voyager LX SWB 4-door van	17240	15371	16306
SE Grand 4-door van	15395	13748	14572
LE Grand 4-door van	18325	16326	17326
Destination charge	515	515	515

SWB denotes short-wheelbase models.

Standard equipment:

2.5-liter TBI engine, 5-speed manual transmission, power steering, liftgate wiper/washer, 5-passenger seating, variable intermittent wipers, tinted glass, left remote mirror, AM/FM radio, P185/75R14 SBR tires. **SE** adds: highback reclining front seats, rear seat (Grand), front folding center armrests, upgraded door panels, power liftgate release. **LE** adds: front air conditioning, 7-passenger seating, added sound insulation, remote mirrors, bodyside moldings, woodgrain exterior applique, upgraded steering wheel. **ES and LX** add: 2.5-liter turbo engine, HD suspension, specific exterior trim, sill extensions, 205/70R15 tires on alloy wheels. **Grand SE** and **LE** have 3.3-liter PFI V-6, 4-speed automatic transmission.

Optional equipment:

	Retail Price	Dealer Invoice	Low Price
2.5-liter turbo engine, SWB	680	578	626
3.0-liter V6, SE & LE SWB	680	578	626
3-speed automatic transmission, SWB . . .	565	480	520
4-speed automatic transmission, SE &			
LE SWB	735	625	676
Requires 3.0-liter V-6.			
Front air conditioning (std. LE)	840	714	773
Rear air conditioning & heater, Grand . . .	560	476	515
Requires front air conditioning.			
Converta-Bed seating, SE SWB	542	461	499
LE SWB	143	122	132
7-passenger seating, base & SE SWB . . .	389	331	358
Popular Value Pkg., SE SWB	966	821	889
SE SWB w/Family Value Pkg.	755	642	695
SE Grand	829	705	763

Light Pkg., cruise control, tilt steering column, forward storage console, overhead console, floormats, tachometer, coolant temperature and oil pressure gauges, 125-mph speedometer, added sound insulation, power rear quarter vent windows, conventional spare tire.

	Retail Price	Dealer Invoice	Low Price
Luxury Value Pkg., SE SWB	2070	1760	1904
SE SWB w/Family Value Pkg.	1765	1500	1624
SE Grand	1903	1618	1751
LE SWB	NC	NC	NC
LE Grand	882	750	811

Popular Pkg. plus rear defogger, lighted visor mirror, power windows and locks, power mirrors, power driver's seat (LE), Infinity I AM/FM cassette, sport steering wheel.

	Retail Price	Dealer Invoice	Low Price
Family Value Pkg., base w/4-cyl.	928	789	854
Base w/V-6	1228	1044	1130
SE SWB	928	789	854

Front air conditioning, rear defogger, dual horns, added sound insulation, Light Pkg.

	Retail Price	Dealer Invoice	Low Price
HD Trailer Tow Pkg., SE	545	463	501
SE w/Popular or Luxury Pkg., LE	441	375	406
SE Grand w/sunroof or Sport Roadwheel			
Pkg.	433	368	398
LE Grand w/sunroof or Sport Roadwheel			
Pkg.	329	280	303
Turbo Sport Pkg., SE SWB	1333	1133	1226
SE SWB w/Popular or Luxury Pkg. . . .	1216	1034	1119
SE SWB w/Trailer Tow Pkg.	1153	980	1061
SE SWB w/Sport Roadwheel Pkg.	865	735	796

2.5-liter turbo engine, tachometer, coolant temperature and oil pressure gauges, 125-mph speedometer, HD suspension, 205/70R15 tires on Eurocast alloy wheels.

Prices are accurate at time of printing; subject to manufacturer's change.

	Retail Price	Dealer Invoice	Low Price
Deluxe Convenience Pkg., base & SE ...	346	294	318
Cruise control, tilt steering column.			
Power Convenience Pkg., SE	425	361	391
Power windows and locks.			
AY4 Sport Roadwheel Pkg., SE & LE ...	468	398	431
205/70R15 tires on alloy wheels, conventional spare tire (LE).			
AYA Sport Roadwheel Pkg. (NA base) ...	442	376	407
205/70R14 tires on alloy wheels.			
Power Sunroof Pkg., SE SWB w/Popular Pkg.	808	687	743
SE SWB w/Luxury Pkg.	724	615	666
SE Grand w/Popular Pkg.	920	782	846
SE Grand w/Luxury Pkg.	836	711	769
LE SWB	601	511	553
LE Grand	713	606	656
Power sunroof, lighted visor mirrors, reading lamp, power rear quarter vent windows, HD brakes, 205/75R15 tires.			
Luxury vinyl trim, base & SE	NC	NC	NC
Leather trim, LE	848	721	780
Woodgrain applique, LE	NC	NC	NC
Rear defogger	165	140	152
Power locks, base & SE	208	177	191
Requires Family or Popular Pkg.			
Sunscreen glass	406	345	374
Luggage rack, base & SE	140	119	129
AM/FM cassette	152	129	140
Inifinity I AM/FM cassette	399	339	367
Infinity II audio system w/EQ, w/Luxury Pkg.	214	182	197
ES	613	521	564
HD suspension	68	58	63
205/70R14 WSW tires	139	118	128
Requires Family, Popular, Luxury or Sport Roadwheel Pkg. on base and SE.			
195/75R15 tires (NA base)	145	123	133
Grand w/rear A/C	NC	NC	NC
SE & LE SWB require Trailer Tow Pkg.; Grand requires Trailer Tow Pkg. or sunroof.			
Conventional spare tire	107	91	98
Wire wheel covers, LE	246	209	226
Requires 205/70R14 tires and Luxury Pkg.			

Chrysler Town & Country

	Retail Price	Dealer Invoice	Low Price
4-door van	$25000	$22200	NA
Destination charge	515	515	515

Standard equipment:

3.3-liter PFI V-6, 4-speed automatic transmission, power steering, front and rear air conditioning, 7-passenger seating with front bucket seats, power driver's seat, quick-release middle and rear bench seats, leather upholstery, power front windows and quarter vents, power locks, cruise control, overhead console, rear defogger, tilt steering column, leather-wrapped steering wheel, remote fuel door and liftgate releases, coolant temperature and oil pressure gauges, voltmeter, trip odometer, rear wiper/washer, intermittent wipers, AM/FM cassette with Infinity speakers, floormats, tinted windshield and front door glass (sunscreen glass on other windows), roof rack, storage drawer under passenger seat, forward storage console, simulated woodgrain exterior applique, 205/70R15 tires on alloy wheels.

Optional equipment:	Retail Price	Dealer Invoice	Low Price
195/75R15 WSW tires	NC	NC	NC
California emissions pkg.	100	85	90

Pontiac Grand Am

Pontiac Grand Am SE

More power and bigger wheels and tires highlight changes to Pontiac's best-selling car. The front-drive Grand Am continues in 2-door coupe and 4-door sedan body styles, each available in base LE and upgraded SE trim. Last year's turbocharged 2.0-liter four has been dropped, replaced as the standard SE engine by the High Output Quad 4 engine, a 16-valve, dual-cam 2.3-liter 4-cylinder rated at 180 horse-

Prices are accurate at time of printing; subject to manufacturer's change.

power. Ordering the optional 3-speed automatic transmission mandates a regular Quad 4 rated at 160 horsepower, 10 more than last year. Replacing 215/60R14 tires on all SEs are 205/55R16 Goodyear Eagle GT + 4s. LE retains as standard a 110-horsepower 2.5-liter four. The optional LE engine is now the regular Quad 4. Last year's 185/80R13 standard LE tires give way to 185/75R14s. And the LE gets a new Sport Option package that includes monochrome exterior paint, fog lamps, and alloy wheels. Among the changes inside, a cassette radio is now an SE standard and

Specifications

	2-door notchback	4-door notchback
Wheelbase, in.	103.4	103.4
Overall length, in.	180.1	180.1
Overall width, in.	66.5	66.5
Overall height, in.	52.5	52.5
Turn diameter, ft.	35.4	35.4
Curb weight, lbs.	2508	2592
Cargo vol., cu. ft.	13.1	13.1
Fuel capacity, gals.	13.6	13.6
Seating capacity	5	5
Front headroom, in.	37.7	37.7
Front shoulder room, in.	52.6	54.7
Front legroom, max., in.	42.9	42.9
Rear headroom, in.	37.1	37.1
Rear shoulder room, in.	55.2	54.1
Rear legroom, min., in.	34.3	34.3

Powertrain layout: transverse front engine/front-wheel drive.

Engines

	ohv I-4	dohc I-4	dohc I-4
Size, liters/cu. in.	2.5/151	2.3/138	2.3/138
Fuel delivery	TBI	PFI	PFI
Horsepower @ rpm	110 @ 5200	160 @ 6200	180 @ 6200
Torque (lbs./ft.) @ rpm	135 @ 3200	155 @ 5200	160 @ 5200
Availability	S[1]	O	S[2]

EPA city/highway mpg

5-speed OD manual	22/33		22/31
3-speed automatic	23/31	23/31	

1. LE.   2. SE.

the driver's power window gets an express-down feature. Grand Am is similar to the Buick Skylark and Oldsmobile Cutlass Calais. The Pontiac is quite unexceptional with the base 2.5-liter engine. Either Quad 4 furnishes a huge performance leap, but these multi-valve fours must be revved over 3500 rpm or so to uncork their power. That can make them ill suited for duty with automatic transmission. While Grand Am has the styling cues of a European sports sedan, it lacks the genuine article's buttoned-down road manners and no-nonsense seats and ergonomics. We applaud the availability of a 4-door body style with the full complement of SE performance pieces, but Pontiac's compact still can't match the interior or trunk space of similarly sized imports.

Prices

Pontiac Grand Am	Retail Price	Dealer Invoice	Low Price
LE 2-door notchback	$10544	$9416	$9616
LE 4-door notchback	10744	9594	9794
SE 2-door notchback	14894	13300	13500
SE 4-door notchback	15194	13568	13768
Destination charge	425	425	425

Standard equipment:

LE: 2.5-liter TBI 4-cylinder engine, 5-speed manual transmission, power steering, rear shoulder belts, tinted glass, dual outside mirrors, AM/FM radio, cloth reclining front bucket seats, remote fuel door release, left visor mirror, 185/75R14 tires. **SE adds:** 2.3-liter DOHC 16-valve PFI HO Quad 4, WS6 sport suspension, monotone exterior treatment, sill moldings, air conditioning, remote decklid release, fog lamps, power windows and locks, split folding rear seat, tachometer, trip odometer, coolant temperature and oil pressure gauges, voltmeter, leather-wrapped steering wheel, shift knob and brake handle, 205/55R16 Goodyear Eagle GT + 4 tires on alloy wheels.

Optional equipment:

2.3-liter Quad 4, LE	660	561	594
SE (credit)	(140)	(119)	(119)
Available only with automatic transmission.			
3-speed automatic transmission	540	459	486
Air conditioning, base	720	612	648
Option Pkg. 1SB, LE	910	774	819
Air conditioning, tilt steering column, intermittent wipers.			

Prices are accurate at time of printing; subject to manufacturer's change.

	Retail Price	Dealer Invoice	Low Price
Option Pkg. 1SC, LE	1105	939	995
Pkg. 1SA plus cruise control.			
Option Pkg. 1SD, LE 2-door	1817	1544	1635
LE 4-door	1922	1634	1730
Pkg. 1SC plus remote decklid release, split folding rear seat, fog lamps, power windows and locks.			
Option Pkg. 1SB, SE	321	273	289
Power driver's seat, power mirrors.			
Value Option Pkg. (VOP) R6A, LE	394	335	355
AM/FM cassette, 195/70R14 tires on alloy wheels.			
Value Option Pkg. R6B, LE	455	387	410
LE 2-door w/Pkg. 1SD	40	34	36
LE 4-door	520	442	468
LE 4-door w/Pkg. 1SD	NC	NC	NC
Power windows and locks, AM/FM cassette.			
Rear defogger	160	136	144
Rally cluster gauges, LE	127	108	114
Decklid luggage rack	115	98	104
Two-tone paint, LE	101	86	91
Power locks, LE 2-door	175	149	158
LE 4-door	215	183	194
Power windows, LE 2-door	240	204	216
LE 4-door	305	259	275
Sport Option Pkg., LE	476	405	428
LE w/VOP R6A	97	82	87
LE w/Pkg. 1SD	379	322	341
Monotone paint treatment, fog lamps, 195/70R14 tires on alloy wheels.			
AM/FM cassette, LE	140	119	126
AM/FM radio w/CD & EQ, LE	545	463	491
LE w/VOP, SE	405	344	365
Removable glass sunroof, SE	350	298	315
195/70R14 tires, LE	114	97	103
Alloy wheels, LE	265	225	239
Warranty enhancements for New York . . .	65	55	59
California emissions pkg.	100	85	90

Pontiac Grand Prix

The first 4-door to wear the Grand Prix name bows as Pontiac's version of the front-drive General Motors W-body car, which also appear in sedan form for '90 as the Chevrolet Lumina, Buick Regal, and Oldsmobile Cutlass Supreme. The sedan shares the Grand Prix coupe's platform and

Pontiac Grand Prix LE

wheelbase, but it has slightly more head and rear leg room. Available initially only in LE trim, an STE (Special Touring Edition) version of the sedan is due early in calender 1990. Along with the Turbo Grand Prix Coupe, it'll have exclusive rights among W-body cars to an optional turbocharged 3.1-liter V-6. Compared to the LE, the STE gets a slightly altered grille and taillights, while its standard features include high-performance tires, alloy wheels, sport suspension, anti-lock brakes, and analog instrumentation. Also for '90, the base Grand Prix coupe has been discontinued, leaving LE, SE, and Turbo trim levels. The limited edition Turbo coupe, introduced during the '89 model year, returns unchanged for '90 with a planned production of 5000. It features a head-up instrument display that projects digital speedometer and turn-signal readouts onto the windshield in front of the driver. The Grand Prix sedan differs little from its Buick, Olds, and Chevy cousins. Its cabin has more of a continental flair, but still doesn't capture the Europeans' ergonomic maturity. Pontiac's sportier suspension tuning gives Grand Prix somewhat more composed road manners than the other W-body cars, especially over bumps and dips, though the differences are subtle. And as with the other W-body cars, Grand Prix works best not with a manual transmission or with the high-revving Quad 4 engine that's standard on the LE, but with an automatic and the 3.1-liter V-6.

Specifications

	2-door notchback	4-door notchback
Wheelbase, in.	107.5	107.5
Overall length, in.	193.9	194.8
Overall width, in.	70.9	70.9
Overall height, in.	52.8	54.3
Turn diameter, ft.	39.0	39.0
Curb weight, lbs.	3186	3250
Cargo vol., cu. ft.	15.0	15.5
Fuel capacity, gals.	16.0	16.0
Seating capacity	6	6
Front headroom, in.	37.8	38.8
Front shoulder room, in.	57.3	57.2
Front legroom, max., in.	42.3	42.4
Rear headroom, in.	36.6	37.6
Rear shoulder room, in.	57.3	57.4
Rear legroom, min., in.	34.8	36.2

Powertrain layout: transverse front engine/front-wheel drive.

Engines

	dohc I-4	ohv V-6	Turbo ohv V-6
Size, liters/cu. in.	2.3/138	3.1/191	3.1/191
Fuel delivery	PFI	PFI	PFI
Horsepower @ rpm	160 @ 6200	140 @ 4800	205 @ 4800
Torque (lbs./ft.) @ rpm	155 @ 5200	180 @ 3600	220 @ 3200
Availability	S	S[1]	S[2]

EPA city/highway mpg

5-speed OD manual		19/28	
3-speed automatic	22/29		
4-speed OD automatic		19/30	16/25

1. SE, STE   2. Grand Prix Turbo.

Prices

Pontiac Grand Prix	Retail Price	Dealer Invoice	Low Price
LE 2-door notchback	$14564	$12569	$12769
LE 4-door notchback	14564	12569	12769
SE 2-door notchback	17684	15261	15461
Destination charge	455	455	455

Standard equipment:

LE: 2.3-liter DOHC 16-valve PFI Quad 4, 3-speed automatic transmission, cloth 40/60 split bench seat with folding armrest and recliners, AM/FM radio, remote fuel door release, tinted glass, left remote and right manual mirrors, coolant temperature gauge, trip odometer, visor mirrors, door pockets, 195/75R14 tires (4-door), 205/65R15 tires (2-door). **SE** adds: 3.1-liter PFI V-6, 4-speed automatic transmission, power windows and locks, AM/FM cassette, articulating bucket seats, power driver's seat, rear bucket seats with pass-through, tachometer, oil pressure gauge, voltmeter, leather-wrapped steering wheel, tilt steering column, seatback pockets, 215/60R16 Goodyear Eagle GT + 4 tires on alloy wheels.

Optional equipment:

	Retail Price	Dealer Invoice	Low Price
3.1-liter V-6, LE	NC	NC	NC
Requires 4-speed automatic transmission.			
4-speed automatic transmission, LE w/V-6 .	200	170	180
SE	640	544	576
5-speed manual transmission, LE 2-door			
w/V-6 (credit)	(440)	(374)	(374)
Anti-lock brakes	925	786	833
LE requires Pkg. 1SE.			
Option Pkg. 1SB, LE	190	162	171
Tilt steering column, intermittent wipers.			
Option Pkg. 1SC, LE 2-door	470	400	423
Pkg. 1SB plus cruise control, tachometer, oil pressure gauge, voltmeter.			
Option Pkg. 1SD, LE 2-door	1603	1363	1443
Pkg. 1SC plus power windows and locks, remote decklid release, custom trim, alloy wheels, AM/FM cassette, power antenna.			
Option Pkg. 1SE, LE 2-door	2162	1838	1946
Pkg. 1SD plus power driver's seat, lighted visor mirrors, power mirrors, remote keyless entry.			
Option Pkg. 1SC, LE 4-door	385	327	347
Pkg. 1SB plus cruise control.			
Option Pkg. 1SD, LE 4-door	1808	1537	1627
Pkg. 1SC plus tachometer, oil pressure gauge, voltmeter, security lighting, power windows and locks, remote decklid release, custom trim, styled steel wheels, AM/FM cassette, power antenna.			
Option Pkg. 1SE, LE 4-door	2487	2114	2238
Pkg. 1SD plus power driver's seat, lighted right visor mirror, power mirrors, remote keyless entry.			
Option Pkg. 1SB, SE	561	477	505
Power antenna, lighted visor mirrors, remote keyless entry, electronic compass with trip computer and service reminder.			
Value Option Pkg. (VOP), LE 2-door	865	735	779
Custom sport bucket seats, AM/FM cassette with EQ, sunroof.			
Value Option Pkg. R6A, LE 4-door	409	348	368
AM/FM cassette, 205/65R15 tires on alloy wheels.			
Value Option Pkg. R6B, LE 4-door	464	394	418
Pkg. R6A plus two-tone paint.			

Prices are accurate at time of printing; subject to manufacturer's change.

CONSUMER GUIDE®   317

	Retail Price	Dealer Invoice	Low Price
Value Option Pkg., SE	975	829	878
Articulating seats with leather trim, sunroof.			
Rear defogger	160	136	144
Two-tone paint, LE	105	89	95
Power locks, LE 2-door	175	149	158
LE 4-door	215	183	194
Power sunroof	650	553	585
Power windows, LE 2-door	240	204	216
LE 4-door	305	259	275
AM/FM cassette, LE	140	119	126
AM/FM cassette w/EQ, LE	400	340	360
Requires Pkg. 1SD or 1SE.			
AM/FM radio w/CD player & EQ, LE . . .	626	532	563
LE 2-door w/VOP, SE	226	192	203
Not available with Quad 4.			
Bucket seats & console, LE	110	94	99
Requires Pkg. 1SC.			
Custom sport bucket seats, LE	140	119	126
Ventura leather articulating seats, SE	450	383	405
Requires Pkg. 1SB.			
Power driver's seat, LE	270	230	243
Requires Pkg. 1SC, 1SD or 1SE.			
Sport Appearance Pkg.			
LE 2-door w/Pkg. 1SB or 1SC	285	242	257
LE 2-door w/Pkg. 1SD or 1SE	160	136	144
LE 4-door w/Pkg. 1SB or 1SC	480	408	432
LE 4-door w/Pkg. 1SD	280	238	252
LE 4-door w/Pkg. 1SE or VOP	160	136	144
SE front fascia with fog lamps, specific moldings, 205/65R15 tires on alloy wheels.			
195/75R14 WSW tires, LE 4-door	72	61	65
205/65R15 tires, LE 4-door	54	46	49
15″ styled wheels, LE 4-door	145	123	131
15″ alloy wheels, LE 2-door	125	106	113
LE 4-door	265	225	239
LE 4-door w/Pkg. 1SD	120	102	108

Pontiac LeMans

Introduction of the '90 version of Pontiac's Korean-built front-drive subcompact has been delayed until early 1990. Pontiac blames the postponement on holdups in the installation of motorized front shoulder belts. When LeMans

Pontiac LeMans GSE

does return, the upscale SE sedan will be dropped, leaving a 4-door sedan in base LE trim and a 3-door hatchback in three equipment levels: stripper Value Leader; mid-line LE; and sporty GSE. Built in Korea by Daewoo Motor Company (partly owned by General Motors), LeMans was designed by GM's Opel division in West Germany. All but the GSE use a 1.6-liter 4-cylinder engine. The GSE comes with a 2.0-liter four. GSE and LE models have a 5-speed manual transmission standard and a 3-speed automatic optional. The Value Leader is available only with a 4-speed manual. For '90, the 1.6-liter cars get a larger master brake cylinder and power-brake booster, and a retuned suspension with a larger front stabilizer bar. The GSE gets quicker-ratio steering. All models except the Value Leader get a revised radio with knob controls instead of levers. LeMans hides its German heritage on the road and shows little cost benefit from being built in Korea. The LE is reasonably surefooted, but is inordinately slow with automatic transmission. While the better-handling GSE's 2.0-liter and 5-speed make for acceptable power, the engine is coarse and noisy, and shift action is rubbery. Fuel economy is a high point, but LeMans in any guise suffers a stiff, jiggly ride on bumpy pavement. The 99.2-inch wheelbase is long for a subcompact, however, so there's more leg room and cargo space than in some rivals.

Specifications

	3-door hatchback	4-door notchback
Wheelbase, in.	99.2	99.2
Overall length, in.	163.7	172.4
Overall width, in.	65.5	65.7
Overall height, in.	53.5	53.7
Turn diameter, ft.	32.8	32.8
Curb weight, lbs.	2136	2235
Cargo vol., cu. ft.	18.8	18.4
Fuel capacity, gals.	13.2	13.2
Seating capacity	5	5
Front headroom, in.	38.8	38.8
Front shoulder room, in.	53.5	53.5
Front legroom, max., in.	42.0	42.0
Rear headroom, in.	38.0	38.0
Rear shoulder room, in.	53.4	53.4
Rear legroom, min., in.	32.8	32.8

Powertrain layout: transverse front engine/front-wheel drive.

Engines

	ohc I-4	ohc I-4
Size, liters/cu. in.	1.6/98	2.0/121
Fuel delivery	TBI	TBI
Horsepower @ rpm	74 @ 5600	96 @ 4800
Torque (lbs./ft.) @ rpm	90 @ 2800	118 @ 3600
Availability	S	S[1]

EPA city/highway mpg

4-speed OD manual	29/38	
5-speed OD manual	31/40	25/31
3-speed automatic	27/33	23/30

1. GSE.

Prices

Pontiac LeMans (1989 prices)	Retail Price	Dealer Invoice	Low Price
Aerocoupe Value Leader 3-door hatchback	$6599	$6104	$6200
Aerocoupe LE 3-door hatchback	7999	7359	7492
LE 4-door notchback	8349	7681	7820
SE 4-door notchback	9749	8774	9036
Aerocoupe GSE 3-door hatchback	9499	8549	8804
Destination charge	315	315	315

Standard equipment:

Value Leader: 1.6-liter TBI 4-cylinder engine, 4-speed manual transmission, power brakes, reclining front bucket seats, rear defogger, tachometer, trip odometer, outboard rear lap/shoulder belts, cargo area cover, 175/70SR13 tires with full-size spare. **LE** adds: 5-speed manual transmission, tinted glass, dual remote mirrors, right visor mirror, AM/FM ST ET with clock, swing-out rear side windows (Aerocoupe; roll-down on 4-door). **SE** adds: 2.0-liter engine, sport suspension, sport seats with height adjusters, 60/40 folding rear seat, tilt steering column, fog lamps, 185/60HR14 tires. **GSE** adds: front air dam with fog lamps, sill extensions, rear spoiler, alloy wheels.

Optional equipment:	Retail Price	Dealer Invoice	Low Price
3-speed automatic transmission (NA VL) .	445	378	409
Air conditioning	680	578	626
Requires power steering; not available on VL).			
Power steering, LE & SE	214	182	197
Cruise control	185	157	170
AM/FM ST ET, VL	307	261	282
AM/FM ST ET cassette, VL	429	365	395
Others	122	104	112
Luggage carrier	95	81	87
Removable sunroof	350	298	322

Pontiac Trans Sport

Pontiac Trans Sport

Pontiac's version of the new General Motors minivan shares with the Chevrolet Lumina APV and the Oldsmobile Silhouette a front-drive layout and a 3.1-liter V-6 hooked to a 3-speed automatic transmission. Trans Sport is available in base and SE versions. Both come with reclining front bucket seats. The base model has a 3-place middle bench with a pair of rear buckets optionally available. Optional on the base model and standard on SE is a 2-2-2 bucket-seat layout. Compared to the base model, the SE comes standard with alloy wheels and larger tires. It also gets a monochrome exterior treatment with a gloss-black roof, lower-body aero moldings, and a load-leveling suspension. In general, GM has achieved a car-like driving feel for its new minivans, though they seem underpowered when called upon for anything more than gentle acceleration. Trans Sport is easy to climb in and out of, and the

Specifications

	4-door van
Wheelbase, in.	109.8
Overall length, in.	194.5
Overall width, in.	74.2
Overall height, in.	65.5
Turn diameter, ft.	42.5
Curb weight, lbs.	3500
Cargo vol., cu. ft.	104.6
Fuel capacity, gals.	20.0
Seating capacity	7
Front headroom, in.	40.2
Front shoulder room, in.	53.5
Front legroom, max., in.	40.7
Rear headroom, in.	38.6
Rear shoulder room, in.	61.6
Rear legroom, min., in.	33.7

Powertrain layout: transverse front engine/front-wheel drive.

Engines

	ohv V-6
Size, liters/cu. in.	3.1/191
Fuel delivery	TBI
Horsepower @ rpm	120 @ 4200
Torque (lbs./ft.) @ rpm	175 @ 2200
Availability	S

EPA city/highway mpg

3-speed automatic	18/23

seatbacks fold down individually to make convenient tables with cup holders. The second- and third-row seats can be tilted forward to increase floor space. Finally, the bucket seats weigh only 34 pounds each and have quick-release mounts that make them easy to remove. The body panels are made of a plastic-like material designed to take minor impacts and spring back without damage. Pontiac modeled the dashboard on that of the Grand Prix and there are plenty of interior storage bins. Overriding all other impressions of the Trans Sport and its sister GM minivans is the snout-nosed styling. It does indeed set them apart visually from box-like rivals, but it also creates an intimidating view from the driver's seat. The driver feels far removed from the road, a problem that's more pronounced in city driving, where maneuvering room may be at a premium.

Prices

Pontiac Trans Sport	Retail Price	Dealer Invoice	Low Price
4-door van	$14995	$13391	—
SE 4-door van	18125	16186	—
Destination charge	500	500	500

Low price not available at time of publication.

Standard equipment:

3.1-liter TBI V-6, 3-speed automatic transmission, power steering, 5-passenger seating (reclining front bucket seats, middle bench seat), tinted glass, tachometer, coolant temperature and oil pressure gauges, voltmeter, trip odometer, AM/FM radio, door pockets, beverage holders, 205/70R14 tires. **SE** adds: 6-passenger seating (three second row and two third row modular seats), air conditioning, pneumatic load leveling, deep-tint glass, AM/FM cassette, leather-wrapped steering wheel, Lamp Group, tilt steering column, cruise control, built-in inflator, 195/70R15 Goodyear Eagle GT + 4 tires on alloy wheels.

Optional equipment:

Air conditioning, base	805	684	—
6-passenger seating, base	525	446	—
Reclining front bucket seats, 2 second row and 2 third row modular seats.			
7-passenger seating, base	675	574	—
Reclining front bucket seats, 3 second row and 2 third row modular seats.			

Prices are accurate at time of printing; subject to manufacturer's change.

	Retail Price	Dealer Invoice	Low Price
Option Pkg. 1SB, base	1195	1016	—
Air conditioning, Lamp Group, cruise control, tilt steering column.			
Option Pkg. 1SC, base	1960	1666	—
Pkg. 1SB plus power windows and locks, power driver's seat.			
Option Pkg. 1SB, SE	765	650	—
Power windows and locks, power driver's seat.			
Rear defogger	160	136	—
Deep-tint glass, base	245	208	—
Power locks	255	217	—
Power windows	240	204	—
Requires power locks.			
AM/FM cassette, base	140	119	—
AM/FM radio w/CD player & EQ, base . . .	516	439	—
SE	376	320	—
Alloy wheels, base	265	225	—
Warranty enhancements for New York . . .	65	55	—
California emissions pkg.	100	85	—

Saab 900

Saab 900 Turbo SPG

Anti-lock brakes and a driver's-side airbag are new standard features on the front-drive 900 series models. Neither was available last year on the 900. The other major change for 1990 is that the fuel tank grows from 16.6 gallons to 18. Last year's lineup returns. The base 900 and the 900S come in 3-door hatchback and 4-door notchback styling with a 128-horsepower 2.0-liter 4-cylinder engine and a choice of 5-speed manual or 3-speed automatic transmissions. The 900 Turbo is available in the hatchback and notchback styling, plus as a convertible with a power top. Turbo models use a 160-horsepower 2.0-liter engine and are available with either a 5-speed manual or 3-speed automatic. At the top of the line is the 900 Turbo SPG, available only as a 3-door hatchback with the 5-speed manual. The SPG's 2.0-liter engine has a new Mitsubishi-made turbocharger and 10 more horsepower (to 175). Anti-lock

Specifications	3-door hatchback	4-door notchback	2-door conv.
Wheelbase, in.	99.1	99.1	99.1
Overall length, in.	184.5	184.3	184.3
Overall width, in.	66.5	66.5	66.5
Overall height, in.	56.1	56.1	55.1
Turn diameter, ft.	35.8	35.8	35.8
Curb weight, lbs.	2732	2787	2967
Cargo vol., cu. ft.	56.5	53.0	9.9
Fuel capacity, gals.	18.0	18.0	18.0
Seating capacity	5	5	4
Front headroom, in.	36.8	36.8	36.8
Front shoulder room, in.	52.2	53.0	52.2
Front legroom, max., in.	41.7	41.7	41.7
Rear headroom, in.	37.4	37.4	NA
Rear shoulder room, in.	53.5	54.5	NA
Rear legroom, min., in.	36.2	36.2	NA

Powertrain layout: longitudinal front engine/front-wheel drive.

Engines	dohc I-4	Turbo dohc I-4	Turbo dohc I-4
Size, liters/cu. in.	2.0/121	2.0/121	2.0/121
Fuel delivery	PFI	PFI	PFI
Horsepower @ rpm	128 @ 6000	160 @ 5500	175 @ 5500
Torque (lbs./ft.) @ rpm	128 @ 3000	188 @ 3000	195 @ 3000
Availability	S[1]	S[2]	S[3]

EPA city/highway mpg

5-speed manual	22/28	22/29	21/28
3-speed automatic	19/22	19/23	

1. 900, 900S   2. Turbo   3. Turbo SPG.

Prices are accurate at time of printing; subject to manufacturer's change.

brakes (ABS) and an airbag as standard were necessary for the 900 to stay competitive in the premium sedan league. The 900 already has one of the best records for occupant protection; ABS and the airbag should help make it even better. The basic design for the Swedish-built 900 is 20 years old, but these cars have aged well. The interiors have ample room for four adults, and there's plenty of luggage space on the hatchback and 4-door sedan. Turbo models provide exceptional acceleration and outstanding passing power, but the base models and 900S have leisurely acceleration by comparison.

Prices

Saab 900	Retail Price	Dealer Invoice	Low Price
3-door hatchback	$16995	—	—
4-door notchback	17515	—	—
S 3-door hatchback	20995	—	—
S 4-door notchback	21545	—	—
Turbo 3-door hatchback	25495	—	—
Turbo 4-door notchback	26045	—	—
Turbo convertible	32995	—	—
Turbo SPG 3-door hatchback	28995	—	—
Destination charge	383	383	383

Dealer invoice and low price not available at time of publication.

Standard equipment:

2.0-liter DOHC 16-valve PFI 4-cylinder engine, 5-speed manual transmission, anti-lock 4-wheel disc brakes, power steering, driver's-side air bag, air conditioning, tachometer, coolant temperature gauge, trip odometer, analog clock, rear defogger, intermittent wipers, power locks, tinted glass, driver's seat tilt/height adjustment, cloth heated reclining front bucket seats, folding rear seat, AM/FM cassette, 185/65TR15 tires. **S** adds: cruise control, folding rear armrest, power windows and mirrors, manual sunroof, alloy wheels. **Turbo** adds: turbocharged engine, sport seats, leather seating surfaces, power sunroof, upgraded stereo with EQ, fog lamps, 185/65HR15 tires. **Turbo SPG** has: higher-output engine, sport suspension, leather-wrapped steering wheel and shift knob, power sunroof, aerodynamic lower body panels, 195/60VR15 tires.

Optional equipment:

3-speed automatic transmission(NA SPG)	580	—	—
Metallic or special black paint	535	—	—

Saab 9000

Saab 9000 CD Turbo

The Saab Direct Ignition system (SDI) is standard this year on the 9000 Turbo models, while a driver's-side airbag is standard on all 9000 models. SDI does away with the distributor and uses a separate ignition coil for each cylinder. Saab says SDI produces higher spark voltage and reduces radio interference. Other changes to Turbo models include a new U.S.-made Garrett turbocharger that's supposed to improve low-speed response. Horsepower on the 2.0-liter turbo engine grows from 160 to 165. The naturally aspirated 2.0-liter engine used in the 9000S is unchanged at 130 horsepower. Last year Saab introduced the 9000 CD Turbo, a notchback 4-door sedan derived from the 9000 5-door hatchback. During the summer a naturally aspirated 9000 CD was added. This year, the 9000 Turbo 5-door gets the CD's softer suspension settings, self-leveling rear shock absorbers, and narrower tires (195/65VR15 instead of 205/55VR15). All 9000 models have front-wheel drive. The naturally aspirated 9000 models have a new manual climate control system, instead of the previous fully automatic system, while the 9000 Turbos have a second-generation automatic system with a new "Off" switch. A driver's-side airbag became standard on Turbo models during 1989; for 1989, it's standard on the 9000S models as well. Anti-lock brakes have been standard on all 9000 models since 1988. Saab sales are slumping partly because the

Swedish automaker only offers 4-cylinder engines at a time when premium-sedan buyers are demanding six cylinders or more.

Specifications

	4-door notchback	5-door hatchback
Wheelbase, in.	105.2	105.2
Overall length, in.	188.2	181.9
Overall width, in.	69.4	69.4
Overall height, in.	55.9	55.9
Turn diameter, ft.	35.8	35.8
Curb weight, lbs.	3022	3004
Cargo vol., cu. ft.	18.1	56.5
Fuel capacity, gals.	17.4	17.4
Seating capacity	5	5
Front headroom, in.	38.5	38.5
Front shoulder room, in.	NA	NA
Front legroom, max., in.	41.5	41.5
Rear headroom, in.	37.4	37.4
Rear shoulder room, in.	NA	NA
Rear legroom, min., in.	38.7	38.7

Powertrain layout: transverse front engine/front-wheel drive.

Engines

	dohc I-4	Turbo dohc I-4
Size, liters/cu. in.	2.0/121	2.0/121
Fuel delivery	PFI	PFI
Horsepower @ rpm	130 @ 6000	165 @ 5500
Torque (lbs./ft.) @ rpm	128 @ 3750	195 @ 3000
Availability	S	S
EPA city/highway mpg		
5-speed OD manual	21/28	20/26
4-speed OD automatic	18/24	18/24

Prices

Saab 9000	Retail Price	Dealer Invoice	Low Price
S 5-door hatchback	$25495	—	—
S 4-door notchback	25995	—	—
Turbo 5-door hatchback	32495	—	—
CD 4-door notchback	32995	—	—
Destination charge	383	383	383

Dealer invoice and low price not available at time of publication.

Standard equipment:

2.0-liter DOHC 16-valve PFI 4-cylinder engine, 5-speed manual transmission, anti-lock 4-wheel disc brakes, power steering, driver's-side airbag, air conditioning, AM/FM cassette, power antenna, trip computer, trip odometer, tachometer, coolant temperature gauge, front and rear reading lights, reclining front bucket seats, driver's seat height/tilt, lumbar and lateral support adjustments, velour upholstery, emergency tensioning front seatbelt retractors, rear shoulder belts, telescopic steering column, power steel sunroof, 195/65TR15 SBR tires on alloy wheels; 4-door has remote decklid release, headlamp wipers and washers. **Turbo and CD** add: turbocharged engine, automatic climate control, leather upholstery, self-leveling rear shock absorbers, power front seats, fog lights, power glass sunroof, upgraded stereo with EQ, remote decklid release (CD), 195/65VR15 tires.

Optional equipment:	Retail Price	Dealer Invoice	Low Price
4-speed automatic transmission	765	—	—
Leather Pkg., S	1995	—	—
Leather seating surfaces, power driver's seat, front fog lamps, power glass sunroof			
Metallic or special black paint	535	—	—

Subaru Justy

Subaru Justy GL 4WD

Subaru's smallest model, the Justy, has a new 5-door hatchback body style as a companion to the carryover 3-door hatchback. Like the 3-door, the new 5-door is available with front-wheel drive or on-demand 4-wheel drive and is built on the same 90-inch wheelbase. For 1990, all but the

Prices are accurate at time of printing; subject to manufacturer's change.

Specifications

	3-door hatchback	5-door hatchback
Wheelbase, in.	90.0	90.0
Overall length, in.	145.5	145.5
Overall width, in.	60.4	60.4
Overall height, in.	55.9	55.9
Turn diameter, ft.	29.5	29.5
Curb weight, lbs.	1820	2045
Cargo vol., cu. ft.	21.9	21.9
Fuel capacity, gals.	9.2	9.2
Seating capacity	4	4
Front headroom, in.	38.0	38.0
Front shoulder room, in.	51.9	51.9
Front legroom, max., in.	41.5	41.5
Rear headroom, in.	37.0	37.0
Rear shoulder room, in.	51.0	51.0
Rear legroom, min., in.	30.2	30.2

Powertrain layout: transverse front engine/front-wheel drive or on-demand 4WD.

Engines

	ohc l-3	ohc l-3
Size, liters/cu. in.	1.2/73	1.2/73
Fuel delivery	2 bbl.	PFI
Horsepower @ rpm	66 @ 5200	73 @ 5600
Torque (lbs./ft.) @ rpm	70 @ 3600	71 @ 2800
Availability	S	S

EPA city/highway mpg

5-speed OD manual	33/37	33/37
ECVT automatic		34/35

base models have multi-point fuel injection instead of a 2-barrel carburetor. With injection, horsepower grows from 66 to 73 for Justy's 1.2-liter 3-cylinder engine. Fuel-injected Justys also get an intermediate front drive shaft to reduce torque steer (pulling to one side in acceleration). Subaru introduced its innovative Electronic Continuously Variable Transmission (ECVT) last year as an option on the front-drive Justy GL. This year it also is available on 4WD models, the first time Subaru has offered automatic on 4WD Justys. ECVT differs from conventional automatics in that it doesn't have three or four forward gears. Instead, a metal belt connects two pulleys that continuously vary the ratio of engine speed to drive shaft speed. Subaru says this "gear-less," infinite spread of ratios is like having a dimmer instead of a 3-way light switch. A 5-speed manual transmission remains standard. Also new for 1990 is a "Fun Justy" appearance package, available on the 3-door, that includes special paint and custom interior trim. Not content to just offer 4WD in a tiny car like the Justy, Subaru now combines 4WD with ECVT, a feature no other car company offers in the U.S. The ECVT gets more performance out of the Justy's 3-cylinder engine than a conventional automatic, but the ECVT Justy has little zip in the 25-to-50-mph range; there's just not enough torque for quick, safe passing. The available 4WD remains Justy's main advantage over other mini-compacts.

Prices

Subaru Justy	Retail Price	Dealer Invoice	Low Price
3-door hatchback	$5866	—	—
GL 3-door hatchback	7251	—	—
GL 4WD 3-door hatchback	7951	—	—
GL 4WD 5-door hatchback	8201	—	—
Destination charge	395	395	395

Dealer invoice and low price not available at time of publication.

Standard equipment:

1.2-liter PFI 3-cylinder engine, 5-speed manual transmission, reclining front bucket seats, one-piece folding rear seatback, 145SR12 tires. **GL** adds: rear wiper/washer, intermittent wipers, bodyside moldings, mud flaps, wheel covers, tachometer, AM/FM radio, rear defogger, visor mirrors, split folding rear seatback, rear luggage shelf, remote hatch release, 165/65SR13 tires.

Optional equipment:

ECVT automatic (NA base)	540	—	—

Subaru Legacy

Subaru introduced the Legacy 4-door sedans and 5-door wagons last spring as its new high-volume models. Legacy is larger and more luxurious than the carryover Subaru Sedan/Wagon/Coupe, which continue for 1990 as the Loyale

Prices are accurate at time of printing; subject to manufacturer's change.

Subaru Legacy L

line. While Loyale is a subcompact, Legacy is a compact, competing in the same league as the Honda Accord, Toyota Camry, Mazda 626, and others. Both the sedan and wagon come in base L and upscale LS trim levels, and with either front-wheel drive or permanently-engaged 4-wheel drive. All models use a 130-horsepower 2.2-liter flat (horizontally opposed) 4-cylinder engine, mated to either a 5-speed manual or 4-speed automatic transmission. Power steering and 4-wheel disc brakes are standard on all models. Anti-lock brakes are optional on 4WD LS models with automatic transmission; later in the year they will also be available with 4WD and the 5-speed manual transmission, and on 4WD L models. All early Legacys were imported from Japan, but production of sedans and wagons started in October at a plant operated jointly by Subaru and Isuzu in Lafayette, Indiana. We timed an LS 4WD wagon with automatic, the heaviest Legacy model, at 10.2 seconds to 60 mph, an impressive showing. Our test wagon also had the optional anti-lock brakes, which helped stop the vehicle from 60 mph in just 123 feet, also quite impressive. We also like Subaru's permanently engaged 4WD systems, which provide outstanding traction without requiring any input from the driver. Legacy is a capable, mainstream car that emerges as a good alternative to the Accord, Camry, and other compacts. Sluggish sales should make most Subaru dealers willing to discount prices.

Specifications

	4-door notchback	5-door wagon
Wheelbase, in.	101.6	101.6
Overall length, in.	177.6	181.1
Overall width, in.	66.5	66.5
Overall height, in.	52.6	53.7
Turn diameter, ft.	33.5	33.5
Curb weight, lbs.	2620[1]	2750[2]
Cargo vol., cu. ft.	14.0	71.0
Fuel capacity, gals.	15.9	15.9
Seating capacity	5	5
Front headroom, in.	38.2	38.2
Front shoulder room, in.	54.1	54.1
Front legroom, max., in.	42.3	42.3
Rear headroom, in.	36.0	37.8
Rear shoulder room, in.	53.7	53.7
Rear legroom, min., in.	35.4	35.6

1. 2830 lbs., 4WD.   2. 2960 lbs., 4WD.

Powertrain layout: longitudinal front engine/front-wheel drive or permanent 4WD.

Engines

	ohc flat-4
Size, liters/cu. in.	2.2/135
Fuel delivery	PFI
Horsepower @ rpm	130 @ 5400
Torque (lbs./ft.) @ rpm	137 @ 4400
Availability	S
EPA city/highway mpg	
5-speed OD manual	23/30
4-speed OD automatic	21/28

Prices

Subaru Legacy	Retail Price	Dealer Invoice	Low Price
L 4-door notchback	$12499	$10933	$11430
LS 4-door notchback	14699	12728	13379
L 4WD 4-door notchback	13699	11972	12522
LS 4WD 4-door notchback	16499	14273	15011
L 5-door wagon	13049	11410	11931
LS 5-door wagon	15249	13200	13878
L 4WD 5-door wagon	14249	12449	13023
LS 4WD 5-door wagon	17049	14745	15509
Destination charge	395	395	395

Prices are accurate at time of printing; subject to manufacturer's change.

Standard equipment:

2.2-liter SOHC 16-valve PFI 4-cylinder engine, 5-speed manual transmission, power steering, 4-wheel disc brakes, Hill-Holder, coolant temperature gauge, trip odometer, tinted glass, remote mirrors, center console, remote fuel door and decklid/liftgate releases, beverage holder, power windows and locks, power mirrors, spot lamps, tilt steering column, driver's-seat lumbar support adjustment, tachometer, intermittent wipers, AM/FM ST ET; wagon has cargo cover, 60/40 split rear seatback, rear wiper/washer, 175/70HR14 tires. **LS** adds: air conditioning, air suspension (4WD automatic), cruise control, driver's-seat height adjustment, rear center armrest (4-door), trunk-through (4-door), variable intermittent wipers, power sunroof. **4WD** models have 185/70HR14 tires.

Optional equipment:	Retail Price	Dealer Invoice	Low Price
4-speed automatic transmission	750	650	683
Anti-lock brakes, LS 4WD automatic	1095	870	959
Value Plus Option Pkg., L	995	850	900

Air conditioning, AM/FM ST ET cassette w/EQ, cruise control.

Subaru Loyale

Subaru Loyale

What used to be Subaru's highest-volume line, the subcompact Sedan/Wagon/3-Door Coupe trio, carries on for 1990 as the Loyale with fewer models and less emphasis, as Subaru shifts its focus to the newer Legacy. Three Loyale body styles are still offered, but the 5-door wagon gets most of the attention since it has been Subaru's best-selling model. Gone are the previous DL, GL, and GL-10 trim levels. The sedan and wagon come in a single price series with standard equipment that falls between that of the old DL and GL, while the 3-Door Coupe comes in sporty RS trim. Two engines are available: a 90-horsepower 1.8-liter flat-4 and a 115-horsepower turbocharged version of the flat-4. As before, all body styles are available with front-wheel drive or 4-wheel-drive (either the on-demand type or permanently engaged 4WD). Loyale has been eclipsed in size, acceleration, and features by the Legacy, but still

Specifications

	3-door hatchback	4-door notchback	5-door wagon
Wheelbase, in.	97.2	97.2	97.0
Overall length, in.	174.6	174.6	176.8
Overall width, in.	65.4	65.4	65.4
Overall height, in.	51.8	52.5	53.0
Turn diameter, ft.	31.5	31.5	31.5
Curb weight, lbs.	2475	2275	2405
Cargo vol., cu. ft.	39.8	14.9	70.3
Fuel capacity, gals.	15.9	15.9	15.9
Seating capacity	5	5	5
Front headroom, in.	37.6	37.6	37.6
Front shoulder room, in.	53.5	53.5	53.5
Front legroom, max., in.	42.2	41.7	41.7
Rear headroom, in.	35.8	36.5	37.7
Rear shoulder room, in.	52.8	53.5	53.5
Rear legroom, min., in.	32.6	35.2	35.2

Powertrain layout: longitudinal front engine/front-wheel drive, or on-demand or permanent 4WD.

Engines

	ohc flat-4	Turbo ohc flat-4
Size, liters/cu. in.	1.8/109	1.8/109
Fuel delivery	TBI	PFI
Horsepower @ rpm	90 @ 5200	115 @ 5200
Torque (lbs./ft.) @ rpm	101 @ 2800	134 @ 2800
Availability	S	S
EPA city/highway mpg		
5-speed OD manual	25/32	22/25
3-speed automatic	24/26	22/24
4-speed OD automatic		20/26

Prices are accurate at time of printing; subject to manufacturer's change.

offers Subaru's famed 4WD systems, all of which are convenient to use and provide great traction. If you don't really need 4WD, then save money and buy a front-drive model. You'll also save on fuel and gain a little acceleration to boot, because the front-drive models are lighter. If you do opt for 4WD, beware that the base 90-horsepower engine is strained by the extra weight, particularly with automatic transmission. Even the turbocharged engine is no ball of fire. The 1990 price structure makes the Loyale line a little less expensive than before, and Subaru has been offering its dealers incentives to spur sales. Among Japanese rivals, Honda and Toyota offer small 4WD wagons, and Toyota also sells a 4WD Corolla sedan, so you don't have to limit your shopping to Subaru if you want all-wheel drive in a small package.

Prices

Subaru Loyale	Retail Price	Dealer Invoice	Low Price
4-door notchback	$9299	—	—
5-door wagon	9999	—	—
4WD 4-door notchback	10374	—	—
4WD 5-door wagon	10999	—	—
4WD RS 3-door hatchback	11024	—	—
Turbo 4-door notchback	11999	—	—
Turbo 5-door wagon	12699	—	—
4WD Turbo 4-door notchback	13049	—	—
4WD Turbo 5-door wagon	13749	—	—
4WD RS 3-door hatchback	13699	—	—
Destination charge	395	395	395

Dealer invoice and low price not available at time of publication.

Standard equipment:

1.8-liter TBI 4-cylinder engine, 5-speed manual transmission, power steering, Hill-Holder (with 5-speed), reclining front bucket seats, remote decklid/liftgate release (exc. wagon), remote fuel door release, 50/50 folding rear seat (exc. 4-door), rear defogger, 175/70SR13 tires. **Turbo** models add: PFI turbocharged engine, 3-speed automatic transmission, 4-wheel disc brakes, uprated suspension, air conditioning, 175/70HR13 tires. **4WD** models have: On-Demand (part-time) 4WD, 185/70SR13 tires. **Turbo 4WD** models have: full-time 4WD, 4-speed automatic transmission, 185/70HR13 tires.

Optional equipment:

3-speed automatic transmission (NA turbos)	550	—	—

Subaru XT

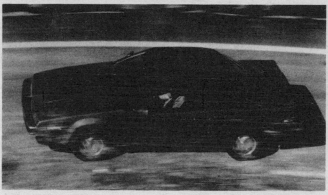

Subaru XT6 4WD

The XT coupe loses its 4-wheel-drive/4-cylinder models, but otherwise is unchanged for 1990. XT is due to be replaced in 1991 and rumors are that it will be a Giugiaro-designed 2-door with a multi-valve 6-cylinder engine producing over 200 horsepower. The current range has a base GL front-drive model with a 97-horsepower 1.8-liter 4-cylinder engine and either a 5-speed manual or 4-speed automatic transmission. Heading the lineup is the XT6, powered by a 145-horsepower 2.7-liter 6-cylinder engine. A front-drive XT6 comes only with a 4-speed automatic transmission. The 4WD XT6 models have a permanently engaged 4WD system and either a 5-speed manual or a 4-speed automatic transmission. Like most of Subaru's engines, the two available in the XT have horizontally opposed cylinders, what is known as a "flat" engine, rather than an inline or V-type. Though the 4-cylinder XT GL looks flamboyant, its 90-horsepower engine generates high fuel economy, not high performance. The XT6 is a different animal. The 6-cylinder engine is smooth and responsive, and works equally well with either automatic or manual transmission. The 4-cylinder, on the other hand, feels anemic with automatic. We also like the permanently engaged 4WD systems available on the XT6, which provide outstanding foul-weather traction without any input required from the driver. XT6 models are pricey, however, and 4WD adds hundreds more, so you're into all-wheel-drive Mitsubishi Eclipse/Eagle Talon territory. We like the Eclipse and Talon better overall, partly because they have a more sensible, more ergonomic interior layout. XT sales are down, so Subaru dealers might be anxious to cut their prices.

Specifications

	2-door notchback
Wheelbase, in.	97.0
Overall length, in.	177.6
Overall width, in.	66.5
Overall height, in.	49.4
Turn diameter, ft.	31.8
Curb weight, lbs.	2455
Cargo vol., cu. ft.	11.6
Fuel capacity, gals.	15.9
Seating capacity	4
Front headroom, in.	37.4
Front shoulder room, in.	52.8
Front legroom, max., in.	43.3
Rear headroom, in.	34.4
Rear shoulder room, in.	52.8
Rear legroom, min., in.	26.2

Powertrain layout: longitudinal front engine/front-wheel drive or permanent 4WD.

Engines

	ohc flat-4	ohc flat-6
Size, liters/cu. in.	1.8/109	2.7/163
Fuel delivery	PFI	PFI
Horsepower @ rpm	97 @ 5200	145 @ 5200
Torque (lbs./ft.) @ rpm	103 @ 3200	156 @ 4000
Availability	S	O

EPA city/highway mpg

5-speed OD manual	25/31	18/25
4-speed OD automatic	23/29	20/28

Prices

Subaru XT	Retail Price	Dealer Invoice	Low Price
GL 2-door notchback	$13071	—	—
XT6 2-door notchback	17111	—	—
4WD XT6 2-door notchback	17951	—	—

	Retail Price	Dealer Invoice	Low Price
Destination charge	395	395	395

Dealer invoice and low price not available at time of publication.

Standard equipment:

GL: 1.8-liter PFI 4-cylinder engine, 5-speed manual transmission, power steering, Hill-Holding (with 5-speed), reclining front bucket seats, driver's-seat lumbar support and height adjustments, power windows and locks, power mirrors, tinted glass, tilt steering column and instrument cluster, remote fuel door and decklid releases, rear defogger, folding rear seat, AM/FM radio, 185/70HR13 tires. **XT6** adds: 2.7-liter PFI 6-cylinder engine, 4-speed automatic transmission (2WD), 5-speed manual transmission (4WD), 4-wheel disc brakes, air suspension (4WD), air conditioning, cruise control, trip computer, upgraded upholstery, AM/FM cassette with EQ, visor mirrors (lighted right), headlamp washers, fog lights, 195/60HR14 tires (2WD), 205/60HR14 tires (4WD), alloy wheels.

Optional equipment:

4-speed automatic transmission, XT6 4WD .	750	—	—

Toyota Camry

Toyota Camry

The optional V-6 engine gains a knock sensor and three horsepower (to 156) as the major mechanical changes for the compact Camry, Toyota's most popular U.S. model. Last year's lineup returns. A front-drive 4-door sedan comes in base, Deluxe, and LE trim, and a front-drive 5-door wagon in Deluxe and LE trim. The All-Trac sedan has a perma-

Prices are accurate at time of printing; subject to manufacturer's change.

nently engaged 4-wheel-drive system, and is available in Deluxe and LE guise. A 115-horsepower 2.0-liter 4-cylinder engine is the base engine and the 2.5-liter V-6 is optional on front-drive Deluxe and LE models. All Camry wagons and some sedans are imported from Japan. A Toyota plant in Kentucky now produces 200,000 Camry sedans per year for sale in the U.S. Other changes for 1990 are that Deluxe models with manual transmission have a tachometer as standard equipment (it was formerly optional) and 60/40 split, folding rear seatbacks are optional on Deluxe sedans.

Specifications

	4-door notchback	5-door wagon
Wheelbase, in.	102.4	102.4
Overall length, in.	182.1	183.1
Overall width, in.	67.4	67.4
Overall height, in.	54.1	54.5
Turn diameter, ft.	34.8	34.8
Curb weight, lbs.	2690[1]	2910
Cargo vol., cu. ft.	14.6	65.2
Fuel capacity, gals.	15.9	15.9
Seating capacity	5	5
Front headroom, in.	37.9	38.2
Front shoulder room, in.	54.3	54.3
Front legroom, max., in.	42.9	42.9
Rear headroom, in.	36.6	37.7
Rear shoulder room, in.	53.7	53.7
Rear legroom, min., in.	34.4	34.4

1. 3086 lbs., All-Trac.

Powertrain layout: transverse front engine/front-wheel drive or permanent 4WD (All-Trac).

Engines

	dohc I-4	dohc V-6
Size, liters/cu. in.	2.0/122	2.5/153
Fuel delivery	PFI	PFI
Horsepower @ rpm	115 @ 5200	156 @ 5600
Torque (lbs./ft.) @ rpm	124 @ 4400	160 @ 4400
Availability	S	O

EPA city/highway mpg

5-speed OD manual	26/34	19/26
4-speed OD automatic	24/31	19/25

The optional Power Package has a new door unlocking system; one turn of the key unlocks the driver's door and a second turn unlocks the other doors. Camry's arch rival in the compact class, the Honda Accord, is new this year, offering a roomier interior and improvements in acceleration, ride, and handling over the previous version. Camry still offers some features not available on Accord, including the V-6 engine, 4WD, station wagon body style, and anti-lock brakes (optional on the LE sedan and wagon with the V-6, and the All-Trac LE). Accord's new 4-cylinder engine is stronger and quieter than Camry's 4-cylinder, but the optional V-6 evens the score for Toyota. Camry has several other virtues: ample passenger room, good assembly quality, a reputation for reliability, and good resale value. And, Toyota dealers should be offering discounts on Camrys.

Prices

Toyota Camry	Retail Price	Dealer Invoice	Low Price
4-door notchback, 5-speed	$11588	$9966	$10777
4-door notchback, automatic	12258	10542	11400
Deluxe 4-door notchback, 5-speed	12388	10555	11471
Deluxe 4-door notchback, automatic	13078	11142	12110
LE 4-door notchback, automatic	14658	12415	13536
All-Trac Deluxe 4-door, 5-speed	14168	12071	13119
All-Trac Deluxe 4-door, automatic	15058	12829	13943
All-Trac LE 4-door, automatic	16648	14101	15374
Deluxe 5-door wagon, automatic	13768	11730	12749
Deluxe V6 4-door notchback, 5-speed	13698	11671	12684
Deluxe V6 4-door notchback, automatic	14388	12259	13323
LE V6 4-door notchback, automatic	16428	13915	15171
Deluxe V6 5-door wagon, automatic	15078	12846	13962
LE V6 5-door wagon, automatic	17218	14584	15901

Dealer invoice and destination charge may vary by region.

Standard equipment:

2.0-liter DOHC 16-valve PFI 4-cylinder engine, 5-speed manual or 4-speed automatic transmission, power steering, coolant temperature gauge, trip odometer, center console with storage, velour reclining front bucket seats with driver's-seat height adjustment, rear shoulder belts, remote fuel door and trunk releases, rear defogger, tinted glass, P185/70SR13 tires. **Deluxe** adds: 2.0-liter DOHC 16-valve PFI 4-cylinder or 2.5-liter DOHC 24-valve PFI V-6 engine, 4-wheel disc brakes (V-6), wide bodyside moldings, dual remote

Prices are accurate at time of printing; subject to manufacturer's change

mirrors, tilt steering column, automatic-off headlamp feature, folding rear seatbacks (wagon), rear wiper/washer (wagon), digital clock, right visor mirror, cup holder. **LE** adds: air conditioning (V-6), power mirrors, tachometer, console armrest, multi-adjustable driver's seat, folding rear armrest, cargo cover (wagon), illuminated entry with fadeout, upper windshield tint band, AM/FM radio with power antenna. **All-Trac** models have full-time 4-wheel drive.

Optional equipment:	Retail Price	Dealer Invoice	Low Price
Anti-lock brakes, LE All-Trac	1280	1024	1152
LE V6	1130	904	1017
Air conditioning (std. LE V6)	825	660	743
Power glass moonroof (NA base)	700	560	630
Cruise control, base	315	258	287
Deluxe & LE	210	168	189
Base includes tilt steering column.			
Power Pkg., Deluxe 4-door	620	496	558
LE	565	452	509
Deluxe wagon	570	457	514
Power windows and locks; Deluxe 4-door includes split folding rear seat; LE includes lighted visor mirrors.			
Power Seat Pkg., LE	230	184	207
Requires Power Pkg. or Value Pkg.			
Leather trim, LE 4-doors	1080	864	972
Includes power height adjustment for driver's seat; requires Power Pkg. or Value Pkg.			
Alloy wheels, LE 4-cyl.	390	312	351
LE V6	410	328	369
All-Trac LE	360	288	324
AM/FM radio, base & Deluxe 4-doors . . .	330	247	289
Deluxe wagon	360	270	315
AM/FM cassette, base & Deluxe 4-doors .	480	360	420
Deluxe wagon	510	382	446
LE	190	142	166
AM/FM cassette w/EQ, LE	470	352	411
Speaker upgrade, 4-doors	140	112	126
Deluxe wagon	170	136	153
Convenience Pkg., base	120	96	108
Conventional spare tire, digital clock.			
Fall 1990 Value Pkg., Deluxe 4-cyl.	1399	1259	1329
Deluxe V6, LE	1190	1008	1099
LE V6	650	551	601
Air conditioning, cruise control, AM/FM cassette, Power Pkg., floormats.			
Split folding rear seat, Deluxe 4-doors . . .	100	80	90
All Weather Guard Pkg., base	55	46	51
California emissions pkg.	70	59	65
Mudguards (std. All-Trac)	30	24	27

Toyota Celica

Toyota Celica GT

The Celica sports coupe has been redesigned for 1990. The wheelbase is the same as the 1986-89 generation's, 99.4 inches, while overall length grows about three inches. A 2-door coupe and Liftback 3-door hatchback went on sale in the fall; a convertible is supposed to arrive in the spring. Base ST models now have a 103-horsepower, dual-cam 1.6-liter engine with 16 valves, the same engine used in most Corollas. GT and GT-S models share a new 130-horsepower 2.2-liter 4-cylinder, also with dual cams and 16 valves. All these models have front-wheel drive and are available with either a 5-speed manual or 4-speed automatic transmission. The 4-wheel-drive Celica All-Trac retains a turbocharged 2.0-liter engine, but has 200 horsepower this year, 10 more than in 1989. The All-Trac, whose 4WD system is permanently engaged, comes only with a 5-speed manual. Anti-lock brakes are optional on the All-Trac and will be available on the GT-S later in the year. A driver's-side airbag is standard on all models. We're surprised at how well the base ST accelerates with the 1.6-liter engine, at least with manual transmission. The optional automatic saps much of the 1.6-liter's vigor. The new 2.2-liter engine is stronger and produces more torque at lower speeds than the 1.6. Even so, the 2.2—like most other multi-valve engines—produces most of its power at higher speeds, which makes it better with manual transmission. For those who want automatic, the 2.2 still delivers adequate acceleration and decent fuel economy. The new Celica's interior provides adequate room for adults in the front seats. As with most sports coupes, the rear seat is too cramped for all but kids. Celicas are pricey, but previous models have been reliable cars with good resale value.

Specifications

	2-door notchback	3-door hatchback
Wheelbase, in.	99.4	99.4
Overall length, in.	176.0	174.0
Overall width, in.	67.1	67.1
Overall height, in.	50.6	50.6
Turn diameter, ft.	36.1	36.1
Curb weight, lbs.	2500	2696[1]
Cargo vol., cu. ft.	12.6	24.7
Fuel capacity, gals.	15.9	15.9
Seating capacity	4	4
Front headroom, in.	37.7	37.7
Front shoulder room, in.	52.0	52.0
Front legroom, max., in.	42.9	42.9
Rear headroom, in.	34.5	33.0
Rear shoulder room, in.	49.2	49.2
Rear legroom, min., in.	26.8	26.8

1. 3272 lbs., All-Trac.

Powertrain layout: transverse front engine/front-wheel drive or permanent 4WD (All-Trac).

Engines	dohc I-4	dohc I-4	Turbo dohc I-4
Size, liters/cu. in.	1.6/97	2.2/132	2.0/122
Fuel delivery	PFI	PFI	PFI
Horsepower @ rpm	103 @ 6000	130 @ 5400	200 @ 6000
Torque (lbs./ft.) @ rpm	102 @ 3200	140 @ 4400	200 @ 3200
Availability	S[1]	S[2]	S[3]

EPA city/highway mpg

5-speed OD manual	28/33	23/29	19/24
4-speed OD automatic	25/33	22/28	

1. ST.   2. GT, GT-S.   3. All-Trac.

Prices

Toyota Celica	Retail Price	Dealer Invoice	Low Price
ST 2-door notchback, 5-speed	$11808	$10096	$10430
ST 2-door notchback, automatic	12478	10665	11020
GT 2-door notchback, 5-speed	13408	11397	11812
GT 2-door notchback, automatic	14078	11966	12402
GT 3-door hatchback, 5-speed	13658	11609	12032
GT 3-door hatchback, automatic	14328	12178	12622
GT 2-door convertible, 5-speed	18318	15570	16137
GT 2-door convertible, automatic	18988	16139	16727
GS-S 2-door notchback, 5-speed	15388	13003	13520
GT-S 2-door notchback, automatic	16138	13636	14178
GT-S 3-door hatchback, 5-speed	15738	13299	13827
All-Trac Turbo 3-door hatchback, 5-speed .	20878	17642	18343

Dealer invoice and destination charge may vary by region.

Standard equipment:

2.0-liter DOHC 16-valve PFI engine, 5-speed manual or 4-speed automatic transmission, power steering, tinted glass, console, rear defogger, remote fuel door and decklid/liftgate releases, fabric reclining front bucket seats, one-piece folding rear seatback, automatic headlamps off, trip odometer, tachometer, coolant temperature and oil pressure gauges, voltmeter, digital clock, AM/FM ST ET, 165SR13 tires. **GT** adds: split folding rear seatback, right visor mirror, pushbutton heating/ventilation controls, power mirrors, memory tilt steering column, cargo cover (3-door), cargo area carpet, 185/70SR13 tires; convertible has power top and power rear windows. **GT** adds: higher-output engine, rear wiper/washer (3-door), variable intermittent wipers, sport seats with power lumbar and lateral supports, tilt/telescopic steering column with memory, 205/60HR14 tires on alloy wheels. **All-Trac Turbo** adds: turbocharged, intercooled engine, permanent 4-wheel drive, 205/60VR14 tires.

Optional equipment:

Anti-lock brakes, GT-S, All-Trac	1130	904	1017
Air conditioning, ST & GT	795	636	716
w/auto temp, GT-S & All-Trac	960	768	864
Power Pkg., ST & GT exc. conv.	415	332	374
Power windows and locks, heated power mirrors.			
Power Pkg., GT conv.	490	392	441
Power windows, locks and mirrors.			
Power Pkg., GT-S	390	312	351
Power windows and locks.			
Power Pkg. 2, GT exc. conv.	390	312	351
Power windows and locks.			

Prices are accurate at time of printing; subject to manufacturer's change

	Retail Price	Dealer Invoice	Low Price
AM/FM ST ET cassette (std. All-Trac) ...	190	142	166
w/EQ, GT & GT-S	430	322	376
w/EQ & diversity antenna, All-Trac	280	210	245
CD player, All-Trac	800	600	700
Alloy wheels, GT	340	272	306
GT conv.	370	296	333
Power sunroof	675	540	608
Cruise control	210	168	189
Color-Keyed Pkg., GT-S	50	40	45
ST	20	16	18
Leather Sport Seat Pkg., GT-S	1550	1240	1395
All-Trac	1160	928	1044
Includes cruise control, power windows and locks.			
Rear wiper/washer, GT 3-door	135	111	123
Tilt/telescopic steering column, GT			
exc. conv.	70	60	65
Rear spoiler, GT	225	180	203
ST Spring Value Pkg. 1 or 2	510	500	510
Pkg. 1: AM/FM ST ET cassette, air conditioner, pinstripe. Pkg. 2 deletes air conditioner and adds sunroof.			
GT Spring Value Pkg.	620	610	620
AM/FM ST ET cassette, air conditioning, cruise control, rear spoiler, GT stripe.			
GT-S Spring Value Pkg. 1	700	690	700
Pkg. 2	1080	1050	700
Pkg. 1: AM/FM ST ET cassette, automatic air conditioning, cruise control, Power Pkg.; Pkg. 2 adds leather seats.			
GT-S Value Pkg. & Leather Sport			
Seat Pkg.	1650	1450	1550

Toyota Corolla/Geo Prizm

Corolla and Prizm are built from the same design and share most major components. One major difference is that all Prizms are built at the New United Motor Manufacturing Inc. plant in California. The Corolla 4-door sedan also is built there, but all Corolla 2-door coupes and 5-door wagons, and some 4-door sedans, are imported from Japan. Here are the changes for both car lines: Toyota has dropped the 90-horsepower, carbureted 1.6-liter 4-cylinder that powered Corolla Deluxe, LE, and SR5 models last year in favor of a 102-horsepower, fuel-injected version of the same en-

Toyota Corolla

Specifications

	2-door notchback	4-door notchback	5-door hatchback	5-door wagon
Wheelbase, in.	95.7	95.7	95.7	95.7
Overall length, in.	172.2	170.3	170.7	171.5
Overall width, in.	65.6	65.2	65.2	65.2
Overall height, in.	49.6	52.4	52.4	54.5
Turn diameter, ft.	31.5	31.5	31.5	31.5
Curb weight, lbs.	2414	2360[1]	2376	2436[2]
Cargo vol., cu. ft.	11.7	12.7	32.2	64.5
Fuel capacity, gals.	13.2	13.2	13.2	13.2
Seating capacity	4	5	5	5
Front headroom, in.	37.9	38.4	38.3	39.6
Front shoulder room, in. . .	52.4	53.2	53.2	53.2
Front legroom, max., in. . .	42.9	40.9	40.9	40.9
Rear headroom, in.	35.3	36.4	35.5	39.3
Rear shoulder room, in. . .	51.0	52.7	52.7	52.7
Rear legroom, min., in. . .	25.8	31.6	31.6	31.6

1. 2650 lbs., Corolla All-Trac.   2. 2736 lbs., Corolla All-Trac.

Powertrain layout: transverse front engine/front-wheel drive or permanent 4WD (Corolla All-Trac).

Engines

	dohc I-4	dohc I-4
Size, liters/cu. in.	1.6/97	1.6/97
Fuel delivery	PFI	PFI
Horsepower @ rpm	102 @ 5800	130 @ 6800
Torque (lbs./ft.) @ rpm	101 @ 4800	105 @ 6000
Availability	S	S[1]

EPA city/highway mpg

5-speed OD manual	28/33	25/31
3-speed automatic	26/29	
4-speed OD automatic	25/33	23/30

1. Corolla GT-S, Prizm GSi.

Prices are accurate at time of printing; subject to manufacturer's change

gine. Last year, the fuel-injected engine came only in the 4-wheel-drive All-Trac models. The sporty Corolla GT-S 2-door gains 15 horsepower and its dual-cam 1.6-liter engine now pumps 130 horsepower. All Corollas have front-wheel drive except the All-Trac sedan and wagon, which have permanently engaged 4WD. Prizm, which is sold through Chevrolet dealers, is available as a 4-door notchback and 5-door hatchback, both with front-wheel drive. The 102-horsepower 1.6 is standard on the base Prizm and LSi. New this fall is a sporty GSi model with the 130-horsepower engine. Corolla and Prizm rank at the top of the subcompact class, along with the Honda Civic, which is slightly less expensive when comparably equipped. We can't tell any difference in quality between Corollas built in the U.S. and those imported from Japan (most Civics are built in North America as well).

Prices

Toyota Corolla	Retail Price	Dealer Invoice	Low Price
4-door notchback, 5-speed	$8748	$7786	$8267
4-door notchback, automatic	9218	8204	8711
Deluxe 4-door notchback, 5-speed	9488	8159	8824
Deluxe 4-door notchback, automatic	9958	8563	9261
LE 4-door notchback, 5-speed	10928	9365	10147
LE 4-door notchback, automatic	11598	9939	10769
Deluxe 5-door wagon, 5-speed	10128	8709	9419
Deluxe 5-door wagon, automatic	10598	9114	9856
All-Trac Deluxe wagon, 5-speed	11838	10189	11014
All-Trac Deluxe wagon, automatic	12608	10842	11725
All-Trac SR5 wagon, 5-speed	13238	11345	12292
All-Trac Deluxe 4-door, 5-speed	10758	9251	10005
All-Trac Deluxe 4-door, automatic	11528	9913	10721

Dealer invoice and destination charge may vary by region.

Standard equipment:

Base and Deluxe: 1.6-liter DOHC 16-valve PFI 4-cylinder engine, 5-speed manual or 3-speed automatic transmission, power brakes, cloth reclining front bucket seats (vinyl on wagons), split folding rear seatback (wagons), tinted glass, console with storage, door map pockets, cup holder, remote fuel door and decklid releases, trip odometer, coolant temperature gauge, 155SR13 tires. **LE adds:** 5-speed manual or 4-speed automatic transmission, tachometer, intermittent wipers, digital clock, AM/FM radio, 60/40 folding rear seatbacks, bodyside molding, remote mirrors, driver's seat height and lumbar support adjustments, upgraded trunk trim, 175/70SR13 all-season tires. **Deluxe All-Trac** models have permanent 4-wheel drive, 5-speed manual or 4-speed automatic transmission. **SR5 All-Trac wagon** adds: power steering, cruise control, digital clock, AM/FM radio, cloth upholstery, tilt steering column, remote mirrors, intermittent wipers, rear wiper.

Optional equipment:	Retail Price	Dealer Invoice	Low Price
Power steering, base & Deluxe	250	214	232
Air conditioning	775	620	698
Convenience Pkg., Deluxe	115	92	104
Remote OS mirrors, digital clock.			
Power sunroof, Deluxe & LE 4-doors	530	424	477
Cruise control & int. wipers (NA base)	210	168	189
Alloy wheels, LE 4-door	370	296	333
SR5 wagon	415	332	374
AM/FM radio w/4 speakers	330	247	289
AM/FM cassette, base & Deluxe 4-doors,			
All-Trac wagon	480	360	420
Deluxe wagons	380	285	333
SR5 wagon	190	142	166
LE	150	112	131
AM/FM radio w/2 speakers, Deluxe	210	157	184
Tilt steering column	85	73	79
Power Pkg., LE 4-door, SR5 wagon	570	456	513
Power windows and locks, power mirrors.			
Two-Tone Paint Pkg., SR5 wagon	320	256	288
Fabric seats, Deluxe wagon	70	60	65
Rear wiper, Deluxe wagon	135	111	123
Exterior Appearance Pkg., LE 4-door,			
All-Trac wagons	85	68	77
Upgrade Speaker Pkg., Deluxe All-Trac wagon	115	92	104
Rear overhead storage shelf, two rear speaker enclosures and wiring (speakers not included).			
Tachometer, 5-speed models	60	48	54
Fall 1990 Value Pkg., Deluxe 4-door	669	602	636
Power steering, digital clock, remote OS mirrors, AM/FM cassette, full wheel covers, floormats, 175/70R13 tires.			
Fall 1990 Value Pkg., LE 4-door	799	719	759
Air conditioning, AM/FM cassette, power windows and locks, power mirrors, color-coordinated bumpers, tilt steering column.			
Fall 1990 Value Pkg., Deluxe 2WD wagon	675	607	641
Deluxe 4WD wagon	659	593	626
Power steering, digital clock, remote OS mirrors, AM/FM cassette, full fabric seats, full wheel covers, 175/70R13 tires (2WD), floormats.			
All Weather Guard Pkg., Deluxe & LE	55	46	51
Base	160	130	145

Prices are accurate at time of printing; subject to manufacturer's change

Toyota Corolla Sport

	Retail Price	Dealer Invoice	Low Price
SR5 2-door notchback, 5-speed	$11068	$9485	$10277
SR5 2-door notchback, automatic	11738	10059	10899
GT-S 2-door notchback, 5-speed	13238	11318	12278

Dealer invoice and destination charge may vary by region.

Standard equipment:

SR5: 1.6-liter DOHC 16-valve PFI 4-cylinder engine, 5-speed manual or 4-speed automatic transmission, cloth reclining front bucket seats, trip odometer, coolant temperature gauge, tachometer, 175/70SR13 tires. **GT-S** adds: higher-output engine, power steering, split folding rear seat, driver's-seat lumbar support and cushion height adjusters, AM/FM radio, power mirrors, oil pressure gauge, voltmeter, tilt steering column, automatic head-lights-off system, power mirrors, leather-wrapped steering wheel, intermittent wipers, 185/60R14 tires.

Optional equipment:

Power steering, SR5	250	214	232
Air conditioning	775	620	698
Power sunroof	530	424	477
Cruise control & int. wipers	210	168	189
Convenience Pkg., SR5	180	151	166
Digital clock, split folding rear seat, driver's-seat lumbar support and cushion height adjusters.			
Alloy wheels, SR5	370	296	333
GT-S	435	348	392
AM/FM radio, SR5	330	247	289
AM/FM cassette, SR5	520	390	455
AM/FM cassette w/EQ, GT-S	430	322	376
Tilt steering column, SR5	85	73	79
Power Pkg.	390	312	351
Power windows and locks.			
Sport seat, GT-S	180	144	162
Exterior Appearance/Convenience Pkg., SR5	355	291	323
Color-coordinated bumper, bodyside moldings, power mirrors, digital clock, driver's-seat lumbar support and cushion height adjusters, split folding rear seat.			
All Weather Guard Pkg.	55	46	51

Geo Prizm

4-door notchback	$10125	$9315	$9515
5-door hatchback	10425	9591	9791
GSi 4-door notchback	11900	10948	11148
GSi 5-door hatchback	12285	11302	11502
Destination charge	335	335	335

Standard equipment:

1.6-liter DOHC PFI 4-cylinder engine, 5-speed manual transmission, velour reclining front bucket seats, tinted glass, door pockets, cup holders, left remote mirror, folding rear seat (hatchbacks), remote fuel door release, bodyside molding, 175/70SR13 SBR tires. **GSi** adds: higher-output engine, power steering, uprated suspension, sport seats, tachometer and oil pressure gauge, rear spoiler, rear wiper/washer (hatchback), left remote and right manual mirrors, AM/FM radio, 185/60HR14 Goodyear Eagle tires on alloy wheels.

Optional equipment:	Retail Price	Dealer Invoice	Low Price
Air conditioning	690	587	621
Power sunroof	530	451	477
Preferred Group 1, base	609	518	548
Power steering, AM/FM radio, left remote and right manual mirrors, full wheel covers.			
Preferred Group 2, base	1074	913	967
Group 1 plus 3-speed automatic transmission.			
Preferred Group 3, base	1554	1321	1399
Group 2 plus air conditioning, 5-speed manual transmission, power locks, remote decklid/hatch release.			
Preferred Group 4, base	2019	1716	1817
Group 3 plus 3-speed automatic transmission.			
LSi Preferred Group 5, base 4-door	2084	1771	1876
Base 5-door	2019	1716	1817
Group 4 plus 5-speed manual transmission, console with storage box, soft-feel steering wheel, visor mirrors, assist grips, split folding rear seat, rear wiper/washer (5-door), tilt steering column.			
LSi Preferred Group 6, base 4-door	2549	2167	2294
Base 5-door	2484	2111	2236
Group 5 plus 3-speed automatic transmission.			
LSi Preferred Group 7, base 4-door	3049	2592	2744
Base 5-door	2984	2536	2686
Group 6 plus power windows, cruise control, intermittent wipers.			
GSi Preferred Group 2	775	659	698
4-speed automatic transmission.			
GSi Preferred Group 3, 4-door	1059	900	953
5-door	909	773	818
Group 2 plus 5-speed manual transmission, air conditioning, split folding rear seat, tilt steering column, remote decklid/hatch release, floormats, visor mirrors.			
GSi Preferred Group 4, 4-door	1834	1559	1651
5-door	1684	1431	1516
Group 3 plus 4-speed automatic transmission.			
GSi Preferred Group 5, 4-door	1904	1618	1714
5-door	1754	1491	1579
Group 4 plus 5-speed manual transmission, AM/FM cassette, power windows and locks, cruise control, intermittent wipers.			

Prices are accurate at time of printing; subject to manufacturer's change

	Retail Price	Dealer Invoice	Low Price
GSi Preferred Group 6, 4-door	2679	2277	2411
5-door	2529	2150	2276
Group 5 plus 4-speed automatic transmission.			
AM/FM cassette	140	119	126
Floormats	40	34	36

Toyota Cressida

Toyota Cressida

Cressida, new last year, is unchanged for 1990. The rear-drive Cressida is still the top-shelf luxury sedan under the Toyota name, but it has been superseded in price and prestige by the Lexus LS 400, the flagship of Toyota's new upscale car division. Cressida comes only as a 4-door notchback sedan in one trim level. Motorized front shoulder belts, with separate manual lap belts, are standard. Antilock brakes are optional. The powertrain consists of a 190-horsepower 3.0-liter 6-cylinder engine and a 4-speed automatic transmission. A standard shift lock requires that the brake pedal be applied before the transmission can be shifted out of Park. We clocked a Cressida at 9.3 seconds in the 0-60-mph test—more than competitive with rivals such as the Acura Legend and Nissan Maxima. The automatic transmission complements the engine with prompt, smooth shifts up and down the speed range. We averaged 22.3 mpg overall in our test, ranging from a low of 17 in the city to an impressive 29 mpg on the highway. Braking was exceptional with the optional anti-lock control. Our test car pulled down from 60 mph in just 119 feet, versus an absolute norm of about 150 feet. In usable passenger room Cressida slightly trails the Mazda 929, another rear-driver, as well as the front-drive Legend and Maxima. Cressida is a little cheaper than either the 929 or the base Legend sedan, but a couple of thousand above even the most expensive Maxima.

Specifications

	4-door notchback
Wheelbase, in.	105.6
Overall length, in.	189.6
Overall width, in.	67.3
Overall height, in.	54.5
Turn diameter, ft.	32.8
Curb weight, lbs.	3417
Cargo vol., cu. ft.	12.0
Fuel capacity, gals.	18.5
Seating capacity	5
Front headroom, in.	38.4
Front shoulder room, in.	54.6
Front legroom, max., in.	42.8
Rear headroom, in.	37.1
Rear shoulder room, in.	54.4
Rear legroom, min., in.	35.0

Powertrain layout: longitudinal front engine/rear-wheel drive.

Engines

	dohc I-6
Size, liters/cu. in.	3.0/180
Fuel delivery	PFI
Horsepower @ rpm	190 @ 5600
Torque (lbs./ft.) @ rpm	185 @ 4400
Availability	S

EPA city/highway mpg

4-speed OD automatic	19/24

Prices

Toyota Cressida	Retail Price	Dealer Invoice	Low Price
4-door notchback	$21498	$17628	$19563

Dealer invoice and destination charge may vary by region.

Prices are accurate at time of printing; subject to manufacturer's change

Standard equipment:

3.0-liter DOHC 24-valve PFI 6-cylinder engine, 4-speed automatic transmission, power steering, 4-wheel disc brakes, automatic climate control, reclining front bucket seats, rear shoulder belts, cruise control, variable intermittent wipers, trip odometer, coolant temperature gauge, tachometer, AM/FM cassette with EQ, power antenna, power windows and locks, heated power mirrors, tilt/telescopic steering column, 205/60R15 tires.

Optional equipment:	Retail Price	Dealer Invoice	Low Price
Anti-lock brakes	1130	904	1017
CD player	700	525	613
Power sunroof	810	648	729
Power Seat Pkg.	540	432	486
Leather/Power Seat Pkg.	1245	996	1121
California emissions pkg.	70	59	

Toyota Supra

Toyota Supra

A driver's-side airbag is standard on Supra this year to meet the federal passive-restraint requirement. In addition, a padded knee bolster has been added to the driver's side of the instrument panel. The airbag is housed in a new 4-spoke steering wheel; the steering column retains its tilt and telescoping features. With the airbag, cruise-control switches have been moved from the steering wheel to a steering-column stalk. The rear-drive Supra comes in

Specifications

	3-door hatchback
Wheelbase, in.	102.2
Overall length, in.	181.9
Overall width, in.	68.7
Overall height, in.	51.2
Turn diameter, ft.	35.4
Curb weight, lbs.	3463
Cargo vol., cu. ft.	12.8
Fuel capacity, gals.	18.5
Seating capacity	4
Front headroom, in.	37.5
Front shoulder room, in.	52.5
Front legroom, max., in.	43.6
Rear headroom, in.	33.9
Rear shoulder room, in.	50.5
Rear legroom, min., in.	24.7

Powertrain layout: longitudinal front engine/rear-wheel drive.

Engines	dohc I-6	Turbo dohc I-6
Size, liters/cu. in.	3.0/180	3.0/180
Fuel delivery	PFI	PFI
Horsepower @ rpm	200 @ 6000	232 @ 5600
Torque (lbs./ft.) @ rpm	188 @ 3600	254 @ 3200
Availability	S	S

EPA city/highway mpg

5-speed OD manual	18/23	17/22
4-speed OD automatic	18/23	18/23

fixed roof or Sport Roof (with removable T-tops) guise with either a 200-horsepower 3.0-liter 6-cylinder or a 232-horsepower, turbocharged 3.0 six. The standard power door locks have a new feature: turning the key once unlocks the driver's door and turning it a second time unlocks the passenger's door. Anti-lock brakes are optional on naturally aspirated and turbo models. The current Supra was introduced as a late 1986 model, so it's an old-timer compared to its primary rival, the Nissan 300ZX, which is new for 1990. The 300ZX Turbo now starts at $33,000, nearly $8000 more than a Supra Turbo. Supra still has much to offer, including strong acceleration, tenacious handling ability, optional anti-lock brakes, an airbag, and a long list of standard comfort and convenience features. With a base curb weight of nearly 3500 pounds, Supra isn't nimble like an MR2, but its wide tires and low stance give it impressive cornering power. In snow, however, the tires have poor traction.

Prices

Toyota Supra	Retail Price	Dealer Invoice	Low Price
3-door hatchback, 5-speed	$22860	$18745	$20803
3-door hatchback, automatic	23610	19360	21485
w/Sport Roof, 5-speed	23930	19623	21777
w/Sport Roof, automatic	24680	20238	22459
Turbo, 5-speed	25200	20664	22932
Turbo, automatic	25950	21279	23615
Turbo w/Sport Roof, 5-speed	26220	21500	23860
Turbo w/Sport Roof, automatic	26970	22115	24543

Dealer invoice and destination charge may vary by region.

Standard equipment:

3.0-liter DOHC 24-valve PFI 6-cylinder engine, 5-speed manual or 4-speed automatic transmission, power steering, 4-wheel disc brakes, driver's-side airbag, automatic climate control, power windows and locks, heated power mirrors, two-can cupholder, tilt/telescopic steering column, fog lights, theft deterrent system, bodyside moldings, tachometer, coolant temperature and oil pressure gauges, voltmeter, trip odometer, variable intermittent wipers, cruise control, console with storage and padded armrest, cloth sport seats, driver's seat power lumbar and lateral support adjustments, folding rear seatbacks, lighted visor mirrors, remote fuel door and hatch releases, automatic-off headlight system, illuminated entry system, tinted glass, rear defogger, cargo cover, AM/FM cassette with EQ, diversity power antenna, 225/50VR16 Goodyear Eagle GT Gatorback tires on alloy wheels. **Turbo** adds: turbocharged, intercooled engine, speed-sensitive power steering, oil cooler, turbo boost gauge, limited-slip differential.

Optional equipment:

Anti-lock brakes	1130	904	1017
Power driver's seat	230	184	207
Sports Pkg., base	795	647	721
Turbo	360	288	324
Electronically modulated suspension, limited-slip differential, progressive power steering.			
White Exterior Appearance Pkg.	40	32	36

	Retail Price	Dealer Invoice	Low Price
CD player	700	525	613
Leather/Power Seat Pkg.	1240	992	1116
California emissions pkg.	70	59	65

Toyota Tercel

Toyota Tercel

The front-drive Tercel subcompact, Toyota's entry-level line, has a smaller roster for 1990. The Deluxe 3-door hatchback and all 5-door hatchbacks are gone. That leaves a 3-door hatchback in EZ and base trim levels, and a 2-door coupe in base and Deluxe trim. The EZ 3-door comes only with a 4-speed manual transmission, the others with a standard 5-speed manual or optional 3-speed automatic. The automatic transmission now has a shift lock that requires the brake pedal be applied to shift out of Park, plus the transmission must be in Park before the ignition key can be removed. Tercels are powered by a carbureted, 78-horsepower 1.5-liter 4-cylinder engine, except for California models with automatic transmission, which have fuel injection and 82 horsepower. The 2-door coupes gain remote trunk and fuel-door releases and a remote outside mirror as standard equipment, while the Deluxe 2-door also adds power steering as standard. As Toyota's smallest, least-expensive model, Tercel's mission is to lure buyers on a tight budget away from the Hyundai Excel, Nissan Sentra, Dodge Omni/Plymouth Horizon, and other low-cost, basic-transportation cars. Several rivals undercut Tercel in price, but few match its admirable record for reliability and durability. Fuel economy is good with automatic transmission, and outstanding with either manual transmission, both of which have overdrive top gears that help stretch a gallon of gas. Acceleration is adequate with manual shift, but barely adequate with automatic. Tercel is a competent small car, but neither its performance nor its price are exceptional. In today's competitive market, you might find a Toyota dealer who's willing to sell one at a big discount.

Specifications

	2-door notchback	3-door hatchback
Wheelbase, in.	93.7	93.7
Overall length, in.	166.7	157.3
Overall width, in.	64.0	64.0
Overall height, in.	51.8	52.6
Turn diameter, ft.	31.2	31.2
Curb weight, lbs.	2020	1990
Cargo vol., cu. ft.	11.0	36.2
Fuel capacity, gals.	11.9	11.9
Seating capacity	5	5
Front headroom, in.	37.8	38.4
Front shoulder room, in.	51.5	51.5
Front legroom, max., in.	40.2	40.2
Rear headroom, in.	35.9	36.6
Rear shoulder room, in.	50.7	51.5
Rear legroom, min., in.	30.8	32.1

Powertrain layout: transverse front engine/front-wheel drive.

Engines

	ohc I-4
Size, liters/cu. in.	1.5/89
Fuel delivery	1 bbl.
Horsepower @ rpm	78 @ 6000
Torque (lbs./ft.) @ rpm	87 @ 4000
Availability	S[1]

EPA city/highway mpg

4-speed OD manual	31/36
5-speed OD manual	30/36
3-speed automatic	29/32

1. Calif. models with automatic transmission have multi-point injection.

Prices

Toyota Tercel	Retail Price	Dealer Invoice	Low Price
Standard 2-door notchback, 5-speed	$7618	$6856	$7237
Standard 2-door notchback, automatic . . .	8078	7270	7674
Deluxe 2-door notchback, 5-speed	9028	7763	8396
Deluxe 2-door notchback, automatic	9498	8168	8833
EZ 3-door hatchback, 4-speed	6488	5936	6212
Standard 3-door hatchback, 5-speed	7558	6878	7218
Standard 3-door hatchback, automatic . . .	8028	7368	7698

Dealer invoice and destination charge may vary by region.

Standard equipment:

EZ: 1.5-liter 12-valve 4-cylinder engine, 4-speed manual transmission, locking fuel door, trip odometer, vinyl reclining front bucket seats, door pockets, folding rear seatback, 145/80SR13 tires on styled steel wheels. **Standard** adds: 5-speed manual or 3-speed automatic transmission, cloth seat inserts, cup holder, door-ajar light, bodyside moldings, rear ashtray. **Deluxe** adds: cloth seat trim, folding rear seatbacks, right visor mirror, rear defogger, tinted glass, 155SR13 tires.

Optional equipment:

Power steering, Standard	250	214	232
Air conditioning (NA EZ)	735	588	662
Rear wiper/washer, Standard hatchbacks .	135	111	123
AM/FM radio	210	157	184
AM/FM cassette	480	360	420
Cargo deck cover, Standard hatchbacks . .	50	41	46
Convenience Pkg., Standard hatchbacks . .	280	225	253

Full wheel covers, intermittent wipers, remote OS mirrors, analog clock, remote fuel door and hatch releases, full fabric seats.

All Weather Guard Pkg., EZ & Std. 2-door .	90	77	84
Standard hatchback & Deluxe 2-door . .	55	46	51
California emissions pkg.	70	59	65

Volkswagen Corrado

Billed as Volkswagen's "first full-blooded sports car," the $17,900 Corrado replaces the Scirocco in VW's North American lineup. Like Scirocco (discontinued here after '88), it's a front-drive, 4-seat hatchback. Corrado's main distinction

Volkswagen Corrado

is a new supercharged version of the 1.8-liter 4-cylinder Golf/Jetta engine, teamed only with a 5-speed manual transmission. The 158-horsepower engine is called "G-Charger" because its crankshaft-driven supercharger is shaped like the letter G. The G-Charger employs a single-cam cylinder head with two valves per cylinder. Corrado is based on the current Golf/Jetta platform and has standard 4-wheel disc brakes with optional anti-lock control. An unusual Corrado feature is a so-called "active" rear spoiler that extends automatically above 45 mph to reduce rear aerodynamic lift; it retracts below 12 mph. A dashboard switch allows manual extension for cleaning. The G-Charger engine is potent for its size and delivers strong passing power, yet almost seems anemic off the line. VW's claim of 7.5 seconds in the 0-60-mph sprint seems optimistic by the seat of our pants. The lack of an automatic transmission will be a drawback for some buyers, and there apparently won't be one soon. Other gripes include poor rearward vision, limited head room even in front, and lots of engine noise. On the plus side, handling is crisp and the power steering is fluid, quick, and properly boosted. It all makes for a car that's fun to drive on tight, winding roads. It's not an outstanding value. For similar money you can get better performance and the bonus of 4-wheel drive in the turbocharged Mitsubishi Eclipse GSX/Eagle Talon TSi.

Specifications

	3-door hatchback
Wheelbase, in.	97.3
Overall length, in.	159.4
Overall width, in.	65.9
Overall height, in.	51.9
Turn diameter, ft.	34.5
Curb weight, lbs.	2660
Cargo vol., cu. ft.	18.6
Fuel capacity, gals.	14.5
Seating capacity	4
Front headroom, in.	37.0
Front shoulder room, in.	53.8
Front legroom, max., in.	41.7
Rear headroom, in.	35.0
Rear shoulder room, in.	50.4
Rear legroom, min., in.	31.2

Powertrain layout: transverse front engine/front-wheel drive.

Engines

	Supercharged ohc I-4
Size, liters/cu. in.	1.8/109
Fuel delivery	PFI
Horsepower @ rpm	158 @ 5600
Torque (lbs./ft.) @ rpm	166 @ 4000
Availability	S

EPA city/highway mpg

5-speed OD manual	21/28

Prices

Volkswagen Corrado	Retail Price	Dealer Invoice	Low Price
3-door hatchback	$17900	$15792	—
Destination charge	320	320	320

Low price not available at time of publication.

Standard equipment:

1.8-liter supercharged PFI 4-cylinder engine, 5-speed manual transmission, 4-wheel disc brakes, velour height-adjustable bucket seats, split folding rear seat, rear shoulder belts, air conditioning, cruise control, power windows

Prices are accurate at time of printing; subject to manufacturer's change

and locks, power mirrors, AM/FM cassette, tachometer, coolant temperature and oil pressure gauges, voltmeter, trip odometer, tilt steering column, rear defogger, tinted glass, leather-wrapped steering wheel and shift knob, cargo cover, visor mirrors (lighted right), speed-activated retractable rear spoiler, fog lamps, intermittent wipers, rear wiper/washer, 195/60VR15 tires on alloy wheels.

Optional equipment:	Retail Price	Dealer Invoice	Low Price
Anti-lock brakes	835	835	835
Leather interior	710	610	—
Metallic paint	165	142	—
Sunroof	695	598	—
California emissions pkg.	97	95	—

Volkswagen Fox

1989 Volkswagen Fox GL Sport

Motorized front shoulder belts are standard on all Fox models this year to meet the federal passive-restraint requirement. Separate lap belts have to be buckled manually. This year's Fox lineup has a base 2-door sedan, GL 4-door sedan, and a GL 3-door wagon with an 81-horsepower 1.8-liter 4-cylinder engine and a 4-speed manual transmission. The

GL Sport 2-door has the same engine, but a 5-speed manual transmission. In addition, the GL Sport has alloy wheels instead of steel wheels. Neither automatic transmission nor power steering is available. The front-drive Fox, built in Brazil, is 5.4 inches longer than the Volkswagen Golf hatchbacks, but 8.3 inches shorter than the Jetta sedans. The base 2-door offers the most value for the money, but there are some benefits to spending more on a Fox, however. GL models have larger tires for better handling, a tachometer that helps you get more out of the frisky engine, and nicer interior furnishings. The GL Sport's 5-speed manual makes Fox easier to drive in traffic. The 4-speed manual has a tall overdrive top gear that keeps the engine well

Specifications

	2-door notchback	4-door notchback	3-door wagon
Wheelbase, in.	92.8	92.8	92.8
Overall length, in.	163.4	163.4	163.4
Overall width, in.	63.0	63.0	63.9
Overall height, in.	53.7	53.7	54.5
Turn diameter, ft.	31.5	31.5	31.5
Curb weight, lbs.	2126	2203	2203
Cargo vol., cu. ft.	9.9	9.9	61.8
Fuel capacity, gals.	12.4	12.4	12.4
Seating capacity	4	4	4
Front headroom, in.	36.6	36.6	36.6
Front shoulder room, in.	51.7	51.7	51.7
Front legroom, max., in.	41.1	41.1	41.1
Rear headroom, in.	35.4	35.4	35.8
Rear shoulder room, in.	52.1	51.1	51.5
Rear legroom, min., in.	30.2	30.2	30.2

Powertrain layout: longitudinal front engine/front-wheel drive.

Engines

	ohc I-4
Size, liters/cu. in.	1.8/109
Fuel delivery	PFI
Horsepower @ rpm	81 @ 5500
Torque (lbs./ft.) @ rpm	93 @ 3250
Availability	S

EPA city/highway mpg

4-speed OD manual	25/30
5-speed OD manual	24/29

Prices are accurate at time of printing; subject to manufacturer's change

below its torque peak, making a downshift to third gear mandatory for passing power. Fuel economy is similar with either transmission (25-30 mpg in urban driving). While all models are agile, the manual steering is quite heavy at low speeds, requiring lots of muscle in tight parking spaces. Fox is too narrow to fit three people in the rear seat without serious cramping, and head room is tight all around. The trunk on the sedans is shallow and a full-size spare tire takes up a lot of cargo space. Despite the flaws, few subcompacts under $10,000 are as fun to drive as Fox.

Prices

Volkswagen Fox	Retail Price	Dealer Invoice	Low Price
2-door notchback	$7225	$6688	$6957
GL Sport 2-door notchback	8595	7819	8207
GL 4-door notchback	8310	7560	7935
GL 3-door wagon	8550	7778	8164
Destination charge	320	320	320

Standard equipment:

1.8-liter PFI 4-cylinder engine, 4-speed manual transmission, cloth reclining front bucket seats, left remote mirror, rear defogger, intermittent wipers, console with coin box and storage bin, analog clock, 155/80SR13 tires. **GL Sport 2-door/GL 4-door** adds: 5-speed manual transmission (2-door); upgraded carpet, velour upholstery, digital clock, door pockets, map light, tachometer, right visor mirror, tinted glass, wide bodyside molding, flip-out rear window, 175/70SR 13 tires, alloy wheels (2-door). **Wagon** deletes tachometer and digital clock and adds: folding rear seat, tonneau cover, analog clock.

Optional equipment:

Air conditioning	715	615	665
Heavy Duty Pkg.	90	78	84
Metallic paint	165	142	154
AM/FM cassette	430	370	400
Radio prep	115	99	107
Rear wiper/washer, wagon	150	129	140
Sunroof	300	258	279

Volkswagen Golf/Jetta

1989 Volkswagen Golf GL

The Golf GTI 16V and Jetta GLI 16V have a larger, more powerful engine this year. The GTI 16V and GLI 16V trade in last year's 123-horsepower 1.8-liter 4-cylinder engine and return for 1990 with a 131-horsepower 2.0-liter 4-cylinder, derived from the base engine used in the Audi 80. Like the engine it replaces, the new 2.0-liter has two overhead cams and four valves per cylinder, and is available only with a 5-speed manual transmission. Golf and Jetta are built on the same front-drive platform and differ mainly in body styling. This year's lineup includes Golf GL hatchbacks and Jetta GL sedans powered by a 100-horsepower 1.8-liter 4-cylinder. Slotted above the GL models are the Golf GTI 3-door hatchback and the Jetta Carat 4-door sedan, both with a 105-horsepower version of the 1.8-liter engine. GL, GTI, and Carat models are available with a 5-speed manual or 3-speed automatic transmission. Rounding out the lineup are the Jetta GL Diesel and Carat Diesel, available only with a 5-speed manual transmission in the 4-door body. The diesel engine, added last summer, is a 52-horsepower 1.6-liter 4-cylinder. A 4-wheel-drive version of the GTI hatchback with the Corrado's supercharged, 158-horsepower engine may be introduced to the U.S. during 1990. It is called the Rallye GTI and has anti-lock disc brakes standard. Golf and Jetta are practical subcompacts that offer sporty handling and a taut, well-controlled ride even on the lowest-priced models. These cars don't sell on their looks, but they look better to us this year because of their lower price tags. A 16-valve model or a Jetta Carat with anti-lock brakes and other extras can be pricey, but a less-expensive GL model with fewer goodies is just as practical and nearly as much fun to drive.

Specifications

	Jetta 2-door notchback	Jetta 4-door notchback	Golf 3-door hatchback	Golf 5-door hatchback
Wheelbase, in.	97.3	97.3	97.3	97.3
Overall length, in.	171.7	171.7	158.0	158.0
Overall width, in.	65.5	65.5	65.5	65.5
Overall height, in.	55.7	55.7	55.7	55.7
Turn diameter, ft.	34.4	34.4	34.4	34.4
Curb weight, lbs.	2305	2305	2194	2246
Cargo vol., cu. ft.	16.6	16.6	39.6	39.6
Fuel capacity, gals.	14.5	14.5	14.5	14.5
Seating capacity	5	5	5	5
Front headroom, in.	38.1	38.1	38.1	38.1
Front shoulder room, in.	53.3	53.3	53.3	53.3
Front legroom, max., in.	39.5	39.5	39.5	39.5
Rear headroom, in.	37.1	37.1	37.5	37.5
Rear shoulder room, in.	53.3	53.3	54.3	54.3
Rear legroom, min., in.	35.1	35.1	34.4	34.4

Powertrain layout: transverse front engine/front-wheel drive.

Engines

	ohc I-4	ohc I-4	dohc I-4	Diesel ohc I-4
Size, liters/cu. in.	1.8/109	1.8/109	2.0/121	1.6/97
Fuel delivery	PFI	PFI	PFI	PFI
Horsepower @ rpm	100 @ 5400	105 @ 5400	131 @ 5800	52 @ 4800
Torque (lbs./ft.) @ rpm	107 @ 3400	110 @ 3400	133 @ 4250	71 @ 2000
Availability	S[1]	S[2]	S[3]	S[4]

EPA city/highway mpg

5-speed OD manual	25/32	25/32	22/28	37/43
3-speed automatic	23/28	23/28		

1. GL models.   2. GTI 8V, Carat.   3. GTI 16V, GLI 16V.   4. Jetta Diesel.

Prices

Volkswagen Golf/GTI	Retail Price	Dealer Invoice	Low Price
GL 3-door hatchback	$8695	$7822	$8259
GL 5-door hatchback	8995	8091	8543

	Retail Price	Dealer Invoice	Low Price
GTI 8V 3-door hatchback	9995	8986	9491
GTI 16V 3-door hatchback	12900	NA	NA
Destination charge	320	320	320

Standard equipment:

GL: 1.8-liter PFI 4-cylinder engine, 5-speed manual transmission, velour height-adjustable reclining front bucket seats, folding rear seat, rear shoulder belts, tachometer, coolant temperature gauge, trip odometer, rear defogger, tinted glass, door pockets, right visor mirror, remote OS mirrors, intermittent wipers, rear wiper/washer, center console with storage, 175/70SR13 tires. **GTI 8V** adds: higher-output engine, power steering, sport suspension, sport seats, upgraded upholstery, 185/60HR14 tires on teardrop-style alloy wheels. **GTI 16V** adds: 2.0-liter DOHC 16-valve engine, 4-wheel disc brakes, Recaro front seats with power height adjustment, trip computer, visor mirrors (lighted right), leather-wrapped steering wheel, tilt steering column, 195/60VR15 tires on BBS alloy wheels.

Optional equipment:

3-speed automatic transmission	505	465	485
Power steering	275	237	256
Air conditioning	805	692	749
Cruise control	225	194	210
Tilt steering column	75	65	70
Metallic paint	165	142	154
Power Pkg.	605	NA	NA
AM/FM cassette	300	258	279
Sound II AM/FM cassette	450	387	419
Sunroof	395	340	368
California emissions pkg.	97	95	96

Volkswagen Jetta

GL 2-door notchback	$9995	$8986	$9491
GL 4-door notchback	10295	9100	9698
GL diesel 4-door notchback	10495	9276	9886
Carat 4-door notchback	10990	9711	10351
Carat diesel 4-door notchback	11190	NA	NA
GLI 16V 4-door notchback	13750	12140	12945
Destination charge	260	260	260

Standard equipment:

GL: 1.8-liter PFI 4-cylinder gas or diesel engine, 5-speed manual transmission, power steering, velour height-adjustable reclining front bucket seats,

Prices are accurate at time of printing; subject to manufacturer's change

rear shoulder belts, tilt steering column, center console with storage, rear defogger, tinted glass, tachometer, coolant temperature gauge, trip odometer, door pockets, rear armrest with storage, right visor mirror, remote OS mirrors, 185/60HR14 tires. **Carat** adds: higher-output engine (gas model), power locks, upgraded upholstery, rear head restraints, time-delay interior light, visor mirrors (lighted right). **GLI 16V** adds: 2.0-liter DOHC 16-valve engine, 4-wheel disc brakes, sport suspension, Recaro front seats with power height adjustment, trip computer, leather-wrapped steering wheel, 185/55VR15 tires on BBS alloy wheels.

Optional equipment:	Retail Price	Dealer Invoice	Low Price
3-speed automatic transmission	505	465	485
Anti-lock brakes	835	835	835
Air conditioning	805	692	749
Alloy wheels	365	314	340
Cold Weather Pkg.	365	NA	NA
Cruise control	225	194	210
Metallic paint	165	142	154
Power Pkg.	450	409	430
AM/FM cassette	300	258	279
Sound II AM/FM cassette	450	387	419
Sunroof	395	340	368
California emissions pkg.	97	95	96

Volkswagen Passat

Passat is a new front-wheel drive model that's scheduled to go on sale in the U.S. by March of 1990. Passat is a well-known name in Europe, but has never been used in the U.S. before. The previous version was called Quantum in the U.S. and was VW's top-rung sedan from 1982 through 1988, essentially a restyled Audi 4000. The new Passat has much different styling than other recent Volkswagens, marked by a grille-less nose and rounded flanks. Prices were released well in advance of the car's introduction: the Passat GL 4-door sedan has a $14,770 base price, while the GL 5-door wagon starts at $15,885. U.S. specifications weren't available, but European models have a wheelbase of 103.3 inches, six inches longer than the Golf/Jetta. Overall length is about 180 inches, giving Passat the dimensions of a compact, close to those of the Toyota Camry and Mitsubishi Galant. U.S. models have a 2.0-liter 4-cylinder en-

Volkswagen Passat (European model)

gine, similar to the 108-horsepower 4-cylinder that's the base engine for the Audi 80. A 5-speed manual transmission is standard on the sedan and a new 4-speed overdrive automatic transmission is optional. The wagon comes only with the automatic. Eventually, Passat also may get a new V-6 engine being developed by Volkswagen. Anti-lock brakes are an $835 option. We haven't driven the Passat so we cannot comment on its performance.

Prices

Volkswagen Passat	Retail Price	Dealer Invoice	Low Price
GL 4-door notchback, 5-speed	$14770	$13037	—
GL 4-door notchback, automatic	15565	13798	—
GL 5-door wagon, automatic	15885	14019	—
Destination charge	320	320	320

Low price not available at time of publication.

Standard equipment:

2.0-liter DOHC 16-valve PFI 4-cylinder engine, 5-speed manual or 4-speed automatic transmission, power steering, air conditioning, cloth reclining front bucket seats, front seat height and lumbar support adjustments, 60/40 folding rear seat, rear armrest, cargo cover (wagon), center console with storage, rear defogger, tinted glass, remote OS mirrors, lighted visor mirrors, radio prep package (four speakers and antenna), tilt steering column, tachometer and trip odometer, intermittent wipers, rear wiper/washer (wagon), wheel covers, 195/60VR14 tires.

Prices are accurate at time of printing; subject to manufacturer's change

Optional equipment:	Retail Price	Dealer Invoice	Low Price
Anti-lock brakes	835	835	835
Cold Climate Pkg.	250	215	—
Heated front seats and windshield washer nozzles.			
Convenience Group	1200	1032	—
Power windows and locks, power mirrors, cruise control, AM/FM cassette with six speakers.			
Metallic paint	165	142	—
Power sunroof	695	598	—
Rear sunshade, 4-door	120	103	—
Leather upholstery	710	610	—
Forged alloy wheels	575	495	—
California emissions pkg.	97	95	—

Volvo 240

Volvo 240 DL

A driver's-side airbag and an under-dashboard knee bolster are new standard feature this year on all 240 models to meet the federal passive-restraint requirement. The GL price series has been dropped and a new base trim level has been added. Prices hadn't been announced for the base 4-door sedan and wagon, but they will be slotted below the DL models and have fewer standard features. Air conditioning, a stereo radio with cassette player, cruise control, and power windows, all standard on the DL, are optional on base models. All models have a 114-horsepower 2.3-liter 4-cylinder engine, and either a 5-speed manual or 4-speed automatic transmission. The rear-drive 240 was introduced in 1975, yet Volvo says these cars accounted for about 40 percent of the company's 1989 U.S. sales, a testament to its enduring popularity. And, Volvo says that despite rumors that a replacement is imminent, it will continue to offer the 240 "as long as it remains popular with the public." The 240 has a reputation for longevity and safety, and this year's standard airbag will provide even better occupant protection. The most recent insurance statistics support the 240's safety reputation: the 4-door sedan has

Specifications

	4-door notchback	5-door wagon
Wheelbase, in.	104.3	104.3
Overall length, in.	189.9	190.7
Overall width, in.	67.3	67.7
Overall height, in.	56.3	57.5
Turn diameter, ft.	32.2	32.2
Curb weight, lbs.	2919	3051
Cargo vol., cu. ft.	14.0	76.0
Fuel capacity, gals.	15.8	15.8
Seating capacity	5	5
Front headroom, in.	37.9	37.9
Front shoulder room, in.	NA	NA
Front legroom, max., in.	40.1	40.1
Rear headroom, in.	36.1	36.8
Rear shoulder room, in.	NA	NA
Rear legroom, min., in.	36.4	36.1

Powertrain layout: longitudinal front engine/rear-wheel drive.

Engines

	ohc I-4
Size, liters/cu. in.	2.3/141
Fuel delivery	PFI
Horsepower @ rpm	114 @ 5400
Torque (lbs./ft.) @ rpm	136 @ 2750
Availability	S

EPA city/highway mpg

5-speed OD manual	21/28
4-speed OD automatic	20/25

Prices are accurate at time of printing; subject to manufacturer's change

fewer injury claims than most mid-size cars, while the wagon has substantially fewer claims. However, the same is true of the Ford Taurus/Mercury Sable sedans and wagons, so you shouldn't limit your shopping to Volvos if safety is your priority. In addition, anti-lock brakes are optional on the Taurus/Sable this year, but they aren't available on the 240. The 240 is still a competent, durable, fairly roomy car that is worth considering.

Prices

Volvo 240	Retail Price	Dealer Invoice	Low Price
DL 4-door notchback, 5-speed	$18450	$15800	$16707
DL 4-door notchback, automatic	19095	16345	17288
DL 5-door wagon, 5-speed	18940	16210	17146
DL 5-door wagon, automatic	19585	16755	17727
DL 4-door w/sunroof, 5-speed	18975	16230	17173
DL 4-door w/sunroof, automatic	19620	16775	17754
Destination charge	350	350	350

Prices for base model not available at time of publication.

Standard equipment:

2.3-liter PFI 4-cylinder engine, 5-speed manual or 4-speed automatic transmission, power steering, 4-wheel disc brakes, driver's-side airbag, power locks, trip odometer, rear defogger, tinted glass, remote OS mirrors, reclining front bucket seats, driver's-seat height adjustment, rear head restraints, 185/70R14 tires (4-door), 185R14 tires (wagon). **DL** adds: air conditioning, AM/FM cassette, power windows.

Optional equipment:

Metallic paint	245	200	217
California emissions pkg.	125	100	110

Volvo 740/760/780

A driver's-side airbag is standard across the board, the 740 models get nose jobs, and turbocharged models have more power this year. A new base 740 trim level has been added with a slightly lower price than the 740 GL. The major

Volvo 740 GLE

difference is that the GL's standard sunroof isn't available on the base. Aerodynamic halogen headlamps, new grilles, and integrated bumpers give the 740 models a new look at the front, while the 740 and 760 wear new taillamps. The 740 and 760 are built from the same rear-drive design and share 4-door sedan and wagon body styles, but differ in standard features and available engines. The 780 is built on the same rear-drive chassis as the others, but comes as a 2-door coupe. The 2.3-liter 4-cylinder engine used in the 740 Turbo and 760 Turbo has a smaller turbocharger, new exhaust manifold, and recalibrated fuel and ignition systems. Horsepower is up by two, and Volvo says maximum turbo boost is now available at 1800 rpm for better low-speed performance. The 780 Turbo uses the same turbocharged engine, but with different electronic controls; this "Turbo +" engine gains 13 horsepower. Anti-lock brakes are optional on the base 740 and 740 GL, and standard on all others. The 700-Series offers luxury-car buyers a choice of three body styles, four engines, and a price spread that runs from $21,000 to $40,000. Unfortunately, you have to go above $25,000 before you get more than ordinary performance. The 114-horsepower engine used in the base 740 and GL is sturdy and economical, but you'll be dusted off by cars that cost half as much. The turbocharged engine provides good off-the-line acceleration and sensational passing power.

Specifications

	780 2-door notchback	740/760 4-door notchback	740/760 5-door wagon
Wheelbase, in.	109.1	109.1	109.1
Overall length, in.	188.8	188.4	188.4
Overall width, in.	69.3	69.3	69.3
Overall height, in.	55.1	55.5	56.5
Turn diameter, ft.	32.2	32.2	32.2
Curb weight, lbs.	3415	2954	3082
Cargo vol., cu. ft.	14.9	16.8	74.9
Fuel capacity, gals.	21.0	15.8[1]	15.8
Seating capacity	4	5	5
Front headroom, in.	37.2	38.6	38.6
Front shoulder room, in.	NA	NA	NA
Front legroom, max., in.	41.0	41.0	41.0
Rear headroom, in.	35.8	37.1	37.6
Rear shoulder room, in.	NA	NA	NA
Rear legroom, min., in.	34.7	34.7	34.7

1. 21.0 gals., 760.

Powertrain layout: longitudinal front engine/rear-wheel drive.

Engines

	ohc I-4	dohc I-4	Turbo ohc I-4	ohc V-6
Size, liters/cu. in.	2.3/141	2.3/141	2.3/141	2.8/173
Fuel delivery	PFI	PFI	PFI	PFI
Horsepower @ rpm	114 @ 5400	153 @ 5700	162 @ 4800[1]	144 @ 5100
Torque (lbs./ft.) @ rpm	136 @ 2750	150 @ 4450	195 @ 3450[1]	173 @ 3750
Availability	S	S	S	S

EPA city/highway mpg

	ohc I-4	dohc I-4	Turbo ohc I-4	ohc V-6
4-speed manual + OD		18/26	20/25	
5-speed OD manual	21/28			
4-speed OD automatic	20/26	18/24	18/21	17/21

1. 780 Turbo has 188 horsepower, 206 lbs/ft torque.

Prices

Volvo 740/760/780	Retail Price	Dealer Invoice	Low Price
740 4-door notchback, 5-speed	$20685	$17580	$18666
740 4-door notchback, automatic	21330	18125	19246
740 5-door wagon, 5-speed	21365	18145	19273
740 5-door wagon, automatic	22010	18690	19854

	Retail Price	Dealer Invoice	Low Price
740 GL 4-door notchback, 5-speed	21700	18130	19429
740 GL 4-door notchback, automatic	22345	18675	20010
740 GL 5-door wagon, 5-speed	22380	18695	20037
740 GL 5-door wagon, automatic	23025	19240	20617
740 GLE 4-door notchback, 4-speed + OD	25440	21210	22756
740 GLE 4-door notchback, automatic	25995	21670	23251
740 GLE 5-door wagon, 4-speed + OD	26120	21775	23363
740 GLE 5-door wagon, automatic	26675	22235	23859
740 Turbo 4-door, 4-speed + OD	25775	21360	22993
740 Turbo 4-door, automatic	26330	21820	23488
740 Turbo 5-door, 4-speed + OD	26455	21925	23600
740 Turbo 5-door, automatic	27010	22385	24095
760 GLE 4-door notchback	33185	26625	29176
760 GLE Turbo 4-door notchback	33965	27260	29866
760 GLE Turbo 5-door wagon	33965	27275	29873
780 2-door notchback	38735	31025	34029
780 Turbo 2-door notchback	39950	32000	35098
Destination charge	350	350	350
Gas Guzzler Tax, 760/780 V-6	500	500	500

Standard equipment:

740 base & GL: 2.3-liter PFI 4-cylinder engine, 5-speed manual or 4-speed automatic transmission, power steering, 4-wheel disc brakes, driver's-side airbag, air conditioning, cloth reclining front bucket seats, power windows and locks, tachometer, coolant temperature gauge, trip odometer, AM/FM cassette, sunroof (GL), 185/70R14 tires. **740 GLE adds:** DOHC 16-valve engine, anti-lock braking system, Supplemental Restraint System, cruise control, 185/65R15 tires on alloy wheels. **740 Turbo adds:** turbocharged, intercooled engine, 4-speed manual plus overdrive or 4-speed automatic transmission, power sunroof, power mirrors, velour and leather upholstery, 195/60R15 tires. **760 adds:** 2.8-liter PFI V-6 or 2.3-liter turbocharged 4-cylinder engine, 4-speed automatic transmission, independent rear suspension, automatic climate control, leather upholstery, power seats, tilt steering column, upgraded stereo with EQ, front map lights, rear reading lights (Turbo). **780 adds:** power moonroof, elm burl accents.

Optional equipment:

Anti-lock brakes, 740 base & GL	1175	945	1034
Leather upholstery, 740	895	735	795
Metallic paint, 740 base & GL	245	200	217
California emissions pkg.	125	100	110

Prices are accurate at time of printing; subject to manufacturer's change

RATINGS CHART

SCALE 5 = Exceptional; 4 = Above average; 3 = Average; 2 = Below average; 1 = Poor

MAKE AND MODEL	Performance							Accommodations						Workmanship		Value	TOTAL
	Acceleration	Economy	Driveability	Ride	Steering/handling	Braking	Noise	Driver seating	Instruments/controls	Visibility	Room/comfort	Entry/exit	Cargo room	Exterior	Interior		
Acura Integra (GS 3-dr)	4	3	4	4	4	5	3	4	4	4	3	3	3	4	4	3	59
Acura Legend (Sedan)	4	2	3	4	4	5	4	4	4	4	4	4	4	4	4	4	62
Audi V8 Quattro	4	2	3	3	5	5	3	4	4	4	4	4	4	5	5	3	62
Audi 80/90 (90)	4	3	4	4	4	5	3	3	4	4	3	3	2	5	5	3	59
Audi 100/200 (200 Quattro)	4	2	4	4	5	5	3	4	4	3	4	4	4	5	4	3	62
BMW 3-Series (325i)	4	3	4	4	4	5	3	3	4	5	3	3	3	5	4	3	60
BMW 5-Series (535i)	5	2	3	4	4	5	4	4	4	4	4	4	4	5	4	3	63
BMW 7-Series (750iL)	5	1	5	5	4	5	5	5	4	4	5	5	4	5	5	3	70
Buick Electra/Oldsmobile Ninety-Eight (ABS)	4	2	4	4	3	5	4	3	3	4	4	4	4	5	4	3	59

Model																
Buick Le Sabre/Oldsmobile Eighty Eight/Pontiac Bonneville (ABS)	4	2	4	4	3	5	4	3	3	5	4	4	4	4	4	61
Buick Riviera and Reatta (Reatta)	4	2	4	3	4	5	3	4	3	4	3	3	4	4	3	56
Buick Skylark/Oldsmobile Cutlass Calais (V-6)	4	2	4	3	3	5	3	3	3	4	3	3	4	3	3	51
Cadillac Allante	4	2	4	3	4	5	3	4	3	3	3	3	4	4	2	53
Cadillac Brougham (5.7)	4	1	4	3	2	3	5	3	2	4	3	2	4	3	3	55
Cadillac De Ville/Fleetwood (ABS)	4	2	4	4	3	5	4	4	3	3	5	4	5	4	4	63
Cadillac Eldorado/Seville (Eldorado, ABS)	4	2	4	3	4	5	4	4	3	3	3	3	5	4	4	58
Chevrolet Astro/GMC Safari	4	1	3	2	3	4	3	3	3	2	5	2	3	4	3	50
Chevrolet Camaro/Pontiac Firebird (IROC-Z)	5	1	3	1	4	4	2	3	3	2	3	2	3	3	3	44
Chevrolet Caprice/Buick Estate/Olds Custom Cruiser (Caprice 4-dr)	4	2	5	4	3	3	5	4	3	4	5	5	4	4	4	63
Chevrolet Cavalier/Pontiac Sunbird (Cavalier 2-dr)	3	3	3	3	3	3	3	3	3	4	3	3	4	4	3	51
Chevrolet Celebrity/Pontiac 6000 (wgn)	3	2	4	3	3	3	3	4	3	4	4	5	4	4	4	57

RATINGS CHART

SCALE 5 = Exceptional; 4 = Above average; 3 = Average; 2 = Below average; 1 = Poor

MAKE AND MODEL	Performance							Accommodations						Workmanship		Value	TOTAL
	Acceleration	Economy	Driveability	Ride	Steering/handling	Braking	Noise	Driver seating	Instruments/controls	Visibility	Room/comfort	Entry/exit	Cargo room	Exterior	Interior		
Chevrolet Corsica/Beretta (Corsica V-6)	4	2	3	3	4	4	3	3	3	4	3	4	3	4	3	3	53
Chevrolet Corvette (ZR-1)	5	1	4	2	5	5	1	3	4	2	3	2	1	3	3	3	47
Chevrolet Lumina (4-dr)	3	2	4	4	4	4	3	3	3	4	4	4	4	4	3	3	56
Chevrolet Lumina APV	3	2	4	4	4	3	4	3	3	2	5	3	5	4	4	3	56
Chrysler Imperial/New Yorker Fifth Avenue	3	2	3	3	3	5	4	3	3	3	4	4	4	4	3	3	54
Chrysler LeBaron (Turbo)	4	2	4	3	4	3	3	4	3	3	3	3	4	4	4	3	54
Chrysler New Yorker (ABS)	3	2	3	4	3	5	4	3	3	3	4	4	4	4	3	3	55
Dodge/Plymouth Colt (wgn)	3	4	3	3	3	3	3	4	4	5	3	3	4	4	4	4	57
Dodge/Plymouth Colt Vista (4WD)	3	3	3	3	4	3	2	4	4	4	4	3	4	4	4	3	55

Model																Total
Dodge Daytona (Shelby)	5	2	4	2	4	4	2	3	4	3	2	2	3	4	3	51
Dodge Dynasty (ABS)	3	2	3	4	3	5	4	3	3	4	4	4	4	3	3	57
Dodge Shadow/Plymouth Sundance (2.5)	3	3	3	3	3	3	3	3	4	3	3	4	4	4	4	53
Eagle Premier/Dodge Monaco (Premier ES)	4	2	4	4	4	3	2	4	4	4	4	4	3	3	4	58
Eagle Summit (LX)	3	4	3	3	4	3	4	5	3	3	3	3	4	3	3	55
Ford Aerostar (3.0)	3	2	4	3	3	3	3	2	5	2	5	4	4	4	3	52
Ford Escort (LX)	3	3	3	3	3	2	3	3	3	3	3	4	4	3	3	51
Ford Festiva	3	5	3	3	3	2	4	3	5	3	2	2	4	4	3	52
Ford LTD Crown Victoria/Mercury Grand Marquis	4	2	5	3	3	5	4	3	4	5	5	4	4	4	4	63
Ford Mustang (GT)	5	2	4	4	3	2	4	3	3	2	3	3	4	3	3	52
Ford Probe (GT, ABS)	4	3	3	4	5	2	3	3	3	2	3	4	4	4	3	52
Ford Taurus/Mercury Sable (3.8)	4	2	4	4	3	3	4	3	4	4	4	4	4	4	4	57
Ford Tempo/Mercury Topaz	2	3	3	3	3	3	4	3	3	3	3	4	4	4	4	51
Ford Thunderbird/Mercury Cougar (SC)	5	2	3	2	4	5	4	4	4	3	3	3	4	4	3	57
Geo Metro	3	5	4	2	3	4	4	3	5	2	3	2	3	3	3	50
Geo Storm, Isuzu Impulse/Stylus (Storm GSi)	4	4	3	2	4	2	3	4	3	2	2	3	4	3	3	50

RATINGS CHART

SCALE 5 = Exceptional; 4 = Above average; 3 = Average; 2 = Below average; 1 = Poor

MAKE AND MODEL	Performance							Accommodations						Workmanship		Value	TOTAL
	Acceleration	Economy	Driveablity	Ride	Steering/handling	Braking	Noise	Driver seating	Instruments/controls	Visibility	Room/comfort	Entry/exit	Cargo room	Exterior	Interior		
Honda Accord (LX 4-dr)	4	3	4	4	4	3	4	4	4	4	4	4	4	4	4	4	62
Honda Civic (LX 4-dr)	3	4	3	3	3	4	3	4	4	5	3	3	3	4	4	4	57
Honda CRX (Si)	4	4	4	2	4	4	1	3	4	2	4	2	3	4	3	4	52
Honda Prelude (Si)	4	3	3	3	4	4	3	3	4	4	2	3	3	4	3	3	53
Hyundai Excel/ Mitsubishi Precis (3-dr)	3	5	3	3	3	3	2	4	3	5	3	3	3	4	4	4	55
Hyundai Sonata (4-cyl)	3	3	3	4	3	3	3	4	4	4	4	3	3	4	3	4	56
Infiniti M30	4	2	4	3	4	5	4	4	4	4	3	4	3	4	4	3	58
Infiniti Q45	5	2	4	4	5	5	4	4	4	4	4	4	4	5	4	4	66
Lexus ES 250	4	3	4	4	4	5	4	3	4	4	4	4	4	4	4	3	62

Model															Total
Lexus LS 400	5	2	5	5	4	5	5	4	4	4	4	4	5	5	4	69
Lincoln Continental	4	2	4	4	3	5	4	4	2	4	4	4	4	4	3	59
Lincoln Mark VII (LSC)	5	2	4	3	4	5	4	3	3	3	3	5	5	4	4	59
Lincoln Town Car	3	1	5	4	3	5	5	3	3	4	5	5	5	4	3	63
Mazda Miata	4	4	4	4	4	4	2	4	4	4	3	4	4	5	5	58
Mazda MPV (V-6)	4	2	4	3	4	4	3	4	3	4	3	4	4	4	4	58
Mazda RX-7	4	2	4	2	4	4	3	3	2	3	2	4	4	4	3	51
Mazda 323/Protege (Protege LX)	4	3	4	3	3	3	3	4	3	3	3	4	4	4	4	57
Mazda 626/MX-6 (626 4-dr)	3	3	3	3	3	4	3	4	4	3	4	4	4	3	3	55
Mazda 929 (ABS)	4	2	4	3	3	5	4	4	4	4	4	4	4	4	4	61
Mercedes-Benz S-Class (560SEL)	5	1	5	4	4	5	4	4	5	5	5	5	5	3	3	67
Mercedes-Benz 190E 2.6	4	2	4	4	4	5	4	3	5	3	3	2	5	4	3	59
Mercedes-Benz 300 (300E)	4	2	4	4	4	5	4	4	4	4	4	5	5	3	3	64
Mercury Tracer (1989 wgn)	3	4	3	3	3	3	2	4	5	3	3	4	4	4	4	56
Mitsubishi Eclipse (GS DOHC)	4	3	4	2	4	4	2	4	2	2	2	4	4	4	4	51
Mitsubishi Galant (LS)	3	3	4	4	3	3	4	4	4	4	3	4	4	4	4	59
Mitsubishi Mirage (4-dr)	3	4	3	3	3	3	4	4	5	3	3	4	3	4	4	56
Mitsubishi Sigma (ABS)	4	2	4	3	5	4	3	4	4	3	3	4	3	3	3	55
Nissan Axxess	3	3	4	4	3	3	4	4	4	4	4	4	4	3	3	58

RATINGS CHART

SCALE 5 = Exceptional; 4 = Above average; 3 = Average; 2 = Below average; 1 = Poor

MAKE AND MODEL	Acceleration	Economy	Driveability	Ride	Steering/handling	Braking	Noise	Driver seating	Instruments/controls	Visibility	Room/comfort	Entry/exit	Cargo room	Exterior	Interior	Value	TOTAL
	Performance							Accommodations						Workmanship			
Nissan Maxima (SE, ABS)	4	2	4	4	4	5	4	4	4	4	4	4	4	4	4	4	63
Nissan Pulsar NX	3	4	3	3	4	3	2	3	4	3	3	2	3	4	4	4	52
Nissan Sentra	3	4	3	3	3	3	2	3	4	5	3	3	3	4	3	3	52
Nissan Stanza (GXE, ABS)	4	3	4	3	4	5	3	4	4	4	3	3	3	4	4	4	59
Nissan 240SX	4	3	4	2	4	3	2	3	4	3	2	2	3	4	4	3	50
Nissan 300ZX (Turbo)	5	2	4	2	5	5	2	4	4	2	3	2	3	5	4	3	55
Oldsmobile Cutlass Ciera/Buick Century (V-6)	4	2	4	3	3	3	3	3	3	4	4	4	4	4	3	4	56
Oldsmobile Cutlass Supreme/Buick Regal (2-dr, V-6)	3	2	4	4	4	4	3	3	3	4	4	3	4	4	3	3	55
Oldsmobile Silhouette	3	2	4	4	4	3	4	3	3	2	5	3	5	4	4	3	56

Model															
Oldsmobile Toronado/Trofeo (Toronado)	4	2	4	4	4	4	4	3	4	3	3	3	4	4	57
Plymouth Acclaim/Dodge Spirit (Acclaim LX)	4	2	4	4	4	3	4	4	4	4	4	4	4	4	60
Plymouth Horizon/Dodge Omni	4	3	4	3	3	3	3	2	3	3	3	3	4	5	55
Plymouth Laser/Eagle Talon (Talon TSi AWD)	5	2	4	5	2	4	4	4	2	2	2	2	4	4	52
Plymouth Voyager/Dodge Caravan/Chrysler Town & Country (Grand Voyager)	4	2	4	4	3	3	3	3	3	5	5	4	4	4	58
Pontiac Grand Am (Quad 4)	4	3	4	2	4	3	3	4	3	3	3	4	4		51
Pontiac Grand Prix (SE)	3	2	3	3	4	3	3	4	4	3	3	4	4		55
Pontiac LeMans (SE)	2	4	3	3	4	2	3	4	4	3	3	3	4		51
Pontiac Trans Sport	3	2	4	4	3	4	3	3	2	5	4	4	4		56
Saab 900 (Turbo 3-dr)	5	2	4	3	4	4	3	5	4	3	3	5	3		57
Saab 9000 CD (Turbo)	5	2	3	4	5	4	4	4	4	4	4	4	4		62
Subaru Justy (ECVT)	3	5	3	2	3	3	5	2	3	3	2	2	4		50
Subaru Legacy (4WD 4-dr)	3	3	4	3	3	4	4	4	4	4	4	3	4		57
Subaru Loyale (4WD wgn)	3	3	4	3	3	4	3	3	5	3	3	4	4		56
Subaru XT (XT6)	4	2	3	4	4	3	3	4	2	2	2	4	4		52
Toyota Camry (V-6, ABS)	4	2	3	3	5	4	4	4	4	4	4	4	4		60
Toyota Celica (GT)	4	3	3	3	4	3	4	3	3	2	3	2	4		53

RATINGS CHART

SCALE 5 = Exceptional; 4 = Above average; 3 = Average; 2 = Below average; 1 = Poor

MAKE AND MODEL	Performance							Accommodations						Workmanship		Value	TOTAL
	Acceleration	Economy	Driveability	Ride	Steering/handling	Braking	Noise	Driver seating	Instruments/controls	Visibility	Room/comfort	Entry/exit	Cargo room	Exterior	Interior		
Toyota Corolla/Geo Prizm (Corolla 4-dr)	3	4	3	4	3	3	3	3	3	5	3	3	3	4	4	4	55
Toyota Cressida (ABS)	4	3	4	4	4	3	5	4	3	5	4	4	3	4	4	3	63
Toyota Supra (Turbo, ABS)	5	2	4	2	4	5	2	5	4	3	2	2	3	4	4	3	54
Toyota Tercel	3	5	3	3	3	3	2	3	3	5	3	3	3	4	3	4	53
Volkswagen Corrado	4	3	3	3	4	4	3	4	3	3	3	2	3	4	4	3	53
Volkswagen Fox (2-dr)	3	4	4	3	3	4	3	3	3	5	3	3	2	4	3	4	54
Volkswagen Golf/Jetta (Jetta Carat, ABS)	4	4	4	3	4	5	3	4	4	3	3	3	3	4	4	4	60
Volvo 240 (4-dr)	3	3	4	4	3	4	3	4	3	5	4	3	3	5	4	4	59
Volvo 740/760/780 (760 Turbo 4-dr)	5	2	3	3	4	5	3	4	4	4	4	4	4	5	4	3	61